DREAMS
and
DESTINY

DREAMS
and
DESTINY

GEDDES &
GROSSET

This edition published 2008

© 2006 Geddes & Grosset
David Dale House, New Lanark, ML11 9DJ

First published 2006, reprinted 2007, 2008

Dictionary of Dreams written and edited by Lily Seafield,
with additional material drawn from
10,000 Dreams Interpreted.

Astrology and Horoscopes written by K White

ISBN 978 1 84205 593 9

Printed and bound in Poland

POLSKABOOK

Dictionary of Dreams

Astrology and Horoscopes

DREAMS

and

DESTINY

DICTIONARY OF DREAMS

Introduction

Why Do We Dream?

Consciousness and unconsciousness

Although it is not known exactly why it is that we dream, in psychoanalysis it has long been recognized that the unconscious has an important role to play. However, this in itself is not terribly helpful as scientists have never been entirely certain as to where consciousness ends and unconsciousness begins. Indeed, the two frequently overlap and there can really be no clear distinction between them.

We may, perhaps, accept that to be conscious means to be awake, aware of our surroundings and in control of our actions. But this does not take into account the fact that much goes on around us in our waking state of which we are generally not aware, or only aware of on a 'less conscious' level. For instance, we may be walking along a busy street, deep in thought, and be completely unaware of the noise of the traffic all around us, until something like the blast of a car horn, or the sound of a collision, alerts us to it.

Furthermore, we do not need to concentrate all the time on moving our legs in order that we might keep on walking, nor do we generally need to concentrate hard on walking in a straight line in order that we might not veer off course and into the road.

Similarly, while we are asleep and are ostensibly 'unconscious', our brains are obviously extremely active. Although we are usually unaware of much of this activity (such as the continuing control over the function of our major organs), dreams are a manifestation of this activity and are often extremely vivid. Therefore, it would seem that the brain is capable of organizing our consciousness into several levels at all times.

The physiological manifestation of the unconscious is also a grey area. However, it is known that a structure situated in the brain stem, known as the reticular formation, acts as an activator for other parts of the brain and may play a part in defining the unconscious. All sensory pathways are linked to the reticular activating system (RAS), so that when a sense receptor is stimulated this also triggers the reticular system, 'awakening' the brain so that it is fully able to respond to messages from the senses.

Sleep

Sleep is essential for the repair of the body and for cell regeneration. People deprived of sleep for lengthy periods generally become quite unwell. However, it is a complicated process, which has been the subject of much research. Broadly speaking, the average night's sleep consists of four or five distinct stages.

1. During stage one, the sleeper begins to relax and will drift in and out of a dozing sleep from which he or she is easily awakened.

2. In stage two, the individual is asleep but can still be easily roused by minor disturbances.

3. By stage three, a state of deep relaxation is reached, and it becomes very difficult to wake the sleeper. During this stage, the eyes often move from side to side.

4. In stage four, 80 per cent of the daily output of growth hormone is released, which helps in the process of repairing body tissues.

The sleeper then proceeds in reverse through the stages, but instead of waking completely after returning to stage 1, he or she will enter a different stage (stage 5), known as REM (rapid eye movement) sleep. It is during this phase that most dreaming occurs. The whole cycle from stages 1–4 and back again takes about 90–100 minutes. During the average night's sleep the cycle will repeat itself 4 or 5 times.

REM sleep

REM sleep takes its name from the characteristic eye movements that take place during this stage. Sleepers who are wakened during this phase will report that they have been dreaming. Research has shown that during REM sleep, the body's major muscle groups seem to be paralysed. This is thought to occur in order to prevent injury or un-controlled movement during sleep.

The length of REM sleep increases with each cycle. Therefore, the longest period of REM sleep and dreaming occurs in the last third of the night. A sleeper whose REM is disrupted will automatically try to increase the time spent in REM sleep the next night to compensate. This may indicate that REM sleep, and therefore dreaming, is essen-tial for wellbeing. Some dreaming does take place outwith REM sleep, but it tends to be much less vivid and somewhat mundane. A sleeper who is wakened during one of these dreams may report that he or she has been 'thinking' rather than dreaming.

Getting the most from sleep

In order to dream well, it is advisable to follow a few simple rules:

1. Decide your optimum amount of sleep and stick to it as much as possible. Most adults need six and a half to eight and a half hours of sleep nightly, but some can get by on as little as five hours. A few will need as much as ten hours. Experiment with varying lengths of sleep. When you have decided how much you need (based on assessment of work performance, levels of irritability and plain tiredness through the day), you should aim to be in bed roughly half an hour before the period of sleep commences.

2. What you have consumed in the hours preceding sleep will di-rectly affect the nature and quality of your dreams. If your diges-tion is working overtime while you sleep, your dreams may be af-fected. It is wise, therefore, to avoid eating wind-producing foods such as raw vegetables, or foods that have a high fat content im-

mediately before you go to bed. Some stimulants, such as caffeine and alcohol, affect the time it takes to fall asleep and the quality of sleep thereafter. Similarly, sleeping tablets seem to suppress REM sleep, which is so vital to our wellbeing.

3. Do as much as possible to eliminate noise and discomfort in the immediate sleeping environment. The immediate environment can affect your dreams; many people will have experienced dreaming that the telephone is ringing, or a fire alarm is sounding, only to find later that they have slept through the noise of the alarm; or they may have dreamt of being restrained only to wake up and find that their sheets have become so entangled that they can hardly move.

Try to adopt a relaxed routine in the hour before bedtime. If the brain is overactive as the head hits the pillow, it will take some time to drift off into a deep, untroubled sleep.

Record your dreams

It is always a good idea to keep a notebook right beside the bed if you want to record your dreams. In this way, you can make a note of your impressions the moment you wake up, before the intrusions of the day cloud or distort your memory.

When people report that they have not dreamt, it is not necessarily the case; it may be that events immediately upon waking (perhaps the alarm clock, the children careering all around, the realization that they might be late for work, etc) were so intrusive that memories of dreams were pushed out of their minds. For this reason, try, if at all possible, to train yourself to wake early, before the alarm clock's sound and before household noises disturb you. You will be more likely to be able to recall your dreams in a peaceful environment. A few pages have been provided at the back of this book witha template showing how you can begin to record your dreams.

Interpreting dreams

Our dreams can often be fantastic, terrifying and hard to comprehend because they do not seem to be contained by the rules of our everyday lives. Some of the most bizarre and disturbing distortions of reality are commonly experienced by dreamers, and the interpretation of these distortions has been given much attention by some eminent psychologists and researchers. Sigmund Freud (1856-1939), the father of psychoanalysis, believed that the unconscious uses symbols in dreams that represent real emotions and feelings. Alfred Adler (1870-1937), originally a follower of Freud, believed that dreams reflect the individual's lifelong drive for power and success. Carl Gustav Jung (1875-1961) was convinced that the symbolism contained in dreams reflected a wider collective unconsciousness and was common to all, regardless of race or culture.

There can be little doubt that dreams do have symbolic significance, and certain archetypal symbols are now quite generally accepted in the field of psychoanalysis. Applying knowledge of these archetypal symbols should do much to enlighten the individual as to the meaning of his or her dreams. Nevertheless, it is important to remember that dreams are very personal, and it is only in the knowledge of the dreamer's own mood and feelings, and also his or her own circumstances, past and present, that dreams become truly meaningful. The A-Z will help you in the process of interpretation if you bear this in mind.

Dream Symbolism

Folklore and dream symbolism

Some of the traditional dream interpretations are ancient indeed. Many were used as mystical tools of prediction. Dream symbolism has its place in the ancient folklore of most cultures and a few are mentioned in this book's A-Z, such as the folklore of gypsies or travelling people, those of the native Americans, the ancient Egyptians, the Chinese, and the early Christians. Many interpretations in this book are included from the work of a strange second century oneirocritic (dream interpreter) and oneiromantic (dream diviner) called Artemidorus Daldianus who wrote a five-volumed book of dream interpretations and predictions. There is also mention of a nineteenth-century astrologer known as Raphael whose speciality was apparently geomancy—the divination by lines or patterns made, for example by a handful of earth. They are virtually unknown now, however, it is interesting to note that although much of the writings of Artemidorus were of the dubious fortune-telling property of dreams, the emphasis, and the emphasis of cultural folklore and the folklore of the gypsy interpreters, was on the analysis of the *symbolism* involved which is also the main factor in modern interpretation and dream analysis.

The language of symbols

Language cannot create thought, but must be created by thought. Thus the first expression of articulate thought must have been through symbols rather than through words, for obviously before attempting speech, man must have perceived objects, and their meaning, use and similarity must have established themselves in his consciousness. Spoken words evolved as expressions of symbols. In this capacity they have remained somewhat incomplete, for they merely express ideas and do not originate them. However, our language is rich in conceptual metaphor. *Life is a journey* is a common everyday conceptual metaphor, eg: 'He came to a point in his life where every day was an uphill struggle.' *Argument is war* is also a commonly expressed metaphor, eg: 'He fought his case valiantly.' *Time* is often expressed as if it is a *resource* eg: 'We're running out of time.'

Conceptual metaphor exemplifies how symbolism is innate in language (for a complete explanation of this theory *see Metaphors We Live By*; George Lakoff and Mark Johnson, University of Chicago Press, 1980). In *The Divided Self* (1960), the Scottish existential psychiatrist R.D. Laing, used this type of conceptual metaphor—in this case life, or life's work, as a quest—to describe Freud's contribution to psychoanalysis:

'Freud was a hero. He descended to the 'Underworld' and met there stark terrors. He carried with him his theory as a Medusa's head which turned these terrors to stone.'

The place of the conceptual metaphor in our language goes some way to explain why subconscious thought expresses itself in the disguised form of symbols.

The interpretation of dream symbols

In *The Interpretation of Dreams* (1900), Freud writes of the subject of symbolism:

'For a few kinds of material a universally applicable dream symbolism has been established on a basis of generally known allusions and equivalents. A good part of this symbolism, moreover, is possessed by the dream in common with the psychoneurosis, and with legends and popular customs.'

In *The World of Dreams* Havelock Ellis (1859-1939) likewise commits himself to symbolism:

'It seems today by no means improbable that amid the absurdities of this popular oneiromancy there are some items of real significance.... Where we are faced with the question of definite and constant symbols, it still remains true that scepticism is often called for. But there can be no manner of doubt that our dreams are full of symbolism.'

Psychoanalysis, therefore, admits that there is some relevance to the traditional symbols of dreams. Jung's fascinating, if somewhat cryptic, work likewise abounds in symbolism. Freud's approach to psychoanalysis and the psychodynamics of personality was by turns thought to be revolutionary and was also thoroughly criticized. His emphasis on sexual drive as the main behaviour-determining agent was thought at the time to be shocking and too restrictive even by some of his colleagues. His work on dream interpretation shows this emphasis on sexual symbolism.

All dream interpretation involves drawing upon personal theories. In the desire to establish hypotheses and to demonstrate theories, the interpreter may draw upon a restricted individual viewpoint, ignoring traditional historical and psychological thought of which they have no experience. In translating the meaning of certain symbols and in fitting them upon certain dreams, interpreters might ignore the history of a symbol throughout the centuries. This history may seem irrelevant to the individual, but it goes some way to explaining the universality of some dream symbols.

Tradition should not be dismissed as the mere perpetuation of superstition. The literature, historical writings, philosophy and traditional folklore of many cultures clearly show that many symbols are typical of many different cultures. Symbolism is purposeful and significant, the outcome of inherited memory, tradition and history as well as the individual's own creativity. Tradition, representing the accumulated reasoning of the race from the inception of thought, is the most universal authority for the interpretation of symbols.

The precise translation of dream symbols is, however, very much dependent on the dreamer's own recognition of what the symbol might mean to him or her personally. If you want to take a more esoteric view of this phenomenon, it is the relation of the symbol to the dreamer's own personal myth (a spiritual view of the human subconscious as encompassing psyche, conscious, unconscious, past life and the past itself) as opposed to the universal myth.

The emotions felt by the dreamer during the dream are also vital to its interpretation, as how the dreamer feels about the dream symbol will apply to what the symbol represents.

Freud argued that in sleep the mind allows suppressed material to come forth in a disguised form—the symbol. The symbol itself is known as the *manifest content* while what the symbol actually represents to the dreamer is the *latent content*. When someone dreams of climbing a high mountain we are aware that this symbolizes a struggle in their life (this corresponds to the conceptual metaphor of life as a journey, and the concept of conquering a mountain links this object as a symbol of a person or an endeavour). The innate symbolism in our language equates the physical exertion of climbing with the mental exertion of an ambition or a problem to be overcome. It is very easy for us to equate the language with the visual image in an interpretation. But only the individual knows what his or her struggle is.

In traditional imagery mountains sometimes signify fear and approaching trouble. To the ancient oneirocritic Artemidorus, this dream would have indicated that the dreamer had, or would have, a great trouble to overcome.

This kind of dream is typical for lots of people (*see* TYPICAL DREAMS). In the interpretation of symbols, which are, after all, merely instinctive records of the human psyche, we must consider not only history, creeds and traditions, but apparent trivialities, all of which combine to explain the soul of the culture from which the symbol emanates.

The origins of symbolism

The scale of symbolism is vast and encompasses all areas of life. The symbol is the primitive expression of speechless man, it is also employed by great minds. Beethoven, Raphael, Michelangelo, Dante and Blake have bequeathed the world symbols that will outlast time. The Wise Men in the East with their frankincense and gold, and the person who wears a poppy on Remembrance Day, are alike symbolists, whatever the expression of the symbol. St John, St Paul, Solomon, Daniel and Ezekiel, the Bible, the Book of the Dead and the Zend Avesta express thought symbolically, while the baseball fan who 'puts it over the plate' does likewise.

Although the civilizing centuries have taught man to think in words, in dreams the mind flies backward to its primitive thought and employs pictures, or symbols. Not only do the Chaldeans, Egyptians and the Biblical oneirocritics utilize the ineradicable human tendency towards symbolism, but modern dream interpreters acknowledge its importance. The perplexing imagery of our dream life continues to fascinate us. Even in modern times dream books are still consulted frequently and with as much interest as ever before.

Traditional folklore and changing society

The symbolism of dreams is merely an effort at expression on the part of the dreaming self. Whether these expressions originate in sexual desire, as maintained by Freudians, or in external stimuli as claimed by physiologists, or from the heights of the human spirit as taught by the mystics, the thought comes from the mind of the individual and is imaged in the language of symbolism. This symbol need bear no immediately obvious interpretation, and it could be that the psyche is represented by a symbol that predates mere speech, but the symbol will have a relevance to the dreamer, and the dreamer and interpreter must work together to find its significance.

The older dream interpreters accepted a simple symbolism founded upon human history and the traditions of the people. Modern interpreters employ reasoning and utilize the unique frame of reference of the individual and the influence of the modern age which brings with it new symbols.

During medieval times and during the renaissance people held a totally different point of view from the ages that preceded them, and both modified symbolic expression. Again racial differences bore their influence. Thus the caverns, mountains and groves were temples and places of worship to Egypt and Greece, while the Hebrews regarded them with suspicion and fear; the Apis, or sacred bull, symbolizing the equinox, at that time in the sign Taurus, was the golden calf, abhorred of the Scriptures, and the serpent, personifying wisdom, was to become accursed of man in Eden.

Gypsy interpreters

Gypsies are the most widely known and the most universally accepted of the traditional mystic dream interpreters. Originally derived from Chaldean, Egyptian and possibly Atlantean sources, their symbolism has been modified, augmented or diminished as the case may be, by time and circumstance. After their descent from their heights of hierophantic teachings, legend and symbol sought the humbler folk. Thus, unconsciously the homely traditions and symbols flourished and scattered to the four winds of civilization, like the seeds of the thistle, the floral prototype of gypsies themselves. Their roots in the subconscious have been deep and permanent, and from these fireside tales have sprung the homely symbols that are most frequently employed in dreams. The universality of the symbols is attributable to the nomadic lifestyle of their preservers, the gypsies. Lacking a written literature, they assimilated local surroundings and drew to themselves the spiritual atmosphere of the varied eras, thus modifying the fundamental significance of the symbols. Early paganism, Hebrewism, Judaism, Christianity, iconoclasm, materialism, each in turn has tinted the mutable science of symbols with the fragments of oral tradition. The scientific colour blindness that has led students to ignore this chameleon quality of symbolism has caused misunderstandings of the symbols themselves.

Christian symbolism—the dove

Symbols can be drawn from many origins. The Christian symbolism of the dove is an emblem of the Holy Ghost. It was the favourite bird of Aphrodite (or Venus) and was thought to be very amorous in nature. It has been pointed out that not only the dove, but the fish and the cross, are all phallic or erotic symbols. This has some truth and a modicum of history as authority, but ignores the changing cultures of intervening centuries and the history of the races that have risen and had their fall since the times of ancient Greece. Unquestionably the dove was originally the symbol of Aphrodite, but it was also the least costly living sacrifice that could be proffered to Jehovah of the Jews, hence for many centuries it was the offering of the poor and the humble—a fitting symbol for Christ, who lived amongst and cared for the humblest of people.

The dream of the dove, while defined by Freud as erotic, is translated by the gypsies as a Holy dream and a good one, and probably in the everyday subconsciousness of the ordinary person, it bears this latter meaning.

The cross

The cross, unquestionably one of the oldest symbols, is of phallic origin. It is now, however, inextricably associated with the Passion and sacrifice of Christ. The image of the sacrifice of Christ and the crucifixion is infinitely more powerful than its original symbolism and has passed into almost every culture in the world. The modern dreamer, Christian or not, who sees a cross in a dream regards it as a symbol of self-sacrifice or of his or her own feelings of religious guilt. Rarely indeed does the dreamer's thought hark back to prehistoric days when the holy emblem bore a phallic significance.

The fish

The adoption of the fish, held by primitive pagans as a symbol of fecundity, was, according to Hulme, adopted by Christians for the reason that the initials of Jesus Christ, the Son of God, are the Greek letters for the word fish. Bishop Kip of California in his work, *The Catacombs of Rome*, corroborates Hulme's theory of the fish as a Christian emblem with the statement that the symbols adopted by the Christians of that day were selected for the purpose of misleading the persecutors of the new faith as well as to convey a message to its followers. They would scarcely suspect beneath the symbol of Aphrodite the meaning that the dove and the fish bore to the followers of Christ.

When dreams 'go by contrary'

The gypsy symbolism lacks the salacious quality usual in that of the Freudian psychologist, and their interpretations manifest a large share of the humour that perhaps the psychologist is lacking. This humour is demonstrated in the interpretation of the dreams that 'go by contrary'. The gypsies also demonstrate a working knowledge of the Bible and a shrewd comprehension of the psychological hypothesis of the subconscious self. The latter is especially surprising in view of the fact that the symbols are old, far older than any possible knowledge of the term subconscious. Dreams of anxiety and loss of property or possessions, for instance, are translated as suggesting thrift on the part of the dreamer, and anxiety indicates the concern that accumulates wealth, while dreams of prodigality and lavishness imply to the shrewd gypsy interpreter a self-complacency and wastefulness that naturally results in poverty.

Since the days of Shakespeare, who undoubtedly was familiar with dreams and their interpretations, a dream of money has implied its loss.

'There is some ill a brewing towards my rest,
For I did dream of Money-bags tonight,'
wails Shylock in *The Merchant of Venice*.

Dreams of hunger, care and poverty seem invariably to bear a contrary meaning, whether from motives of consolation to the dreamer or whether through the establishment of symbolism in the days of gypsy supremacy when the witch was sent for to comfort my lady in her bower, we may not decide.

The knowledge of the medieval gypsy

The invariably happy omen of every dream relating to the farmer or to agricultural implements pictures the medieval gypsy looking with longing eyes upon the land that he might not own. Implements of trade, especially the trades of the town, on the other hand imply discomfort and contempt. Female domestic occupations evidently rouse the disdain of the wandering tribes, for to dream of a distaff, spindle, needle, pin or any other symbol of a purely feminine occupation implies gossip and mischief.

Apart from these there is still a certain natural and obvious symbolism that establishes itself even more strongly than symbols of past traditions. These symbols are derived from a knowledge of the powers of nature and of natural history, and in gypsy dream interpretations these take, and hold precedence. The goose appears in dreams, not as the sacred bird of the Greeks and Romans, but as an emblem of stupidity; insects denote hurts and stings and animals generally signify misfortune in accord with the naturalist's knowledge of the proclivities of the beasts themselves. Sometimes this natural symbolism is tinged with humour as in the dream of soap which is held to signify transient worries, while the dream of yeast is another example of practical homely symbolism.

Morality

Rigid morality is the general tone of the gypsy translation, the morality of children's fairy tales and of folklore in which the villain is discovered and punished and the good man rewarded. The virtue of hard work is implied in that all manner of work prognosticates success, even when superficial worldly judgment might argue the contrary. A dream of a workhouse is one that forecasts a legacy.

Falsity of every description is fiercely frowned upon by the old-world morality of the dream books. Wigs, false hair and teeth, rouge, etc, invariably connote evil or evil conditions. Physical indulgence is likewise disapproved, and dreams of eating or of food invariably predict illness; whether from a sternly moral disapprobation of gluttony or whether from the modern theory of a physical dream as implying a physical desire, it is impossible to say. Cynical knowledge of human nature is implied in the interpretation of the dream of servants and inferiors into a prediction of hostility, and the interchangeable dreams of tombs and weddings might bring a smile of agreement from the sceptic. With some dream interpreters dreams of marriage herald death, and dreams of death predict a wedding. The phallic and erotic symbols of modern interpreters are invariably translated as ominous dreams by the gypsy.

Artemidorus Daldianus

The list of dream symbols in the following A–Z includes interpretations from several sources. Of the ancient oneirocritics and oneiromantics, Artemidorus Daldianus is the one most generally cited, with Raphael (pen name of Robert Cross Smith, astrologer and writer of a *Royal Book of Dreams, 1830*) following in importance.

Artemidorus was the 'great lawgiver of the dream world', says one writer upon the subject, and his *Oneirocritica,* a record from the interpretations of the Greeks, Assyrians and Egyptians, was once the statute book of dreams.

He lived in the second century AD under the Emperor Antoninus Pius, and claimed to have gathered his dream lore from ancient and established sources.

He gives certain rules for dream interpretation that it may be well to remember, not only in dream interpretation, but in forming judgment upon the efforts of others in this direction.

'In giving judgment on dreams we are to take notice that dreams are proportioned according to the condition of the party dreaming. Thus those of persons of eminency, be they good or bad, will be great—that is, if good, they signify great benefit; but if bad great misery. If the party that dreams be of a mean condition, the dreams, with their events, will be mean also; if poor, their dreams will be very inconsiderable. For the rules of dreaming are not general and therefore cannot satisfy all persons at once, but often, according to times and persons, admit of various interpretations ...

Moreover, all those things which are done by us and to us, and towards us only, we must think that they appertain to us particularly. And on the contrary, that all such things as are not done by us, nor towards us, nor in us, shall happen to others; and yet, notwithstanding, if they be our friends, and the dreams signify good, the joy shall come to us; and if contrary, then the contrary; but if they be our enemies, we ought to think and judge accordingly.'

It is interesting to note that this ancient fortune-teller places an importance on the individual's interpretation of the symbol. We may not believe the predictive element of dream content as Artemidorus did but, through the ages, it is surprising to note the similarities between the ancients and the moderns in the approach to dream interpretation.

This book

This book is a curious, possibly eccentric, combination of ancient and modern knowledge regarding dream symbolism. Oneiromancy sits alongside psychotherapy; traditional folklore and fortune telling are neighbours to Freud and Jung.

What all – ancient and modern – would agree upon is that the best interpreter of the dream is the dreamer him- or herself.

So, use the following A–Z of dream symbolism as a guide, as an amusement, or as inspiration on your journey into the world of the subconscious. But never forget the importance of the dreamer's role in untangling the mysteries of the sleeping mind.

A–Z of the
Language of Dreams

A

abandonment someone who dreams of being abandoned by close family may be experiencing greater personal and sexual freedom than he or she has had before. Dreams of being abandoned may also reflect feelings of being unwanted or unloved, feelings of emotional isolation.

abbey this dream is one of comfort, peace of mind, etc. The symbolism of sanctuary is obvious.

abbot, abbess, hermit, monk, nun, or priest to dream of becoming one denotes calmness in passion. Merely to dream of one indicates pride, or malice of which the dreamer will be the victim. The significance of this dream is evidently due to the regard in which the clergy of past ages held their gypsy brethren.

abdomen to see your abdomen in a dream, foretells that you will have great expectations, but you must curb hard-headedness and redouble your energies on your labour, as pleasure is approaching to your hurt. To see your abdomen shrivelled, foretells that you will be persecuted and defied by false friends. To see it swollen, you will have tribulations, but you will overcome them and enjoy the fruits of your labour. To see blood oozing from the abdomen, foretells an accident or tragedy in your family. The abdomen of children in an unhealthy state, portends that contagion will pursue you. *See* BODY, BELLY.

abduction if the dreamer is the abductor, the dream indicates a desire for power. Individuals who dream of being abducted are probably going through troublesome times, and may have a feeling of being carried away by events.

abject to dream that you are abject, denotes that you will be the recipient of gloomy tidings, which will cause a relaxation in your strenuous efforts to climb the heights of prosperity. To see others abject, is a sign of bickering and false dealings among your friends.

abortion a dream of abortion dreamt by a man reflects feelings of guilt, not necessarily in connection with parenthood or actual abortion. When dreamt by a woman, abortion dreams can indicate anxiety about starting out on something new.

above to see anything hanging above you, and about to fall, implies danger; if it falls upon you it may be ruin or sudden disappointment. If it falls near, but misses you, it is a sign that you will have a narrow escape from loss of money, or other misfortunes may follow. Should it be securely fixed above you, so as not to imply danger, your condition will improve after threatened loss.

abroad a dream of foreign travel may represent the dreamer's desire to be free of the constraints of his or her present environment, whether by making new friends or significantly altering his or her lifestyle.

Absalom to dream of Absalom, is significant of distressing incidents. You may unconsciously fall a victim to error, and penetrate some well beloved heart with keen anguish and pain over the committal of immoral actions and the outraging of innocence. No flower of purity will ever be too sacred for you to breathe a passionate breath upon. To dream of this, or any other disobedient character, is a warning against immoral tendencies. A father is warned by this dream to be careful of his children.

abscess, boil, running sore, etc to dream of having any of these afflictions indicates good fortune and good health, preceded by a temporary sickness (Raphael). These dreams may reflect illnesses in corresponding parts of the body. This interpretation is attributable to the theory that these visitations clear the system of impurities, thereby conferring comfort after sickness. *See also* ULCER.

absence to grieve over the absence of any one in your dreams, denotes that repentance for some hasty action will be the means of securing you life-long friendships. If you rejoice over the absence of friends, it denotes that you will soon be well rid of an enemy.

absinthe to come under the influence of absinthe in dreams, denotes that you will lead a merry and foolish pace with innocent companions, and waste your inheritance in prodigal lavishness on the siren, selfish fancy. For a young woman to dream that she drinks absinthe with her lover warns her to resist his persuasions to illicit consummation of their love. If she dreams she is drunk, she will yield up her favours without strong persuasion. (This dream typifies that you are likely to waste your energies in pleasure.)

abundance to dream that you are possessed with an abundance; foretells that you will have no occasion to reproach Fortune, and that you will be independent of her future favours; but your domestic happiness may suffer a collapse under the strain you are likely to put upon it by your infidelity.

abuse to dream of abusing a person, means that you will be unfortunate in your affairs, losing good money through over-bearing persistency in business relations with others. To feel yourself abused, you will be molested in your daily pursuits by the enmity of others. For a young woman to dream that she hears abusive language, foretells that she will fall under the ban of some person's jealousy and envy. If she uses the language herself, she will meet with unexpected rebuffs, that may fill her with mortification and remorse for her past unworthy conduct toward friends.

abyss if the dream involves feelings of fear, then it probably represents some loss of control, death or failure, or it may symbolize the dreamer's failure to face up to certain situations. If no fear is present, then a dream of falling into an abyss can represent the potential of going beyond preconceptions and experience. An abyss indicates impending danger, a dream of warning (Artemidorus) or an erotic dream of warning (Freud). This dream may be interpreted as a symptom of vertigo, due to apoplexy, etc. *See also* PRECIPICE.

acacia flowers a dream of rest and tranquillity, say the gypsy dreamers. This is an erotic dream according to Freud, while flower symbolists proclaim the blossom as signifying 'rest to the heart'. The Egyptians held it as sacred to woman.

academy to visit an academy in your dreams, denotes that you will regret opportunities that you have let pass through sheer idleness and indifference. To think you own, or are an inmate of one, you will find that you are to meet easy defeat of aspirations. You will take on knowledge, but be unable to rightly assimilate and apply it. For a young woman or any person to return to an academy after having finished there, signifies that demands will be made which the dreamer may find himself or her self unable to meet.

acceptance for a business man to dream that his proposition has been accepted, foretells that he will succeed in making a trade, which heretofore looked as if it would prove a failure. For a lover to dream that he has been accepted by his sweetheart, denotes that he will happily wed the object of his own and others' admiration.

If this dream has been occasioned by over-anxiety and weakness, the contrary may be expected. The elementary influences often play pranks upon weak and credulous minds by lying, and deceptive utterances. Therefore the dreamer should live a pure life, fortified by a strong will, thus controlling his destiny by expelling from it involuntary intrusions.

accident obviously, such a dream could have a link with a real accident experienced by the dreamer, but if no such experience has taken place, then the dream is probably due to anxiety. A dream of an accident at sea, for example, can signify the end of a long-term relationship and the accompanying feelings of insecurity. If someone dreams of coming to grief in an accident it may be that he or she is in fact punishing him or herself for something. Dreaming of an accident befalling somebody else may be indicative of negative feelings towards that person. To dream of injuring any part of the body may indicate suffering in that part (Raphael). In this case the dream is attributable to physical stimuli.

accolades *see* APPLAUSE.

accordion to dream of hearing the music of an accordion, denotes that you will engage in amusement which will win you from sadness and retrospection. You will by this means be enabled to take up your burden more cheerfully.

For a young woman to dream that she is playing an accordion, portends that she will win her lover by some sad occurrence; but, notwithstanding which, the same will confer lasting happiness upon her union. If the accordion gets out of tune, she will be saddened by the illness or trouble of her lover.

accounts to dream of having accounts presented to you for payment, you will be in a dangerous position. You may have recourse to law to disentangle yourself. If you pay the accounts, you will soon effect a compromise in some serious dispute.

To hold accounts against others, foretells that disagreeable contingencies will arise in your business, marring the smoothness of its management.

For a young woman book-keeper to dream of footing up accounts, denotes that she will have trouble in business, and in her love affairs; but some worthy person will persuade her to account for his happiness. She will be much respected by her present employers.

accuse to dream that you accuse any one of a mean action, denotes that you will have quarrels with those under you, and your dignity will be thrown from a high pedestal.

If you are accused, you are in danger of being guilty of distributing scandal in a sly and malicious way. *See* similar words in following chapters.

aches to dream that you have aches, denotes that you are halting too much in your business, and that some other person is profiting by your ideas.

For a young woman to dream that she has the heartache, foretells that she will be in sore distress over the laggardly way her lover prosecutes his suit. If it is the backache, she will encounter illness through careless exposure. If she has the headache, there will be much disquietude of mind for the risk she has taken to rid herself of rivalry.

This dream is usually due to physical causes and is of little significance.

acid dreaming of acid may indicate that something is weighing heavily on the dreamer's conscience, i.e. 'burning into' his or her mind.

acorns the saying about great oak trees growing from little acorns has some validity in the world of dreams, where the acorn is a symbol of potential for great growth, whether it be mental, physical or spiritual. This is a good dream according to Artemidorus, denoting health, wealth and happiness. If single it denotes a happy marriage. Acorns were regarded in certain parts of Europe as a symbol of wellbeing. They also bore a certain significance as associated with the sacred fire in the worship of Zeus at Dodona.

acquaintance to meet an acquaintance, and converse pleasantly with him, foretells that your business will run smoothly, and there will be but little discord in your domestic affairs.

If you seem to be disputing, or engaged in loud talk, humiliations and embarrassments will whirl seethingly around you.

If you feel ashamed of meeting an acquaintance, or meet him at an inopportune time, it denotes that you will be guilty of illicitly conducting yourself, and other parties will let the secret out.

For a young woman to think that she has an extensive acquaintance, signifies that she will be the possessor of vast interests, and her love will be worthy the winning. If her circle of acquaintances is small, she will be unlucky in gaining social favours.

After dreaming of acquaintances, you may see or hear from them.

acquittal to dream that you are acquitted of a crime, denotes that you are about to come into possession of valuable property, but there is danger of a law suit before obtaining possession.

To see others acquitted, foretells that your friends will add pleasure to your labours.

acrobat to dream of seeing acrobats, denotes that you will be prevented from carrying out hazardous schemes by the foolish fears of others.

To see yourself performing acrobatics, you will have a sensation to answer for, and your existence will be made almost unendurable by the guying of your enemies.

To see women performing acrobatics, denotes that your name will be maliciously and slanderously handled. Also your business interests will be hindered.

For a young woman to dream that she sees acrobats in tights, signifies that she will court favour of men.

acting dreams of acting and giving a poor performance suggest a lack of self-confidence about something. Dreams of performing may also point to the part which a person plays in life, the act he or she puts on in front of other people.

actor and actress to see in your dreams an actress, denotes that your present state will be one of unbroken pleasure and favour.

To see one in distress, you will gladly contribute your means and influence to raise a friend from misfortune and indebtedness.

If you think yourself one, you will have to work for subsistence, but your labours will be pleasantly attended.

If you dream of being in love with one, your inclination and talent will be allied with pleasure and opposed to downright toil.

To see a dead actor, or actress, your good luck will be overwhelmed in violent and insubordinate misery.

To see them wandering and penniless, foretells that your affairs will undergo a change from promise to threatening of failure. To those enjoying domestic comforts, it is a warning of revolution and faithless vows.

For a young woman to dream that she is engaged to an actor, or about to marry one, foretells that her fancy will bring remorse after the glamour of pleasure has vanished.

If a man dreams that he is sporting with an actress, it foretells that private broils with his wife, or sweetheart, will make him more misery than enjoyment.

actions what one is doing with one's body in a dream may be significant.

dancing a dream involving dancing is generally taken to be symbolic of the interaction of people on an emotional or sexual level, even as the precursor to sexual intercourse. It can also reflect feelings of elation, joy or victory that the dreamer experiences in life.

kneeling may denote a feeling of humility or even worthlessness on the part of the dreamer.

lying down may suggest relaxation, passivity, or a denial of responsibilities.

running may suggest a strong sensation of the life force within, and exuberance. Running away suggests avoidance, either of emotions, fears or responsibilities, depending on the context of the dream. A fortunate dream of advantageous journeys and elevation in rank unless the dreamer falls, in which case misfortune is denoted (gypsy folklore).

turning turning round and round in circles suggests indecision and lack of direction. Turning to face in another direction suggests a decision to make changes in waking life.

Adam and Eve to dream of Adam and Eve, foretells that some eventful occasion will rob you of the hope of success in your affairs.

To see them in the garden, Adam dressed in his fig leaf, but Eve perfectly nude save for an Oriental coloured serpent ornamenting her waist and abdomen, signifies that treachery and ill faith will combine to overthrow your fortune.

To see or hear Eve conversing with the serpent, foretells that artful women will reduce you to the loss of fortune and reputation.

adamant to dream of adamant, denotes that you will be troubled and defeated in some desire that you held as your life.

adder to dream of seeing an adder strike, and a friend, who is dead but seems to be lying down and breathing, rises partly to a sitting position when the adder strikes at him, and then both disappearing into some bushes nearby, denotes that you will be greatly distressed over the ill luck of friends, and a loss threatened to yourself.

For a young woman to see an adder, foretells a deceitful person is going to cause her trouble. If it runs from her, she will be able to defend her character in attacks made on her.

addition to dream of struggling over addition, denotes that you will have a struggle to overcome difficult situations, which will soon prominently assume formidable shapes in your business transactions.

To find some error in addition, shows that you will be able to overcome enemies by fortunately discerning their intention before they have executed their design.

To add figures with a machine, foretells that you will have a powerful ally who will save you from much oppression.

If you fail to read the figures, you will lose fortune by blind speculation.

admiration, adoration to admire others in a dream will not necessarily represent admiration of any one person in real life; it is more likely to represent finding and submitting to some sort of guiding spirit or influence.

admonishment to admonish your child, or son, or some young person, denotes that your generous principles will keep you in favour, and fortune will be added to your gifts.

adoption to see your adopted child, or parent, in your dreams, indicates that you will amass fortune through the schemes and speculations of strangers.

To dream that you or others are adopting a child, you will make an unfortunate change in your abode.

adulation to dream that you seek adulation, foretells that you will pompously fill unmerited positions of honour.

If you offer adulation, you will expressly part with some dear belonging in the hope of furthering material interests.

adultery, affairs a dream of adultery may relate to a similar situation in real life, or may merely be a sign of unresolved guilt about something completely unrelated. Occasionally, dreams of committing adultery may be indicative of a simple yearning to do just that, but they may also indicate anxiety. A dream of adultery committed by one's spouse may reflect fears of just such a thing, or may reflect the dreamer's fears of his or her sexual allure.

advancement to dream of advancing in any engagement, denotes your rapid ascendancy to preferment and to the consummation of affairs of the heart.

To see others advancing, foretells that friends will hold positions of favour near you.

adventure the wild, wonderful and sometimes terrifying adventures that occur in dreams are often a simple release from the reality of our lives, which is usually rather more mundane. If the adventure is terrifying, this normally reflects a desire to escape from a restrictive situation, while being afraid to do so.

adversary to dream that you meet or engage with an adversary, denotes that you will promptly defend any attacks on your interest. Sickness may also threaten you after this dream.

If you overcome an adversary, you will escape the effect of some serious disaster. *See* ENEMIES.

adversity to dream that you are in the clutches of adversity, denotes that you will have failures and continued bad prospects.

To see others in adversity, portends gloomy surroundings, and the illness of some one will produce grave fears of the successful working of plans.

The old dream books give this as a sign of coming prosperity. This definition is untrue. There are two forces at work in man, one from within and the other from without. They are from two distinct spheres; the animal mind influenced by the personal world of carnal appetites, and the spiritual mind from the realm of universal Brotherhood, present antagonistic motives on the dream consciousness. If these two forces were in harmony, the spirit or mental picture from the dream mind would find a literal fulfilment in the life of the dreamer.

The pleasurable sensations of the body cause the spirit anguish. The selfish enrichment of the body impoverishes the spirit influence upon the Soul. The trials of adversity often cause the spirit to rejoice and the flesh to weep. If the cry of the grieved spirit is left on the dream mind it may indicate to the dreamer worldly advancement, but it is hardly the theory of the occult forces, which have contributed to the contents of this book.

advertisement to dream that you are getting out advertisements, denotes that you will have to resort to physical labour to promote your interest, or establish your fortune.

To read advertisements, denotes that enemies will overtake you, and defeat you in rivalry.

advice to dream that you receive advice, denotes that you will be enabled to raise your standard of integrity, and strive by honest means to reach independent competency and moral altitude.

To dream that you seek legal advice, foretells that there will be some transactions in your affairs which will create doubt of their merits and legality.

advocation to dream that you advocate any cause, denotes that you will be faithful to your interests, and endeavour to deal honestly with the public, as your interests affect it, and be loyal to your promises to friends.

aeroplane *See* JOURNEY.

affliction to dream that affliction lays a heavy hand upon you and calls your energy to a halt, foretells that some disaster is surely approaching you.

To see others afflicted, foretells that you will be surrounded by many ills and misfortunes.

affluence to dream that you are in affluence, foretells that you will make fortunate ventures, and will be pleasantly associated with people of wealth. To young women, a vision of weird and fairy affluence is ominous of illusive and evanescent pleasure. They should study more closely their duty to friends and parents. After dreams of this nature they are warned to cultivate a love for home life. *See* WEALTH.

Africa to dream that you are in Africa surrounded by Cannibals, foretells that you will be oppressed by enemies and quarrelsome persons.

For a woman to dream of African scenes, denotes she will make journeys which will prove lonesome and devoid of pleasure or profit.

afternoon for a woman to dream of an afternoon, denotes she will form friendships which will be lasting and entertaining. A cloudy, rainy afternoon, implies disappointment and displeasure. See also TIME.

afternoon/evening may represent the later years of life.

daylight/daytime may represent the conscious self.

morning may represent childhood.

night its blackness may represent that which is unknown, perhaps that which lies in the future. According to the mood of the dream, night may represent a time of fear, or a time of peace and rest.

agate to see agate in a dream, signifies a slight advancement in business affairs.

age to dream of age, portends failures in any kind of undertaking.

To dream of your own age, indicates that perversity of opinion will bring down upon you the indignation of relatives.

For a young woman to dream of being accused of being older than she is, denotes that she will fall into bad companionship, and her denial of stated things will be brought to scorn. To see herself looking aged, intimates possible sickness, or unsatisfactory ventures. If it is her lover she sees aged, she will be in danger of losing him.

aggression/hostility to dream of being an aggressor is often a simple expression of anger which the dreamer has been forced to suppress in waking life. It is worth reflecting upon why the dream anger is directed towards a particular person or group of people. A woman who dreams of an aggressive man may have a deep-seated fear of sexual assault, while an aggressive woman in a man's dream may, in reality, be a symbol for the unresolved fear of his mother.

agony this is not as good a dream, as some would wish you to believe. It portends worry and pleasure intermingled, more of the former than of the latter.

To be in agony over the loss of money, or property, denotes that disturbing and imaginary fears will rack you over the critical condition of affairs, or the illness of some dear relative. *See* WEEPING.

air this dream denotes a withering state of things, and bodes no good to the dreamer.

To dream of breathing hot air suggests that you will be influenced to evil by oppression.

To feel cold air, denotes discrepancies in your business, and incompatibility in domestic relations.

To feel oppressed with humidity, some curse will fall on you that will prostrate and close down on your optimistic views of the future.

alabaster to dream of alabaster, foretells success in marriage and all legitimate affairs. To break an alabaster figure or vessel, denotes sorrow and repentance. For a young woman to lose an alabaster box containing incense, signifies that she will lose her lover or property through carelessness of her reputation.

alarm bell to hear a bell in your sleep, denotes that you will have cause for anxiety.

album to dream of an album, denotes you will have success and true friends.

For a young woman to dream of looking at photographs in an album, foretells that she will soon have a new lover who will be very agreeable to her.

alcohol dreams of being drunk and incapable may point to excesses of some sort in the life of the dreamer, or may express a subconscious fear of losing control.

alcohol to be given to drinking alcohol in your dreams, omens ill-natured rivalry and contention for small possession. To think you have quit drinking, or find that others have done so, shows that you will rise above present estate and rejoice in prosperity.

alley loss of property is augured here, a plausible interpretation from the gypsy standpoint, while the Freudian erotic meaning is less obvious.

alligator *see* ANIMALS.

alloy to dream of alloy, denotes your business will vex you in its complications. For a woman to dream of alloy, is significant of sorrow and trouble completely hiding pleasure.

almanac to dream of an almanac, means variable fortunes and illusive pleasures. To be studying the signs, foretells that you will be harassed by small matters taking up your time.

almond to dream of eating an almond symbolizes future enjoyment and travelling in distant lands. If the almonds are bitter the journey will be unhappy. The almond has always been a sacred symbol throughout the orient and can be traced etymologically to *al monde*, meaning Lord of the World, sole protecting Lord.

almond tree a dream of success (Raphael). A symbol with religious connotations, as the almond has. Freudians contend that dreams of trees bear an erotic meaning.

altar to dream of seeing a priest at the altar, denotes quarrels and unsatisfactory states in your business and home. To see a marriage, sorrow to friends, and death to old age.

An altar would hardly be shown you in a dream, accept to warn you against the commission of error. Repentance is also implied.

aluminium to dream of aluminium, denotes contentment with any fortune, however small. For a woman to see her aluminium ornaments or vessels tarnished, foretells strange and unexpected sorrow, and loss will befall her.

amateur to dream of seeing an amateur actor on the stage, denotes that you will see your hopes pleasantly and satisfactorily fulfilled. If they play a tragedy, evil will be disseminated through your happiness. If there is an indistinctness or distorted images in the dream, you are likely to meet with quick and decided defeat in some enterprise apart from your regular business.

ambush to dream that your are attacked from ambush, denotes that you have lurking secretly near you a danger, which will soon set upon and overthrow you if you are heedless of warnings.

If you lie in ambush to revenge yourself on others, you will unhesitatingly stoop to debasing actions to defraud your friends.

America high officials should be careful of State affairs, others will do well to look after their own person, for some trouble is at hand after this dream.

amethyst seen in a dream, represents contentment with fair business.

For a young woman to lose an amethyst, foretells broken engagements and slights in love.

ammonia seen in a dream, means displeasure will be felt by the dreamer at the conduct of a friend. Quarrels and disruptions of friendships will follow this dream.

For a young woman to see clear bottles of ammonia, foretells she will be deceived in the character and intentions of some person whom she considers friendly.

ammunition to dream of ammunition, foretells the undertaking of some work, which promises fruitful completion. To dream your ammunition is exhausted, denotes fruitless struggles and endeavours.

amputation ordinary amputation of limbs, denotes small offices lost; the loss of entire legs or arms, unusual depression in trade. To seamen, storm and loss of property. Afflicted persons should be warned to watchfulness after this dream.

anchor hope fulfilled is the general dream interpretation, endorsed by Christian symbolism. The Japanese hold it as an emblem of security and safety.

anecdote to dream of relating an anecdote, signifies that you will greatly prefer gay companionship to that of intellect, and that your affairs will prove as unstable as yourself.

For a young woman to hear anecdotes related, denotes that she will be one of a merry party of pleasure-seekers.

angel an angel appearing in a dream is possibly a symbol for the mother of the dreamer, or at least those aspects of the dreamer's mother which exercised a benevolent or benign influence over his or her life. A purely Christian symbol of protection, divine grace, etc, to the dreamer it prophecies peace and unspeakable happiness.

anger to dream of anger, denotes that some awful trial awaits you. Disappointments in loved ones, and broken ties, of enemies may make new attacks upon your property or character.

To dreams that friends or relatives are angry with you, while you meet their anger with composure, denotes you will mediate between opposing friends, and gain their lasting favour and gratitude.

angling to dream of catching fish is good. If you fail to catch any, it will be bad for you.

animals dreams of animals are often a reflection of 'the animal within' the dreamer, i.e. motivations and impulses that are of an instinctive rather than an intellectual nature. Certain animals are thought to have special significance.

Freud attached sexual significance to dreams of animals; dream interpreters, however, regard the dream of a number of domestic animals as foretelling happiness, while wild animals symbolize enemies.

alligator/crocodile a cunning, dangerous enemy. Being attacked by an alligator indicates the dreamer's insecurity and fear of an enemy. Freudians would translate this as an erotic dream.

antelope seeing antelopes in a dream, foretells your ambitions will be high, but may be realised by putting forth great energy. For a young woman to see an antelope miss its footing and fall from a height, denotes the love she aspires to will prove her undoing.

animals (ctd.)

ape or *monkey* a dream of deceit, treacherous friends and associates (Artemidorus). Plato taught that the soul of a bad jester would return as an ape. It may be a modern symbol of uncleanness, lust, cunning, and malice. It was, however, an emblem of wisdom in Egypt and of the god Thoth, patron of the art of writing.

ass a dream of patience that will enable the dreamer to overcome all obstacles. A Christian symbol of humility and patient endurance.

baby animals all of us still have certain needs for nurturing which we never grow out of. We all need to be cared for, to a certain extent. These needs are often represented by baby animals in dreams. Alternatively, baby animals could represent immaturity.

bear a bear may be a symbol of motherhood, or perhaps possessiveness. It can signify a rich, powerful enemy. To overcome a bear in your dream is a favourable sign (Artemidorus). Although the cult of Artemis worshipped the she-bear, in Christian thought the ferocious animals are usually suspect. The bear is a modern symbol of ferocity and surliness. A dream of this kind also has a sexual significance.

boar storms and tempests are predicted by this dream, as is trouble caused by evil-minded people (Artemidorus). A Christian symbol of impurity. A sexual symbol of power and oppression (Freud).

camel this is a dream of burdens patiently borne (Artemidorus). The camel is a modern symbol of patience and submission.

cat cats symbolize the elegant and mysterious aspects of some people. Cats also represent intuitiveness. A dream of a cat may be an unfavourable one of treachery and deceit. To be scratched by a cat symbolizes bad luck, but to kill one is a good omen denoting triumph over enemies (Artemidorus). The image of a cat in a dream expresses an angry, discontented mood. The cat was worshipped as a symbol of the sun god in Egypt. The same word, Mau, stands for both cat and light. The Hebrew horror of the gods of the Egyptians is therefore expressed in their interpretation of the cat as a symbol of deceit and treachery. To dream of a *black cat* or any black animal is unfortunate, for these are associated with evil spirits (Artemidorus). The Chinese attach especial misfortune to the symbol of the black cat.

animals (ctd.)

American Indians hold it as a symbol of good luck. The *kitten* symbolizes joy, peace and happiness at home; to be scratched by one, however, predicts an unhappy married life (gypsy folklore).

cattle a dream of a herd of cattle is a dream of prosperity (gypsy folklore); a dream of plenty in proportion to the number seen (Artemidorus). 'Cattle over a thousand hills,' we read as the symbol of success in the Old Testament. The *cow* is a symbol of the earth as mother of all things.

beaver to dream of seeing beavers, foretells that you will obtain comfortable circumstances by patient striving. If you dream of killing them for their skins, you will be accused of fraud and improper conduct toward the innocent.

badger to dream of a badger, is a sign of luck after battles with hardships.

bull represents urges of a sexual nature, i.e. animal lust. It can also represent aggressive impulsiveness ('like a bull at a gate'). Violent enemies and slander are forecast by this dream (Artemidorus). A dream of a bull, as with many dreams of animals is an erotic dream (Freud and Jung). To be attacked by one can be interpreted as an omen or as an erotic dream.

chameleon this dream indicates that the dreamer is being cheated mercilessly (gypsy folklore).

clam to dream of digging for them is a good omen, denoting thrift (gypsy folklore).

crab signifies a ruinous lawsuit (gypsy folklore); a modern expression for an ill-tempered person; the tenacity of the crab has become symbolic.

deer dissensions, disputes and quarrels with one's sweetheart (gypsy folklore). It can also be an erotic dream (Jung). To dream of a *fawn* denotes inconstancy (gypsy folklore). The fawn is a symbol of fleetness and timidity. To kill a *hart* in your dreams forecasts an inheritance from an old man, also the overcoming of fugitive and deceitful enemies. A running hart shows wealth through subtlety (Artemidorus).

animals (ctd.)

dog dogs appear quite frequently in people's dreams. Their symbolism rather depends on the way they appear in the dreams. Thus, friendly dogs can represent faithfulness and friendship, either of the dreamer or another person, whilst vicious dogs can represent aggression and betrayal. The dog is a modern symbol of fidelity. *Bulldogs* represent faithful, loyal friends (gypsy folklore). To dream of following *hounds* denotes unprofitable pursuits (gypsy folklore). To be bitten by one predicts an injury from a friend (gypsy folklore). Jung and Freud classify all dreams of animals or of being bitten by animals as erotic, or sex dreams.

dolphin out of water, a dream of the loss of sweetheart or friend; swimming it augurs unexpected adventure. In medieval art it symbolizes social love. The dolphin was anciently held as the special friend of man and the saviour of the shipwrecked.

donkey/ass/mule the most basic life-force within the dreamer, i.e. the reflexes which are necessary for life may be represented by an ass or a donkey. To dream that mules are savage and mad and that they hurt denotes deceit by someone of your own household (Artemidorus).

earthworm a dream of secret enemies (gypsy folklore).

eels a warning to beware of uncertain speculations (gypsy folklore). 'As slippery as an eel,' is the old simile for a rogue.

elephant a fortunate dream forecasting riches (gypsy folklore). The elephant is a symbol of power and wisdom. In India the god of wisdom is elephant-headed.

elk a dream of good luck (gypsy folklore).

ferret a dream of enemies deep and sly (gypsy folklore). The symbol is founded on the reputation of the ferret as being a sly and wicked creature.

fish fish in dreams represent the unconscious motivations or impulses of human beings, either individual or collective, and are often closely connected with the unconscious drive to procreate. Fish may represent unknown aspects of the self that are as yet undiscovered or not yet understood, or may symbolize a supreme being, such as the Christ figure. Dreaming of eating fish can be symbolic of an attempt to find

animals (ctd.)

the hidden self by delving deep into the unconscious. Fish can predict much pleasure, and comparative independence (Raphael). Originally an emblem of sex and of fecundity it was adopted by the Christians as a symbol of Christ and the church.

frogs a lucky dream, forecasting good to all conditions (Artemidorus). The frog is a symbol of transformation, regeneration, new life, resurrection. However, if the feeling that accompanies the dream of frogs is revulsion then the dreamer must consider what aspect of their life might be making them unhappy.

goat a dream of enemies, trials and deceit (Artemidorus). The goat is an emblem of lewdness and wickedness in Christian symbolism.

hare a dream of wealth resulting from fertility of resource and address. The hair is a symbol of nimbleness, wit and cleverness in gypsy folklore and African lore.

hedgehog a dream forecasting the meeting with an old friend whom you have not seen for years (gypsy folklore). The hedgehog is a gypsy emblem of honesty and loyalty.

hog avarice and greed are indicated by a dream of a hog (Artemidorus). The hog is a symbol of sensuality.

horse the appearance of a horse in a dream is generally thought to represent human dynamic energy, whether mental or physical, sexual or creative. A wounded or a dying horse will therefore represent the weakening or fading of power in some way. Dreaming of running away from a horse or horses can mean a fear of the dreamer's own potential in some way, whether this be his or her sexuality or intellectual, spiritual or physical potential. Jung regarded this as an erotic dream. To dream of riding signifies success (gypsy folklore).

hyena a dream of cruel sorrow (gypsy folklore). The hyena is a symbol of ferocity.

jackal this dream denotes an enemy who will backbite and bring trouble (gypsy folklore). An Egyptian symbol of judgement, and of watchfulness over sacred things, the jackal was evidently held in horror by the faiths that succeeded those of Egypt.

animals (ctd.)

kangaroo dreaming of kangaroos signifies prolonged worries. To kill one is a lucky dream (gypsy folklore). Wild animals generally symbolize misfortune with gypsy interpreters. Freud and Jung, however, attach to them an erotic significance.

leeches to dream of leeches being applied denotes sickness (Raphael). As an ancient and popular remedy, the application of leeches would indicate a subconsciousness of illness, though this is unlikely in the modern age.

leopard to dream of a leopard signifies dangers and difficulties and as many changes as there are spots on his coat (gypsy folklore). The leopard is the symbol of watchfulness and alertness, also treachery.

lion lions mean power, particularly the power and strength brought on by anger and aggression. This is also true of a dream of a *wolf*. Dreaming of a lion is said to denote discourse with a great king or commander. Combat with a lion forecasts a quarrel with some great adversary Strength, majesty and courage are symbolized by the lion.

lizard misfortune through secret enemies is denoted by this dream (Artemidorus). The lizard is the medieval symbol of misfortune and ill-luck.

lobsters foretell sorrows and troubles (gypsy folklore).

lynx a dream warning you that you are watched by a keen-eyed enemy (Artemidorus).

mare for a man to dream of seeing a young mare denotes marriage to a beautiful, young, rich woman. An ill-shapen mare denotes a disadvantageous alliance (Artemidorus).

mouse a dream of mice denotes envious slanderers and poverty (gypsy folklore).

otter a dream of disagreeable and dangerous acquaintances.

oysters 'To dream of opening and eating oysters shows great hunger, or a living earned through pains and difficulty.' (Artemidorus).

oyster shells empty oyster shells signify loss, disappointment and worry (gypsy folklore).

animals (ctd.)

ox in a dream signifies the yoke of obedience. A pair of fat oxen predicts a year of plenty, lean oxen are an omen of scarcity and famine. Oxen ploughing a field predict gain and plenty (Artemidorus). The symbolism is plainly drawn from Pharaoh's dream of the kine. The ox symbolized patience, strength and sacrifice, in Christian art.

panther a dream predicting the approach of evil, a lawsuit (gypsy folklore); the panther is the symbol of watchfulness and alertness.

pig a dream both good and bad. Dreaming of a pig may denote false friends, but a faithful lover (gypsy folklore). The pig is a Chinese lucky symbol, but is regarded as an emblem of greed.

porcupine a dream auguring the handling of a delicate affair (gypsy folklore).

racoon to dream of a racoon is a sign of rain (gypsy folklore). The Ainu, the aboriginal people of Japan, prayed to the skulls of these animals during drought to bring on rain. To increase the storm they donned gloves and caps of racoon skin and danced.

rat dreaming of many rats signifies enemies through whom the dreamer will suffer losses, trouble and anxiety. To kill rats, however, is a good dream (Raphael).

reindeer always a lucky dream (gypsy folklore). The association with the Christmas legends accounts for this interpretation.

salamander a dream of assurance that neither man nor elements can harm you (gypsy folklore). The symbolism here is derived from the traditional belief that mythical beasts was that they lived in fire.

salmon a dream denoting division in the family (gypsy folklore).

scorpions misfortunes through secret enemies (gypsy folklore). The scorpion is an ancient symbol of war.

shark this dream denotes an enemy. If the shark eats you, the enemy will ruin you (gypsy folklore).

sheep/lamb to dream of sheep predicts prosperity and enjoyment. If they are scattered they signify persecution (gypsy folklore). The *lamb* was an early Christian symbol for the church. A dream of a ewe-lamb symbolizes a faithful and precious friendship (gypsy

animals (ctd.)

folklore). 'A possession greatly prized' in scriptural symbolism. A dream of a lamb is always a favourable dream except to dream of slaying a lamb, this denotes moral torment. To own a lamb denotes comfort, peace and happiness (gypsy folklore).

shellfish to find shells empty, loss of time and credit; to find them full, hope of success. To gather them, merry making and sport.

shrimp a dream of grief and distraction.

snail to see a snail in your dream foretells honourable promotion. If it shows its horns it denotes infidelity, adultery, want of chastity, etc. (Artemidorus).

snake could reflect fears of plots against the dreamer or sexual anxiety. *See also* REPTILE and SERPENT.

spiders to dream of a spider foretells money. For a spider to spin its web before your face augurs a fortune (Raphael). The spider is the symbol of shrewdness, perseverance and foresight. To dream of seeing the upper part of a room covered with spiders may be a symptom of headache.

stag a dream denoting gain and profit (gypsy folklore). The stag can be a symbol of solitude (Christian).

tiger this is the dream of an enemy. To escape from the chase of a tiger is a good omen; otherwise the dream predicts ruin (Raphael).

toad a dream denoting a malicious enemy. To kill a toad is said to predict success and triumph (gypsy folklore). The symbol of malice.

tortoise a dream signifying success through long toil and perseverance (gypsy folklore). See Aesop's fable of the hare and the tortoise.

trout a dream denoting money, the larger the trout the more the money (gypsy folklore).

viper enemies who strive to injure you symbolize an unfaithful partner (gypsy folklore). The symbolism here derives from the fable of the man who nourished a viper.

walrus to dream of a walrus denotes a wasted life (gypsy folklore).

weasel a dream of a weasel is said to forecast friendship for malicious persons (gypsy folklore). The symbolism derives from the weasel being an emblem of malice.

whale a dream warning the dreamer of danger (gypsy folklore).

animals (ctd.)

wildcat a warning to beware of enemies who have gained your confidence (gypsy folklore).

worms to dream of seeing worms in the path predicts death to the dreamer or to his friends (gypsy folklore). Worms were a medieval symbol of death and decay.

zebra a dream denoting misplaced friendship and ingratitude.

anniversary dreams usually indicate a happy time within the family, a get-together or a reunion.

annoyance this dream denotes that you have enemies who are at work against you. Annoyances experienced in dreams are apt to find speedy fulfilment in the trifling incidents of the following day.

antelope see animals.

ants *see* INSECTS.

anus *see* BODY.

anvil an anvil usually indicates prosperity despite obstacles (Raphael). It is an emblem of the primal force.

anxiety a dream of this kind is occasionally a good omen, denoting, after threatening states, success and rejuvenation of mind; but if the dreamer is anxious about some momentous affair, it indicates a disastrous combination of business and social states.

ape *see* ANIMALS.

apparition take unusual care of all depending upon you. Calamity awaits you and yours. Both property and life are in danger. Young people should be decidedly upright in their communications with the opposite sex. Character is likely to be rated at a discount.

appetite dreams involving appetite are generally sexually orientated. Dreams of loss of appetite can mean loss of libido, while hunger or thirst represent great sexual desire.

applause, accolades this is generally a wish-fulfilment dream. The dreamer seeks recognition for something which he or she has achieved. Some would believe that such a dream can foretell good fortune of some kind.

apple tree alive and flourishing, good news; dead, bad tidings. In mystic literature, the apple is the tree of life.

apples *see* FRUIT.

apprentice to dream that you serve as an apprentice, foretells you will have a struggle to win a place among your companions

apricot *see* FRUIT.

April to dream of the month of April, signifies that much pleasure and profit will be your allotment. If the weather is miserable, it is a sign of passing ill luck.

apron to dream of an apron, signifies a zigzag course, for a young woman. For a school girl to dream that her apron is loosened, or torn, implies bad lessons, and lectures in propriety from parents and teachers.

arch an arch in a dream, denotes your rise to distinction and the gaining of wealth by persistent effort. To pass under one, foretells that many will seek you who formerly ignored your position.

For a young woman to see a fallen arch, denotes the destruction of her hopes, and she will be miserable in her new situation.

archbishop to see an archbishop in dreams, is a sign of coming death. Gypsy outlaws established this unwholesome symbolism for the mighty prelate.

architect architects drawing plans in your dreams, denotes a change in your business, which will be likely to result in loss to you.

For a young woman to see an architect, foretells she will meet rebuffs in her aspirations and manoeuvres to make a favourable marriage.

arms *see* BODY.

aroma for a young woman to dream of a sweet aroma, denotes she will soon be the recipient of some pleasure or present.

arrested to see respectable-looking strangers arrested, foretells that you desire to make changes, and new speculations will be subordinated by the fear of failure. If they resist the officers, you will have great delight in pushing to completion the new enterprise. *See* PRISONER.

arrow this is an ominous dream if the arrow is directed towards the dreamer, or penetrates his body. It indicates that you feel that someone may be plotting against you (Artemidorus). An interpretation obviously derived from the significance of the arrow in warfare.

Freudians regard this as a sex dream, probably tracing the symbolism to the arrows of Eros or Cupid.

art gallery to visit an art gallery, portends unfortunate unions in domestic circles. You will struggle to put forth an appearance of happiness, but will secretly care for other associations.

ascend if you reach the extreme point of ascent, or top of steps, without stumbling, it is good; otherwise, you will have obstacles to overcome before the good of the day is found.

asceticism to dream of asceticism, denotes that you will cultivate strange principles and views, rendering yourself fascinating to strangers, but repulsive to friends.

ashes a dream of trouble and misfortune at hand. Ashes are a Christian symbol of mourning and grief.

Asia to dream of visiting Asia is assurance of change, but no material benefits from fortune will follow.

asp this is an unfortunate dream. Females may lose the respect of honourable and virtuous people. Deadly enemies are at work to defame character. Sweethearts will wrong each other.

asparagus to dream of asparagus, signifies prosperous surroundings and obedience from servants and children. To eat it, denotes interrupted success.

ass *see* ANIMALS.

assassin if you are the one to receive the assassin's blow, you will not surmount all your trials.

To see another, with the assassin standing over him with blood stains, portends that misfortune will come to the dreamer.

To see an assassin under any condition is a warning that losses may befall you through secret enemies.

assistance giving assistance to any one in a dream, foretells you will be favoured in your efforts to rise to higher position.

If any one assists you, you will be pleasantly situated, and loving friends will be near you.

astral dreams of the astral, denote that your efforts and plans will culminate in worldly success and distinction. A spectre or picture of your astral self brings heart-rending tribulation.

asylum to dream of an asylum, denotes sickness and unlucky dealings, which cannot be overcome without great mental struggle.

atlas to dream you are looking at an atlas, denotes that you will carefully study interests before making changes or journeys.

atonement means joyous communing with friends. Courting among the young will meet with happy consummation. The sacrifice or atonement of another for your waywardness, is portentous of the humiliation of self or friends through your open or secret disregard of duty. A woman after this dream is warned of approaching disappointment.

attic to dream that you are in an attic, denotes that you are entertaining hopes which will fail of materialisation.

For a young woman to dream that she is sleeping in an attic, foretells that she will fail to find contentment in her present occupation.

attorney to see an attorney at the bar, denotes that disputes of a serious nature will arise between parties interested in worldly things. Enemies are stealing upon you with false claims. If you see an attorney defending you, your friends will assist you in coming trouble, but they will cause you more worry than enemies.

auction to dream of an auction in a general way, is good. If you hear the auctioneer crying his sales, it means bright prospects and fair treatment from business ventures.

To dream of buying at an auction, signifies close deals to tradesmen, and good luck in live stock to the farmer. Plenty, to the housewife is the omen for women. If there is a feeling of regret about the dream, you are warned to be careful of your business affairs.

August to dream of the month of August, denotes unfortunate deals, and misunderstandings in love affairs.

For a young woman to dream that she is going to be married in August, is an omen of sorrow in her early wedded life.

aunt *see* UNCLE.

aura to dream of discussing any subject relating to aura, denotes that you will reach states of mental unrest, and work to discover the power which influences you from within.

author for an author to dream that his manuscript has been rejected by the publisher, denotes some doubt at first, but finally his work will be accepted as authentic and original.

To dream of seeing an author over his work, perusing it with anxiety, denotes that you will be worried over some literary work either of your own or that of some other person.

automobile to dream that you ride in an automobile, denotes that you will be restless under pleasant conditions, and will make a change in your affairs. There is grave danger of impolitic conduct intimated through a dream of this nature.

If one breaks down with you, the enjoyment of a pleasure will not extend to the heights you contemplate.

To find yourself escaping from the path of one, signifies that you will do well to avoid some rival as much as you can honestly allow.

For a young woman to look for one, she will be disappointed in her aims to entice some one into her favour.

autumn for a woman to dream of autumn, denotes she will obtain property through the struggles of others. If she thinks of marrying in autumn, she will be likely to contract a favourable marriage and possess a cheerful home.

awake to dream that you are awake, denotes that you will experience strange happenings which will throw you into gloom.

To pass through green, growing fields, and look upon landscape, in your dreams, and feel that it is an awaking experience, signifies that there is some good and brightness in store for you, but there will be disappointments intermingled between the present and that time.

axe to see an axe in a dream denotes death. Freud designates this as an erotic dream, although the interpretation is rather hazy. Amongst primitive races the axe was the symbol for God or the Divine Being. Later it became a symbol of solar power, with modern times, however, its symbolism altered and it became a crudely murderous weapon.

B

baby animals *see* ANIMALS.

baby babies appear quite frequently in dreams. A crying baby is generally thought to represent illness of some kind. Babies also represent one's responsibilities. Dreaming of looking after a baby and something dreadful happening to it can mean that you are frightened of making a mess of things. Dreaming of giving a baby to someone else to look after will mean shedding one's responsibilities, delegating, or perhaps even letting someone else take the blame.

baby carriages, prams to dream of a baby carriage, denotes that you will have a congenial friend who will devise many pleasurable surprises for you.

Bacchus, bacchanalians the interpretation given by Artemidorus of dreaming of Bacchus, the god of wine and drunken revelry, is of a bad year for wine and grape growers.

bachelor for a man to dream that he is a bachelor, is a warning for him to keep clear of women.

For a woman to dream of a bachelor, denotes love not born of purity. Justice goes awry. Politicians lose honour.

back to see your own back in your dream indicates misfortune, uneasiness of mind, sickness, etc. This may be a dream incited by backache, and its attendant discomfort that draws the dreamer's attention to that portion of the anatomy.

Artemidorus saw such a dream as a prediction of the love of a child or success in love.

backbite to dream that you are victimized by a scandal promises high success, the favour of great persons. A dream of CONTRARY MEANING, probably inspired by the interpreter's knowledge of the subconscious.

backgammon to dream of playing backgammon, denotes that you will, while visiting, meet with unfriendly hospitality, but will unconsciously win friendships which will endure much straining.

If you are defeated in the game, you will be unfortunate in bestowing your affections, and your affairs will remain in an unsettled condition.

bacon to dream of eating bacon is good, if someone is eating with you and hands are clean.

Rancid bacon, is dullness of perception and unsatisfactory states will worry you.

To dream of curing bacon is bad, if not clear of salt and smoke. If clear, it is good.

badger *see* ANIMALS.

bag *see* SACK.

baggage a dream of weariness, fatigue, an overburdened conscience. This dream might have religious significance being symbolic of the burden of sin.

Baghavad Ghitta to dream of the Baghavad, foretells for you a season of seclusion; also rest to the exhausted faculties. A pleasant journey for your advancement will be planned by your friends. Little financial advancement is promised in this dream.

bagpipes a dream forecasting increase in family and fortune (gypsy folklore). A Carpathian legend was that whenever someone played the bagpipes all things that he desired would grow about him.

bail if the dreamer is seeking bail, unforeseen troubles will arise; accidents are likely to occur; unfortunate alliances may be made.

If you go bail for another, about the same conditions, though hardly as bad.

bailiff shows a striving for a higher place, and a deficiency in intellect. If the bailiff comes to arrest, or make love, false friends are trying to work for your money.

bakery to dream of a bakery, demands caution in making changes in one's career. Pitfalls may reveal themselves on every hand.

For a young woman to dream that she is in a bakery, portends that her character will be assailed. She should exercise great care in her social affairs.

baking is unpropitious for a woman. Ill health and the care of many children; meanness and poverty of supporters are indicated.

balcony for lovers to dream of making sad adieus on a balcony, long and perhaps final separation may follow. Balcony also denotes unpleasant news of absent friends.

bald to see a bald-headed man, denotes that people are out to swindle you, but by keeping wide awake, you will outwit them.

For a man to dream of a bald-headed woman, insures him to have a vixen for wife.

A bald hill, or mountain, indicates famine and suffering in various forms.

For a young woman to dream of a bald-headed man, is a warning to her to use her intelligence against listening to her next marriage offer.

Bald-headed babies signify a happy home, a loving companion, and obedient children.

ball, dance a very satisfactory omen, if beautiful and gaily-dressed people are dancing to the strains of entrancing music. If you feel gloomy and distressed at the inattention of others, a death in the family may be expected soon.

ballet indicates infidelity in the marriage state; also failures in business, and quarrels and jealousies among sweethearts.

balloon in gypsy folklore this dream symbolizes unsuccessful schemes.

balm a dream that denotes sickness but certain recovery (Artemidorus). This may be a dream incited by discomfort in some part of the body.

bamboo a dream of dissension in the family circle in gypsy folklore. Probably originating in the use of rattan or bamboo for purposes of chastisement.

bananas *see* FRUIT.

banishment evil pursues the unfortunate dreamer. If you are banished to foreign lands, death will be your portion at an early date. To banish a child, means perjury of business allies. It is a dream of fatality.

bank to see vacant tellers, foretells business losses. Giving out gold money, denotes carelessness; receiving it, great gain and prosperity.

To see silver and bank-notes accumulated, increase of honour and fortune. You will enjoy the highest respect of all classes.

bankrupt denotes partial collapse in business, and weakening of the brain faculties. A warning to leave speculations alone.

banner to see the banner of your native country symbolizes misfortune to a loved one or a fatal journey in gypsy folklore. Another representation is that of a military emblem; to see it flying against a clear sky signifies victory over enemies.

banquet it is good to dream of a banquet. Friends will wait to do you favours. To dream of yourself, together with many gaily-attired guests, eating from costly plate and drinking wine of fabulous price and age, foretells enormous gain in enterprises of every nature, and happiness among friends.

To see inharmonious influences, strange and grotesque faces or empty tables, is ominous of grave misunderstandings or disappointments.

bantam to see bantam chickens in your dream, denotes your fortune will be small, yet you will enjoy contentment. If they appear sickly, or exposed to wintry storms, your interests will be impaired.

baptism to dream of baptism, signifies that your character needs strengthening by the practice of temperance in advocating your opinions to the disparagement of your friends.

To dream that you are an applicant, signifies that you will humiliate your inward self for public favour.

To dream that you see John the Baptist baptising Christ in the Jordan, denotes that you will have a desperate mental struggle between yielding yourself to labour in meagre capacity for the sustenance of others, or follow desires which might lead you into wealth and exclusiveness.

To see the Holy Ghost descending on Christ, is significant of resignation to duty and abnegation of self.

If you are being baptised with the Holy Ghost and fire, it means that you will be thrown into a state of terror over being discovered in some lustful engagement.

bar to dream of tending a bar, denotes that you will resort to some questionable mode of advancement.

Seeing a bar, denotes activity in communities, quick uplifting of fortunes, and the consummation of illicit desires; the dreamer who dreams of a public house or ale house should be very cautious of his affairs. Enemies are watching him.

barber to dream of a barber, denotes that success will come through struggling and close attention to business. For a young woman to dream of a barber, foretells that her fortune will increase, though meagrely.

barefoot to dream that you have become barefoot is a dream of success and prosperity (gypsy folklore).

barley bread in gypsy folklore, to dream of eating barley bread denotes health, contentment, etc. It is plainly a dream of healthy hunger and its gratification.

barley fields in gypsy folklore, to walk through them indicates trouble and pain to the dreamer. This is distinctly the symbol of gypsies, in view of the penalties attached to damaging the farmer's crops.

barmaid for a man to dream of a barmaid, denotes that his desires run to low pleasures, and he will scorn purity.

For a young woman to dream that she is a barmaid, foretells that she will be attracted to fast men, and that she will prefer irregular pleasures to propriety.

barn if well filled with ripe and matured grain, and perfect ears of corn, with fat stock surrounding it, it is an omen of great prosperity. If empty, the reverse may be expected.

barometer to see a barometer in a dream, foretells a change will soon take place in your affairs, which will prove profitable to you. If it is broken, you will find displeasing incidents in your business, arising unexpectedly.

barrel *see* CASK.

baseball to see baseball in your dream, denotes you will be easily contented, and your cheerfulness will make you a popular companion.

For a young woman to dream that she is playing baseball, means much pleasure for her, but no real profit or comfort.

basement to dream that you are in a basement, foretells that you will see prosperous opportunities abating, and with them, pleasure will dwindle into trouble and care. *See* CELLAR.

basin for a young woman to dream of bathing in a basin, foretells her womanly graces will win her real friendships and elevations.

basket to dream of seeing or carrying a basket, signifies that you will meet unqualified success, if the basket is full; but empty baskets indicate discontent and sorrow.

bass voice to dream that you have a bass voice, denotes you will detect some discrepancy in your business, brought about by the deceit of some one in your employ. For the lover, this foretells estrangements and quarrels.

basting to dream of basting meats while cooking, denotes you will undermine your own expectations by folly and selfishness. For a woman to baste her sewing, omens much vacation owing to her extravagance.

bath baths generally represent a kind of moral cleansing, a kind of 'washing away of guilt'. The dreamer may desire to alter his or her habits and adapt a healthier lifestyle.

bathing a dream of bathing in clean, clear water is a dream of great good fortune, in muddy water, the reverse is true (Artemidorus).

bathroom to see white roses in a bathroom, and yellow ones in a box, denote that sickness will interfere with pleasure; but more lasting joys will result from this disappointment.

For a young woman to dream of a bathroom, foretells that her inclinations trend too much toward light pleasures and frivolities.

bats the unfortunate dreamer of this animal will suffer sorrows and calamities. Death of parents and friends, loss of limbs or sight, may follow after a dream of these ghoulish monsters. A white bat is almost a sure sign of death.

battle a battle, or taking part in battles, usually signifies struggles which the dreamer faces in his or her life. To overcome indicates triumph (gypsy folklore). Evidently the realities of warfare were too grim and too close to admit the rule of contraries to apply to this dream, to which modern interpreters, however, attach an erotic meaning.

bay tree a palmy leisure awaits you in which you will meet many pleasing varieties of diversions. Much knowledge will be reaped in the rest from work. It is generally a good dream for everybody.

bayonet to dream of a bayonet, signifies that enemies will hold you in their power, unless you get possession of the bayonet.

beacon light a dream indicating deliverance from care and trouble (Artemidorus).

beads this dream denotes success, good fortune, honour and wealth (gypsy folklore). The symbolism is derived from the property of amulet beads to avert misfortune and the evil eye.

beans an unfortunate dream. To eat them augurs illness, to see them growing predicts contentions and quarrels (Artemidorus). An erotic dream according to more recent authority. The symbolism may derive from the Flamen Diates at Rome, the Egyptian priests, the ancient Hebrews and the Pythagoreans who were forbidden to eat them.

bear *see* ANIMALS.

beard to see one in a dream denotes health. If it is a long one it represents gain. A beard on a woman, however, is a disagreeable omen (Artemidorus). The beard symbolizes the male sex and according to Freudians is an erotic symbol representing the genitalia.

beasts *see* ANIMALS.

beating it bodes no good to dream of being beaten by an angry person; family jars and discord are signified.

To beat a child, ungenerous advantage is taken by you of another; perhaps the tendency will be to cruelly treat a child.

beauty in any form is pre-eminently good. A beautiful woman brings pleasure and profitable business. A well formed and beautiful child, indicates love reciprocated and a happy union.

beaver *see* ANIMALS.

bed fellow to dream that you do not like your bed fellow, foretells that some person who has claims upon you, will censure and make your surroundings unpleasant generally.

If you have a strange bed fellow, your discontent will worry all who come near you. If you think you have any kind of animal in bed with you, there will be unbounded ill luck overhanging you.

bed *see* FURNITURE.

bedbugs seen in your dreams, they indicate continued sickness and unhappy states. Fatalities are intimated if you see them in profusion.

To see bedbugs simulating death, foretells unhappiness caused by illness. To mash them, and water appears instead of blood, denotes alarming but not fatal illness or accident. To see bedbugs crawling up white walls, and you throw scalding water upon them, denotes grave illness will distress you, but there will be useless fear of fatality.

If the water fails to destroy them, some serious complication with fatal results is not improbable.

bed-chamber to see one newly furnished, a happy change for the dreamer. Journeys to distant places, and pleasant companions.

bedroom *see* HOUSE.

bee *see* INSECTS.

beef if raw and bloody, cancers and tumours of a malignant nature will attack the subject. Be on your guard as to bruises and hurts of any kind.

To see, or eat cooked beef, anguish surpassing human aid is before you. Loss of life by horrible means will occur. Beef properly served under pleasing surroundings denotes harmonious states in love and business, if otherwise, evil is foreboded, though it may be of a trifling nature.

beer fateful of disappointments if drinking from a bar. To see others drinking, work of designing intriguers will displace your fairest hopes.

To habitué's of this beverage, harmonious prospectives are foreshadowed, if pleasing, natural and cleanly conditions survive. The dream occurrences frequently follow in the actual.

beetles *see* INSECTS.

beetroot to see them growing abundantly, harvest and peace will obtain in the land; eating them with others, is full of good tidings.

If they are served in soiled or impure dishes, distressful awakenings will disturb you.

beggar to see an old, decrepit beggar, is a sign of bad management, and unless you are economical, you will lose much property. Scandalous reports will prove detrimental to your fame.

To give to a beggar, denotes dissatisfaction with present surroundings.

To dream that you refuse to give to a beggar is altogether bad.

beheading to dream of being beheaded, overwhelming defeat or failure in some undertaking will soon follow.

To see others beheaded, if accompanied by a large flow of blood, death and exile are portended.

behind *see* POSITION.

belladonna strategic moves will bring success in commercial circles. Women will find rivals in society; vain and fruitless efforts will be made for places in men's affections.

Taking it, denotes misery and failure to meet past debts.

bellman fortune is hurrying after you. Questions of importance will be settled amicably among disputants. To see him looking sad some sorrowful event or misfortune may soon follow.

bellows working a bellows, denotes a struggle, but a final triumph over poverty and fate by energy and perseverance.

To dream of seeing a bellows, distant friends are longing to see you.

To hear one, occult knowledge will be obtained by the help of powerful means. One fallen into disuse, portends you have wasted energies under misguiding impulses.

bells a good dream under most conditions (gypsy folklore). They were believed by the ancients to disperse storms, to drive away pestilence and devils, and to put out fire. In Christian symbolism bells represent the exorcism of evil spirits.

In modern times, however, subject to the context of the dream, the bells can be interpreted as alarm bells, warning the dreamer of something he or she should be paying heed to, or something that he or she is in danger of overlooking.

belly it is bad to dream of seeing a swollen mortifying belly, it indicates desperate sickness. To see anything moving on the belly, prognosticates humiliation and hard labour. *See* ABDOMEN, BODY.

belt to dream that you have a new style belt, denotes you are soon to meet and make engagements with a stranger, which will demoralise your prosperity. If it is out of date, you will be meritedly censured for rudeness.

bench distrust debtors and confidants if you dream of sitting on one. If you see others doing so, happy reunions between friends who have been separated through misunderstandings are suggested.

bequest after this dream, pleasures of consolation from the knowledge of duties well performed, and the health of the young is assured.

bereavement to dream of the bereavement of a child, warns you that your plans will meet with quick frustration, and where you expect success there will be failure.

Bereavement of relatives, or friends, denotes disappointment in well matured plans and a poor outlook for the future.

bet betting on races, beware of engaging in new undertakings. Enemies are trying to divert your attention from legitimate business.

Betting at gaming tables, denotes that immoral devices will be used to wring money from you.

bible to dream of the Bible, foretells that innocent and disillusioned enjoyment will be proffered for your acceptance.

To dream that you vilify the teachings of the Bible, forewarns you that you are about to succumb to resisted temptations through the seductive persuasiveness of a friend.

bicycle journey *see* JOURNEY.

bicycle to dream of riding a bicycle up hill, signifies bright prospects. Riding it down hill, if the rider be a woman, calls for care regarding her good name and health; misfortune hovers near.

bigamy for a man to commit bigamy, denotes loss of manhood and failing mentality. To a woman, it predicts that she will suffer dishonour unless very discreet.

bill to dream that you receive a bill, warns you to look after your affairs and correct all tendency towards neglect of business and love.

billiards foretell coming troubles to the dreamer. Law suits and contentions over property. Slander will get in her work to your detriment. If you see table and balls idle, deceitful comrades are undermining you.

bird's nest to dream of finding a nest with eggs indicates profit. A nest that is empty, disappointment (Artemidorus); here the symbolism is that of nature itself.

birds birds can signify many things in dreams. Birds in general are thought to represent some aspects of the human being, particularly intellect and spirituality. Some say that a bird in flight represents sexuality, particularly sexual freedom. Freudians regard dreams of birds as erotic dreams. Other interpreters give them varied meanings according to the nature of the birds.

caged birds represent frustration and confinement. *See also* CAGE.

blackbird both in dream lore and in symbolism these birds indicate slander, suspicion and trouble.

chicken for a mother to dream of seeing a brood of chickens under a hen warns her that despite her care some of her offspring will stray (Artemidorus). This dream is traceable to maternal anxiety.

cock a dream denoting pride, success and power, combined with watchfulness (gypsy folklore). The cock is a modern symbol of vigilance, formerly held sacred to the sun. The cock was also the herald of Apollo. A dream of a cock crowing warns of a false friend, or a betrayal (gypsy folklore). The symbolic connection here is with Christ's betrayal.

crane a dream denoting wickedness on the part of the dreamer (gypsy folklore); the symbolism here is probably derived from the well-known destructiveness of these birds among the fish and smaller varieties of their own species. To the Egyptians it was a symbol of the dawn and of regeneration, while to the Japanese it denotes longevity. Freudians regard it as bearing an erotic significance.

crow a symbol representing death. This is an invariably ill-omened dream. Artemidorus holds it as the dream of an adulterer. Raphael labels it the sign of a funeral. Cicero was warned of his own death by a number of crows circling about his head.

cuckoo a dream predicting disappointment in love (gypsy folklore). The cuckoo, according to Dr Samuel Johnson, is the symbol of faithlessness.

dove the symbol of peace in dreams, just as in life. The dream of a dove is a fortunate one denoting happiness and fidelity at home (Artemidorus). Originally an erotic symbol as the bird of Aphrodite, it later became the bird of holiness, symbolizing the sacrificial offerings of the Hebrews.

birds (ctd.)

duck a dream of profit and pleasure (gypsy folklore). A symbol of good fortune (Chinese).

eagle power, freedom, perception and domination. An eagle rushing through the air denotes successful undertakings; flying overhead, dignity and honours. To a pregnant woman this dream augurs the birth of a prodigy.

falcon to have one on the wrist denotes honour (gypsy folklore).

goose a sexist interpretation from Raphael is that for a single man this dream predicts a silly and incompetent wife. Modern nursery lore represents the goose as an emblem of silliness, despite that fowl's illustrious reputation in both Rome and Egypt. The cackling of geese denotes good luck and speedy success in business (Artemidorus). The symbolism derives from Roman history, referring to the cackling geese that saved the city.

hawk the dream of the commencement of a new enterprise. If the hawk darts downwards you will succeed, but if a little bird attacks the hawk you will fail (gypsy folklore). The hawk was the ancient symbol of the sun, of intelligence and good luck and also of enterprise. The hawk was the bird of Horus.

humming bird travel in a foreign land and success is symbolized by a dream of this little creature fluttering from flower to flower.

jackdaw to dream that one crosses your path symbolizes the meeting of bitter enemies. To catch one signifies success in defying enemies.

lark a lucky dream forecasting health and prosperity (Raphael). The lark is the symbol of joy and of praise.

magpie a dream of deceit (gypsy folklore). The bird itself symbolizes deceit and misfortune.

ostrich long futile conversations are here denoted (gypsy folklore). The symbolism here is connected with the legend of the stupidity of the ostrich.

owl a dream of an owl denotes unhappiness, sickness and discontent. The hooting of an owl in a dream denotes death (gypsy folklore). The Romans regarded the owl as the bird of wisdom, yet it was an evil portent. In Christian art they symbolize mourning and desolation.

birds (ctd.)

parrot this bird denotes the revelation of secrets, also eavesdropping (gypsy folklore).

partridge to a man this dream indicates dealings with malicious and amoral women (Artemidorus). This bird has ever been held as the symbol of foolishness.

peacock to see one spreading its tail denotes wealth and a handsome wife. For a woman this is a dream forecasting the promotion of her husband to popular favour.

To a young woman it symbolizes vanity and the attempted seduction by an unworthy man (gypsy folklore). The early Christians held it as the symbol of immortality. It was also the bird of Juno, who cursed whosoever should pluck its feathers that their children should never be well, nor should men come for their daughters— hence the superstition attached to these feathers. They are the modern symbol of pomp and vanity.

pheasants a dream of inexhaustible happiness. To carry one in the hand denotes health, profit and glory. To eat one in a dream is a reference to surfeit of food and indigestion (Raphael).

pigeon wild pigeons signify dissolute women. Tame pigeons denote honest women and matrons (Artemidorus). For symbolism of pigeon *see dove.*

quail a dream denoting bad news, misfortune (Artemidorus). The word quail was once synonymous for prostitute, owing to the salacious character attributed to the bird.

raven a raven is a symbol of trouble and mischief. In gypsy folklore it is said to be a sign of infidelity. In some cultures the raven is a symbol of knowledge. It was once associated with the god of light, poetry, music, healing and prophecy, Apollo. Modern symbolism regards it as a symbol, of misfortune.

robin a dream of happiness and joy (gypsy folklore). The symbolism derives from the robin being a Christmas bird.

rook a dream auguring business promptly concluded (gypsy folklore).

singing birds foretell joy and delight.

small birds signify lawsuits.

birds (ctd.)

sparrow a good fortune will attend whatever you have in view after this dream (Raphael).

stork a dream of change, possibly loss (gypsy folklore).

swallow news from afar is forecast by this dream. A swallow's nest is a symbol of domestic happiness (gypsy folklore).

swan a white swan denotes wealth and happiness; a black one, grief (Raphael). The swan was a sacred bird of the ancients, although it was a medieval symbol of hypocrisy as the swan has white feathers and black meat. In Norse legend, however, they were held as sacred and still are in Eastern Europe.

turkeys a dream denoting triumph over enemies (gypsy folklore).

turtle dove fidelity, gentleness and good housekeeping in the marriage partner (gypsy folklore).

vulture an evil dream of people trying to destroy your reputation and malevolent rivalry and revenge (gypsy folklore). Here the symbolism is derived from the Scriptures; ancient Hebrews held the vulture in abhorrence, while in Egypt it was the symbol of maternity and of the protection of Isis.

to catch birds with lime denotes unfair triumph over enemies. *See also* FEATHERS.

birth dreams of birth taking place can mean some sort of fresh start or major change in the life of the dreamer. For a woman, dreams of giving birth may be wish-fulfilment.

birthday presents receiving happy surprises, means a multitude of high accomplishments. Working people will advance in their trades.

Giving birthday presents, denotes small deferences, if given at a fete or reception.

birthday represents happiness or good fortune.

biscuits eating or baking them, indicates ill health and family peace ruptured over silly disputes.

bishop to dream of a bishop, teachers and authors will suffer great mental worries, caused from delving into intricate subjects.

To the tradesman, foolish buying, in which he is likely to incur loss of good money.

For one to see a bishop in his dreams, hard work will be his patrimony, with chills and ague as attendant. If you meet the approval of a much admired bishop, you will be successful in your undertakings in love or business.

bite this dream omens ill.

black cat *see* ANIMALS.

black *see* COLOURS.

blackberries to dream of blackberries denotes many ills. To gather them is unlucky. Eating them denotes losses.

blackbirds *see* BIRDS.

blackboard to see in your dreams writing in white chalk on a blackboard, denotes ill tidings of some person prostrated with some severe malady, or your financial security will be swayed by the panicky condition of commerce.

blacksmith to see a blacksmith in a dream, means laborious undertakings will soon work to your advantage.

bladder to dream of your bladder, denotes you will have heavy trouble in your business if you are not careful of your health and the way you spend your energies.

To see children blowing up bladders, foretells your expectations will fail to give you much comfort.

blankets in your dream means treachery if soiled. If new and white, success where failure is feared, and a fatal sickness will be avoided through unseen agencies.

blasphemy denotes an enemy creeping into your life, who under assumed friendship will do you great harm.

To dream you are cursing yourself, means evil fortune. To dream you are cursed by others, signifies relief through affection and prosperity.

bleating to hear young animals bleating in your dreams, foretells that you will have new duties and cares, though not necessarily unpleasant ones.

bleeding to dream of bleeding, denotes death by horrible accidents and malicious reports about you. Fortune will turn against you.

blind man's buff to dream that you are playing at blind man's buff, denotes that you are about to engage in some weak enterprise which will likely humiliate you, besides losing money for you.

blind to dream of being blind, denotes a sudden change from affluence to almost abject poverty.

To see others blind, denotes that some worthy person will call on you for aid.

blindfold for a woman to dream that she is blindfolded, means that disturbing elements are rising around to distress and trouble her. Disappointment will be felt by others through her.

blood *see* BODY.

blood stone to dream of seeing a blood stone, denotes that you will be unfortunate in your engagements. For a young woman to receive one as a gift, denotes she will suffer estrangement from one friend, but will, by this, gain one more worthy of her.

blossoming trees an invariable dream of gladness and also of prosperity (Artemidorus). Undoubtedly the symbolism is taken from the gladness of spring, as associated with these blossoms.

blotting paper to dream of using blotting paper, signifies you will be deceived into the betrayal of secrets which will seriously involve a friend.

To see worn blotting paper, denotes continued disagreements in the home or among friends.

blows denotes injury to yourself. If you receive a blow, brain trouble will threaten you. If you defend yourself, a rise in business will follow.

blue *see* COLOURS.

blushing for a young woman to dream of blushing, denotes she will be worried and humiliated by false accusations. If she sees others blush, she will be given to flippant raillery which will make her unpleasant to her friends.

boa-constrictor to dream of this is just about the same as to dream of the devil; it indicates stormy times and much bad fortune. Disenchantment with humanity will follow. To kill one is good.

boar *see* ANIMALS.

boarding house to dream of a boarding house, foretells that you will suffer entanglement and disorder in your enterprises, and you are likely to change your residence.

boasting to hear boasting in your dreams, you will sincerely regret an impulsive act, which will cause trouble to your friends. To boast to a competitor, foretells that you will be unjust, and will use dishonest means to overcome competition.

boat journey *see* JOURNEY.

boat signals forecast bright prospects, if upon clear water. If the water is unsettled and turbulent, cares and unhappy changes threaten the dreamer. If with a gay party you board a boat without an accident, many favours will be showered upon you. Unlucky the dreamer who falls overboard while sailing upon stormy waters.

boat, canoe, sailboat, ship, etc seen in a clear stream, this is a dream of happiness. To see one sink indicates disappointment, to fall from one, great dangers, to sail on smooth water, happiness and prosperity; on muddy water, trouble (Raphael). *See also* JOURNEY.

bobbin to dream of bobbins, denotes that important work will devolve on you, and your interests will be adversely affected if you are negligent in dispatching the same work.

body to dream that your body is robust denotes authority, that it is weak denotes failing or infirmity of the part in question (Artemidorus). The body is generally considered to be representative of the individual. Parts of the body therefore represent aspects of that person.

anus represents the individual's ability to express him or herself and to give of him or herself.

arms represent the potential in the individual for caring and affection. To dream of losing the right arm signifies the death of father, son or brother; of the left arm, of the mother, daughter or sister. To dream that the arms are withered predicts suffering in health and fortune; that they have grown strong indicates success. The latter part of this interpretation is based upon possible physical stimuli, and subsequent effects on the body.

body (ctd.)

blood can represent menstruation and thus womanhood, or the individual's essential being, the spirit which flows through him or her. To see a quantity of gore or congealed blood is said to predict dreadful calamity or death.

eyes the perceptive abilities of the dreamer. This is a dream predicting success through foresight (Artemidorus). The symbol of the eye is eternal vigilance.

finger to dream of losing a finger shows trouble (gypsy folklore).

hands signify creativity, perhaps sexual creativity.

head the idea which the dreamer has of him or herself, his or her intentions, wishes and beliefs.

heart to dream of the heart as sick or suffering augurs illness dangerous in proportion to the suffering. To dream of an injury to the heart portends danger. Dreaming of heart disease may well be attributable to physical conditions.

knees to fall upon the knees symbolizes a need for help (gypsy folklore).

mouth representative of the dreamer's needs and their fulfilment. It may represent the female genitalia.

nose the intuitive qualities of the dreamer. To dream of a great, fair nose is fortunate and is said to signify subtlety, prominent acquaintances and great personages. Dreaming of a nose longer than ordinary promises wealth and power. Two noses augur discord and quarrels. A stopped-up nose indicates deceit in a domestic circle (Artemidorus). The Egyptian priests believed that a wart on the nose indicated knowledge in proportion to the size of the wart.

penis the essential being of the man; the driving force behind his existence. *See also* GENITALS.

teeth the things with which we bite, and therefore the dreamer's ability to be aggressive. Dreams of teeth falling out indicate a fear of loss of power and of growing old and dying. To dream of loose teeth denotes personal sickness. To lose a tooth denotes the death of a friend or relative. For all the teeth to fall out forecasts your own death (gypsy folklore). *See also* TYPICAL DREAMS.

body (ctd.)

throat to dream of cutting someone's throat augurs unwitting injury to that person (gypsy folklore). *See also* TYPICAL DREAMS.

vagina womanhood, femininity, procreative abilities.

wrist to dream of hurting the wrist predicts a future injury through a foolish act (gypsy folklore).

bog denotes burdens under whose weight you feel that endeavours to rise are useless. Illness and other worries may oppress you.

boil *see* ABSCESS.

boiler to dream of seeing a boiler out of repair, signifies you will suffer from bad management or disappointment. For a woman to dream that she goes into a cellar to see about a boiler foretells that sickness and losses will surround her.

bolts to dream of bolts, signifies that formidable obstacles will oppose your progress.

If the bolts are old or broken, your expectations will be eclipsed by failures.

bomb shell to dream of bomb shells, foretells anger and disputes, ending in law suits. Many displeasing incident{s?} follow this dream.

bones human bones are an omen of death in the family (Artemidorus). They are a Christian symbol of death and mortality.

bonnet denotes much gossiping and slanderous insinuations, from which a woman should carefully defend herself.

For a man to see a woman tying her bonnet, denotes unforeseen good luck near by. His friends will be faithful and true.

A young woman is likely to engage in pleasant and harmless flirtations if her bonnet is new and of any colour except black.

Black bonnets, denote false friends of the opposite sex.

book books in dreams represent wisdom and learning. A book that cannot be opened will signify a secret that cannot be revealed. Open books mean opportunities for learning and changes for the better in one's life. This is a dream predicting the acquisition of both knowledge and wisdom (Artemidorus). The book is a Christian symbol of hidden wisdom and of learning.

book store to visit a book store in your dream, foretells you will be filled with literary aspirations, which will interfere with your other works and labours.

bookcase to see a bookcase in your dreams, signifies that you will associate knowledge with your work and pleasure. Empty bookcases, imply that you will be put out because of lack of means or facility for work.

boots if new, they symbolize a happy future. Boots or shoes are symbols of luck.

borrowing is a sign of loss and meagre support. For a banker to dream of borrowing from another bank, a run on his own will leave him in a state of collapse, unless he accepts this warning. If another borrows from you, help in time of need will be extended or offered you. True friends will attend you.

bosom for a young woman to dream that her bosom is wounded, foretells that some affliction is threatening her.

To see it soiled or shrunken, she will have a great disappointment in love and many rivals will vex her. If it is white and full she is soon to be possessed of fortune. If her lover is slyly observing it through her sheer corsage, she is about to come under the soft persuasive influence of a too ardent wooer.

bottle dreaming of a bottle, especially if it is one full of wine, denotes joy, celebration and drinking to someone's health. A broken bottle symbolizes disappointment (Artemidorus).

bouquet to dream of a bouquet beautifully and richly coloured, denotes a legacy from some wealthy and unknown relative; also, pleasant, joyous gatherings among young folks.

To see a withered bouquet, signifies sickness and death.

bow *see* ARROW.

box to dream of opening a box and of looking for something that you cannot find augurs disappointment in money matters (gypsy folklore). The interpretation here is derived from a knowledge of the subconscious desire to search for and to find money, an anxiety dream. It can also signify a coffin and death.

If the dreamer dreams of a plant box or a window box, the dream denotes long life, prosperity and a happy family (Artemidorus). It is a symbol of long life, perpetual hope.

bracelet dreaming of a bracelet is supposed to be a prediction of a wealthy marriage. A dream of an amulet is a dream of happiness and success.

brain this dream symbolizes sickness, loss of reputation, or some kind of weakness (gypsy folklore).

brambles or **briars** a dream of desire in love, a wish for the unattainable (Artemidorus). It is interesting to note that Freud and modern interpreters corroborate this interpretation, that thorned bushes symbolize that which is sexually unattainable.

branches branches with leaves and buds symbolize happiness and joy.

brandy to dream of brandy, foretells that while you may reach heights of distinction and wealth, you will lack that innate refinement which wins true friendship from people whom you most wish to please.

brass to dream of brass, denotes that you will rise rapidly in your profession, but while of apparently solid elevation you will secretly fear a downfall of fortune.

braying hearing an ass bray, is significant of unwelcome tidings or intrusions.

bread for a woman to dream of eating bread, denotes that she will be afflicted with children of stubborn will, for whom she will spend many days of useless labour and worry.

To dream of breaking bread with others, indicates an assured competence through life.

To see a lot of impure bread, want and misery will burden the dreamer. If the bread is good and you have access to it, it is a favourable dream.

break any dream of breakage implies misfortune.

limb to break a limb denotes sickness.

furniture denotes loss of money.

mirror to break a mirror or looking glass is a symbol of death.

window a broken window is a prediction of danger of fire (gypsy folklore).

The logic of these interpretations is plain, the breaking of a limb is a forewarning of pain, possibly not yet noted by the waking consciousness, fear of financial loss readily expressed in the destruction of property. By the same token the warning of fire, subconsciously read and noted while the consciousness was unaware might readily be construed as a broken window, symbolizing a means of escape. The superstition of a broken mirror as predicting misfortune predates written history.

breakfast is favourable to persons engaged in mental work. To see a breakfast of fresh milk and eggs and a well filled dish of ripe fruit, indicates hasty, but favourable changes.

If you are eating alone, it means you will fall into your enemies' trap. If you are eating with others it is good. *See* MEALS.

breath to come close to a person in your dreaming with a pure and sweet breath, commendable will be your conduct, and a profitable consummation of business deals will follow.

Breath if fetid, indicates sickness and snares.

Losing one's breath, denotes signal failure where success seemed assured.

brewing to dream of being in a vast brewing establishment, means unjust persecution by public officials, but you will eventually prove your innocence and will rise far above your persecutors.

Brewing in any way in your dreams, denotes anxiety at the outset, but usually ends in profit and satisfaction.

briars to see yourself caught among briars, black enemies are weaving cords of calumny and perjury intricately around you and will cause you great distress, but if you succeed in disengaging yourself from the briars, loyal friends will come to your assistance in every emergency.

brick in a dream, indicates unsettled business and disagreements in love affairs. To make them you will doubtless fail in your efforts to amass great wealth.

bride or **bridegroom**, **bridesmaids**, **ushers**, these dreams may have an erotic interpretation. According to Raphael they are dreams denoting grief and disappointment (but he invariably places an unfortunate interpretation upon all dreams of an erotic nature). The appearance of a bride or bridegroom in a dream will tell the dreamer something about his or her thoughts and desires in relation to finding a lifelong partner. Seeing someone else as a bride or bridegroom may mean that you fear losing their friendship to someone else.

bridge dreams of bridges denote changes, how you view the bridge in the dream will explain how you feel about the particular transition taking place.

crossing a bridge to see oneself crossing the bridge denotes work and possible anxiety in store.

broken bridge a broken or rickety bridge is an expression of fear about possible trouble ahead and a warning to take no steps on an unknown road.

falling may be stimulated by physical reasons (*see also* TYPICAL DREAMS). The symbolism of a bridge spanning water is obviously the subconscious hope of success. Falling expresses the anticipation of failure.

bridle bits to see bridle bits in your dreams, foretells you will subdue and overcome any obstacle opposing your advancement or happiness. If they break or are broken you will be surprised into making concessions to enemies.

bridle to dream of a bridle, denotes you will engage in some enterprise which will afford much worry, but will eventually terminate in pleasure and gain. If it is old or broken you will have difficulties to encounter, and the probabilities are that you will go down before them.

A blind bridle signifies you will be deceived by some wily enemy, or some woman will entangle you in an intrigue.

brimstone to dream of brimstone, foretells that discreditable dealings will lose you many friends. if you fail to rectify the mistakes you are making.

To see fires of brimstone, denotes you will be threatened with loss by contagion in your vicinity.

bronchitis to dream that you are affected with bronchitis, foretells you will be detained from pursuing your views and plans by unfortunate complications of sickness in your home.

To suffer with bronchitis in a dream, denotes that discouraging prospects of winning desired objects will soon loom up before you.

bronze for a woman to dream of a bronze statue, signifies that she will fail in her efforts to win the person she has determined on for a husband.

If the statue simulates life, or moves, she will be involved in a love affair, but no marriage will occur. Disappointment to some person may follow the dream.

To dream of bronze serpents or insects, foretells you will be pursued by envy and ruin. To see bronze metals, denotes your fortune will be uncertain and unsatisfactory.

brood *see* BIRDS.

brooks clear and near the house, an honourable office in which the dreamer will practice benevolence; muddy brooks indicate loss. Dried up brooks augur ruin to their owners (Artemidorus).

broom to dream of brooms, denotes thrift and rapid improvement in your fortune, if the brooms are new. If they are seen in use, you will lose in speculation. For a woman to lose a broom, foretells that she will prove a disagreeable and slovenly wife and housekeeper.

broth denotes the sincerity of friends. They will uphold you in all instances. If you need pecuniary aid it will be forthcoming. To lovers, it promises a strong and lasting attachment. To make broth, you will rule your own and others' fate.

brothel to dream of being in a brothel, denotes you will encounter disgrace through your material indulgence.

brothers to see your brothers, while dreaming, full of energy, you will have cause to rejoice at your own, or their good fortune; but if they are poor and in distress, or begging for assistance, you will be called to a deathbed soon, or some dire loss will overwhelm you or them.

brown *see* COLOURS.

brush to dream of using a hair-brush, denotes you will suffer misfortune from your mismanagement. To see old hair brushes, denotes sickness and ill health. To see clothes brushes, indicates a heavy task is pending over you.

If you are busy brushing your clothes, you will soon receive reimbursement for laborious work. To see miscellaneous brushes, foretells a varied line of work, yet withal, rather pleasing and remunerative.

buckle to dream of buckles, foretells that you will be beset with invitations to places of pleasure, and your affairs will be in danger of chaotic confusion.

buffalo if a woman dreams that she kills a lot of buffaloes, she will undertake a stupendous enterprise, but by enforcing will power and leaving off material pleasures, she will win commendation from men, and may receive long wished for favours. Buffalo, seen in a dream, augurs obstinate and powerful but stupid enemies. They will boldly declare against you but by diplomacy you will escape much misfortune.

bugle to hear a bugle indicates unexpected good news (Artemidorus).

bugs to dream of bugs denotes that some disgustingly revolting complications will rise in your daily life. Families will suffer from the carelessness of servants, and sickness may follow.

buildings to see large and magnificent buildings, with green lawns stretching out before them, is significant of a long life of plenty, and travels and explorations into distant countries.

Small and newly built houses, denote happy homes and profitable undertakings; but, if old and filthy buildings, ill health and decay of love and business will follow.

bull see ANIMALS.

bulldog see ANIMALS.

bullock denotes that kind friends will surround you, if you are in danger from enemies. Good health is promised you. See ANIMALS.

buoy this dream is a warning of danger ahead (gypsy folklore).

burden to dream that you carry a heavy burden, signifies that you will be tied down by oppressive weights of care and injustice, caused from favouritism shown your enemies by those in power. But to struggle free from it, you will climb to the topmost heights of success.

burglary dreaming of being burgled often means a fear of losing something precious, either something material such as one's home, or something more metaphysical, such as one's independence or self-confidence. *See also* TYPICAL DREAMS.

burial *see* CONTRARY MEANING.

buried alive to dream that you are buried alive. denotes that you are about to make a great mistake, which your opponents will quickly turn to your injury. If you are rescued from the grave, your struggle will eventually correct your misadventure.

burns stand for tidings of good. To burn your hand in a clear and flowing fire, denotes purity of purpose and the approbation of friends. To burn your feet in walking through coals, or beds of fire, denotes your ability to accomplish any endeavour, however impossible it may be to others. Your usual good health will remain with you, but, if you are overcome in the fire, it represents that your interests will suffer through treachery of supposed friends.

burr to dream of burrs, denotes that you will struggle to free self from some unpleasant burden, and will seek a change of surroundings.

butcher to dream of a butcher cutting up meat denotes trouble and sickness (gypsy folklore). It may be a dream of physical stimuli originating in the organ the butcher seems to be cutting.

butter to dream of eating fresh, golden butter, is a sign of good health and plans well carried out; it will bring unto you possessions, wealth and knowledge.

To eat rancid butter, denotes a competency acquired through struggles of manual labour.

To sell butter, denotes small gain.

butterfly *see* INSECTS.

buttermilk drinking buttermilk, denotes sorrow will follow some worldly pleasure, and some imprudence will impair the general health of the dreamer.

To give it away, or feed it to pigs, is bad still.

To dream that you are drinking buttermilk made into oyster soup, denotes that you will be called on to do some very repulsive thing, and ill luck will confront you. There are quarrels brewing and friendships threatened. If you awaken while you are drinking it, by discreet manoeuvring you may effect a pleasant understanding of disagreements.

buttons to dream of sewing bright shining buttons on a uniform, betokens to a young woman the warm affection of a fine looking and wealthy partner in marriage. To a youth, it signifies admittance to military honours and a bright career.

Dull, or cloth buttons, denotes disappointments and systematic losses and ill health.

The loss of a button, and the consequent anxiety as to losing a garment, denotes prospective losses in trade.

buzzard to dream that you hear a buzzard talking, foretells that some old scandal will arise and work you injury by your connection with it.

To see one sitting on a railroad, denotes some accident or loss is about to descend upon you. To see them fly away as you approach, foretells that you will be able to smooth over some scandalous disagreement among your friends, or even appertaining to yourself.

To see buzzards in a dream, portends generally salacious gossip or that unusual scandal will disturb you.

C

cab to ride in a cab in dreams, is significant of pleasant avocations, and average prosperity you will enjoy.

To ride in a cab at night, with others, indicates that you will have a secret that you will endeavour to keep from your friends.

To ride in a cab with a woman, scandal will couple your name with others of bad repute.

To dream of driving a public cab, denotes manual labour, with little chance of advancement.

cabbage to dream of cabbages growing denotes health and long life. The eating of them denotes sorrow, loss and illness (gypsy folklore). The former version of the dream, like all dreams of growing things, is optimistic, the latter may be an indication that you are bored and see your life as dull.

cabin the cabin of a ship is rather unfortunate to be in in a dream. Some mischief is brewing for you. You will most likely be engaged in a law suit, in which you will lose from the instability of your witness. For log cabin, see HOUSE.

cable to dream of a cable, foretells the undertaking of a decidedly hazardous work, which, if successfully carried to completion, will abound in riches and honour to you.

To dream of receiving cablegrams, denotes that a message of importance will reach you soon, and will cause disagreeable comments.

cackle to hear the cackling of hens denotes a sudden shock produced by the news of an unexpected death in your neighbourhood, Sickness will cause poverty.

cage without birds a dream of a cage denotes trouble. With birds the dream denotes contentment and happiness. A cage with the door open and the bird flown, the dream signifies desertion by the lover or husband. To see a bird escape augurs an elopement (Artemidorus). Cages, and things in cages, generally represent restrictions or frustrations to individuals, perhaps to their ambitions or their sexual desires. *See also* BIRDS; ENCLOSURE.

cakes batter or pancakes, denote that the affections of the dreamer are well placed, and a home will be bequeathed to him or her.

To dream of sweet cakes, is gain for the labouring and a favourable opportunity for the enterprising. Those in love will prosper.

Pound cake is significant of much pleasure either from society or business. For a young woman to dream of her wedding cake is the only bad luck cake in the category. Baking them is not so good an omen as seeing them or eating them.

calendar to dream of keeping a calendar, indicates that you will be very orderly and systematic in habits throughout the year.

To see a calendar, denotes disappointment in your calculations.

calm to see calm seas, denotes successful ending of doubtful undertaking.

To feel calm and happy, is a sign of a long and well-spent life and a vigorous old age.

calomel to dream of calomel shows some person is seeking to deceive and injure you through the unconscious abetting of friends. For a young woman to dream of taking it, foretells that she will be victimised through the artful designing of persons whom she trusts. If it is applied externally, she will close her eyes to deceit in order to enjoy a short season of pleasure.

calves to dream of calves peacefully grazing on a velvety lawn, foretells to the young, happy, festive gatherings and enjoyment. Those engaged in seeking wealth will see it rapidly increasing. *see* CATTLE, ANIMALS.

camel *see* ANIMALS.

cameo brooch to dream of a cameo brooch, denotes some sad occurrence will soon claim your attention.

camera to dream of a camera, signifies that changes will bring undeserved environments. For a young woman to dream that she is taking pictures with a camera, foretells that her immediate future will have much that is displeasing and that a friend will subject her to acute disappointment.

camp to dream of camping in the open air, you may expect a change in your affairs, also prepare to make a long and wearisome journey.

To see a camping settlement, many of your companions will remove to new estates and your own prospects will appear gloomy.

For a young woman to dream that she is in a camp, denotes that her lover will have trouble in getting her to name a day for their wedding, and that he will prove a kind husband. If in a military camp she will marry the first time she has a chance.

A married woman after dreaming of being in a soldier's camp is in danger of having her husband's name sullied, and divorce courts may be her destination.

campaign to dream of making a political one, signifies your opposition to approved ways of conducting business, and you will set up original plans for yourself regardless of enemies' working against you. Those in power will lose.

If it is a religious people conducting a campaign against sin, it denotes that you will be called upon to contribute from your private means to sustain charitable institutions.

For a woman to dream that she is interested in a campaign against fallen women, denotes that she will surmount obstacles and prove courageous in time of need.

canal to see the water of a canal muddy and stagnant-looking, portends sickness and disorders of the stomach and dark designs of enemies. But if its waters are clear a placid life and the devotion of friends is before you.

For a young woman to glide in a canoe across a canal, denotes a chaste life and an adoring husband. If she crossed the canal on a bridge over clear water and gathers ferns and other greens on the banks, she will enjoy a life of ceaseless rounds of pleasure and attain to high social distinction. But if the water be turbid she will often find herself tangled in meshes of perplexity and will be the victim of nervous troubles.

canary birds to dream of this sweet songster, denotes unexpected pleasures. For the young to dream of possessing a beautiful canary, denotes high class honours and a successful passage through the literary world, or a happy termination of love's young dream.

To dream one is given you, indicates a welcome legacy. To give away a canary, denotes that you will suffer disappointment in your dearest wishes.

To dream that one dies, denotes the unfaithfulness of dear friends.

Advancing, fluttering, and singing canaries, in luxurious apartments, denotes feasting and a life of exquisite refinement, wealth, and satisfying friendships. If the light is weird or unnaturally bright, it augurs that you are entertaining illusive hopes. Your over-confidence is your worst enemy. A young woman after this dream should beware, lest flattering promises react upon her in disappointment. Fairy-like scenes in a dream are peculiarly misleading and treacherous to women.

cancer to have one successfully treated in a dream, denotes a sudden rise from obscure poverty to wealthy surroundings.

To dream of a cancer, denotes illness of some one near you, and quarrels with those you love. Depressions may follow to the man of affairs after this dream.

To dream of a cancer, foretells sorrow in its ugliest phase. Love will resolve itself into cold formality, and business will be worrying and profitless.

candle to see one being lit forecasts a birth. To exhibit a lighted candle predicts contentment and prosperity. To dream of making candles symbolizes joy and satisfaction. To see a candle burning brilliantly denotes prosperity, health to invalids, and marriage to single people. A dimly burning candle shows sickness, sadness and decay (Artemidorus). The symbolism is that of the sacred flame, the vital spark, with the sacredness invariably depending upon the fiery element.

Men who dream of flickering candles may have concerns about their sexual potency.

Brightly burning candles may mean a desire on the part of the dreamer to find fulfilment in a spiritual way.

candlestick this dream forecasts an invitation to a wedding (Artemidorus). Here the ecclesiastical association is apparent. The candlestick is an emblem of Christ and His church, and a near universal symbol of ceremonial faith.

candy to dream of making candy, denotes profit accruing from industry.

To dream of eating candy implies social pleasures and much love-making among the young and old. Sour candy is a sign of illness.

To receive a box of bonbons, signifies to a young person that he or she will be the recipient of much adulation. It generally means prosperity. If you send a box you will make a proposition, but will meet with disappointment.

cane to see cane growing in your dream, foretells favourable advancement will be made toward fortune. To see it cut, denotes absolute failure in all undertakings.

canker to dream of seeing canker on anything, is an omen of evil. It foretells death and treacherous companions for the young. Sorrow and loneliness to the aged.

Cankerous growths in the flesh, denote future distinctions either as head of State or stage life.

The last definition is not consistent with other parts of this book, but I let it stand, as I find it among my automatic writings.

cannon *see* WEAPONS.

cannon-ball this means that secret enemies are uniting against you. For a maid to see a cannon-ball, denotes that she will have a soldier sweetheart. For a youth to see a cannon-ball, denotes that he will be called upon to defend his country.

canoe *see* BOAT.

canon *see* CAVE.

canopy to dream of a canopy or of being beneath one, denotes that false friends are influencing you to undesirable ways of securing gain. You will do well to protect those in your care.

cap for a woman to dream of seeing a cap, she will be invited to take part in some festivity.

For a girl to dream that she sees her sweetheart with a cap on, denotes that she will be bashful and shy in his presence.

To see a prisoner's cap, denotes that your courage is failing you in time of danger.

To see a miner's cap, you will inherit a substantial competency.

captain to dream of seeing a captain of any company, denotes your noblest aspirations will be realised. If a woman dreams that her lover is a captain, she will be much harassed in mind from jealousy and rivalry.

captive a dream of being held captive may mean that you are unhappy in a relationship or in a place of work and feel restricted. *See also* CHAINS; ENCLOSURE; IMPRISONMENT.

car journey *see* JOURNEY.

car to dream of seeing cars, denotes journeying and changing in quick succession. To get on one shows that travel which you held in contemplation will be made under different auspices than had been calculated upon.

To miss one, foretells that you will be foiled in an attempt to forward your prospects.

To get off of one, denotes that you will succeed with some interesting schemes which will fill you with self congratulations.

To dream of sleeping-cars, indicates that your struggles to amass wealth is animated by the desire of gratifying selfish and lewd principles which should be mastered and controlled.

To see street-cars in your dreams, denotes that some person is actively interested in causing you malicious trouble and disquiet.

To ride on a car, foretells that rivalry and jealousy will enthral your happiness.

To stand on the platform of a street-car while it is running, denotes you will attempt to carry on an affair which will be extremely dangerous, but if you ride without accident you will be successful.

If the platform is up high, your danger will be more apparent, but if low, you will barely accomplish your purpose.

cardinal it is unlucky to dream you see a cardinal in his robes. You will meet such misfortunes as will necessitate your removal to distant or foreign lands to begin anew your ruined fortune. For a woman to dream this is a sign of her downfall through false promises. If priest or preacher is a spiritual adviser and his services are supposed to be needed, especially in the hour of temptation, then we find ourselves dreaming of him as a warning against approaching evil.

cards to play them in a dream denotes quarrels and deception of which the dreamer will be a dupe (gypsy folklore).

carnival to dream that you are participating in a carnival, portends that you are soon to enjoy some unusual pleasure or recreation. A carnival when masks are used, or when incongruous or clownish figures are seen, implies discord in the home; business will be unsatisfactory and love unrequited.

carp this symbol denotes good luck through work (gypsy folklore). The carp is a Japanese emblem of endurance.

carpenter to see carpenters at their labour, foretells you will engage in honest endeavours to raise your fortune, to the exclusion of selfish pastime or so-called recreation.

carpet to see a carpet in a dream, denotes profit, and wealthy friends to aid you in need.

To walk on a carpet, you will be prosperous and happy.

To dream that you buy carpets, denotes great gain. If selling them, you will have cause to go on a pleasant journey, as well as a profitable one.

For a young woman to dream of carpets, shows she will own a beautiful home and servants will wait upon her.

carriage to see a carriage, implies that you will be gratified, and that you will make visits.

To ride in one, you will have a sickness that will soon pass, and you will enjoy health and advantageous positions.

To dream that you are looking for a carriage, you will have to labour hard, but will eventually be possessed with a fair competency.

carrot to dream of carrots, portends prosperity and health For a young woman to eat them, denotes that she will contract an early marriage and be the mother of several hardy children.

cart to dream of riding in a cart, ill luck and constant work will employ your time if you would keep supplies for your family.

To see a cart, denotes bad news from kindred or friends.

To dream of driving a cart, you will meet with merited success in business and other aspirations.

For lovers to ride together in a cart, they will be true in spite of the machinations of rivals.

cartridge to dream of cartridges, foretells unhappy quarrels and dissension. Some untoward fate threatens you or some one closely allied to you. If they are empty, there will be foolish variances in your associations.

carving to dream of carving a fowl, indicates you will be poorly off in a worldly way. Companions will cause you vexation from continued ill temper.

Carving meat, denotes bad investments, but, if a change is made, prospects will be brighter.

cash box to dream of a full cash box, denotes that favourable prospects will open around you. If empty, you will experience meagre reimbursements.

cash to dream that you have plenty of cash, but that it has been borrowed, portends that you will be looked upon as a worthy man, but that those who come in close contact with you will find that you are mercenary and unfeeling.

For a young woman to dream that she is spending borrowed money, foretells that she will be found out in her practice of deceit, and through this lose a prized friend. *See* MONEY.

cashier to see a cashier in your dream, denotes that others will claim your possessions. If you owe any one, you will practice deceit in your designs upon some wealthy person.

cask to see one filled, denotes prosperous times and feasting. If empty, your life will be void of any joy or consolation from outward influences.

castle castles represent security. The more heavily fortified the castle, the greater the dreamer's desire is for security. It may mean the protection of things that are important to dreamers or the protection of the dreamers themselves.

A dream of a castle is generally a good one. To enter one indicates pleasant hopes. However, to see one burned denotes misfortune, an accident, sickness or death to the owner (gypsy folklore).

castor oil to dream of castor oil, denotes that you will seek to overthrow a friend who is secretly abetting your advancement.

castoria to dream of castoria, denotes that you will fail to discharge some important duty, and your fortune will seemingly decline to low stages.

castration a man who dreams of castration undoubtedly fears failure and losing his status as a man. Women who dream of castration are probably embroiled in bitter relationships with men and seek to somehow disempower them.

cat *see* ANIMALS.

catechism to dream of the catechism, foretells that you will be offered a lucrative position, but the strictures will be such that you will be worried as to accepting it.

caterpillar *see* INSECTS.

cathedral to dream of a vast cathedral with its domes rising into space, denotes that you will be possessed with an envious nature and unhappy longings for the unattainable, both mental and physical; but if you enter you will be elevated in life, having for your companions the learned and wise.

cattle *see* ANIMALS.

cauliflower to dream of eating it, you will be taken to task for neglect of duty. To see it growing, your prospects will brighten after a period of loss. For a young woman to see this vegetable in a garden, denotes that she will marry to please her parents and not herself.

cavalry to dream that you see a division of cavalry, denotes personal advancement and distinction. Some little sensation may accompany your elevation.

cave or cavern, canon, grotto, crypt obscurity and misfortune are interpreted from these symbols (gypsy folklore). Caves and grottoes have an ancient and sacred symbolism, while popular tradition peopled them with dragons and other evil creatures. The cave is often seen as the door to the subconscious; the further you go in, the closer you get to your individual subconscious being. Freud saw the dream of the cave as reflecting sexual desires or a wish to return to the womb.

cedar to dream of cedar denotes happiness, joy and peace (Artemidorus). The cedar of Lebanon, by its height, perfume and healing qualities, was a symbol of goodness and of the Virgin.

celery to dream of seeing fresh, crisp stalks of celery, you will be prosperous and influential beyond your highest hopes.

To see it decaying, a death in your family will soon occur.

To eat it, boundless love and affection will be heaped upon you.

For a young woman to eat it with her lover, denotes she will come into rich possessions.

celestial signs to dream of celestial signs, foretells unhappy occurrences will cause you to make unseasonable journeys. Love or business may go awry, quarrels in the house are also predicted if you are not discreet with your engagements. *See* ILLUMINATION.

cellar to dream you are in a cellar shows that you are threatened with illness (gypsy folklore). *See also* HOUSE, HOME.

cemeteries cemeteries represent what has gone before; this may in fact be dead people or figures from the past, or it may be a period in the individual's life, or one small incident that is over and done with. Dreams of cemeteries are also prompting the dreamer to think of death and the afterlife and, therefore, spirituality and religious beliefs. The universal acceptance of this as a dream of prosperity suggests either the spirit of contrariety found in certain dream interpretations, or symbolism derived from the morbidity of certain early Christian sects.

chaff a dream of abortive or worthless schemes (Artemidorus).

chains a dream warning you against the conspiracy of enemies, from which, however, you will escape (Artemidorus). *See also* CAPTIVE; ENCLOSURE.

chair maker to dream of seeing a chair maker, denotes that worry from apparently pleasant labour will confront you.

chair *see* FURNITURE.

chairman to dream that you see the chairman of any public body, foretells you will seek elevation and be recompensed by receiving a high position of trust. To see one looking out of humour you are threatened with unsatisfactory states.

If you are a chairman, you will be distinguished for your justice and kindness to others.

chalice a dream of high ideals and strivings never to be attained in the flesh. This symbolism derives from the chalice as the emblem of the priestly order and of the Grail.

chalk for a woman to dream of chalking her face, denotes that she will scheme to obtain admirers.

To dream of using chalk on a board, you will attain public honours, unless it is the blackboard; then it indicates ill luck.

To hold hands full of chalk, disappointment is foretold.

challenge if you are challenged to fight a duel, you will become involved in a social difficulty wherein you will be compelled to make apologies or else lose friendships.

To accept a challenge of any character, denotes that you will bear many ills yourself in your endeavour to shield others from dishonour.

chamber to find yourself in a beautiful and richly furnished chamber implies sudden fortune, either through legacies from unknown relatives or through speculation. For a young woman, it denotes that a wealthy stranger will offer her marriage and a fine establishment. If the chamber is plainly furnished, it denotes that a small competency and frugality will be her portion.

chambermaid to see a chambermaid, denotes bad fortune and decided changes will be made.

For a man to dream of making love to a chambermaid, shows he is likely to find himself an object of derision on account of indiscreet conduct and want of tact.

chameleon *see* ANIMALS.

champion to dream of a champion, denotes you will win the warmest friendship of some person by your dignity and moral conduct.

chandelier to dream of a chandelier, portends that unhoped-for success will make it possible for you to enjoy pleasure and luxury at your caprice.

To see a broken or ill-kept one, denotes that unfortunate speculation will depress your seemingly substantial fortune. To see the light in one go out, foretells that sickness and distress will cloud a promising future.

chapel to dream of a chapel, denotes dissension in social circles and unsettled business.

To be in a chapel, denotes disappointment and change of business.

For young people to dream of entering a chapel, implies false loves and enemies. Unlucky unions may entangle them.

charcoal to dream of charcoal unlighted, denotes miserable situations and bleak unhappiness. If it is burning with glowing coals, there is prospects of great enhancement of fortune, and possession of unalloyed joys.

chariot to dream of riding in a chariot, foretells that favourable opportunities will present themselves resulting in your good if rightly used by you.

To fall or see others fall from one, denotes displacement from high positions.

charity to dream of giving charity, denotes that you will be harassed with supplications for help from the poor and your business will be at standstill.

To dream of giving to charitable institutions, your right of possession to paving property will be disputed. Worries and ill health will threaten you.

For young persons to dream of giving charity, foreshows they will be annoyed by deceitful rivals. To dream that you are an object of charity, omens that you will succeed in life after hard times with misfortunes.

charity, charitable acts will bring evil if given or taken unwillingly. Otherwise, a good dream.

chastise to dream of being chastised, denotes that you have not been prudent in conducting your affairs.

To dream that you administer chastisement to another, signifies that you will have an ill-tempered partner either in business or marriage.

For parents to dream of chastising their children, indicates they will be loose in their manner of correcting them, but they will succeed in bringing them up honourably.

cheated to dream of being cheated in business, you will meet designing people who will seek to close your avenues to fortune.

For young persons to dream that they are being cheated in games, portend they will lose their sweethearts through quarrels and misunderstandings.

cheese to dream of eating cheese, denotes great disappointments and sorrow. No good of any nature can be hoped for. Cheese is generally a bad dream.

chemise for a woman to dream of a chemise, denotes she will hear unfavourable gossip about herself.

cheques to dream of palming off false cheques on your friends, denotes that you will resort to subterfuge in order to carry forward your plans.

To receive cheques you will be able to meet your payments and will inherit money.

To dream that you pay out cheques, denotes depression and loss in business.

cherries *see* FRUIT.

cherubs to dream you see cherubs, foretells you will have some distinct joy, which will leave an impression of lasting good upon your life.

To see them looking sorrowful or reproachful, foretells that distress will come unexpectedly upon you.

chess *see* GAMES.

chestnuts to dream of handling chestnuts, foretells losses in a business way, but indicates an agreeable companion through life.

Eating them, denotes sorrow for a time, but final happiness.

For a young woman to dream of eating or trying her fortune with them, she will have a well-to-do lover and comparative plenty.

chickens *see* BIRDS.

chiffonier to see or search through a chiffonier, denotes you will have disappointing anticipations. To see one in order, indicates pleasant friends and entertainment.

chilblain to dream of suffering with chilblains, denotes that you will be driven into some bad dealing through over-anxiety of a friend or partner. This dream also portends your own illness or an accident.

childbed to dream of giving child birth, denotes fortunate circumstances and safe delivery of a handsome child.

For an unmarried woman to dream of being in childbed, denotes unhappy changes from honour to evil and low estates.

children to dream of children indicates success (Artemidorus). Children symbolize Christ's love and beneficence. Dreaming that you are a child expresses feelings of immaturity or insecurity.

chimes to dream of Christmas chimes, denotes fair prospects for business men and farmers.

For the young, happy anticipations fulfilled. Ordinary chimes, denotes some small anxiety will soon be displaced by news of distant friends.

chimney to dream of one, especially if a fire is lit, denotes domestic joy (Artemidorus).

china for a woman to dream of painting or arranging her china, foretells she will have a pleasant home and be a thrifty and economical matron.

china store for a china merchant to dream that his store looks empty, foretells he will have reverses in his business, and withal a gloomy period will follow. *see* CROCKERY.

chocolate to dream of chocolate, denotes you will provide abundantly for those who are dependent on you. To see chocolate candy, indicates agreeable companions and employment. If sour, illness or other disappointments will follow. To drink chocolate, foretells you will prosper after a short period of unfavourable reverses.

choir to dream of a choir, foretells you may expect cheerful surroundings to replace gloom and discontent. For a young woman to sing in a choir, denotes she will be miserable over the attention paid others by her lover.

cholera a dream telling of the likelihood of serious illness (Artemidorus).

Christ to dream of Christ indicates that you are seeking religious consolation or commitment. To dream of Christ on the cross symbolizes trouble and sorrow and may be an expression of religious guilt.

Christmas tree to dream of a Christmas tree, denotes joyful occasions and auspicious fortune. To see one dismantled, foretells some painful incident will follow occasions of festivity.

chrysanthemum to dream that you gather white chrysanthemums, signifies loss and much perplexity; coloured ones, betokens pleasant engagements.

To see them in bouquets, denotes that love will be offered you, but a foolish ambition will cause you to put it aside. To pass down an avenue of white chrysanthemums, with here and there a yellow one showing among the white, foretells a strange sense of loss and sadness, from which the sensibilities will expand and take on new powers. While looking on these white flowers as you pass, and you suddenly feel your spirit leave your body and a voice shouts aloud 'Glory to God, my Creator', foretells that a crisis is pending in your near future. If some of your friends pass out, and others take up true ideas in connection with spiritual and earthly needs, you will enjoy life in its deepest meaning. Often death is near you in these dreams.

church service a dream of listening to mass, or church music with a feeling of inner peace and satisfaction denotes contentment with one's religious beliefs.

church to dream of building one is an expression of divine love. To dream of entering one symbolizes honourable conduct and benevolence. To talk in one or see it desecrated symbolizes envy, lies and sin. In gypsy folklore to go to church in mourning predicts a wedding; to go in white predicts a funeral (gypsy folklore).

churchyard to dream of walking in a churchyard, if in winter, denotes that you are to have a long and bitter struggle with poverty, and you will reside far from the home of your childhood, and friends will be separated from you; but if you see the signs of springtime, you will walk up in into pleasant places and enjoy the society of friends.

For lovers to dream of being in a churchyard means they will never marry each other, but will see others fill their places.

churning to dream of churning, you will have difficult tasks set you, but by diligence and industry you will accomplish them and be very prosperous. To the farmer, it denotes profit from a plenteous harvest; to a young woman, it denotes a thrifty and energetic husband.

cider to dream of cider, denotes fortune may be won by you if your time is not squandered upon material pleasure. To see people drinking it, you will be under the influence of unfaithful friends.

cipher to dream of reading cipher, indicates that you are interested in literary researches, and by constant study you will become well acquainted with the habits and lives of the ancients.

circle to dream of a circle, denotes that your affairs will deceive you in their proportions of gain. For a young woman to dream of a circle, warns her of indiscreet involvement to the exclusion of marriage.

cistern to dream of a cistern, denotes you are in danger of trespassing upon the pleasures and rights of your friends. To draw from one, foretells that you will enlarge in your pastime and enjoyment in a manner which may be questioned by propriety.

To see an empty one, foretells despairing change from happiness to sorrow.

city a busy city predicts riches; a deserted city predicts plague (gypsy folklore). The city is the maternal symbol of woman, who fosters the inhabitants as children (Jung).

city council to dream of a city council, foretells that your interests will clash with public institutions and there will be discouraging outlooks for you.

city hall to dream of a city hall, denotes contentions and threatened law suits.

To a young woman this dream is a foreboding of unhappy estrangement from her lover by her failure to keep virtue inviolate.

clairvoyance to dream of being a clairvoyant and seeing yourself in the future, denotes signal changes in your present occupation, followed by a series of unhappy conflicts with designing people.

To dream of visiting a clairvoyant, foretells unprosperous commercial states and unhappy unions.

clam *see* ANIMALS.

claret cup and punch to dream of claret cup or punch, foretells that you will be much pleased with the attention shown you by new acquaintances.

claret to dream of drinking claret, denotes you will come under the influence of ennobling association. To dream of seeing broken bottles of claret, portends you will be induced to commit immoralities by the false persuasions of deceitful persons.

clarinet to dream of a clarinet, foretells that you will indulge in frivolity beneath your usual dignity. If it is broken, you will incur the displeasure of a close friend.

clay to dream of clay, denotes isolation of interest and probable insolvency. To dig in a clay bank, foretells you will submit to extraordinary demands of enemies. If you dig in an ash bank and find clay, unfortunate surprises will combat progressive enterprises or new work. Your efforts are likely to be misdirected after this dream.

Women will find this dream unfavourable in love, social and business states, and misrepresentations will overwhelm them.

clergyman to dream that you send for a clergyman to preach a funeral sermon, denotes that you will vainly strive against sickness and to ward off evil influences, but they will prevail in spite of your earnest endeavours.

If a young woman marries a clergyman in her dream, she will be the object of much mental distress, and the wayward hand of fortune will lead her into the morass of adversity. *see* MINISTER.

climb a dream predicting successfully overcoming obstacles, and final promotion, honour, etc. (Artemidorus). An interpretation of the character whose subconscious desire is for attainment. *See also* TYPICAL DREAMS.

cloak a dream denoting the concealment of poverty, etc (gypsy folklore).

clock to dream of a clock denotes misfortune (gypsy folklore). The symbolism probably derives from the common superstition attached to the timepiece that it stops at the death of a member of the family, etc.

cloister to dream of a cloister, omens dissatisfaction with present surroundings, and you will soon seek new environments. For a young woman to dream of a cloister, foretells that her life will be made unselfish by the chastening of sorrow.

closeness *see* POSITION.

clothes clothes in dreams may represent the way in which the dreamer appears to the world and to his or herself, his or her self-image and attitudes and the way in which he or she is seen in relationship to other people. Someone who dreams of being wrapped up in a large overcoat, for example, might be protecting, or seeking to protect, him or herself from others, or hiding some aspect of him or herself. Alternatively, such clothing may be representative of the loving protection that the dreamer feels from another, e.g., a mother or a lover.

C*olours* of clothing may also be symbolic in dreams, just as we often dress in different colours according to our mood. Thus, dark dreary colours can be symbolic of unpleasant feelings or occurrences, and black may symbolize death.

Underwear can symbolize the dreamer's feelings about his or her sexuality. *See also* COLOURS.

There is rich symbolism regarding clothing in folklore too. Dreams of clothes, denote that enterprises will be successes or failures, as the clothing seems to be whole and clean, or soiled and threadbare.

Fine clothing, but out of date, foretells that you will have fortune, but you will scorn progressive ideas. If you reject out-of-date apparel, you will outgrow present environments and enter into new relations, new enterprises and new loves, which will transform you into a different person.

To see yourself or others clothed in white, denotes eventful changes, and you will nearly always find the change bearing sadness.

To walk with a person wearing white, proclaims that person's illness or distress, unless it be a young woman or child, then you will have pleasing surroundings for a season at least.

To see yourself, or others, dressed in black, portends quarrels, disappointments, and disagreeable companions; or, if it refers to business, the business will fall short of expectations.

To see yellow clothing, foretells approaching gaieties and financial progress. Seen as a flitting spectre, in an unnatural light, the reverse may be expected. You will be fortunate if you dream of yellow cloth.

clothes (ctd.)

To dream of blue clothing, signifies carrying forward to victory your aspirations, through energetic, insistent efforts. Friends will loyally support you.

To dream of crimson clothing, foretells that you will escape formidable enemies by a timely change in your expressed intention.

To see green clothing, is a hopeful sign of prosperity and happiness.

To see many coloured clothes, foretells swift changes, and intermingling of good and bad influences in your future.

To dream of misfitting clothing, intimates crosses in your affections, and that you are likely to make a mistake in some enterprise.

To see old or young in appropriate clothing, denotes that you will undertake some engagement for which you will have no liking, and which will give rise to many cares.

For a woman to dream that she is displeased with her clothing, foretells that she will find many rivalries in her quest for social distinction.

To admire the clothing of others, denotes that she will have jealous fears of her friends.

To dream of the loss of any article of clothing, denotes disturbances in your business and love affairs.

For a young woman to dream of being attired in a gauzy black costume, foretells she will undergo chastening sorrow and disappointment.

For a young woman to dream that she meets another clothed in a crimson dress with a crepe mourning veil over her face, foretells she will be outrivaled by one she hardly considers her equal, and bitter disappointment will sour her against women generally.

The dreamer interpreting the dream of clothing should be careful to note whether the objects are looking natural. If the faces are distorted and the light unearthly, though the colours are bright, beware; the miscarriage of some worthy plan will work you harm. There are few dreams in which the element of evil is wanting, as there are few enterprises in waking life from which the element of chance is obviated.

clouds to dream of heavy clouds signifies threatened misfortune. Light, opaque clouds denote mystery (gypsy folklore). Clouds are sometimes symbolic of the majesty of God, at other times of doubt and obscurity.

cloven foot to dream of a cloven foot, portends some unusual ill luck is threatening you, and you will do well to avoid the friendship of strange persons.

clover walking through fields of fragrant clover is a propitious dream. It brings all objects desired into the reach of the dreamer. Fine crops is portended for the farmer and wealth for the young. Blasted fields of clover brings harrowing and regretful sighs.

To dream of clover, foretells prosperity will soon enfold you. For a young woman to dream of seeing a snake crawling through blossoming clover, foretells she will be early disappointed in love, and her surroundings will be gloomy and discouraging, though to her friends she seems peculiarly fortunate.

clown to dream of a clown predicts misfortune and disgrace (gypsy folklore). The attitude of the medieval world towards the jesters explains this interpretation. To dream that you are a clown reflects the feeling that you are making a fool of yourself in a situation.

club a dream predicting suffering and misfortune (gypsy folklore). Freud regarded it as a phallic symbol. It symbolized strength and power amongst the ancients, bearing no erotic significance. To the Christians it became an emblem of suffering and of martyrdom.

coach to dream of riding in a coach, denotes continued losses and depressions in business. Driving one implies removal or business changes.

coal-hod to dream of a coal-hod, denotes that grief will be likely to fill a vacancy made by reckless extravagance. To see your neighbour carrying in hods, foretells your surroundings will be decidedly distasteful and inharmonious.

coals to dream of coals denotes trouble, loss and hunger (Raphael). Secret love is the interpretation attached to this dream by Freud. 'With coal no fire so hotly glows as secret love, which no one knows.' (Freud, *Interpretation of Dreams*).

coat to dream of wearing another's coat, signifies that you will ask some friend to go security for you. To see your coat torn, denotes the loss of a close friend and dreary business.

To see a new coat, portends for you some literary honour.

To lose your coat, you will have to rebuild your fortune lost through being over-confident in speculations. *See* CLOTHES.

coat-of-arms to dream of seeing your coat-of-arms, is a dream of ill luck. You will never possess a title.

cock *see* BIRDS.

cockade this dream denotes that foes will bring disastrous suits against you. Beware of titles.

cockchafer *see* BEETLE.

cock-crowing to dream of hearing a cock crowing in the morning, is significant of good. If you be single, it denotes an early marriage and a luxurious home.

To hear one at night is despair, and cause for tears you will have.

To dream of seeing cocks fight, you will leave your family because of quarrels and infidelity. This dream usually announces some unexpected and sorrowful events. The cock warned the Apostle Peter when he was about to perjure himself. It may also warn you in a dream when the meshes of the world are swaying you from 'the straight line' of spiritual wisdom.

cocktail to drink a cocktail while dreaming, denotes that you will deceive your friends as to your inclinations and enjoy the companionship of fast men and women while posing as a serious student and staid home lover. For a woman, this dream portends fast living and an ignoring of moral and set rules.

cocoa to dream of cocoa, denotes you will cultivate distasteful friends for your own advancement and pleasure.

coconut in dreams, warns you of fatalities in your expectations, as sly enemies are encroaching upon your rights in the guise of ardent friends. Dead coconut trees are a sign of loss and sorrow. The death of some one near you may follow.

coffee house to see or visit a coffee house in your dreams, foretells that you will unwisely entertain friendly relations with persons known to be your enemies. Designing women may intrigue against your morality and possessions.

coffee mill to see a coffee mill in your dreams, denotes you are approaching a critical danger, and all your energy and alertness will have to stand up with obduracy to avert its disastrous consequences. To hear it grinding, signifies you will hardly overthrow some evil pitted against your interest.

coffee to dream of drinking coffee, denotes the disapproval of friends toward your marriage intentions. If married, disagreements and frequent quarrels are implied.

To dream of dealing in coffee, portends business failures. If selling, sure loss. Buying it, you may with ease retain your credit.

For a young woman to see or handle coffee she will be made a by-word if she is not discreet in her actions.

To dream of roasting coffee, for a young woman it denotes escape from evil by luckily marrying a stranger.

To see ground coffee, foretells successful struggles with adversity. Parched coffee, warns you of the evil attentions of strangers.

Green coffee, denotes you have bold enemies who will show you no quarter, but will fight for your overthrow.

coffin this dream is unlucky. You will, if you are a farmer, see your crops blasted and your cattle lean and unhealthy. To business men it means debts whose accumulation they are powerless to avoid. To the young it denotes unhappy unions and death of loved ones.

To see one, indicates disastrous losses and the early dissolution of a dear relative.

To see your own coffin in a dream, business defeat and domestic sorrow may be expected.

To dream of a coffin moving of itself, denotes sickness and marriage in close conjunction. Sorrow and pleasure intermingled. Death may follow this dream, but there will also be good.

To see your corpse in a coffin, signifies brave efforts will be crushed in defeat and ignominy,

To dream that you find yourself sitting on a coffin in a moving hearse, denotes desperate if not fatal illness for you or some person closely allied to you.

Quarrels with the opposite sex is also indicated. You will remorsefully consider your conduct toward a friend.

To see one, strewn with flowers in a church, denotes an unfortunate marriage.

coins to dream of gold, denotes great prosperity and much pleasure derived from sight-seeing and ocean voyages.

Silver coin is unlucky to dream about. Dissension will arise in the most orderly families.

For a maiden to dream that her lover gives her a silver coin, signifies she will be jilted by him.

Copper coins, denotes despair and physical burdens. Nickel coins, imply that work of the lowest nature will devolve upon you.

If silver coins are your ideal of money, and they are bright and clean, or seen distinctly in your possession, the dream will be a propitious one.

coke (coal derivative) to dream of coke, denotes affliction and discord will enter your near future.

coke oven to see coke ovens burning, foretells some unexpected good fortune will result from failure in some enterprise.

cold to dream of suffering from cold, you are warned to look well to your affairs. There are enemies at work to destroy you. Your health is also menaced.

collar to dream of wearing a collar, you will have high honours thrust upon you that you will hardly be worthy of. For a woman to dream of collars, she will have many admirers, but no sincere ones, She will be likely to remain single for a long while.

college to dream of a college, denotes you are soon to advance to a position long sought after. To dream that you are back in college, foretells you will receive distinction through some well favoured work.

colliery or coal-mine to dream of being in a coal-mine or colliery and seeing miners, denotes that some evil will assert its power for your downfall; but if you dream of holding a share in a coal-mine, it denotes your safe investment in some deal.

For a young woman to dream of mining coal, foreshows she will become the wife of a real-estate dealer or dentist.

collision to dream of a collision, you will meet with an accident of a serious type and disappointments in business.

For a young woman to see a collision, denotes she will be unable to decide between lovers, and will be the cause of wrangles.

colonel to dream of seeing or being commanded by a colonel, denotes you will fail to reach any prominence in social or business circles.

If you are a colonel, it denotes you will contrive to hold position above those of friends or acquaintances.

colours it is possible to dream in vivid technicolor, muted colours or monochrome, or one may have a dream in which one colour predominates, most commonly white or black. The colours in a dream can have considerable significance, depending on the state of mind of the dreamer and the context of the dream. *See also* CLOTHES.

black is the colour of the dark, hidden, gloomy and secret. It may be symbolic of death or of a fear of death. The dreamer may be feeling sad or depressed.

blue is a spiritual colour, it may symbolize hope and faithfulness, or reasoning and higher intellect. A predominance of dark and/or dull blues, however, can signify depression.

brown is associated with excrement, dreariness and depression, but also with money, or even gold.

green is associated with growth, both physical and spiritual, and also with things that grow.

red is associated with anger, danger and warning. It may also be a symbol of sexual arousal in certain contexts.

white is associated with purity, cleanliness and innocence. It also has connections with illumination of the mind. White liquid, in certain contexts, may symbolize semen.

column an unfortunate dream (gypsy folklore). Freud regards this dream as bearing a phallic significance. Christians regard the column as an emblem of the Passion.

combat to dream of engaging in combat, you will find yourself seeking to ingratiate your affections into the life and love of some one whom you know to be another's, and you will run great risks of losing your good reputation in business. It denotes struggles to keep on firm ground. For a young woman to dream of seeing combatants, signifies that she will have choice between lovers, both of whom love her and would face death for her.

combing to dream of combing one's hair, denotes the illness or death of a friend or relative. Decay of friendship and loss of property is also indicated by this dream. *see* HAIR.

comedy to dream of being at a light play, denotes that foolish and short-lived pleasures will be indulged in by the dreamer.

To dream of seeing a comedy, is significant of light pleasures and pleasant tasks.

comet a dream of death and illness (Artemidorus). The omen is apparent in legend connected with these heavenly bodies.

comic songs to hear comic songs in dreams, foretells you will disregard opportunity to advance your affairs and enjoy the companionship of the pleasure loving. To sing one, proves you will enjoy much pleasure for a time, but difficulties will overtake you.

command to dream of being commanded, denotes that you will be humbled in some way by your associates for scorn shown your superiors.

To dream of giving a command, you will have some honour conferred upon you. If this is done in a tyrannical or boastful way disappointments will follow.

commandment to dream of receiving commands, foretells you will be unwisely influenced by persons of stronger will than your own. To read or hear the Ten Commandments read, denotes you will fall into errors from which you will hardly escape, even with the counsels of friends of wise and unerring judgement.

commerce to dream that you are engaged in commerce, denotes you will handle your opportunities wisely and advantageously. To dream of failures and gloomy outlooks in commercial circles, denotes trouble and ominous threatening of failure in real business life.

committee to dream of a committee, foretells that you will be surprised into doing some distasteful work. For one to wait on you, foretells some unfruitful labour will be assigned you.

companion to dream of seeing a wife or husband, signifies small anxieties and probable sickness.

To dream of social companions, denotes light and frivolous pastimes will engage your attention hindering you from performing your duties.

compass to dream of a compass, denotes you will be forced to struggle in narrow limits, thus making elevation more toilsome but fuller of honour.

To dream of the compass or mariner's needle, foretells you will be surrounded by prosperous circumstances and honest people will favour you.

To see one pointing awry, foretells threatened loss and deception.

completion to dream of completing a task or piece of work, denotes that you will have acquired a competency early in life, and that you can spend your days as you like and wherever you please.

For a young woman to dream that she has completed a garment, denotes that she will soon decide on a husband.

To dream of completing a journey, you will have the means to make one whenever you like.

complexion to dream that you have a beautiful complexion is lucky. You will pass through pleasing incidents.

To dream that you have bad and dark complexion, denotes disappointment and sickness.

composing to see in your dreams a composing stick, foretells that difficult problems will disclose themselves, and you will be at great trouble to meet them.

concert to dream of a concert of a high musical order, denotes delightful seasons of pleasure, and literary work to the author. To the business man it portends successful trade, and to the young it signifies unalloyed bliss and faithful loves.

Ordinary concerts such as engage ballet singers, denote that disagreeable companions and ungrateful friends will be met with. Business will show a falling off.

concubine for a man to dream that he is in company with a concubine, forecasts he is in danger of public disgrace, striving to keep from the world his true character and state of business.

For a woman to dream that she is a concubine, indicates that she will degrade herself by her own improprieties.

For a man to dream that his mistress is untrue, denotes that he has old enemies to encounter. Expected reverses will arise.

confectionery to dream of impure confectionery, denotes that an enemy in the guise of a friend will enter your privacy and discover secrets of moment to your opponents.

confetti to dream of confetti obstructing your view in a crowd of merry-makers, denotes that you will lose much by first seeking enjoyment, and later fulfil tasks set by duty.

conflagration to dream of a conflagration, denotes, if no lives are lost, changes in the future which will be beneficial to your interests and happiness.

conflict any sort of conflict that is dreamt about has to be considered in the light of what is going on in the life of the dreamer. Victory in conflict, while dreaming, may be wish-fulfilment and some sort of compensation for the individual's inability to overcome a struggle in daily life.

conjurer to dream of a conjuror, denotes unpleasant experience will beset you in your search for wealth and happiness.

conjuring to dream that you are in a hypnotic state or under the power of others, portends disastrous results, for your enemies will enthral you; but if you hold others under a spell you will assert decided will power in governing your surroundings.

For a young woman to dream that she is under strange influences, denotes her immediate exposure to danger, and she should beware.

To dream of seeing hypnotic and slight-of-hand performances, signifies worries and perplexities in business and domestic circles, and unhealthy conditions of state.

conscience to dream that your conscience censures you for deceiving some one, denotes that you will be tempted to commit wrong and should be constantly on your guard.

To dream of having a quiet conscience, denotes that you will stand in high repute.

conspiracy to dream that you are the object of a conspiracy, foretells you will make a wrong move in the directing of your affairs.

consumption to dream that you have consumption, denotes that you are exposing yourself to danger. Remain with your friends.

contempt to dream of being in contempt of court, denotes that you have committed business or social indiscretion and that it is unmerited.

To dream that you are held in contempt by others, you will succeed in winning their highest regard, and will find yourself prosperous and happy. But if the contempt is merited, your exile from business or social circles is intimated.

contrary meaning some dreams, according to the ancient oneirocritics and the gypsy interpreters, have a contrary meaning to the expected interpretation. This is the case for some dreams of VIOLENCE, DEATH, burial and financial gain or loss. For example, violence may signify deep affection, and dreaming of a burial may in fact denote a WEDDING. The dream of a wedding may also signify a FUNERAL. A dream of great RICHES may signify imminent POVERTY and vice versa.

convent to dream of seeking refuge in a convent, denotes that your future will be signally free from care and enemies, unless on entering the building you encounter a priest. If so, you will seek often and in vain for relief from worldly cares and mind worry.

For a young girl to dream of seeing a convent, her virtue and honestly will be questioned.

convention to dream of a convention, denotes unusual activity in business affairs and final engagement in love. An inharmonious or displeasing convention brings you disappointment.

convict to dream of seeing convicts, denotes disasters and sad news. To dream that you are a convict, indicates that you will worry over some affair; but you will clear up all mistakes.

For a young woman to dream of seeing her lover in the garb of a convict, indicates she will have cause to question the character of his love.

cooking stove to see a cooking stove in a dream, denotes that much unpleasantness will be modified by your timely interference. For a young woman to dream of using a cooking stove, foretells she will be too hasty in showing her appreciation of the attention of some person and thereby lose a closer friendship.

cooking to cook a meal, denotes some pleasant duty will devolve on you. Many friends will visit you in the near future. If there is discord or a lack of cheerfulness you may expect harassing and disappointing events to happen.

cooling board for a young woman to see a cooling board in her dreams, foretells sickness and quarrels with her lover. To dream of some living person as dead and rising up from a cooling board, denotes she will be indirectly connected with that person in some trouble, but will find out that things will work out satisfactorily.

To see her brother, who has long since been dead, rising from a cooling board, warns her of complications which may be averted if she puts forth the proper will and energy in struggling against them.

copper plate seen in a dream, is a warning of discordant views causing unhappiness between members of the same household.

copper to dream of copper, denotes oppression from those above you in station.

copperas to dream of copperas, foretells unintentional wrong will be done you which will be distressing and will cause you loss.

coppersmith to dream of a coppersmith, denotes small returns for labour, but withal contentment.

copying to dream of copying, denotes unfavourable workings of well tried plans.

For a young woman to dream that she is copying a letter, denotes she will be prejudiced into error by her love for a certain class of people.

coral to dream of coral, is momentous of enduring friend ship which will know no weariness in alleviating your trouble. Coloured coral is meant in this dream.

White coral, foretells unfaithfulness and warning of love.

cords *see* ROPE.

cork to dream of drawing corks at a banquet, signifies that you will soon enter a state of prosperity, in which you will revel in happiness of the most select kind.

To dream of medicine corks, denotes sickness and wasted energies.

To dream of seeing a fishing cork resting on clear water, denotes success. If water is disturbed you will be annoyed by unprincipled persons.

To dream that you are corking bottles, denotes a well organised business and system in your living.

For a young woman to dream of drawing champagne corks, indicates she will have a gay and handsome lover who will lavish much attention and money on her. She should look well to her reputation and listen to the warning of parents after this dream.

corkscrew a dream signifying an inquisitive friend.

corn a dream of riches (Artemidorus). Ears of corn are a symbol of the Holy Eucharist (Clement). An ear of corn is also the symbol of Horus bringing light and plenty to the world.

corn and corn-field to dream of passing through a green and luxurious corn-field, and seeing full ears hanging heavily, denotes great wealth for the farmer. It denotes fine crops and rich harvest and harmony in the home. To the young it promises much happiness and true friends, but to see the ears blasted, denotes disappointments and bereavements.

To see young corn newly ploughed, denotes favour with the powerful and coming success. To see it ripe, denotes fame and wealth. To see it cribbed, signifies that your highest desires will be realised.

To see shelled corn, denotes wealthy combines and unstinted favours.

To dream of eating green corn, denotes harmony among friends and happy unions for the young.

corner this is an unfavourable dream if the dreamer is frightened and secretes himself in a corner for safety.

To see persons talking in a corner, enemies are seeking to destroy you. The chances are that some one whom you consider a friend will prove a traitor to your interest.

cornet seen or heard in a dream, denotes kindly attentions from strangers.

cornmeal to see cornmeal, foretells the consummation of ardent wishes. To eat it made into bread, denotes that you will unwittingly throw obstructions in the way of your own advancement.

corns to dream that your corns hurt your feet, denotes that some enemies are undermining you, and you will have much distress; but if you succeed in clearing your feet of corns, you will inherit a large estate from some unknown source.

For a young woman to dream of having corns on her feet, indicates she will have to bear many crosses and be coldly treated by her sex.

cornucopia a dream of abundance (gypsy folklore), the Horn of Plenty of ancient tradition.

coronation to dream of a coronation, foretells you will enjoy acquaintances and friendships with prominent people. For a young woman to be participating in a coronation, foretells that she will come into some surprising favour with distinguished personages. But if the coronation presents disagreeable incoherence in her dreams, then she may expect unsatisfactory states growing out of anticipated pleasure.

corpse to dream of a corpse is fatal to happiness, as this dream indicates sorrowful tidings of the absent, and gloomy business prospects. The young will suffer many disappointments and pleasure will vanish.

To see a corpse placed in its casket, denotes immediate troubles to the dreamer.

To see a corpse in black, denotes the violent death of a friend or some desperate business entanglement.

To see a battle-field strewn with corpses, indicates war and general dissatisfaction between countries and political factions.

To see the corpse of an animal, denotes unhealthy situation, both as to business and health.

To see the corpse of any one of your immediate family, indicates death to that person, or to some member of the family, or a serious rupture of domestic relations, also unusual business depression. For lovers it is a sure sign of failure to keep promises of a sacred nature.

To put money on the eyes of a corpse in your dreams, denotes that you will see unscrupulous enemies robbing you while you are power-less to resent injury. If you only put it on one eye you will be able to recover lost property after an almost hopeless struggle. For a young woman this dream denotes distress and loss by unfortunately giving her confidence to designing persons.

For a young woman to dream that the proprietor of the store in which she works is a corpse, and she sees while sitting up with him that his face is clean shaven, foretells that she will fall below the standard of perfection in which she was held by her lover. If she sees the head of the corpse falling from the body, she is warned of secret enemies who, in harming her, will also detract from the interest of her employer. Seeing the corpse in the store, foretells that loss and unpleasantness will offset all concerned. There are those who are not conscientiously doing the right thing. There will be a gloomy outlook for peace and prosperous work.

corpulence for a person to dream of being corpulent, indicates to the dreamer bountiful increase of wealth and pleasant abiding places.

To see others corpulent, denotes unusual activity and prosperous times.

If a man or woman sees himself or herself looking grossly corpulent, he or she should look well to their moral nature and impulses. Beware of either concave or convex telescopically or microscopically drawn pictures of yourself or others, as they forebode evil.

corridor dreams about buildings or parts of buildings, such as corridors, are often very symbolic. The corridor may be interpreted as the birth canal, a passage from one stage of life to another, or a means of escape from a situation. Bunyan had a dream of a long narrow corridor leading to the sunny side of a far mountain through which he had great difficulty in passing. This signified a difficult religious journey and is said by the poet Southey to have inspired the former's work *The Pilgrim's Progress*.

corset to dream of a corset, denotes that you will be perplexed as to the meaning of attentions won by you. If a young woman is vexed over undoing or fastening her corset, she will be strongly inclined to quarrel with her friends under slight provocations.

Cossack to dream of a Cossack, denotes humiliation of a personal character, brought about by dissipation and wanton extravagance.

cot to dream of a cot, foretells some affliction, either through sickness or accident. Cots in rows signify you will not be alone in trouble, as friends will be afflicted also.

cotton cap it is a good dream, denoting many sincere friends.

cotton cloth to see cotton cloth in a dream, denotes easy circumstances. No great changes follow this dream.

For a young woman to dream of weaving cotton cloth, denotes that she will have a thrifty and enterprising husband. To the married it denotes a pleasant yet a humble abode.

cotton gin to dream of a cotton gin, foretells you will make some advancement toward fortune which will be very pleasing and satisfactory. To see a broken or dilapidated gin, signifies misfortune and trouble will overthrow success.

cotton to dream of young growing cotton-fields, denotes great business and prosperous times. To see cotton ready for gathering, denotes wealth and abundance for farmers.

For manufacturers to dream of cotton, means that they will be benefited by the advancement of this article.

For merchants, it denotes a change for the better in their line of business.

To see cotton in bales, is a favourable indication for better times.

To dream that cotton is advancing, denotes an immediate change from low to high prices, and all will be in better circumstances.

couch to dream of reclining on a couch, indicates that false hopes will be entertained. You should be alert to every change of your affairs, for only in this way will your hopes be realised.

cough to dream that you are aggravated by a constant cough indicates a state of low health; but one from which you will recuperate if care is observed in your habits.

To dream of hearing others cough, indicates unpleasant surroundings from which you will ultimately emerge.

counsellor to dream of a counsellor, you are likely to be possessed of some ability yourself, and you will usually prefer your own judgement to that of others. Be guarded in executing your ideas of right.

countenance to dream of a beautiful and ingenuous countenance, you may safely look for some pleasure to fall to your lot in the near future; but to behold an ugly and scowling visage, portends unfavourable transactions.

counter to dream of counters, foretells that active interest will debar idleness from infecting your life with unhealthy desires. To dream of empty and soiled counters, foretells unfortunate engagements which will bring great uneasiness of mind lest your interest will be wholly swept away.

counterfeit money to dream of counterfeit money, denotes you will have trouble with some unruly and worthless person. This dream always omens evil, whether you receive it or pass it.

counterpane is very good to dream of, if clean and white, denoting pleasant occupations for women; but if it be soiled you may expect harassing situations. Sickness usually follows this dream.

counting to dream of counting your children, and they are merry and sweet-looking, denotes that you will have no trouble in controlling them, and they will attain honourable places.

To dream of counting money, you will be lucky and always able to pay your debts; but to count out money to another person, you will meet with loss of some kind. Such will be the case, also, in counting other things. If for yourself, good; if for others, usually bad luck will attend you.

country to dream of being in a beautiful and fertile country, where abound rich fields of grain and running streams of pure water, denotes the very acme of good times is at hand. Wealth will pile in upon you, and you will be able to reign in state in any country. If the country be dry and bare, you will see and hear of troublous times. Famine and sickness will be in the land.

courtship bad, bad, will be the fate of the woman who dreams of being courted. She will often think that now he will propose, but often she will be disappointed. Disappointments will follow illusory hopes and fleeting pleasures. For a man to dream of courting, implies that he is not worthy of a companion.

cousin dreaming of one's cousin, denotes disappointments and afflictions. Saddened lives are predicted by this dream.

To dream of an affectionate correspondence with one's cousin, denotes a fatal rupture between families.

cow *see* ANIMALS.

cowslip to dream of gathering cowslips, portends unhappy ending of seemingly close and warm friendships; but seeing them growing, denotes a limited competency for lovers. This is a sinister dream.

To see them in full bloom, denotes a crisis in your affairs. The breaking up of happy homes may follow this dream.

coxcomb to dream of a coxcomb, denotes a low state of mind. The dreamer should endeavour to elevate his mind to nobler thoughts.

crab *see* ANIMALS.

cradle to dream of a cradle, with a beautiful infant occupying it, portends prosperity and the affections of beautiful children.

To rock your own baby in a cradle, denotes the serious illness of one of the family.

For a young woman to dream of rocking a cradle is portentous of her downfall. She should beware of gossiping.

crane *see* BIRDS.

crape to dream of seeing crape hanging from a door, denotes that you will hear of the sudden death of some relative or friend.

To see a person dressed in crape, indicates that sorrow, other than death, will possess you. It is bad for business and trade. To the young, it implies lovers' disputes and separations.

cravat or tie this might predict a sore throat. To take off or remove a tie or cravat indicates the cure of a cold (gypsy folklore). This dream refers to a troublesome partner from whom the dreamer longs to be freed (Freud). *See also* CLOTHES.

crawfish deceit is sure to assail you in your affairs of the heart, if you are young, after dreaming of this backward-going thing.

crawl to dream that you are crawling on the ground, and hurt your hand, you may expect humiliating tasks to be placed on you.

To crawl over rough places and stones, indicates that you have not taken proper advantage of your opportunities. A young woman, after dreaming of crawling, if not very careful of her conduct, will lose the respect of her lover.

To crawl in mire with others, denotes depression in business and loss of credit. Your friends will have cause to censure you.

cream to dream of seeing cream served, denotes that you will be associated with wealth if you are engaged in business other than farming.

To the farmer, it indicates fine crops and pleasant family relations. To drink cream yourself, denotes immediate good fortune. To lovers, this is a happy omen, as they will soon be united.

credit to dream of asking for credit, denotes that you will have cause to worry, although you may be inclined sometimes to think things look bright.

To credit another, warns you to be careful of your affairs, as you are likely to trust those who will eventually work you harm.

creek to dream of a creek, denotes new experiences and short journeys. If it is overflowing, you will have sharp trouble, but of brief period.

If it is dry, disappointment will be felt by you, and you will see another obtain the things you intrigued to secure.

cremate to dream of seeing bodies cremated, denotes enemies will reduce your influence in business circles. To think you are being cremated, portends distinct failure in enterprises, if you mind any but your own judgement in conducting them.

crescent a dream interpreted as signifying successful love. The symbol of Isis and of motherhood. In Egypt it is used as an emblem of the Virgin Mary.

crew to dream of seeing a crew getting ready to leave port, some unforeseen{sic} circumstance will cause you to give up a journey from which you would have gained much.

To see a crew working to save a ship in a storm, denotes disaster on land and sea. To the young, this dream bodes evil.

cricket *see* INSECTS.

cries to hear cries of distress, denotes that you will be engulfed in serious troubles, but by being alert you will finally emerge from these distressing straits and gain by this temporary gloom.

To hear a cry of surprise, you will receive aid from unexpected sources.

To hear the cries of wild beasts, denotes an accident of a serious nature.

To hear a cry for help from relatives, or friends, denotes that they are sick or in distress.

criminal to dream of associating with a person who has committed a crime, denotes that you will be harassed with unscrupulous persons, who will try to use your friendship for their own advancement.

To see a criminal fleeing from justice, denotes that you will come into the possession of the secrets of others, and will therefore be in danger, for they will fear that you will betray them, and consequently will seek your removal.

crochet work to dream of doing crochet work, foretells your entanglement in some silly affair growing out of a too great curiosity about other people's business. Beware of talking too frankly with over-confidential women.

crockery to dream of having an abundance of nice, clean crockery, denotes that you will be a tidy and economical housekeeper.

To be in a crockery store, indicates, if you are a merchant or business man, that you will look well to the details of your business and thereby experience profit. To a young woman, this dream denotes that she will marry a sturdy and upright man. An untidy store, with empty shelves, implies loss.

crocodile as sure as you dream of this creature, you will be deceived by your warmest friends. Enemies will assail you at every turn.

To dream of stepping on a crocodile's back, you may expect to fall into trouble, from which you will have to struggle mightily to extricate yourself. Heed this warning when dreams of this nature visit you. Avoid giving your confidence even to friends.

crocodile *see* ANIMALS.

cross roads to dream of cross roads, denotes you will be unable to hold some former favourable opportunity for reaching your desires. If you are undecided which one to take, you are likely to let unimportant matters irritate you in a distressing manner. You will be better favoured by fortune if you decide on your route. It may be after this dream you will have some important matter of business or love to decide.

cross to dream of a cross predicts success and honour; to carry it, trouble (Artemidorus). The dreamer may be seeking the comfort of religious consolation.

cross-bones to dream of cross-bones, foretells you will be troubled by the evil influence of others, and prosperity will assume other than promising aspects.

To see cross-bones as a monogram on an invitation to a funeral, which was sent out by a secret order, denotes that unnecessary fears will be entertained for some person, and events will transpire seemingly harsh, but of good import to the dreamer.

crossroads dreaming of crossroads may have associations with taking major decisions in life and of choosing from between two or more options as to which course of action to take.

croup to dream that your child has the croup, denotes slight illness, but useless fear for its safety. This is generally a good omen of health and domestic harmony.

crow *see* BIRDS.

crowd of people importunity, excitement (gypsy folklore). 'This dream is a sign of great excitement in the unconscious, especially in persons outwardly calm.' (Jung).

crown A dream of reward among all people. 'To bear a gold crown on the head signifies the friendship of your liege, honour, pleasure and many gifts' (Artemidorus). The unvarying symbol of reward.

crucifix to see a crucifix in a dream, is a warning of distress approaching, which will involve others beside yourself. To kiss one, foretells that trouble will be accepted by you with resignation.

For a young woman to possess one, foretells she will observe modesty and kindness in her deportment, and thus win the love of others and better her fortune.

crucifixion if you chance to dream of the crucifixion, you will see your opportunities slip away, tearing your hopes from your grasp, and leaving you wailing over the frustration of desires.

cruelty to dream of cruelty being shown you, foretells you will have trouble and disappointment in some dealings. If it is shown to others, there will be a disagreeable task set for others by you, which will contribute to you own loss.

crust to dream of a crust of bread, denotes incompetence, and threatened misery through carelessness in appointed duties.

crutches an adverse dream predicting illness (Artemidorus).

crying to dream of crying, is a forerunner of illusory pleasures, which will subside into gloom, and distressing influences affecting for evil business engagements and domestic affairs.

To see others crying, forebodes unexpected calls for aid from you.

cryst *see* CAVE.

crystal to dream of crystal in any form, is a fatal sign of coming depression either in social relations or business transactions. Electrical storms often attend this dream, doing damage to town and country.

For a woman to dream of seeing a dining-room furnished in crystal, even to the chairs, she will have cause to believe that those whom she holds in high regard no longer deserve this distinction, but she will find out that there were others in the crystal-furnished room, who were implicated also in this sinister dream.

cuckoo *see* BIRDS.

cucumber a dream symbolizing serious indisposition (gypsy folklore). Freud believed that dreams about food had a clear sexual significance and the cucumber may be a rather too obvious phallic symbol. If a man has this dream he may fear sexual inadequacy; for a woman it could express a wish for a masculine kind of power.

cunning to dream of being cunning, denotes you will assume happy cheerfulness to retain the friendship of prosperous and gay people. If you are associating with cunning people, it warns you that deceit is being practised upon you in order to use your means for their own advancement.

cupboards *see* FURNITURE; HOUSE.

cupid a dream of love and happiness (Artemidorus)

currying a Horse To dream of currying a horse, signifies that you will have a great many hard licks to make both with brain and hand before you attain the heights of your ambition; but if you successfully curry him you will attain that height, whatever it may be.

curtains to dream of curtains, foretells that unwelcome visitors will cause you worry and unhappiness. Soiled or torn curtains seen in a dream means disgraceful quarrels and reproaches.

cushion to dream of reclining on silken cushions, foretells that your ease will be procured at the expense of others; but to see the cushions, denotes that you will prosper in business and love-making. For a young woman to dream of making silken cushions, implies that she will be a bride before many months.

custard for a married woman to dream of making or eating custard, indicates she will be called upon to entertain an unexpected guest. A young woman will meet a stranger who will in time become a warm friend. If the custard has a sickening sweet taste, or is insipid, nothing but sorrow will intervene where you had expected a pleasant experience.

custom-house to dream of a custom-house, denotes you will have rivalries and competition in your labours.

To enter a custom-house, foretells that you will strive for, or have offered you, a position which you have long desired.

To leave one, signifies loss of position, trade or failure of securing some desired object.

cut to dream of a cut, denotes sickness or the treachery of a friend will frustrate your cheerfulness.

cymbal hearing a cymbal in your dreams, foretells the death of a very aged person of your acquaintance. The sun will shine, but you will see it darkly because of gloom.

cypress a dream of sorrow and mourning (Artemidorus).

D

daffodils a gypsy dream of good health and good news.

dagger a dream featuring a small pointed dagger denotes injustice and persecution (gypsy folklore). A Christian symbol of martyrdom. *See also* WEAPONS.

To dream of someone stabbing you with a poniard, denotes that secret enemies will cause you uneasiness of mind.

If you attack any person with one of these weapons, you will unfortunately suspect your friends of unfaithfulness.

Dreaming of poniards, omens evil.

dagger foretells death and suffering, unless you dream of grasping it firmly, which symbolizes success. Jung interprets the dagger as a phallic symbol.

dahlia to see dahlias in a dream, if they are fresh and bright, signifies good fortune to the dreamer. S*ee* BOUQUET

dairy to dream of a dairy is a good dream both to the married and unmarried.

daisy a good dream in spring or summer, predicting a true lover, but a bad one in winter or autumn (Raphael). The daisy symbolizes the eye of day and the sun.

damask rose to dream of seeing a damask rosebush in full foliage and bloom, denotes that a wedding will soon take place in your family, and great hopes will be fulfilled.

For a lover to place this rose in your hair, foretells that you will be deceived. If a woman receives a bouquet of damask roses in springtime, she will have a faithful lover; but if she received them in winter, she will cherish blasted hopes.

damson this is a peculiarly good dream if one is so fortunate as to see these trees lifting their branches loaded with rich purple fruit and dainty foliage; one may expect riches compared with his present estate. To dream of eating them at any time, forebodes grief.

dancing master to dream of a dancing master, foretells you will neglect important affairs to pursue frivolities. For a young woman to dream that her lover is a dancing master, portends that she will have a friend in accordance with her views of pleasure and life.

dancing see ACTIONS.

dandelion this dream denotes secret enemies at work against you (gypsy folklore). The interpretation probably derived from the fact that farmers regard the flower as a nuisance.

danger dreaming of being in some sort of danger or of having a strong sense of danger is one of the ways in which particular anxieties may be manifested in dreams. This may be a fear of letting oneself go emotionally or sexually and so risking betrayal or loss, or it may be fear of coping with some hurdle that is being, or is about to be, encountered in life. Such dreams need to be considered closely in the light of what is going on in the dreamer's life and his or her personal fears, whether acknowledged or hitherto subconscious.

darkness the darkness represents the unknown and also what is depressing or even feared. However, where darkness is dreamt of in association with feelings of warmth and comfort, it may be symbolic of the time before birth and the safety of the womb. A dream of warning against treachery, false friends, and a wilful blindness to reason and good sense (Artemidorus).

dates *see* FRUIT.

daughter to dream of your daughter, signifies that many displeasing incidents will give way to pleasure and harmony. If in the dream, she fails to meet your wishes, through any cause, you will suffer vexation and discontent.

daughter-in-law to dream of your daughter-in-law, indicates some unusual occurrence will add to happiness, or disquiet, according as she is pleasant or unreasonable.

David to dream of David, of Bible fame, denotes divisions in domestic circles, and unsettled affairs, will tax heavily your nerve force.

day a dream of a clear day is a good omen (Artemidorus).

daybreak to watch the day break in a dream, omens successful undertakings, unless the scene is indistinct and weird; then it may imply disappointment when success in business or love seems assured.

daylight, daytime *see* TIME.

dead people when one dreams of a person who is already dead, one is likely to be trying to resolve feelings about that person that are as yet unresolved. *See also* TYPICAL DREAMS.

death dreaming of the death of someone may indicate feelings of anger towards that person, even a desire to sever relations with him or her and thus be free of them. It is not likely to mean, however, that the dreamer wishes the person dead.

Dreaming of one's own death may be an attempt to deal with one's own uncertainties and fears about death or it may signify a wish to free oneself of certain current responsibilities or problems. *See also* CONTRARY MEANINGS; TYPICAL DREAMS.

debt is rather a bad dream, foretelling worries in business and love, and struggles for a competency; but if you have plenty to meet all your obligations, your affairs will assume a favourable turn.

December to dream of December, foretells accumulation of wealth, but loss of friendship. Strangers will occupy the position in the affections of some friend which was formerly held by you.

deck to dream of being on a ship and that a storm is raging, great disasters and unfortunate alliances will overtake you; but if the sea is calm and the light distinct, your way is clear to success. For lovers, this dream augurs happiness. *See* BOAT.

decorate to dream of decorating a place with bright-hued flowers for some festive occasion, is significant of favourable turns in business, and, to the young, of continued rounds of social pleasures and fruitful study.

To see the graves or caskets of the dead decorated with white flowers, is unfavourable to pleasure and worldly pursuits.

To be decorating, or see others decorate for some heroic action, foretells that you will be worthy, but that few will recognise your ability.

deed to dream of seeing or signing deeds, portends a law suit, to gain which you should be careful in selecting your counsel, as you are likely to be the loser. To dream of signing any kind of a paper, is a bad omen for the dreamer.

deer *see* ANIMALS.

déjà vu this means literally 'seen before', and is a phenomenon whereby the individual will recognize something that they encounter in life as having been seen in a dream before. In many cases the person or place will have been seen before but has simply not been remembered. Nevertheless, there are cases in which people will, for example, know what is about to happen or recognize where they are going on a journey because they remember similar events or places from their dream life. There is no simple explanation as to why this happens, but it is believed by some that feelings of *déjà vu* are connected with reincarnation and are not so much rooted in dreams as in a previous life of the individual concerned.

delay to be delayed in a dream, warns you of the scheming of enemies to prevent your progress.

delicacies see VIANDS.

delight to dream of experiencing delight over any event, signifies a favourable turn in affairs. For lovers to be delighted with the conduct of their sweethearts, denotes pleasant greetings.

To feel delight when looking on beautiful landscapes, prognosticates to the dreamer very great success and congenial associations.

deluge overwhelming business loss (Artemidorus). Financial affairs are usually indicated by storms, rain, etc. *See also* RAIN.

demand to dream that a demand for charity comes in upon you, denotes that you will be placed in embarrassing situations, but by your persistency you will fully restore your good standing. If the demand is unjust, you will become a leader in your profession. For a lover to command you adversely, implies his, or her, leniency.

dentist to dream of a dentist working on your teeth, denotes that you will have occasion to doubt the sincerity and honour of some person with whom you have dealings.

To see him at work on a young woman's teeth, denotes that you will soon be shocked by a scandal in circles near you.

departure dreaming of leaving somewhere or somebody has significance in relation to changes in the dreamer's life, a 'leaving behind' of old attitudes maybe, or a major change in lifestyle.

derrick seen in a dream, indicate strife and obstruction in your way to success.

descent dreams of going down from a high place towards the ground may be symbolic of a descent 'back down to earth' in terms of one's approach to life or some particular problem. Dreaming of descending into the depths of a tunnel or cave can either mean an attempt by the individual to reach deeper within the mind and increase self-awareness, or it may represent a returning to the experience of life within the womb.

desert loss of friends and wealth are shown by this dream (Artemidorus). Loneliness and isolation are symbolized.

desk to be using a desk in a dream, denotes unforeseen ill luck will rise before you. To see money on your desk, brings you unexpected extrication from private difficulties.

despair to be in despair in dreams, denotes that you will have many and cruel vexations in the working world.

To see others in despair, foretells the distress and unhappy position of some relative or friend.

detective to dream of a detective keeping in your wake when you are innocent of charges preferred, denotes that fortune and honour are drawing nearer to you each day; but if you feel yourself guilty, you are likely to find your reputation at stake, and friends will turn from you. For a young woman, this is not a fortunate dream.

devil the worst possible dream (gypsy folklore). Dreaming of the devil is a subconscious expression of guilt.

devotion for a farmer to dream of showing his devotion to God, or to his family, denotes plenteous crops and peaceful neighbours. To business people, this is a warning that nothing is to be gained by deceit.

For a young woman to dream of being devout, implies her chastity and an adoring husband.

dew to feel the dew falling on you in your dreams, portends that you will be attacked by fever or some malignant disease; but to see the dew sparkling through the grass in the sunlight, great honours and wealth are about to be heaped upon you. If you are single, a wealthy marriage will soon be your portion.

diadem to dream of a diadem, denotes that some honour will be tendered you for acceptance.

diamonds to dream of owning diamonds is a very propitious dream, signifying great honour and recognition from high places.

For a young woman to dream of her lover presenting her with diamonds, foreshows that she will make a great and honourable marriage, which will fill her people with honest pride; but to lose diamonds, and not find them again, is the most unlucky of dreams, foretelling disgrace, want and death.

For a sporting woman to dream of diamonds, foretells for her many prosperous days and magnificent presents. For a speculator, it denotes prosperous transactions. To dream of owning diamonds, portends the same for sporting men or women.

Diamonds are omens of good luck, unless stolen from the bodies of dead persons, when they foretell that your own unfaithfulness will be discovered by your friends.

dice a dream of enmity, quarrels and business vicissitudes (gypsy folklore).

dictionary to dream that you are referring to a dictionary, signifies you will depend too much upon the opinion and suggestions of others for the clear management of your own affairs, which could be done with proper dispatch if your own will was given play.

difficulty this dream signifies temporary embarrassment for business men of all classes, including soldiers and writers. But to extricate yourself from difficulties, foretells your prosperity.

For a woman to dream of being in difficulties, denotes that she is threatened with ill health or enemies. For lovers, this is a dream of contrariety, denoting pleasant courtship.

digging to dig in clean ground denotes thrift and good luck; in dirty or wet ground, trouble; to dig for gold and find large lumps, good fortune; to fail to find it, disappointment (Raphael). Most dreams of honest toil are of favourable augury. *See also* MUD.

dinner to dream that you eat your dinner alone, denotes that you will often have cause to think seriously of the necessaries of life.

For a young woman to dream of taking dinner with her lover, is indicative of a lovers' quarrel or a rupture, unless the affair is one of harmonious pleasure, when the reverse may be expected.

To be one of many invited guests at a dinner, denotes that you will enjoy the hospitalities of those who are able to extend to you many pleasant courtesies.

dirt to dream of seeing freshly stirred dirt around flowers or trees, denotes thrift and healthful conditions abound for the dreamer.

To see your clothes soiled with unclean dirt, you will be forced to save yourself from contagious diseases by leaving your home or submitting to the strictures of the law.

To dream that some one throws dirt upon you, denotes that enemies will try to injure your character.

disaster to dream of being in any disaster from public conveyance, you are in danger of losing property or of being maimed from some malarious disease.

For a young woman to dream of a disaster in which she is a participant, foretells that she will mourn the loss of her lover by death or desertion.

To dream of a disaster at sea, denotes unhappiness to sailors and loss of their gains. To others, it signifies loss by death; but if you dream that you are rescued, you will be placed in trying situations, but will come out unscathed.

To dream of a railway wreck in which you are not a participant, you will eventually be interested in some accident because of some relative or friend being hurt, or you will have trouble of a business character.

disease to dream that you are diseased, denotes a slight attack of illness, or of unpleasant dealings with a relative.

For a young woman to dream that she is incurably diseased, denotes that she will be likely to lead a life of single blessedness.

disgrace to be worried in your dream over the disgraceful conduct of children or friends, will bring you unsatisfying hopes, and worries will harass you. To be in disgrace yourself, denotes that you will hold morality at a low rate, and you are in danger of lowering your reputation for uprightness. Enemies are also shadowing you.

dish to dream of handling dishes, denotes good fortune; but if from any cause they should be broken, this signifies that fortune will be short-lived for you.

To see shelves of polished dishes, denotes success in marriage.

To dream of dishes, is prognostic of coming success and gain, and you will be able to fully appreciate your good luck. Soiled dishes, represent dissatisfaction and an unpromising future.

disinherited to dream that you are disinherited, warns you to look well to your business and social standing.

For a young man to dream of losing his inheritance by disobedience, warns him that he will find favour in the eyes of his parents by contracting a suitable marriage. For a woman, this dream is a warning to be careful of her conduct, lest she meet with unfavourable fortune.

dispute to dream of holding disputes over trifles, indicates bad health and unfairness in judging others.

To dream of disputing with learned people, shows that you have some latent ability, but are a little sluggish in developing it.

distaff a favourable dream (gypsy folklore). The distaff used to be a symbol of women's work.

distance *see* POSITION.

ditch to dream of falling in a ditch, denotes degradation and personal loss; but if you jump over it, you will live down any suspicion of wrong-doing.

dividend to dream of dividends, augments successful speculations or prosperous harvests. To fail in securing hoped-for dividends, proclaims failure in management or love affairs.

diving to dream of diving in clear water, denotes a favourable termination of some embarrassment. If the water is muddy, you will suffer anxiety at the turn your affairs seem to be taking.

To see others diving, indicates pleasant companions. For lovers to dream of diving, denotes the consummation of happy dreams and passionate love.

divining rods to see a divining rod in your dreams, foretells ill luck will dissatisfy you with present surroundings.

divorce to dream of being divorced, denotes that you are not satisfied with your companion, and should cultivate a more congenial atmosphere in the home life. It is a dream of warning.

For women to dream of divorce, denotes that a single life may be theirs through the infidelity of lovers.

docks to dream of being on docks, denotes that you are about to make an unpropitious journey. Accidents will threaten you. If you are there, wandering alone, and darkness overtakes you, you will meet with deadly enemies, but if the sun be shining, you will escape threatening dangers.

doctor this is a most auspicious dream, denoting good health and general prosperity, if you meet him socially, for you will not then spend your money for his services. If you be young and engaged to marry him, then this dream warns you of deceit.

To dream of a doctor professionally, signifies discouraging illness and disagreeable differences between members of a family.

To dream that a doctor makes an incision in your flesh, trying to discover blood, but failing in his efforts, denotes that you will be tormented and injured by some evil person, who may try to make you pay out money for his debts. If he finds blood, you will be the loser in some transaction.

dog *see* ANIMALS.

dolphin *see* ANIMALS.

dome to dream that you are in the dome of a building, viewing a strange landscape, signifies a favourable change in your life. You will occupy honourable places among strangers.

To behold a dome from a distance, portends that you will never reach the height of your ambition, and if you are in love, the object of your desires will scorn your attention.

dominoes to dream of playing at dominoes, and lose, you will be affronted by a friend, and much uneasiness for your safety will be entertained by your people, as you will not be discreet in your affairs with women or other matters that engage your attention.

If you are the winner of the game, it foretells that you will be much courted and admired by certain dissolute characters, bringing you selfish pleasures, but much distress to your relatives.

donkey *see* ANIMALS.

doomsday to dream that you are living on, and looking forward to seeing doomsday, is a warning for you to give substantial and material affairs close attention, or you will find that the artful and scheming friends you are entertaining will have possession of what they desire from you, which is your wealth, and not your sentimentality.

To a young woman, this dream encourages her to throw aside the attention of men above her in station and accept the love of an honest and deserving man near her.

door bell to dream you hear or ring a door bell, foretells unexpected tidings, or a hasty summons to business, or the bedside of a sick relative.

doors doors in dreams can represent opportunities or paths available to the dreamer in life. Thus, a closed door may represent an option that is no longer available to the dreamer, while an open door beckons the dreamer to take a chance or to move forward into a new 'room' in life.

dove *see* BIRDS.

dowry to dream that you fail to receive a dowry, signifies penury and a cold world to depend on for a living. If you receive it, your expectations for the day will be fulfilled. The opposite may be expected if the dream is superinduced by the previous action of the waking mind.

dragon A dream of sudden changes in the worldly condition, riches and treasure (Raphael). In Christian art the dragon symbolizes Satan, or sin. The Chinese regard a dragon, or winged serpent, as the symbol of the Infinite Intelligence, keeping ward over the Tree of Knowledge. A dragon was also the standard of the Welsh, of the West Saxons, of the Phoenicians and of the Chinese Manchu dynasty. The Celts use the word dragon to signify a chief, a dictator in time of danger, and probably the dream interpretation is derived from this symbol.

drama to see a drama, signifies pleasant reunions with distant friends.

To be bored with the performance of a drama, you will be forced to accept an uncongenial companion at some entertainment or secret affair.

To write one, portends that you will be plunged into distress and debt, to be extricated as if by a miracle.

draughts, checkers to dream of playing draughts, you will be involved in difficulties of a serious character, and strange people will come into your life, working you harm.

To dream that you win the game, you will succeed in some doubtful enterprise.

draw-knife to see or use a draw-knife, portends unfulfilled hopes or desires.

Some fair prospect will loom before you, only to go down in mistake and disappointment.

dreaming of a dream it may happen, particularly in unpleasant dreams, that dreamers 'interrupt themselves' to give themselves reassurance—'it's only a dream'—or to tell themselves, 'this has happened in a dream before'. It may be that what is being dreamt about is particularly hard for the dreamer to cope with, so the unconscious mind is helping the dreamer to keep the dream safely within the confines of the dream world so that it does not have to be faced up to in 'real life'.

To dream of relating a dream indicates that something unusual is about to happen (Raphael). Evidently a struggle on the part of the subconscious to bring the matter before the consciousness.

dregs a dream of poverty, failure and loss (gypsy folklore).

dressing to think you are having trouble in dressing, while dreaming, means some evil persons will worry and detain you from places of amusement.

If you can't get dressed in time for a train, you will have many annoyances through the carelessness of others. You should depend on your own efforts as far as possible, after these dreams, if you would secure contentment and full success.

drinking for a woman to dream of hilarious drinking, denotes that she is engaging in affairs which may work to her discredit, though she may now find much pleasure in the same. If she dreams that she fails to drink clear water, though she uses her best efforts to do so, she will fail to enjoy some pleasure that is insinuatingly offered her.

driving to dream of driving a carriage, signifies unjust criticism of your seeming extravagance. You will be compelled to do things which appear undignified.

To dream of driving a public cab, denotes menial labour, with little chance for advancement. If it is a wagon, you will remain in poverty and unfortunate circumstances for some time. If you are driven in these conveyances by others, you will profit by superior knowledge of the world, and will always find some path through difficulties. If you are a man, you will, in affairs with women, drive your wishes to a speedy consummation. If a woman, you will hold men's hearts at low value after succeeding in getting a hold on them. *See* CAB or CARRIAGE.

dromedary to dream of a dromedary, denotes that you will be the recipient of unexpected beneficence, and will wear your new honours with dignity; you will dispense charity with a gracious hands. To lovers, this dream foretells congenial dispositions.

dropsy to dream of being afflicted with the dropsy, denotes illness for a time, but from which you will recover with renewed vigour. To see others thus afflicted, denotes that you will hear from the absent shortly, and have tidings of their good health.

drought this is-an evil dream, denoting warring disputes between nations, and much bloodshed therefrom. Shipwrecks and land disasters will occur, and families will quarrel and separate; sickness will work damage also. Your affairs will go awry, as well.

drown an unfortunate dream predicting illness (gypsy folklore). A dream evidently due to some physical cause affecting the breathing apparatus. *See also* WATER.

drugs or drugstore this may be a dream predicting illness (gypsy folklore). Another reason may be that this is a dream inspired by the subconscious knowledge of need.

drum a dream of strife and war (gypsy folklore).

drunk this is an unfavourable dream if you are drunk on heavy liquors, indicating profligacy and loss of employment. You will be disgraced by stooping to forgery or theft.

If drunk on wine, you will be fortunate in trade and love-making, and will scale exalted heights in literary pursuits. This dream is always the bearer of aesthetic experiences.

To see others in a drunken condition, foretells for you, and probably others, unhappy states.

Drunkenness in all forms is unreliable as a good dream. All classes are warned by this dream to shift their thoughts into more healthful channels.

duck *see* BIRDS.

duet to dream of hearing a duet played, denotes a peaceful and even existence for lovers. No quarrels, as is customary in this sort of thing. Business people carry on a mild rivalry. To musical people, this denotes competition and wrangling for superiority.

To hear a duet sung, is unpleasant tidings from the absent; but this will not last, as some new pleasure will displace the unpleasantness.

dulcimer to dream of a dulcimer, denotes that the highest wishes in life will be attained by exalted qualities of mind. To women, this is significant of a life free from those petty jealousies which usually make women unhappy.

dumb to dream of being dumb, indicates your inability to persuade others into your mode of thinking, and using them for your profit by your glibness of tongue. To the dumb, it denotes false friends.

dungeon to dream of being in a dungeon, foretells for you struggles with the vital affairs of life but by wise dealing you will disenthrall yourself of obstacles and the designs of enemies. For a woman this is a dark foreboding; by her wilful indiscretion she will lose her position among honourable people.

To see a dungeon lighted up, portends that you are threatened with entanglements of which your better judgement warns you.

dunghill to dream of a dunghill, you will see profits coming in through the most unexpected sources. To the farmer this is a lucky dream, indicating fine seasons and abundant products from soil and stock. For a young woman, it denotes that she will unknowingly marry a man of great wealth.

dusk this is a dream of sadness; it portends an early decline and unrequited hopes. Dark outlook for trade and pursuits of any nature is prolonged by this dream.

dust a dream of temporary calamity (gypsy folklore). Dust is the Christian symbol of humility and woe, but its effects are obviously temporary and easily thrown aside. To dream of dust covering you, denotes that you will be slightly injured in business by the failure of others. For a young woman, this denotes that she will be set aside by her lover for a newer flame. If you free yourself of the dust by using judicious measures, you will clear up the loss.

dwarf this is a very favourable dream. If the dwarf is well formed and pleasing in appearance, it omens you will never be dwarfed in mind or stature. Health and good constitution will admit of your engaging in many profitable pursuits both of mind and body.

To see your friends dwarfed, denotes their health, and you will have many pleasures through them.

dye to see the dyeing of cloth or garments in process, your bad or good luck depends on the colour. Blues, reds and gold, indicate prosperity; black and white, indicate sorrow in all forms.

dying to dream of dying, foretells that you are threatened with evil from a source that has contributed to your former advancement and enjoyment.

To see others dying, forebodes general ill luck to you and to your friends.

To dream that you are going to die, denotes that unfortunate inattention to your affairs will depreciate their value. Illness threatens to damage you also.

To see animals in the throes of death, denotes escape from evil influences if the animal be wild or savage.

It is an unlucky dream to see domestic animals dying or in agony.

[As these events of good or ill approach you they naturally assume these forms of agonising death, to impress you more fully with the joyfulness or the gravity of the situation you are about to enter on awakening to material responsibilities, to aid you in the mastery of self which is essential to meeting all conditions with calmness and determination.] *See* DEATH.

dynamite to see dynamite in a dream, is a sign of approaching change and the expanding of one's affairs. To be frightened by it, indicates that a secret enemy is at work against you, and if you are not careful of your conduct he will disclose himself at an unexpected and helpless moment.

dynamo to dream of a dynamo, omens successful enterprises if attention is shown to details of business. One out of repair, shows you are nearing enemies who will involve you in trouble.

E

eagle *see* BIRDS.

earrings to see earrings in dreams, omens good news and interesting work is before you. To see them broken, indicates that gossip of a low order will be directed against you.

ears to dream of seeing ears, an evil and designing person is keeping watch over your conversation to work you harm.

earth as the earth is the source for growth, so earth in dreams signifies where we are coming from, our family roots, and social background. A universally portentous dream (gypsy folklore). The earth as the symbol of the universal mother is curiously at variance with this interpretation of the oneirocritics. It is only to be accounted for by the hypothesis that in their anxiety to escape all implication of idolatry and paganism, the gypsies reversed the symbols of the ancient creeds.

earthquake losses, broken ties, bereavements (gypsy folklore); nature's own symbolism.

earthworm *see* ANIMALS.

earwig to dream that you see an earwig or have one in your ear, denotes that you will have unpleasant news affecting your business or family relations.

eating eating is seen as the satisfying of a hunger, of a sexual or emotional nature. The sharing of food in dreams may be symbolic of the giving and receiving of love, the sharing of affection and/or bodies.

ebony if you dream of ebony furniture or other articles of ebony, you will have many distressing disputes and quarrels in your home.

echo false news and absurdity are hereby indicated (Artemidorus). Dreaming of an echo is likely to be a signal that you are lacking in confidence in some respect.

eclipse Dreaming of an eclipse of the sun predicts a great loss. An eclipse of the moon is not a bad dream as such but whatever your wish is you will not attain it (Artemidorus). The symbolism here is apparent.

ecstasy to dream of feeling ecstasy, denotes you will enjoy a visit from a long-absent friend. If you experience ecstasy in disturbing dreams you will be subjected to sorrow and disappointment.

education to dream that you are anxious to obtain an education, shows that whatever your circumstances in life may be there will be a keen desire for knowledge on your part, which will place you on a higher plane than your associates. Fortune will also be more lenient to you.

To dream that you are in places of learning, foretells for you many influential friends.

eels *see* ANIMALS.

eggs eggs are symbolic of the potential of the individual, which has yet been untapped. A dream meaning happiness; broken eggs, however, predict quarrels and lawsuits; fresh eggs, good news (Artemidorus). An ancient symbol of creation the egg has been held as an emblem of good fortune by all races.

eight *see* NUMBERS.

ejaculation ejaculation is the ultimate end of the sexual act, the final release. Dreams of ejaculation are undeniably sexual and probably represent wish-fulfilment. Ejaculation or, for the female, orgasm while asleep will indicate that the individual has been having a dream that is tied to his or her sexuality, though this may not be immediately apparent through the remembered content of the dream.

elbows to see elbows in a dream, signifies that arduous labours will devolve upon you, and for which you will receive small reimbursements.

For a young woman, this is a prognostic of favourable opportunities to make a reasonably wealthy marriage. If the elbows are soiled, she will lose a good chance of securing a home by marriage.

elderberries *see* FRUIT.

election to dream that you are at an election, foretells you will engage in some controversy which will prove detrimental to your social or financial standing.

electricity to dream of electricity, denotes there will be sudden changes about you, which will not afford you either advancement or pleasure. If you are shocked by it you will face a deplorable danger.

To see live electrical wire, foretells that enemies will disturb your plans, which have given you much anxiety in forming. To dream that you can send a package or yourself out over a wire with the same rapidity that a message can be sent, denotes you will finally overcome obstacles and be able to use your enemies' plans to advance yourself.

elephant *see* ANIMALS.

elevator to dream of ascending in an elevator, denotes you will swiftly rise to position and wealth, but if you descend in one your misfortunes will crush and discourage you. If you see one go down and think you are left, you will narrowly escape disappointment in some undertaking. To see one standing, foretells threatened danger.

elixir of life to dream of the elixir of life, denotes that there will come into your environments new pleasures and new possibilities.

elk *see* ANIMALS.

elopement to dream of eloping is unfavourable. To the married, it denotes that you hold places which you are unworthy to fill, and if your ways are not rectified your reputation will be at stake. To the unmarried, it foretells disappointments in love and the unfaithfulness of men.

To dream that your lover has eloped with some one else, denotes his or her unfaithfulness.

To dream of your friend eloping with one whom you do not approve, denotes that you will soon hear of them contracting a disagreeable marriage.

eloquent if you think you are eloquent of speech in your dreams, there will be pleasant news for you concerning one in whose interest you are working.

To fail in impressing others with your eloquence, there will be much disorder in your affairs.

embalming to see embalming in process, foretells altered positions in social life and threatened poverty. To dream that you are looking at yourself embalmed, omens unfortunate friendships for you, which will force you into lower classes than you are accustomed to move in.

embankment to dream that you drive along an embankment, foretells you will be threatened with trouble and unhappiness. If you continue your drive without unpleasant incidents arising, you will succeed in turning these foreboding to useful account in your advancement. To ride on horseback along one, denotes you will fearlessly meet and overcome all obstacles in your way to wealth and happiness. To walk along one, you will have a weary struggle for elevation, but will &ally reap a successful reward.

embracing to dream of embracing your husband or wife, as the case may be, in a sorrowing or indifferent way, denotes that you will have dissension and accusations in your family, also that sickness is threatened.

To embrace relatives, signifies their sickness and unhappiness.

For lovers to dream of embracing, foretells quarrels and disagreements arising from infidelity. If these dreams take place under auspicious conditions, the reverse may be expected.

If you embrace a stranger, it signifies that you will have an unwelcome guest.

embroidery if a woman dreams of embroidering, she will be admired for her tact and ability to make the best of everything that comes her way. For a married man to see embroidery, signifies a new member in his household, For a lover, this denotes a wise and economical wife.

emerald the dream indicates wealth, a rise in the world (gypsy folklore). Persians used it as a charm against the devil, it also bestows knowledge of the future.

emotion remembering the emotions that were felt while dreaming is essential in unravelling the meaning behind the content of any dream.

emperor to dream of going abroad and meeting the emperor of a nation in your travels, denotes that you will make a long journey, which will bring neither pleasure nor much knowledge.

employee to see one of your employees denotes crosses and disturbances if he assumes a disagreeable or offensive attitude. If he is pleasant and has communications of interest, you will find no cause for evil or embarrassing conditions upon waking.

employment this is not an auspicious dream. It implies depression in business circles and loss of employment to wage earners. It also denotes bodily illness.

To dream of being out of work, denotes that you will have no fear, as you are always sought out for your conscientious fulfilment of contracts, which make you a desired help.

Giving employment to others, indicates loss for yourself. All dreams of this nature may be interpreted as the above.

empress to dream of an empress, denotes that you will be exalted to high honours, but you will let pride make you very unpopular.

To dream of an empress and an emperor is not particularly bad, but brings one no substantial good.

enchantment to dream of being under the spell of enchantment, denotes that if you are not careful you will be exposed to some evil in the form of pleasure. The young should heed the benevolent advice of their elders.

To resist enchantment, foretells that you will be much sought after for your wise counsels and your liberality.

To dream of trying to enchant others, portends that you will fall into evil.

enclosure dreams of being enclosed may have connections with the barriers that the individual puts up against the world, the protective 'shell' that is used as a barricade against fears or hurt.

If unpleasant feelings are felt, the dreamer could be facing restrictions to his or her actions and feelings in life and feeling frustrated because of this. *See also* CAGE; CAPTIVE; CHAINS; IMPRISONMENT.

encyclopaedia to dream of seeing or searching through encyclopaedias, portends that you will secure literary ability to the losing of prosperity and comfort.

enemy to dream that you overcome enemies, denotes that you will surmount all difficulties in business, and enjoy the greatest prosperity.

If you are defamed by your enemies, it denotes that you will be threatened with failures in your work. You will be wise to use the utmost caution in proceeding in affairs of any moment.

To overcome your enemies in any form, signifies your gain. For them to get the better of you is ominous of adverse fortunes. This dream may be literal.

engagement to dream of a business engagement, denotes dullness and worries in trade.

For young people to dream that they are engaged, denotes that they will not be much admired.

To dream of breaking an engagement, denotes a hasty, and an unwise action in some important matter or disappointments may follow.

engine to dream of an engine, denotes you will encounter grave difficulties and journeys, but you will have substantial friends to uphold you.

Disabled engines stand for misfortune and loss of relatives.

engineer to see an engineer, forebodes weary journeys but joyful reunions.

English to dream, if you are a foreigner, of meeting English people, denotes that you will have to suffer through the selfish designs of others.

entertainment to dream of an entertainment where there is music and dancing, you will have pleasant tidings of the absent, and enjoy health and prosperity. To the young, this is a dream of many and varied pleasures and the high regard of friends.

entrails a bad dream predicting sickness (gypsy folklore).

envelope seen in a dream, omens news of a sorrowful cast.

envy to dream that you entertain envy for others, denotes that you will make warm friends by your unselfish deference to the wishes of others.

If you dream of being envied by others, it denotes that you will suffer some inconvenience from friends overanxious to please you.

epaulet a dream of dignity (gypsy folklore).

epicure to dream of sitting at the table with an epicure, denotes that you will enjoy some fine distinction, but you will be surrounded by people of selfish principles.

To dream that you an epicure yourself, you will cultivate your mind, body and taste to the highest polish.

For a woman to dream of trying to satisfy an epicure, signifies that she will have a distinguished husband, but to her he will be a tyrant.

epidemic to dream of an epidemic, signifies prostration of mental faculties and worry from distasteful tasks. Contagion among relatives or friends is foretold by dreams of this nature.

equator good weather and fine crops are promised to the farmer by this dream; to others, abundance (gypsy folklore). The tropical heat here symbolizes fruitfulness.

ermine this dream symbolizes a rise to honour and dignity (gypsy folklore). The ermine symbolizes royalty.

errands to go on errands in your dreams, means congenial associations and mutual agreement in the home circle. For a young woman to send some person on an errand, denotes she will lose her lover by her indifference to meet his wishes.

escape dreams of escape may represent a desire to find release from particular circumstances in one's life, or may mean a recovery from depression or even illness.

Dreaming of something escaping from you could be a reminder of something that has been overlooked, or a missed opportunity.

estate to dream that you come into the ownership of a vast estate, denotes that you will receive a legacy at some distant day, but quite different to your expectations. For a young woman, this dream portends that her inheritance will be of a disappointing nature. She will have to live quite frugally, as her inheritance will be a poor man and a house full of children.

Europe to dream of travelling in Europe, foretells that you will soon go on a long journey, which will avail you in the knowledge you gain of the manners and customs of foreign people. You will also be enabled to forward your financial standing. For a young woman to feel that she is disappointed with the sights of Europe, omens her inability to appreciate chances for her elevation. She will be likely to disappoint her friends or lover.

eve to dream of this ancient character, denotes your hesitancy to accept this ancient story as authentic, and you may encounter opposition in business and social circles because of this doubt.

For a young woman to dream that she impersonates Eve, warns her to be careful. She may be wiser than her ancient relative, but the Evil One still has powerful agents in the disguise of a handsome man. Keep your eye on innocent Eve, young man. That apple tree still bears fruit, and you may be persuaded, unwittingly, to share the wealth of its products.

evening dreams of evening may be symbolic of the 'setting of the sun' in one's life, i.e. approaching old age. Alternatively, they can represent times of peace and rest, the calm after the storm and the final relaxation after a period of struggle. *See also* TIME.

evergreen this dream denotes boundless resources of wealth, happiness and learning. It is a free presentiment of prosperity to all classes.

ewe-lamb *see* ANIMALS.

exams while exam dreams commonly start in adolescence (a period marked by real anxiety about school exams for most people) they can be repeated over and over again throughout the rest of the dreamer's life, almost always occurring at times of particular stress. The dreams have similar scenarios for most people—turning up at an exam to find that it is not the exam that you have prepared for, looking at the exam paper and finding that it is written in some incomprehensible script or foreign language, discovering that you have to sit an exam for which you have attended no classes, etc. Such dreams are always a pointer to real-life stress and an indication to the dreamer that this stress is a problem that must be dealt with. *See also* TYPICAL DREAMS.

exchange denotes profitable dealings in all classes of business. For a young woman to dream that she is exchanging sweethearts with her friend, indicates that she will do well to heed this as advice, as she would be happier with another.

excrement excrement is thought by some to be symbolic of wealth. The link between excrement and wealth has its origins in the belief of early alchemists that all the necessary ingredients for making gold were to be found in faecal matter.

Dreaming of incontinence may indicate a fear of letting oneself go in some way, perhaps a fear of one's emotions.

Excrement in dreams can also signify feelings of disgust towards the self or another, depending upon the context of the dream in which it appears. *See also* MUD.

execution a person who dreams of his or her own execution may be depressed and suffering from severely diminished self-esteem. This could be a way of seeking self-punishment.

exile for a woman to dream that she is exiled, denotes that she will have to make a journey which will interfere with some engagement or pleasure.

explosion dreams of explosion can represent outbursts of anger from which the dreamer feels prevented or inhibited in real life. Such dreams may be symbolic of orgasm, EJACULATION and the culmination of sexual desire.

eyebrows denotes that you will encounter sinister obstacles in your immediate future.

eyeglass to dream of seeing or wearing an eyeglass, denotes you will be afflicted with disagreeable friendships, from which you will strive vainly to disengage yourself. For a young woman to see her lover with an eyeglass on, omens disruption of love affairs.

eyes *see* BODY.

F

fables to dream of reading or telling fables, denotes pleasant tasks and a literary turn of mind. To the young, it signifies romantic attachments.

To hear, or tell, religious fables, denotes that the dreamer will become very devotional.

face this dream is favourable if you see happy and bright faces, but significant of trouble if they are disfigured, ugly, or frowning on you.

To a young person, an ugly face foretells lovers' quarrels; or for a lover to see the face of his sweetheart looking old, denotes separation and the breaking up of happy associations.

To see a strange and weird-looking face, denotes that enemies and misfortunes surround you.

To dream of seeing your own face, denotes unhappiness; and to the married, threats of divorce will be made.

To see your face in a mirror, denotes displeasure with yourself for not being able to carry out plans for self-advancement. You will also lose the esteem of friends.

failure like EXAM dreams, dreams of failure are generally linked to fears and problems in the dreamer's life. The dreamer may be coming to realize that what he or she is striving for in real life is, in fact, impossible. However, the dream may simply be an expression of fears that the dreamer feels unable to admit to. *See also* EXAMS.

fainting to dream of fainting, signifies illness in your family and unpleasant news of the absent.

If a young woman dreams of fainting, it denotes that she will fall into ill health and experience disappointment.

fair this dream predicts coming into the company of many people through whom you will profit (gypsy folklore). Here the gypsy interprets according to his own custom and tradition.

fairy a dream of riches and independence to the poor, to the rich it shows temptation (gypsy folklore). The providence of nursery legend and mythology, their dream symbolism is apparent.

faithless to dream that your friends are faithless, denotes that they will hold you in worthy esteem. For a lover to dream that his sweetheart is faithless, signifies a happy marriage.

fakir to dream of an Indian fakir, denotes uncommon activity and phenomenal changes in your life. Such dreams may sometimes be of gloomy import.

falcon *see* BIRDS.

falling dreams of falling are quite common. Often the dreamer dreams of falling and then wakes up before hitting the ground. Falling can represent any one of several things. Where the dreamer falls and lands, the dream may be sexually related, the fall representing the act of intercourse. Alternatively, a fall in a dream may represent a 'fall from grace' in the dreamer's life; the dreamer has let him or herself down in some way. Approaching some sort of edge and falling over may indicate that the dreamer is heading for problems in life, while dreaming of being in danger from falling can mean that the dreamer has real fears of potential disaster. *See also* TYPICAL DREAMS.

falling leaves *see* TREE.

fame to dream of being famous, denotes disappointed aspirations. To dream of famous people, portends your rise from obscurity to places of honour.

family for most people the attitudes and values that they grow up with are related to and even dependent on their family. Whether an individual grows up to accept or to reject the values and attitudes of his or her family, it is generally true to say that they have built up their own set of values based on what they have seen and learnt within the context of family life. Equally, the way in which an individual behaves in relation to other people will, in all probability, be rooted in the patterns of behaviour of his or her parents and siblings.

Family figures in dreams may well represent themselves, but they can also represent that part of the dreamer that has its foundations in that particular family member. Thus, a man may have a dream about his mother in which he is perhaps resolving some of his feelings towards her; this dream involves a straight representation of his mother. Or he may have a dream in which his mother represents, perhaps, the caring and nurturing aspect of himself.

Generalizations as to what the appearance of a family member in a dream might mean can have little meaning without first some knowledge of the context of the dream, the dreamer's background, and the influences that have come to bear on his or her life through the family.

Even the fact that an individual may lack a family background (in the traditional sense) is of relevance.

famine to dream of a famine, foretells that your business will be unremunerative and sickness will prove a scourge. This dream is generally bad.

If you see your enemies perishing by famine, you will be successful in competition. If dreams of famine should break in wild confusion over slumbers, tearing up all heads in anguish, filling every soul with care, hauling down Hope's banners, sombre with omens of misfortune and despair, your waking grief more poignant still must grow ere you quench ambition and envy overthrow.

famish to dream that you are famishing, foretells that you are meeting disheartening failure in some enterprise which you considered a promising success. To see others famishing, brings sorrow to others as well as to yourself.

fan a dream of pride (gypsy folklore). A Japanese emblem of authority, power, royalty.

farewell to dream of bidding friends farewell denotes a change in business (gypsy folklore).

farm to dream of taking a farm denotes advancement; to visit a farm and partake of its products, good health (gypsy folklore). Obviously an interpretation derived from the rural districts.

fat to dream of growing fat signals affliction, physical or otherwise (gypsy folklore). It may be the result of physical stimuli, probably the plethora attendant upon certain ailments.

fates to dream of the fates, unnecessary disagreements and unhappiness is foretold. For a young woman to dream of juggling with fate, denotes she will daringly interpose herself between devoted friends or lovers.

father to dream of your father, signifies that you are about to be involved in a difficulty, and you will need wise counsel if you extricate yourself therefrom.

If he is dead, it denotes that your business is pulling heavily, and you will have to use caution in conducting it.

For a young woman to dream of her dead father, portends that her lover will, or is, playing her false.

father-in-law to dream of your father-in-law, denotes contentions with friends or relatives. To see him well and cheerful, foretells pleasant family relations.

fatigue to feel fatigued in a dream, foretells ill health or oppression in business. For a young woman to see others fatigued, indicates discouraging progress in health.

favour to dream that you ask favours of anyone, denotes that you will enjoy abundance, and that you will not especially need anything. To grant favours, means a loss.

fawn *see* ANIMALS.

fear fear is like all the other emotions that we experience while dreaming in that it can give a real clue as to the dreamer's state of mind, or the dreamer's true response to a situation, or an occurrence in his or her life. Dreaming gives people an opportunity to express feelings that they might otherwise be unable to express properly. Thus, while a person may present a brave, cheerful or perhaps angry face to the world, in dreams he or she can express the fear that lies behind the outward persona. The content of a nightmare, therefore, is not necessarily as enlightening as the fear that has been felt by the person who has had the nightmare. *See also* MONSTER; PANIC.

fear to feel that you are afraid to proceed with some affair, or continue a journey, denotes that you will find trouble in your household, and enterprises will be unsuccessful.

To see others afraid, denotes that some friend will be deterred from performing some favour for you because of his own difficulties.

For a young woman to dream that she is afraid of a dog, there will be a possibility of her doubting a true friend.

feast to dream of a feast, foretells that pleasant surprises are being planned for you. To see disorder or misconduct at a feast, foretells quarrels or unhappiness through the negligence or sickness of some person. To arrive late at a feast, denotes that vexing affairs will occupy you.

feathers white feathers foretell success; dark feathers, the reverse (Artemidorus). Feathers are a symbol of power, and in Egypt the emblem of truth, goodness and knowledge. *See also* BIRDS.

February to dream of February, denotes continued ill health and gloom, generally. If you happen to see a bright sunshiny day in this month, you will be unexpectedly and happily surprised with some good fortune.

feeble to dream of being feeble, denotes unhealthy occupation and mental worry. Seek to make a change for yourself after this dream.

feet to dream of seeing your own feet, is ominous of despair. You will be overcome by the will and temper of another. To see others' feet, denotes that you will maintain your rights in a pleasant, but determined way, and win for yourself a place above the common walks of life.

To dream that you wash your feet, denotes that you will let others take advantage of you.

To dream that your feet are hurting you, portends troubles of a humiliating character, as they usually are family quarrels.

To see your feet swollen and red, you will make a sudden change in your business by separating from your family. This is an evil dream, as it usually foretells scandal and sensation.

fence to dream of climbing to the top of a fence, denotes that success will crown your efforts.

To fall from a fence, signifies that you will undertake a project for which you are incapable, and you will see your efforts come to naught.

To be seated on a fence with others, and have it fall under you, denotes an accident in which some person will be badly injured.

To dream that you climb through a fence, signifies that you will use means not altogether legitimate to reach your desires.

To throw the fence down and walk into the other side, indicates that you will, by enterprise and energy, overcome the most stubborn of barriers between you and success.

To see stock jumping a fence, if into your enclosure, you will receive aid from unexpected sources; if out of your lot, loss in trade and other affairs may follow.

To dream of building a fence, denotes that you are, by economy and industry, laying a foundation for future wealth. For a young woman, this dream denotes success in love affairs; or the reverse, if she dreams of the fence falling, or that she falls from it.

ferns to see ferns in dreams, foretells that pleasant hours will break up gloomy foreboding. To see them withered, indicates that much and varied illness in your family connections will cause you grave unrest.

ferret *see* ANIMALS.

ferry to wait at a ferry for a boat and see the waters swift and muddy, you will be baffled in your highest wishes and designs by unforeseen circumstances.

To cross a ferry while the water is calm and clear, you will be very lucky in carrying out your plans, and fortune will crown you.

festival to dream of being at a festival, denotes indifference to the cold realities of life, and a love for those pleasures that make one old before his time. You will never want, but will be largely dependent on others.

fever an evil dream of ambitious desires, extravagance, etc (gypsy folklore). The restlessness and delirium accompanying fever would justify this interpretation of a dream undoubtedly attributable to a physical condition.

A sickly condition of the dreamer is sometimes implied by this dream. To dream that you are shaking with an ague, signifies that you will suffer from some physical disorder, and that fluctuating opinions of your own affairs may bring you to the borders of prostration.

To see others thus affected, denotes that you will offend people by your supreme indifference to the influences of others.

fiddle to dream of a fiddle, foretells harmony in the home and many joyful occasions abroad. *see* violin.

fields a dream of fertile fields denotes prosperity; barren fields, disappointment (gypsy folklore).

fiend to dream that you encounter a fiend, forebodes reckless living and loose morals. For a woman, this dream signifies a blackened reputation.

To dream of a fiend, warns you of attacks to be made on you by false friends. If you overcome one, you will be able to intercept the evil designs of enemies.

fife to dream of hearing a fife, denotes that there will be an unexpected call on you to defend your honour, or that of some person near to you.

To dream that you play one yourself, indicates that whatever else may be said of you, your reputation will remain intact. If a woman has this dream, she will have a soldier husband.

fighting dreams of fighting are indicative of internal emotional, sexual or moral conflict on the part of the dreamer. It may reflect the dreamer's struggle for independence or freedom from a particular situation.

figs *see* FRUIT.

figure to dream of figures, indicates great mental distress and wrong. You will be the loser in a big deal if not careful of your actions and conversation.

filbert this is a favourable dream, denoting a peaceful and harmonious domestic life and profitable business ventures.

To dream of eating them, signifies to the young, delightful associations and many true friends.

file to dream that you see a file, signifies that you will transact some business which will prove unsatisfactory in the extreme.

To see files, to store away bills and other important papers, foretells animated discussions over subjects which bear relation to significant affairs, and which will cause you much unrest and disquiet. Unfavourable predictions for the future are also implied in this dream.

finger *see* BODY.

finger-nails to dream of soiled finger-nails, forebodes disgrace in your family by the wild escapades of the young.

To see well-kept nails, indicates scholarly tastes and some literary attainments; also, thrift.

fire budget to dream of a fire budget, denotes disagreement over small matters.

fire fire can symbolize great passions; anger, a consuming desire for something, or, quite simply, lust. In certain contexts, fire can symbolize enlightenment. A dream of fire can be one of health and happiness. To be burned, however, signifies calamity (gypsy folklore). Sacred to primitive man it symbolizes fructifying strength and heat, the life-giving element. *See also* FLAMES.

firebrand or torch to dream of a firebrand is good for young people to whom it signifies love and pleasure; to see another hold a firebrand is an ill dream for one who would be secret (Artemidorus).

fire-engine to see a fire-engine, denotes worry under extraordinary circumstances, but which will result in good fortune. To see one broken down, foretells accident or serious loss For a young woman to ride on one, denotes she will engage in some unladylike and obnoxious affair.

fireman to see a fireman in your dreams, signifies the constancy of your friends. For a young woman to see a fireman meet with an accident, implies grave danger is threatening a close friend.

fireworks to see fireworks, indicates enjoyment and good health. For a young woman, this dream signifies entertainment and pleasant visiting to distant places.

firmament to dream of the firmament filled with stars, denotes many crosses and almost superhuman efforts ere you reach the pinnacle of your ambition. Beware of the snare of enemies in your work.

To see the firmament illuminated and filled with the heavenly hosts, denotes great spiritual research, but a final pulling back on Nature for sustenance and consolation. You will often be disappointed in fortune also.

To see people you know in the firmament, signifies that they are about to commit some unwise act through you, and others must be the innocent sufferers. Great disasters usually follow this dream. *see* ILLUMINATION.

fish market to visit a fish market in your dream, brings competence and pleasure.

To see decayed fish, foretells distress will come in the guise of happiness.

fish *see* ANIMALS.

fisherman to dream of a fisherman, denotes you are nearing times of greater prosperity than you have yet known.

fishhooks to dream of fishhooks, denotes that you have opportunities to make for yourself a fortune and an honourable name if you rightly apply them.

fish-net to dream of a fish-net, portends numerous small pleasures and gains. A torn one, represents vexatious disappointments.

fish-pond to dream of a fish-pond, denotes illness through dissipation, if muddy. To see one clear and well stocked with fish, portends profitable enterprises and extensive pleasures. To see one empty, proclaims the near approach of deadly enemies.

For a young woman to fall into a clear pond, omens decided good fortune and reciprocal love. If muddy, the opposite is foretold.

fits to dream of having fits, denotes that you will fall a prey to ill health and will lose employment.

To see others in this plight, denotes that you will have much unpleasantness in your circle, caused by quarrels from those under you.

five *see* NUMBERS.

flag to dream of your national flag, portends victory if at war, and if at peace, prosperity.

For a woman to dream of a flag, denotes that she will be ensnared by a soldier.

To dream of foreign flags, denotes ruptures and breach of confidence between nations and friends.

To dream of being signalled by a flag, denotes that you should be careful of your health and name, as both are threatened.

flames to dream of flames denotes happiness (gypsy folklore). Flames are a Christian symbol of zeal, fervour. *See also* FIRE.

flax spinning foretells you will be given to industrious and thrifty habits.

flax to see flax in a dream, prosperous enterprises are denoted.

fleas *see* INSECTS.

fleet to dream of a fleet of vessels promises fulfilment of hopes (gypsy folklore). Ships symbolize hopes both in ancient and modern symbolism.

flies *see* INSECTS.

flight to dream of flight, signifies disgrace and unpleasant news of the absent.

For a young woman to dream of flight, indicates that she has not kept her character above reproach, and her lover will throw her aside.

To see anything fleeing from you, denotes that you will be victorious in any contention.

floating dreaming of floating suggests a certain loss of control, involuntary or otherwise, and the idea of letting oneself be carried along by life rather than living it in a more active fashion. *See also* TYPICAL DREAMS.

floods *see* DELUGE.

flour to dream of flour, denotes a frugal but happy life. For a young woman to dream that she sees flour on herself, denotes that she will be ruled by her husband, and that her life will be full of pleasant cares.

To dream of dealing in flour, denotes hazardous speculations.

flowers flowers in dreams will often have strong sexual meanings. In general, they are symbolic of life and growth; also of beauty, love and tenderness. More specifically, a blossoming flower may represent the female genitalia, a bud the penis or vagina. Damaged flowers may symbolize damaged innocence, loss of purity/virginity, while wilting flowers may indicate the decline of sexual/reproductive powers. Joy is indicated by dreaming of flowers in season, but usually the dream augurs disappointment, white flowers are but slightly unfortunate; yellow flowers forecast painful difficulties; red flowers indicate death (gypsy folklore). Freud regards this as a purely erotic dream. In Christian symbolism flowers symbolize immortality; cut flowers, however, are emblematic of death. *See also* TREE.

flute to dream of hearing notes from a flute, signifies a pleasant meeting with friends from a distance, and profitable engagements.

For a young woman to dream of playing a flute, denotes that she will fall in love because of her lover's engaging manners.

flux to dream of having flux, or thinking that you are thus afflicted, denotes desperate or fatal illness will overtake you or some member of your family. To see others thus afflicted, implies disappointment in carrying out some enterprise through the neglect of others. In-harmonious states will vex you.

flying machine to dream of seeing a flying machine, foretells that you will make satisfactory progress in your future speculations. To see one failing to work, foretells gloomy returns for much disturbing and worrisome planning.

flying to dream of flying is to dream of release from the influences that are holding one back. These may be practical difficulties, such as lack of money, stifling of creativity in one's job, or family commitments. It could also indicate repressive emotions or a lack of belief in oneself. For some, dreaming of flying may indicate a desire for sexual release. Flying signifies freedom and independence and also the ability to take a different view of the world and of other people. Invariably a happy dream, auguring beautiful things to come. Modern dream interpreters, however, classify it as a typical dream induced by vertigo, etc. *See also* TYPICAL DREAMS.

fly-trap to see a fly-trap in a dream, is signal of malicious designing against you. To see one full of flies, denotes that small embarrassments will ward off greater ones.

foal to dream of a foal, indicates new undertakings in which you will be rather fortunate.

fog dreaming of fog indicates a problem of perception for the dreamer and a need to look at something more closely in order to understand it fully. A dream of uncertainty (gypsy folklore).

food food represents nourishment, whether for the body, the mind or the spirit. Dreaming of eating food is symbolic, therefore, of satisfying some desire for nourishment of some sort. Thus, to dream of sharing a meal with someone may represent the sharing of mutual love and respect or it may represent the act of sexual nourishing, i.e. sexual intercourse.

foot-log to dream of crossing a clear stream of water on a foot-log, denotes pleasant employment and profit. If the water is thick and muddy, it indicates loss and temporary disturbance. For a woman this dream indicates either a quarrelsome husband, or one of mild temper and regular habits, as the water is muddy or clear.

To fall from a foot-log into clear water, signifies short widowhood terminating in an agreeable marriage. If the water is not clear, gloomy prospects. *see* BRIDGE.

forehead to dream of a fine and smooth forehead, denotes that you will be thought well of for your judgement and fair dealings.

An ugly forehead, denotes displeasure in your private affairs.

To pass your hand over the forehead of your child, indicates sincere praises from friends, because of some talent and goodness displayed by your children.

For a young woman to dream of kissing the forehead of her lover, signifies that he will be displeased with her for gaining notice by indiscreet conduct.

foreign countries dreams of foreign lands may be indicative of new experiences in life.

foreigner to dream of a stranger pleasing you, denotes good health and pleasant surroundings; if he displeases you, look for disappointments. To dream you are a foreigner, denotes abiding friendships.

forest a dream of dire trouble and sorrow (Artemidorus). The legends that people the forests with witches, ogres and giants account for this interpretation. To dream that you are hiding in a forest suggests that you are guilty about something or have a secret. Being lost in the forest expresses feelings that you are going in the wrong direction in life. If the forest is covered in brown, dead leaves this may express the feeling that a situation or a relationship is unsatisfactory.

forge a dream of brilliant success through hard work (gypsy folklore).

fork to dream of a fork, denotes that enemies are working for your displacement. For a woman, this dream denotes unhappy domestic relations, and separation for lovers.

form to see anything ill formed, denotes disappointment. To have a beautiful form, denotes favourable conditions to health and business.

forsaking for a young woman to dream of forsaking her home or friend, denotes that she will have troubles in love, as her estimate of her lover will decrease with acquaintance and association.

fort to dream of defending a fort, signifies your honour and possessions will be attacked, and you will have great worry over the matter.

To dream that you attack a fort and take it, denotes victory over your worst enemy, and fortunate engagements.

fortress to dream that you are confined in a fortress, denotes that enemies will succeed in placing you in an undesirable situation.

To put others in a fortress, denotes your ability to rule in business or over women.

fortune-telling to dream of telling, or having your fortune told, it dictates that you are deliberating over some vexed affair, and you should use much caution in giving consent to its consummation. For a young woman, this portends a choice between two rivals. She will be worried to find out the standing of one in business and social circles. To dream that she is engaged to a fortune-teller, denotes that she has gone through the forest and picked the proverbial stick. She should be self-reliant, or poverty will attend her marriage.

fountain to dream of a clear fountain indicates abundance to well persons and health to invalids (Artemidorus). The fountain is a symbol of the gospel and of miraculous healing waters. *See also* WATER.

four *see* NUMBERS.

fowl to dream of seeing fowls, denotes temporary worry or illness. For a woman to dream of fowls, indicates a short illness or disagreement with her friends. *See* CHICKEN, BIRDS.

fox to dream of chasing a fox, denotes that you are engaging in doubtful speculations and risky love affairs.

If you see a fox slyly coming into your yard, beware of envious friendships; your reputation is being slyly assailed.

To kill a fox, denotes that you will win in every engagement.

fratricide success will never attend the dreamer of this dream (Raphael). The interpretation of what is evidently regarded as a wish dream.

fraud to dream that you are defrauding a person, denotes that you will deceive your employer for gain, indulge in degrading pleasures, and fall into disrepute.

If you are defrauded, it signifies the useless attempt of enemies to defame you and cause you loss.

To accuse some one of defrauding you, you will be offered a place of high honour.

freckles for a woman to dream that her face is freckled, denotes that many displeasing incidents will insinuate themselves into her happiness. If she sees them in a mirror, she will be in danger of losing her lover to a rival.

friend to dream of friends being well and happy, denotes pleasant tidings of them, or you will soon see them or some of their relatives.

To see your friend troubled and haggard, sickness or distress is upon them.

To see your friends dark-coloured, denotes unusual sickness or trouble to you or to them. To see them take the form of animals, signifies that enemies will separate you from your closest relations.

To see your friend who dresses in sombre colours in flaming red, foretells that unpleasant things will transpire, causing you anxiety if not loss, and that friends will be implicated.

To dream you see a friend standing like a statue on a hill, denotes you will advance beyond present pursuits, but will retain former impressions of justice and knowledge, seeking these through every change. If the figure below be low, you will ignore your friends of former days in your future advancement. If it is on a plane or level with you, you will fail in your ambition to reach other spheres. If you seem to be going from it, you will force yourself to seek a change in spite of friendly ties or self-admonition.

To dream you see a friend with a white cloth tied over his face, denotes that you will be injured by some person who will endeavour to keep up friendly relations with you.

To dream that you are shaking hands with a person who has wronged you, and he is taking his departure and looks sad, foretells you will have differences with a close friend and alienation will perhaps follow. You are most assuredly nearing loss of some character.

fright to dream that you are frightened, foretells that you will sustain an injury through an accident.

To see others frightened, brings you close to misery and distressing scenes. Dreams of this nature are frequently caused by nervous and feverish conditions, either from malaria or excitement. When such is the case, the dreamer is warned to take immediate steps to remove the cause. Such dreams or reveries only occur when sleep is disturbed.

frogs *see* ANIMALS.

frost to a man in business, a dream of frost predicts difficulties in trade. To others it may symbolize love nipped in the bud, etc. *See also* ICE.

fruit fruit, like flowers, are symbolically linked with life, growth and sex. Fruits, in particular, are associated with reproduction and coming to maturity or ripeness. A dream of unripe fruit may represent sexual immaturity. *See also* ORCHARD; TREE.

apples ripe apples symbolize success in trade, love, etc. Green apples symbolize the contrary. The gypsy influence is distinctly traceable in the folklore of the apple as a symbol. It confers immortal youth in the fairytale, golden apples, love apples, etc, while in Christian symbolism it represents the fall from Eden, the sin that made Christ's coming necessary. It may denote a cunning and dangerous enemy. The apple has long been regarded as a symbol of sexual love and Freudians translate this as an erotic dream.

apricots dreams of seeing apricots growing, denote that the future, though seemingly rosy hued, holds masked bitterness and sorrow for you. To eat them signifies the near approach of calamitous influences. If others eat them, your surroundings will be unpleasant and disagreeable to your fancies.

bananas to dream of eating them denotes misfortune (gypsy folklore). A Melanesian legend, that the banana was the cause of human mortality, may be the source of the symbolism.

fruit (ctd.)

cherries to dream of cherries growing denotes health and fertility. To gather them indicates deception by a woman; to eat them denotes love (Artemidorus).

dates a dream of dates denotes either strong and powerful enemies or admirers of the opposite sex (Artemidorus).

elderberries a dream of good luck, speedy marriage and success financially (Raphael). The fruit of the sacred elder, these berries were highly esteemed by the ancient Prussians as symbols of good fortune.

figs a dream of joy and pleasure. Dreaming of figs out of season denotes grief. To eat figs predicts loss of fortune or shame and dry figs signify the slipping away of wealth, but success in married life (gypsy folklore). In sacred symbolism they denote prosperity. They were held as sacred by the Romans, a symbol of fruitfulness and life, and also an erotic symbol.

gooseberries many offspring and the accomplishment of plans are denoted by this dream (Raphael). The gooseberry is an ancient symbol of reproduction and fertility.

grapes eating grapes denotes cheerfulness and profit. Treading grapes indicates the overthrow of enemies; gathering white grapes, gain; gathering black grapes, damage (Artemidorus). They are the symbol of joy, happiness and fertility.

greengages to dream of eating these plums denotes trouble and grief.

melon to a sick person this is a dream of recovery by reason of the juiciness which dispels fever (gypsy folklore). This is a dream originating in physical stimuli indicative of coolness and moisture after fever.

olives to dream of gathering them denotes peace, delight, happiness to all conditions. Eating olives predicts a rise in circumstance (gypsy folklore). They are the emblem of peace and plenty.

oranges a dream of tears and anxiety (gypsy folklore); the symbolism is obscure.

peaches to dream of them in season denotes contentment, wealth and pleasure (Artemidorus). They are a Chinese symbol of longevity and good fortune. The peach-tree was also the symbol of the Paradise of Osiris.

fruit (ctd.)

pears a dream denoting sickness (Raphael). It was held as an emblem of the human heart.

pineapple someone who dreams of pineapples will soon receive an invitation to a celebration or a wedding. This dream also denotes prosperity and good health (gypsy folklore).

plums green plums forecast sickness; ripe ones are fortunate. To dream of picking plums from the ground and finding that they are rotten indicates false friends, poverty and disgrace. (Raphael).

pomegranate to dream of gathering them ripe denotes fortune through an influential person. Unripe pomegranates foretell sickness and scandal (gypsy folklore). The pomegranate was the Christian symbol of the resurrection and of fertility. With the golden bells they form part of the symbolic robe of the Israelite high priest.

prunes a dream denoting health and joy (gypsy folklore).

raspberries to dream of eating them denotes remorse and sorrow (Raphael). Raspberries look a bit like miniature hearts and for this reason were christened the berries of Eraspe, or Father Eros.

strawberries indicate good luck or a happy marriage (gypsy folklore).

vines to walk under or to pick their fruit is a dream of abundance, wealth and fecundity (gypsy folklore). The spiritual symbol of fruitfulness.

watermelon a dream of sickness (gypsy folklore).

fruit seller to dream of a fruit seller, denotes you will endeavour to recover your loss too rapidly and will engage in unfortunate speculations.

F

funeral the funeral of a relative or a great lord is a good dream; betokening either a wealthy marriage or a fortune through relatives (Artemidorus). A wish dream (Freud). *See also* CONTRARY MEANING; TYPICAL DREAMS.

furnace to dream of a furnace, foretells good luck if it is running. If out of repair, you will have trouble with children or hired help. To fall into one, portends some enemy will overpower you in a business struggle.

furniture/furnishings furniture in dreams may represent, in general, our emotional baggage, or the feelings and attitudes with which our lives have become furnished through our upbringing and our interaction with others.

More specifically, certain items of furniture are thought to be significant in their own way.

bed, for example, may represent one's life as one has made it and one's level of happiness within that life. It may symbolize relations with other people, sexual or otherwise according to the context, marriage, occupation, etc. In some cases, where the mood of the dream is depressing, a bed or lying in bed may signify illness or a need for peace and retreat from the pressures of the outside world. Dreaming of *lying in bed* and watching things going on all around can indicate a certain passivity in one's approach to life. *See also* MATTRESS.

cupboards or *wardrobes* often hold sexual significance; the cupboard can be the womb. Finding something in a cupboard may signify discovering some aspect of one's sexual self. Alternatively, the cupboard may simply represent the mind, the depths of the cupboard standing for the deepest recesses of the psyche. Locked cupboards indicate secrets, or hidden thoughts; an aspect of the self that is hidden from the world or that is unacknowledged by the individual.

chair dreaming of sitting in a chair may reflect a rather passive role in life for the dreamer, or a relaxed attitude.

furs to dream of dealing in furs, denotes prosperity and an interest in many concerns.

To be dressed in fur, signifies your safety from want and poverty.

To see fine fur, denotes honour and riches. For a young woman to dream that she is wearing costly furs, denotes that she will marry a wise man.

future dreaming of events that are about to happen is a phenomenon that is much written about but, as yet, is little understood. It is believed by some to be a manifestation of the subconscious link between human beings, whereby strong feelings towards a person may give us an insight into the direction his or her life is taking them. However, this does not fully explain such dreams, as some dreams like this are not about people who are linked to the dreamer in any obvious way. Cynics would explain the phenomenon as being no more than coincidence.

G

gadflies *see* INSECTS.

gaiter to dream of gaiters, foretells pleasant amusements and rivalries.

gale to dream of being caught in a gale, signifies business losses and troubles for working people.

gallows paradoxically the gypsies saw this dream as fortunate, the dreamer will rise proportionately to the height of the gallows (gypsy folklore).

gambling *see* GAMES.

games games in dreams can reflect the individual's attitude to life and the strategies that he or she develops to cope with certain situations.

Competitive games can symbolize a sense of struggle within the dreamer, a feeling of having to overcome competition from others to achieve goals in life.

Games like *chess* are indicative of a more intellectual approach, a consideration of strategies to employ in working towards one's ends.

Dreaming of *gambling* may be indicative of a certain recklessness in the general behaviour of the dreamer and can serve as a warning to change one's ways.

gangrene to dream that you see any one afflicted with gangrene, foretells the death of a parent or near relative.

garbage to see heaps of garbage in your dreams, indicates thoughts of social scandal and unfavourable business of every character. For females this dream is ominous of disparagement and desertion by lovers.

garden gardens in dreams represent the 'inner person', the feelings and ideas that 'grow' within the individual. Thus, an untidy garden can be seen as a mind that lacks order and perhaps suffers from indecision or lack of purpose; alternatively, it may represent a person who does not listen or pay attention to his or her inner self (i.e. a neglected garden equals a neglected self). A very tidy, symmetrically arranged garden might be seen as a sign of a highly ordered mind, very controlled, perhaps inhibited, while a beautiful garden can reflect a happy state of mind and contentment. Some would say a beautiful garden shows great happiness in the future, while an overgrown or untidy garden points to aspects of the individual's life needing attention.

gardener a dream of good luck and speedy success (gypsy folklore); agriculturists generally connote good fortune in gypsy symbolism.

garlands a dream of triumph (gypsy folklore).

garlic to dream of passing through a garlic patch, denotes a rise from penury to prominence and wealth. To a young woman, this denotes that she will marry from a sense of business, and love will not be considered.

To eat garlic in your dreams, denotes that you will take a sensible view of life and leave its ideals to take care of themselves.

garret to dream of climbing to a garret, denotes your inclination to run after theories while leaving the cold realities of life to others less able to bear them than yourself. To the poor, this dream is an omen of easier circumstances. To a woman, it denotes that her vanity and selfishness should be curbed.

garter for a lover to find his lady's garter, foretells that he will lose caste with her. He will find rivals.

For a woman to dream that she loses her garter, signifies that her lover will be jealous and suspicious of a handsomer person.

For a married man to dream of a garter, foretells that his wife will hear of his clandestine attachments, and he will have a stormy scene.

For a woman to dream that she is admiring beautiful jewelled garters on her limbs, denotes that she will be betrayed in her private movements, and her reputation will hang in the balance of public opinion. If she dreams that her lover fastens them on her, she will hold his affections and faith through all adverse criticisms.

gas lamps to see a gas lamp, denotes progress and pleasant surroundings. To see one explode, or out of order other wise, foretells you are threatened with unseasonable distress.

gas to dream of gas, denotes you will entertain harmful opinions of others, which will cause you to deal with them unjustly, and you will suffer consequent remorse. To think you are asphyxiated, denotes you will have trouble which you will needlessly incur through your own wastefulness and negligence. To try to blow gas out, signifies you will entertain enemies unconsciously, who will destroy you if you are not wary.

To extinguish gas, denotes you will ruthlessly destroy your own happiness. To light it, you will easily find a way out of oppressive ill fortune.

gasoline to dream of gasoline, denotes you have a competency coming to you through a struggling source.

gate a gate, or gates, may be interpreted as the entrance to the dreamer's inner self, the way in to the unconscious motivations of the individual. To go through the gate is to take the opportunity to increase one's self-awareness.

A gate may also be seen as the way into the dreamer's conscious desires, the way to achieve his or her ultimate aims. The interpretation of the dream will very much, depend on whether the gate lies open or closed, what, if anything, is seen to lie beyond the gate, and how the dreamer feels about his or her life at the time of dreaming.

gauze to dream of being dressed in gauze, denotes uncertain fortune. For a lover to see his sweetheart clothed in filmy material, suggests his ability to influence her for good.

geese *see* BIRDS.

gems a dream forecasting a rise in social position (gypsy folklore). *See also* JEWELS.

genealogical tree to dream of your genealogical tree, denotes you will be much burdened with family cares, or will find pleasure in other domains than your own. To see others studying it, foretells that you will be forced to yield your rights to others. If any of the branches are missing, you will ignore some of your friends because of their straightened circumstances.

genitals genitals in dreams are often symbols of the dreamer's sexual self; a woman, for example, may dream that she has a penis, and this could be interpreted as her experiencing the male part of herself. *See also* BODY.

geography to dream of studying geography, denotes that you will travel much and visit places of renown. *See* ATLAS.

ghosts ghosts in dreams may either represent the dreamer's individual self, memories of the past that may be tormenting the dreamer, or things that he or she may feel guilty about.

Dreaming of the ghost of a person who is well known to the dreamer may point to the fact that the dreamer is still influenced, whether consciously or subconsciously, by the attitudes and opinions that the dead person had.

giants giants frequently appear in the dreams of children; they most likely represent grownups (who do seem huge to young children). Adults who dream of giants are possibly harking back to their childhood. Alternatively, and particularly if the dream is frightening, the giant may be like a MONSTER and so represent something of which the dreamer has a deep-seated fear and which looms large in his or her thoughts. *See also* MONSTER; OGRE.

gifts the giving and receiving of gifts in dreams should not be seen in a material sense but as the giving and receiving of love or the sharing of thoughts and ideas, or even actions that have certain effects on people. What is given, of course, need not always be pleasant; a nasty gift could be interpreted as something hurtful that is done by the 'giver' in the dream to the 'receiver'. *See also* PRESENTS.

gig to run a gig in your dream, you will have to forego a pleasant journey to entertain unwelcome visitors. Sickness also threatens you. *See* CART.

girdle to dream of wearing a girdle, and it presses you, denotes that you will be influenced by designing people.

To see others wearing velvet, or jewelled girdles, foretells that you will strive for wealth more than honour.

For a woman to receive one, signifies that honours will be conferred upon her.

girls to dream of seeing a well, bright-looking girl, foretells pleasing prospects and domestic joys. If she is thin and pale, it denotes that you will have an invalid in your family, and much unpleasantness.

For a man to dream that he is a girl, he will be weak-minded, or become an actor and play female parts.

glasshouse to see a glasshouse, foretells you are likely to be injured by listening to flattery. For a young woman to dream that she is living in a glasshouse, her coming trouble and threatened loss of reputation is emphasised.

glass to dream that you are looking through glass, denotes that bitter disappointments will cloud your brightest hopes.

To see your image in a mirror, foretells unfaithfulness and neglect in marriage, and fruitless speculations.

To see another face with your own in a mirror indicates that you are leading a double life. You will deceive your friends.

To break a mirror, portends an early and accidental death.

To break glass dishes, or windows, foretells the unfavourable termination to enterprises.

To receive cut glass, denotes that you will be admired for your brilliancy and talent.

To make presents of cut glass ornaments, signifies that you will fail in your undertakings.

For a woman to see her lover in a mirror, denotes that she will have cause to institute a breach of promise suit.

For a married woman to see her husband in a mirror, is a warning that she will have cause to feel anxiety for her happiness and honour.

To look clearly through a glass window, you will have employment, but will have to work subordinately. If the glass is clouded, you will be unfortunately situated.

If a woman sees men, other than husband or lover, in a looking glass, she will be discovered in some indiscreet affair which will be humiliating to her and a source of worry to her relations.

For a man to dream of seeing strange women in a mirror, he will ruin his health and business by foolish attachments.

glass-blower to dream that you see glass-blowers at their work, denotes you will contemplate change in your business, which will appear for the better, but you will make it at a loss to yourself.

gleaning to see gleaners at work at harvest time, denotes prosperous business, and, to the farmer, a bountiful yield of crops. If you are working with the gleaners, you will come into an estate, after some trouble in establishing rights. For a woman, this dream foretells marriage with a stranger.

gloomy to be surrounded by many gloomy situations in your dream, warns you of rapidly approaching unpleasantness and loss. *See* DESPAIR.

gloves to dream of wearing new gloves, denotes that you will be cautious and economical in your dealings with others, but not mercenary. You will have law suits, or business troubles, but will settle them satisfactorily to yourself.

If you wear old or ragged gloves, you will be betrayed and suffer loss.

If you dream that you lose your gloves, you will be deserted and earn your own means of livelihood.

To find a pair of gloves, denotes a marriage or new love affair.

For a man to fasten a lady's glove, he has, or will have, a woman on his hands who threatens him with exposure.

If you pull your glove off, you will meet with poor success in business or love.

goat *see* ANIMALS.

goblet if you dream that you drink water from a silver goblet, you will meet unfavourable business results in the near future.

To see goblets of ancient design, you will receive favours and benefits from strangers.

For a woman to give a man a glass goblet full of water, denotes illicit pleasures.

God one need not be a religious person to dream of God, or even of meeting God in some shape or form. Someone who dreams of God may indeed be in the process of analysing his or her own religious beliefs in life, particularly in relation to life and death; nevertheless, the God in the dream may simply be representative of some figure of authority in the dreamer's life. This may reassure the dreamer that responsibility does not lie with him or her alone, i.e. the buck does not stop with him or her. Alternatively, it may act as a reminder to the dreamer that the power to change things, or the ultimate control, does not actually lie in his or her hands.

Lastly, the appearance of God in a dream can take the place, to a certain extent, of the dreamer's conscience, bringing to the dreamer's attention the moral responsibility that he or she must bear for his or her actions. *See also* RELIGION.

goggles to dream of goggles, is a warning of disreputable companions who will wheedle you into lending your money foolishly.

For a young woman to dream of goggles, means that she will listen to persuasion which will mar her fortune.

gold gold in dreams rarely foretells untold wealth. It is more likely to represent things of a metaphysical nature that one values in life. Thus, false or tarnished gold will stand for values that are not worth having. To dream of gold embroidered garments indicates joy and honour, to wear a gold crown signifies royal favour; to gather up gold and silver signifies deceit and loss. To dream of pockets full of gold betokens but little money (Artemidorus). Gold was the emblem of the sun and of the goodness of God.

gold leaves to dream of gold leaves, signifies a flattering future is before you.

goldfish to dream of goldfish, is a prognostic of many successful and pleasant adventures. For a young woman, this dream is indicative of a wealthy union with a pleasing man. If the fish are sick or dead, heavy disappointments will fall upon her.

golf to be playing golf or watching the game, denotes that pleasant and successive wishing will be indulged in by you. To see any unpleasantness connected with golf, you will be humiliated by some thoughtless person.

gondola *see* BOAT.

gong to hear the sound of a gong while dreaming, denotes false alarm of illness, or loss will vex you excessively.

goodbye to dream of bidding cheerful adieus to people, denotes that you will make pleasant visits and enjoy much social festivity; but if you are saying goodbye in a sad or doleful way, you will endure loss and bereaving sorrow.

If say goodbye to home and country, you will travel in the nature of an exile from fortune and love.

To throw kisses of farewell to loved ones, or children, foretells that you will soon have a journey to make, but there will be no unpleasant accidents or happenings attending your trip.

goose *see* BIRDS.

gooseberries *see* FRUIT.

gore *see* BODY.

gossip to dream of being interested in common gossip, you will undergo some humiliating trouble caused by overconfidence in transient friendships.

If you are the object of gossip, you may expect some pleasurable surprise.

gout if you dream of having the gout, you will be sure to be exasperated beyond endurance by the silly conduct of some relative, and suffer small financial loss through the same person.

gown if you dream that you are in your night-gown, you will be afflicted with a slight illness. If you see others thus clad, you will have unpleasant news of absent friends. Business will receive a back set.

If a lover sees his sweetheart in her night gown, he will be superseded.

grain a dream of prosperity. To see large grain bins in a storehouse is a symbol of plenty. A field of grain denotes profit; to harvest grain predicts wealth; to carry it signifies weariness (Artemidorus).

grammar to dream that you are studying grammar, denotes you are soon to make a wise choice in momentous opportunities.

gramophone to dream of hearing the gramophone, foretells the advent of some new and pleasing comrade who will lend himself willingly to advance your enjoyment. If it is broken, some fateful occurrence will thwart and defeat delights that you hold in anticipation.

grandparents to dream of meeting your grandparents and conversing with them, you will meet with difficulties that will be hard to surmount, but by following good advice you will overcome many barriers.

grapes *see* FRUIT.

grass to dream of walking through fields of grass signifies happiness and fortune. To dream of grasses such as sorrel lettuce, etc, denotes grief and embarrassment. To eat grass symbolizes sorrow and sickness. Dead or withered grass denotes misfortune (gypsy folklore).

grasshopper *see* INSECTS.

grave dreams of graves may be indicative of the dreamer's coming to terms with his or her own mortality, or the grave in the dream may represent some aspect of the dreamer's life, or character, that has changed or been overcome.

gravel to dream of gravel, denotes unfruitful schemes and enterprises.

If you see gravel mixed with dirt, it foretells you will unfortunately speculate and lose good property.

gravy to dream of eating gravy, portends failing health and disappointing business.

grease to dream you are in grease, is significant of travels being enjoyed with disagreeable but polished strangers.

Greek to dream of reading Greek, denotes that your ideas will be discussed and finally accepted and put in practical use. To fail to read it, denotes that technical difficulties are in your way.

green *see* COLOURS.

greengages *see* FRUIT.

greyhound is a fortunate object to see in your dream. If it is following a young girl, you will be surprised with a legacy from unknown people. If a greyhound is owned by you, it signifies friends where enemies were expected.

grindstone success through toil is indicated by this dream (gypsy folklore).

groans if you hear groans in your dream, decide quickly on your course, for enemies are undermining your business. If you are groaning with fear, you will be pleasantly surprised at the turn for better in your affairs, and you may look for pleasant visiting among friends.

groceries to dream of general groceries, if they are fresh and clean, is a sign of ease and comfort.

grotto *see* CAVE.

ground to fall to the ground predicts humiliation and disgrace (gypsy folklore).

grove this dream denotes trouble but to a lesser degree than the dream of a FOREST (gypsy folklore).

guardian to dream of a guardian, denotes you will be treated with consideration by your friends. For a young woman to dream that she is being unkindly dealt with by her guardian, foretells that she will have loss and trouble in the future.

guilt like many emotions experienced while dreaming, the guilt that a dreamer is feeling may well be guilt that is being repressed, or should be felt, for the dreamer's thoughts, words or deeds in real life.

guitar to dream of listening to a guitar signifies happiness (gypsy folklore).

gulls to dream of gulls, is a prophecy of peaceful dealings with ungenerous persons. Seeing dead gulls, means separation for friends.

gun to dream of a gun is an expression of anxiety about a sexual experience. To hear the report of a gun denotes the death of a friend, a slander, enmity and loss (gypsy folklore). A dream of a pistol is one which predicts attacks from secret enemies (gypsy folklore). *See also* WEAPONS.

gutter to dream of a gutter, is a sign of degradation. You will be the cause of unhappiness to others.

To find articles of value in a gutter, your right to certain property will be questioned.

gymnast to dream of a gymnast, denotes you will have misfortune in speculation or trade.

gypsies dreaming of gypsies may indicate an unexpressed desire for more freedom in life. This may be physical freedom or freedom of the intellect or the spirit.

H

haggard to see a haggard face in your dreams, denotes misfortune and defeat in love matters.

To see your own face haggard and distressed, denotes trouble over female affairs, which may render you unable to meet business engagements in a healthy manner.

hail to dream of hail denotes sorrow and trouble, with tempest and thunder it denotes afflictions. It predicts tranquillity to the poor, however, for during storms they rest (Artemidorus).

hair dreams of hair refer to the dreamer's feelings about their freedom and their standing in life.

long hair someone who dreams of having long, flowing locks may have a yearning for more freedom than he or she currently has. If a man dreams that he has long hair like a woman this reflects feelings of effeminacy and weakness. If the hair is longer and darker than usual, this predicts an increase of riches.

black and short hair this dream is said to predict misfortune.

dishevelled hair this denotes annoyances and sorrows.

hair falling out denotes subconscious feelings of insecurity. A bald-headed woman symbolizes famine; a bald-headed man, abundance, riches and health (gypsy folklore). If the hair is thinner than usual then this predicts affliction and poverty.

hair in a tangle this dream symbolizes quarrels in which the dreamer is the losing party, possibly the outcome of a lawsuit.

white hair to dream that you have white hair denotes high honour. Seeing it grow white may predict loss of fortune.

hair-dresser should you visit a hair-dresser in your dreams, you will be connected with a sensation caused by the indiscretion of a good looking woman. To a woman, this dream means a family disturbance and well merited censures.

For a woman to dream of having her hair coloured, she will narrowly escape the scorn of society, as enemies will seek to blight her reputation.

To have her hair dressed, denotes that she will run after frivolous things, and use any means to bend people to her wishes.

hairy hands to dream that your hands are covered with hair like that of a beast, signifies you will intrigue against innocent people, and will find that you have alert enemies who are working to forestall your designs.

halter to dream that you put a halter on a young horse, shows that you will manage a very prosperous and clean business. Love matters will shape themselves to suit you.

To see other things haltered, denotes that fortune will be withheld from you for a while. You will win it, but with much toil.

ham to dream of seeing hams, signifies you are in danger of being treacherously used. To cut large slices of ham, denotes that all opposition will be successfully met by you. To dress a ham, signifies you will be leniently treated by others.

To dream of dealing in hams, prosperity will come to you. Also good health is foreboded.

To eat ham, you will lose something of great value. To smell ham cooking, you will be benefited by the enterprises of others.

hammer a dream of oppression (Artemidorus). 'Like a hammer that breaketh the rock in pieces,' *Jeremiah xxiii.*

hammer to dream of a hammer, denotes you will be burdened with some unprofitable yet not unpleasant pursuit. To use one, denotes that officiousness will be shown by you toward your friends.

handbills to post them denotes dishonour. To read them denotes labour without reward.

handcuffs to find yourself handcuffed, you will be annoyed and vexed by enemies. To see others thus, you will subdue those oppressing you and rise above your associates.

To see handcuffs, you will be menaced with sickness and danger.

To dream of handcuffs, denotes formidable enemies are surrounding you with objectionable conditions. To break them, is a sign that you will escape toils planned by enemies.

handkerchiefs to dream of handkerchiefs, denotes flirtations and contingent affairs.

To lose one, omens a broken engagement through no fault of yours.

To see torn ones, foretells that lovers' quarrels will reach such straits that reconciliation will be improbable if not impossible.

To see them soiled, foretells that you will be corrupted by indiscriminate associations.

To see pure white ones in large lots, foretells that you will resist the insistent flattery of unscrupulous and evil-minded persons, and thus gain entrance into high relations with love and matrimony.

To see them coloured, denotes that while your engagements may not be strictly moral, you will manage them with such ingenuity that they will elude opprobrium.

If you see silk handkerchiefs, it denotes that your pleasing and magnetic personality will shed its radiating cheerfulness upon others, making for yourself a fortunate existence.

For a young woman to wave adieu or a recognition with her handkerchief, or see others doing this, denotes that she will soon make a questionable pleasure trip, or she may knowingly run the gauntlet of disgrace to secure some fancied pleasure.

hands *see* BODY.

handsome to see yourself handsome-looking in your dreams, you will prove yourself an ingenious flatterer.

To see others appearing handsome, denotes that you will enjoy the confidence of fast people.

handwriting to dream that you see and recognise your own handwriting, foretells that malicious enemies will use your expressed opinion to foil you in advancing to some competed position.

hanging to dream of being hanged predicts success in proportion to the size of the gibbet. If the dreamer is ill he will find joy and contentment. The dream of condemning another to be hanged signifies anger with someone. The Persians and Egyptians interpreted the dream of hanging as predicting riches, honour and respect. To dream of being delivered from being hanged forecasts downfall in estate and dignity (Artemidorus).

hare *see* ANIMALS.

harem to dream that you maintain a harem, denotes that you are wasting your best energies on low pleasures. Life holds fair promises, if your desires are rightly directed.

If a woman dreams that she is an inmate of a harem, she will seek pleasure where pleasure is unlawful, as her desires will be toward married men as a rule. If she dreams that she is a favourite of a harem, she will be preferred before others in material pleasures, but the distinction will be fleeting.

harlequin to dream of a harlequin cheating you, you will find uphill work to identify certain claims that promise profit to you. If you dream of a harlequin, trouble will beset you.

To be dressed as a harlequin, denotes passionate error and unwise attacks on strength and purse. Designing women will lure you to paths of sin.

harlot to dream of being in the company of a harlot, denotes ill-chosen pleasures and trouble in your social circles, and business will suffer depression. If you marry one, life will be threatened by an enemy.

harness to dream of possessing bright new harness, you will soon prepare for a pleasant journey.

harp to hear the sad sweet strains of a harp, denotes the sad ending to what seems a pleasing and profitable enterprise.

To see a broken harp, betokens illness, or broken troth between lovers.

To play a harp yourself, signifies that your nature is too trusting, and you should be more careful in placing your confidence as well as love matters.

harpies tribulation and pain caused by envious persons, malice and treachery (Artemidorus).

hart *see* ANIMALS.

harvest a dream of prosperity (gypsy folklore).

harvesters many harvesters denote success in trade; to see them idle is a symbol of scarcity (gypsy folklore).

hash to dream you are eating hash, many sorrows and vexations are foretold.

You will probably be troubled with various little jealousies and contentions over mere trifles, and your health will be menaced through worry.

For a woman to dream that she cooks hash, denotes that she will be jealous of her husband, and children will be a stumbling block to her wantonness.

hassock to dream of a hassock, forebodes the yielding of your power and fortune to another. If a woman dreams of a hassock, she should cultivate spirit and independence.

hat to dream of losing your hat, you may expect unsatisfactory business and failure of persons to keep important engagements.

For a man to dream that he wears a new hat, predicts change of place and business, which will be very much to his advantage. For a woman to dream that she wears a fine new hat, denotes the attainment of wealth, and she will be the object of much admiration.

For the wind to blow your hat off, denotes sudden changes in affairs, and somewhat for the worse.

hatchet a warning to expect peril or death (gypsy folklore).

hate to dream that you hate a person, denotes that if you are not careful you will do the party an inadvertent injury or a spiteful action will bring business loss and worry.

If you are hated for unjust causes, you will find sincere and obliging friends, and your associations will be most pleasant. Otherwise, the dream forebodes ill.

hatred to dream that you abhor a person, denotes that you will entertain strange dislike for some person, and your suspicion of his honesty will prove correct. To think yourself held in abhorrence by others, predicts that your good intentions to others will subside into selfishness. For a young woman to dream that her lover abhors her, foretells that she will love a man who is in no sense congenial.

hawk see BIRDS.

hawthorn a dream of constancy (gypsy folklore).

hay or hay-cart this dream denotes success through diligence (gypsy folklore), and is an agricultural symbol of prosperity.

head see BODY.

headache a dream of trouble, illness, and poverty (gypsy folklore). The physical stimuli account for this interpretation.

headgear to dream of seeing rich headgear, you will become famous and successful. To see old and worn headgear, you will have to yield up your possessions to others.

health a bad omen for the sick (gypsy folklore), evidently due to physical stimuli.

hearse to dream of a hearse, denotes uncongenial relations in the home, and failure to carry on business in a satisfactory manner. It also betokens the death of one near to you, or sickness and sorrow.

If a hearse crosses your path, you will have a bitter enemy to overcome.

heart *see* BODY.

heat heat is generally thought to symbolize the heat of strong feelings, either sexual arousal, romantic love or perhaps anger. It should be considered within the context of the dream. The dream may also have a physical cause.

heather or **heath** a dream of hope; if withered or dry, frustrated hopes (gypsy folklore).

heaven a beautiful and auspicious dream. To ascend thereto symbolizes grandeur and glory (Artemidorus). This need not be a religious dream. It could signify that you aspire to something better in life; this may be for spiritual reasons or something as mundane as wanting a new job.

hedgehog *see* ANIMALS.

hedges when green, this signifies prosperity; when thorny and impenetrable, dangers and difficulties (gypsy folklore). Freud would have given this symbol a sexual significance, signifying the dreamer's fear of sex, or feelings that it is forbidden.

height dreams of being at a great height, on top of a mountain or a particularly high building maybe, point to feelings of isolation on the part of the dreamer. It may indicate achievement or success, but this could be success that makes the dreamer stand out from his or her peers. *See also* MOUNTAIN and POSITION.

A dream of looking up at something that is high above may indicate a feeling of smallness in the general scheme of things.

heir to dream that you fall heir to property or valuables, denotes that you are in danger of losing what you already possess. and warns you of coming responsibilities. Pleasant surprises may also follow this dream.

hell a dream denoting mental agony or bodily pain (gypsy folklore).

helmet to dream of seeing a helmet, denotes threatened misery and loss will be avoided by wise action.

hemp seed to see hemp seed in dreams, denotes the near approach of a deep and continued friendship. To the business man, is shown favourable opportunity for money-making.

hemp to dream of hemp, denotes you will be successful in all undertakings, especially large engagements. For a young woman to dream that some accident befalls her through cultivating hemp, foretells the fatal quarrel and separation from her friend.

hen *see* BIRDS.

herbs to dream of hemlock, henbane and other poisonous herbs denotes that you are in danger, but to dream of useful herbs is a good omen (gypsy folklore). This might be a dream caused by physical stimuli induced by the odours of herbs or other strong smelling scents.

herd of cattle *see* ANIMALS.

herdsman a dream of damage to the rich and profit to the poor (Raphael). Here the interpretation is based on reason, for what would be gain to one is loss to the other.

hermaphrodite dreaming of having the physical characteristics of both sexes is likely to be either an indication of a need to explore one's own sexuality or an expression, within the safety and privacy of one's dreams, of aspects of one's sexuality that one may well be prohibited from expressing, or too inhibited to express, in real life.

hermit *see* ABBOT.

heron or **crane** *see* BIRDS.

herring to dream of seeing herring, indicates a tight squeeze to escape financial embarrassment, but you will have success later.

hickory-nuts trouble from creditors.

hidden to dream that you have hidden away any object, denotes embarrassment in your circumstances.

To find hidden things, you will enjoy unexpected pleasures.

For a young woman to dream of hiding objects, she will be the object of much adverse gossip, but will finally prove her conduct orderly.

hiding a dreamer who hides may indeed be a dreamer who has something to hide, or who thinks he or she has something to hide. The dreamer may wish to hide his or her true feelings from someone, or may possess a characteristic of which he or she is ashamed. If the predominant emotion felt while dreaming of hiding is fear, then this may indicate that the dreamer is frightened of letting his or her true emotions be felt or shown.

hieroglyphs seen in a dream, foretells that wavering judgement in some vital matter may cause you great distress and money loss. To be able to read them, your success in overcoming some evil is foretold.

high school to dream of a high school, foretells ascension to more elevated positions in love, as well as social and business affairs. For a young woman to be suspended from a high school, foretells she will have troubles in social circles.

high tide to dream of high tide is indicative of favourable progression in your affairs.

hills climbing a hill in a dream is indicative of a struggle of some sort in real life, either to achieve something or simply to maintain the status quo. Going downhill at speed in a dream suggests a loss of control, or at least a feeling that one is losing control in real life. Gently rolling, fertile, green hills may have a sexual meaning, suggesting in particular the female body, the breasts and belly of a woman of child-bearing years. To dream of climbing a steep hill and reaching the top, difficulties overcome; to fail to reach the top, disappointment; distant green hills, hope, promise (Artemidorus). *See also* TYPICAL DREAMS.

hips to dream that you admire well-formed hips, denotes that you will be upbraided by your wife.

For a woman to admire her hips, shows she will be disappointed in love matters.

To notice fat hips on animals, foretells ease and pleasure.

For a woman to dream that her hips are too narrow, omens

sickness and disappointments. If too fat, she is in danger of losing her reputation.

hissing to dream of hissing persons, is an omen that you will be displeased beyond endurance at the discourteous treatment shown you while among newly made acquaintances. If they hiss you, you will be threatened with the loss of a friend.

history to dream that you are reading history, indicates a long and pleasant recreation.

hives to dream that your child is affected with hives, denotes that it will enjoy good health and be docile.

To see strange children thus affected, you will be unduly frightened over the condition of some favourite.

hoe to dream of seeing a hoe, denotes that you will have no time for idle pleasures, as there will be others depending upon your work for subsistence.

To dream of using a hoe, you will enjoy freedom from poverty by directing your energy into safe channels.

For a woman to dream of hoeing, she will be independent of others, as she will be self-supporting. For lovers, this dream is a sign of faithfulness.

To dream of a foe striking at you with a hoe, your interests will be threatened by enemies, but with caution you will keep aloof from real danger.

hog *see* ANIMALS.

holes holes in dreams very possibly have sexual significance, symbolizing in all probability the vagina and womb. Emerging from a hole may therefore be indicative of the process of being born, while entering a hole may be either an expression of desire to return to the safety of the womb or a symbol for the act of penetration in sexual intercourse.

Other interpretations of holes in dreams include death, the unknown and the subconscious.

To determine the significance of a hole in a dream, it must be considered along with the other elements of the dream and the dreamer's current life and mood.

holiday to dream of a holiday, foretells interesting strangers will soon partake of your hospitality. For a young woman to dream that she is displeased with a holiday, denotes she will be fearful of her own attractions in winning a friend back from a rival.

holly this is a good omen in a dream (gypsy folklore). Holly is a traditional symbol of joy.

holy communion to dream that you are taking part in the Holy Communion, warns you that you will resign your independent opinions to gain some frivolous desire.

If you dream that there is neither bread nor wine for the supper, you will find that you have suffered your ideas to be proselytised in vain, as you are no nearer your goal.

If you are refused the right of communion and feel worthy, there is hope for your obtaining some prominent position which has appeared extremely doubtful, as your opponents are popular and powerful. If you feel unworthy, you will meet with much discomfort.

To dream that you are in a body of Baptists who are taking communion, denotes that you will find that your friends are growing uncongenial, and you will look to strangers for harmony.

home dreams of home may indicate security and contentment, or may have a more sinister meaning; it all depends on the experiences that the dreamer has had of home. Houses generally represent the psyche of the dreamer, so the state of the home and how the dreamer feels to be there is very important.

To dream that you can't find your home, you will completely lose faith in the integrity of others. If you have no home in your dreams, you will be unfortunate in your affairs, and lose by speculation. To change your home, signifies hurried tidings and that hasty journeys will be made by you. For a young woman to dream that she has left her home, is significant of slander and falsehoods being perpetrated against her.

homesick to dream of being homesick, foretells you will lose fortunate opportunities to enjoy travels of interest and pleasant visits.

homicide to dream that you commit homicide, foretells that you will suffer great anguish and humiliation through the indifference of others, and your gloomy surroundings will cause perplexing worry to those close to you. To dream that a friend commits suicide, you will have trouble in deciding a very important question. *See* KILL.

homosexuality one does not have to be homosexual in order to dream that one is homosexual or taking part in a homosexual act. Dreams give us the opportunity to explore aspects of our personalities and our sexuality that we feel, for one reason or another, prevented from exploring in real life. Dreams of homosexual love may be wish-fulfilment but are not necessarily so. We all need the love of people of both sexes, and yet we may feel inhibited from acknowledging that what we need from people of our own sex is love, even if this is not sexual love but the love of friendship, brotherhood, sisterhood or the love between parents and children.

honey a dream of prosperity (Artemidorus). 'A land flowing with milk and honey,' was the promised land of the Hebrews. *See also* BEES.

honeysuckle to see or gather, honeysuckle, denotes that you will be contentedly prosperous and your marriage will be a singularly happy one.

hood for a young woman to dream that she is wearing a hood, is a sign she will attempt to allure some man from rectitude and bounden duty.

hook to dream of a hook, foretells unhappy obligations will be assumed by you.

hoop to dream of a hoop, foretells you will form influential friendships. Many will seek counsel of you. To jump through, or see others jumping through hoops, denotes you will have discouraging outlooks, but you will overcome them with decisive victory.

hops a dream of peace and plenty (gypsy folklore). The soothing influence of hops is well known and the symbolism may well be derived from this.

hornet a dream of vexations (gypsy folklore). *See also* INSECTS and STING.

horns a dream of wearing horns denotes dominion and grandeur (Artemidorus). Horns have ever been worn by priests and rulers of barbarous tribes as symbols of state and power. Jung and Freud attach to them a phallic significance.

horoscope to dream of having your horoscope drawn by an astrologist, foretells unexpected changes in affairs and a long journey; associations with a stranger will probably happen.

If the dreamer has the stars pointed out to him, as his fate is being read, he will find disappointments where fortune and pleasure seem to await him.

horseradish to dream of horseradish, foretells pleasant associations with intellectual and congenial people. Fortune is also expressed in this dream. For a woman, it indicates a rise above her present station.

To eat horseradish, you will be the object of pleasant raillery.

horror feelings of horror are, like any emotion that can be felt in a dream, genuine feelings. They should be validated, not in relation to the content of the dream, but in relation to that aspect of, or occurrence in, the life of the dreamer to which the dream symbol is alluding.

horse chestnut a dream denoting home quarrels and worries.

horse see ANIMALS.

horseshoe a peculiar dream denoting fortune in business and home affairs (gypsy folklore). A world symbol of good fortune.

horse-trader to dream of a horse-trader, signifies great profit from perilous ventures.

To dream that you are trading horses, and the trader cheats you, you will lose in trade or love. If you get a better horse than the one you traded, you will better yourself in fortune.

hospital an unfortunate dream (Raphael). This dream may be a warning from your subconscious that you are working too hard or are getting run down.

hostel (for homeless) for a young woman to dream of a hostel, denotes she will meet failure in her efforts to contract a worldly marriage.

hostility see AGGRESSION.

hotel to dream of living in a hotel, denotes ease and profit.

To visit women in a hotel, your life will be rather on a dissolute order.

To dream of seeing a fine hotel, indicates wealth and travel.

If you dream that you are the proprietor of a hotel, you will earn all the fortune you will ever possess.

To work in a hotel, you could find a more remunerative employment than what you have.

To dream of hunting a hotel, you will be baffled in your search for wealth and happiness.

hounds *see* ANIMALS.

house the house in a dream is thought to be symbolic of the self, its separate rooms all representing aspects of the self. Thus, the *cellar* and cupboards are the 'hidden self', the deeper recesses of the mind, or the aspects of oneself that one keeps hidden from others. The *bedroom* can either be the parts of one's mind to which one retreats when stressed, or it can be the aspects of the self that one shares with few others; the intimate, sexual self. The *kitchen* is the source of all nourishment, the way in which one seeks and finds fulfilment of all needs, physical and mental. The *walls* of the house are one's mental protection against life. *See also* WALL. To build a house predicts profit, and to be in a strange house denotes change (gypsy folklore).

housekeeper to dream that you are a housekeeper, denotes you will have labours which will occupy your time, and make pleasure an ennobling thing. To employ one, signifies comparative comfort will be possible for your obtaining.

howls to hear howls in a dream is an omen of death (gypsy folklore). Popular superstition concerning howls is responsible for this interpretation.

hugging if you dream of hugging, you will be disappointed in love affairs and in business.

For a woman to dream of hugging a man, she will receive advances of a doubtful character from men.

humidity to dream that you are overcome with humidity, foretells that you will combat enemies fiercely, but their superior force will submerge you in overwhelming defeat. *see* AIR.

humming bird *see* BIRDS.

hunchback to dream of a hunchback, denotes unexpected reverses in your prospects.

hungry dreams of feeling hungry may point to some unfulfilled need in the dreamer's life.

hunting if you dream of hunting, you will struggle for the unattainable.

If you dream that you hunt game and find it, you will overcome obstacles and gain your desires. *see* GAIN.

hurricane to hear the roar and see a hurricane heading towards you with its frightful force, you will undergo torture and suspense, striving to avert failure and ruin in your affairs.

If you are in a house which is being blown to pieces by a hurricane, and you struggle in the awful gloom to extricate some one from the falling timbers, your life will suffer a change. You will move and remove to distant places, and still find no improvement in domestic or business affairs.

If you dream of looking on debris and havoc wrought by a hurricane, you will come close to trouble, which will be averted by the turn in the affairs of others.

To see dead and wounded caused by a hurricane, you will be much distressed over the troubles of others.

husband to dream that your husband is leaving you, and you do not understand why, there will be bitterness between you, but an unexpected reconciliation will ensue. If he mistreats and upbraids you for unfaithfulness, you will hold his regard and confidence, but other worries will ensue and you are warned to be more discreet in receiving attention from men.

If you see him dead, disappointment and sorrow will envelop you.

To see him pale and careworn, sickness will tax you heavily, as some of the family will linger in bed for a time.

To see him gay and handsome, your home will be filled with happiness and bright prospects will be yours. If he is sick, you will be mistreated by him and he will be unfaithful.

To dream that he is in love with another woman, he will soon tire of his present surroundings and seek pleasure elsewhere.

To be in love with another woman's husband in your dreams, denotes that you are not happily married, or that you are not happy unmarried, but the chances for happiness are doubtful.

For an unmarried woman to dream that she has a husband, denotes that she is wanting in the graces which men most admire.

To see your husband depart from you, and as he recedes from you he grows larger, inharmonious surroundings will prevent immediate congeniality. If disagreeable conclusions are avoided, harmony will be reinstated.

For a woman to dream she sees her husband in a compromising position with an unsuspected party, denotes she will have trouble through the indiscretion of friends. If she dreams that he is killed while with another woman, and a scandal ensues, she will be in danger of separating from her husband or losing property. Unfavourable conditions follow this dream, though the evil is often exaggerated.

hut to dream of a hut, denotes indifferent success.

To dream that you are sleeping in a hut, denotes ill health and dissatisfaction.

To see a hut in a green pasture, denotes prosperity, but fluctuating happiness.

hyacinth a dream denoting riches (gypsy folklore).

hydra to see a hydra or seven-headed serpent signifies temptation (Artemidorus). *See also* SERPENT and MONSTER.

hydrophobia to dream that you are afflicted with hydrophobia, denotes enemies and change of business.

To see others thus afflicted, your work will be interrupted by death or ungrateful dependence.

To dream that an animal with the rabies bites you, you will be betrayed by your dearest friend, and much scandal will be brought to light.

hyena *see* ANIMALS.

hymns to dream of hearing hymns sung, denotes contentment in the home and average prospects in business affairs. *See* SINGING.

hypocrite to dream that anyone has acted the hypocrite with you, you will be turned over to your enemies by false friends.

To dream that you are a hypocrite, denotes that you will prove yourself a deceiver and be false to friends.

hyssop a dream signifying labour, trouble, sickness and weakness. To physicians, however, the dream is a favourable one (Artemidorus).

I

ice cream to dream that you are eating ice cream, foretells you will have happy success in affairs already undertaken. To see children eating it, denotes prosperity and happiness will attend you most favourably.

For a young woman to upset her ice cream in the presence of her lover or friend, denotes she will be flirted with because of her unkindness to others. To see sour ice cream, denotes some unexpected trouble will interfere with your pleasures. If it is melted, your anticipated pleasure will reach stagnation before it is realised.

ice ice is symbolic of physical or emotional coldness. It may point to lack of love or loss of libido. The dreamer should consider his or her life to try to understand where this coldness originates. It may be a result of the sleeper's body becoming too cold. *See also* FROST.

icicles to a young woman this is a prediction of marriage to an old and wealthy man (gypsy folklore).

ideal for a young woman to dream of meeting her ideal, foretells a season of uninterrupted pleasure and contentment. For a bachelor to dream of meeting his ideal, denotes he will soon experience a favourable change in his affairs.

idiot to dream of turning into an idiot and going mad predicts favour with princes and also gain and pleasure through things of the world (Artemidorus).

idle if you dream of being idle, you will fail to accomplish your designs.

To see your friends in idleness, you will hear of some trouble affecting them.

For a young woman to dream that she is leading an idle existence, she will fall into bad habits, and is likely to marry a shiftless man.

idols should you dream of worshipping idols, you will make slow progress to wealth or fame, as you will let petty things tyrannise over you.

To break idols, signifies a strong mastery over self, and no work will deter you in your upward rise to positions of honour.

To see others worshipping idols, great differences will rise up between you and warm friends.

To dream that you are denouncing idolatry, great distinction is in store for you through your understanding of the natural inclinations of the human mind.

illness dreams of illness may be the dreamer's first 'admission' that all is not well. The problem is not so frequently a physical one as one within the mind. It is possible that the illness represents unpleasant feelings of some sort (guilt, loneliness, etc) that may have been festering for some time, or even depression. Alternatively, to dream of being ill (and hence of needing to be cared for) can denote a need for attention, affection or real caring in the dreamer. A dream of someone else being ill is possibly an exploration of the dreamer's feelings towards that person; the outcome of the 'illness', the dreamer's emotions and the part that he or she plays in the scenario will all, therefore, be of significance.

illumination some great joy at hand is predicted by this dream (gypsy folklore).

image if you dream that you see images, you will have poor success in business or love.

To set up an image in your home, portends that you will be weak minded and easily led astray. Women should be careful of their reputation after a dream of this kind. If the images are ugly, you will have trouble in your home. *See also* PHOTOGRAPH.

imitation to dream of imitations, means that persons are working to deceive you. For a young woman to dream some one is imitating her lover or herself, foretells she will be imposed upon, and will suffer for the faults of others.

implements to dream of implements, denotes unsatisfactory means of accomplishing some work. If the implements are broken, you will be threatened with death or serious illness of relatives or friends, or failure n business.

imprisonment the person who dreams of being imprisoned is very possibly suffering from some form of restriction to his or her independence in real life; problems such as restrictive family relationships (particularly those between parents and their children), claustrophobic love affairs, or guilty feelings may be holding the dreamer back from achieving freedom of action, movement or even thought. *See also* ENCLOSURE and CAPTIVE.

imps a dream denoting disappointment (gypsy folklore). The imp is a symbol of malice.

inauguration to dream of inauguration, denotes you will rise to higher position than you have yet enjoyed. For a young woman to be disappointed in attending an inauguration, predicts she will fail to obtain her wishes.

incantation to dream you are using incantations, signifies unpleasantness between husband and wife, or sweethearts. To hear others repeating them, implies dissembling among your friends.

incense a dream of flatterers, parasites, etc (gypsy folklore).

incest to dream of incestuous practices, denotes you will fall from honourable places, and will also suffer loss in business.

incoherent to dream of incoherency, usually denotes extreme nervousness and excitement through the oppression of changing events.

income to dream of coming into the possession of your income, denotes that you may deceive some one and cause trouble to your family and friends.

To dream that some of your family inherits an income, predicts success for you.

For a woman to dream of losing her income, signifies disappointments in life. To dream that your income is insufficient to support you, denotes trouble to relatives or friends.

To dream of a portion of your income remaining, signifies that you will be very successful for a short time, but you may expect more than you receive.

increase to dream of an increase in your family, may denote failure in some of your plans, and success to another.

To dream of an increase in your business, signifies that you will overcome existing troubles.

independent to dream that you are very independent, denotes that you have a rival who may do you an injustice.

To dream that you gain an independence of wealth, you may not be so successful at that time as you expect, but good results are promised.

India rubber to dream of India rubber, denotes unfavourable changes in your affairs. If you stretch it, you will try to establish a greater business than you can support.

indifference to dream of indifference, signifies pleasant companions for a very short time.

For a young woman to dream that her sweetheart is indifferent to her, signifies that he may not prove his affections in the most appropriate way. To dream that she is indifferent to him, means that she will prove untrue to him.

indigence a dream of becoming indigent indicates sudden gain (gypsy folklore). This is probably based upon the caution of the provident and therefore successful person.

indigestion to dream of indigestion, indicates unhealthy and gloomy surroundings.

indigo to see indigo in a dream, denotes you will deceive friendly persons in order to cheat them out of their be longings. To see indigo water, foretells you will be involved in an ugly love affair.

indistinct if in your dreams you see objects indistinctly, it portends unfaithfulness in friendships, and uncertain dealings.

indulgence for a woman to dream of indulgence, denotes that she will not escape unfavourable comment on her conduct.

industry to dream that you are industrious, denotes that you will be unusually active in planning and working out ideas to further your interests, and that you will be successful in your undertakings.

For a lover to dream of being industriously at work, shows he will succeed in business, and that his companion will advance his position.

To see others busy, is favourable to the dreamer.

infants to dream of seeing a newly born infant, denotes pleasant surprises are nearing you. For a young woman to dream she has an infant, foretells she will be accused of indulgence in immoral pastime. To see an infant swimming, portends a fortunate escape from some entanglement.

infection as in the case of illness dreams, dreams of infections such as ABSCESSES, boils or festering wounds may reflect something within the mind of the dreamer that is bothering him or her, thus 'infecting' his or her thoughts. This may be no more than an irritation that has to be dealt with, but it can also be something of a more serious nature; for example, guilty feelings or negative feelings towards another person for one reason or another.

infernal things to dream of an infernal spirit is a bad sign, indicating death to the sick, melancholy to the healthy, also anger, tumults, illness (Artemidorus). This dream is conceded by physiologists to result from outward stimuli. It may be a subconscious expression of guilt.

infirm to dream of seeing a person becoming infirm, indicates you, yourself, will become so (gypsy folklore). A dream inspired by physical weakness.

infirmary to dream that you leave an infirmary, denotes your escape from wily enemies who will cause you much worry. *See* HOSPITAL.

influence if you dream of seeking rank or advancement through the influence of others, your desires will fail to materialise; but if you are in an influential position, your prospects will assume a bright form.

To see friends in high positions, your companions will be congenial, and you will be free from vexations.

inheritance to dream that you receive an inheritance, foretells that you will be successful in easily obtaining your desires. *See* ESTATE.

injury to dream of an injury being done you, signifies that an unfortunate occurrence will soon grieve and vex you. *see* HURT.

ink to see ink spilled over one's clothing, many small and spiteful meanness will be wrought you through envy.

If a young woman sees ink, she will be slandered by a rival.

To dream that you have ink on your fingers, you will be jealous and seek to injure some one unless you exercise your better nature. If it is red ink, you will be involved in a serious trouble.

To dream that you make ink, you will engage in a low and debasing business, and you will fall into disreputable associations.

To see bottles of ink in your dreams, indicates enemies and unsuccessful interests.

ink-stand empty ink-stands denote that you will narrowly escape public denunciation for some supposed injustice.

To see them filled with ink, if you are not cautious, enemies will succeed in calumniation.

inn to dream of an inn, denotes prosperity and pleasures, if the inn is commodious and well furnished.

To be at a dilapidated and ill kept inn, denotes poor success, or mournful tasks, or unhappy journeys.

inquest to dream of an inquest, foretells you will be unfortunate in your friendships.

inquisition to dream of an inquisition, bespeaks for you an endless round of trouble and great disappointment.

If you are brought before an inquisition on a charge of wilfulness, you will be unable to defend yourself from malicious slander.

insane to dream of being insane forebodes disastrous results to some newly undertaken work, or ill health may change your prospects.

To see others insane, denotes disagreeable contact with suffering and appeals from the poverty-stricken. The utmost care should be taken of the health after this dream.

inscription to dream you see an inscription, foretells you will shortly receive unpleasant communications. If you are reading them on tombs, you will be distressed by sickness of a grave nature. To write one, you will lose a valued friend.

insects depending on how the insects are perceived in the dream, the interpretation of their appearance can differ. Buzzing flies may represent nothing more than a nagging problem within the dreamer's mind. The appearance of insects accompanied by feelings of displeasure or disgust will therefore reflect something about which the dreamer is more troubled. The problem may be a sexual one, in that the dreamer may associate both insects and sex with feelings of distaste. In some dreams, insects or small creatures may be representative of one's children; thus, the mother who dreams of insects flying away from her may be dealing with her feelings about her children

insects (ctd.)

gaining independence and leaving the family home. A dream that may signify illness and loss (Artemidorus).

ants to the tradesman this dream augurs success. In medieval symbolism ants typify industry. Plato says the souls of unimaginative persons return to earth as ants.

bee a dream signifying both good and bad: good if the bees do not sting, bad if they sting. Seeing bees indicates profit to country people and trouble to the rich.

beekeeping to dream of keeping bees augurs profit.

flying a bee flying about the ears signifies harassment by enemies.

honey and wax such a dream symbolizes sickness or a recovery from sickness. If you dream of bees making honey in the house this predicts dignity, eloquence and success to the occupants.

industrious bees their hard work is auspicious to ploughmen and to those profiting from this industry, to others this dream signifies trouble by reason of the noise they make.

stinging bees to be stung by a bee denotes vexation and trouble. Wounds or injuries are indicated by the position of their STING.

Some bee symbolism may derive from classical mythology. Jupiter is said to have been nourished by bees, and in his infancy Pindar was supposedly fed on honey instead of milk. They were sacred to Artemis and they appear on her statues and on her coins. Mahomet admits bees to Paradise. In modern Christian art bees symbolize industry. *See also* STING.

beetles this dream signifies that you believe some slander is circulating concerning you. To kill the beetle is to overcome this slander (Raphael). The symbolism surrounding the beetle is ancient indeed. It was held as sacred by the Egyptians as a symbol of virility, new life and of eternity. The beetle has been known to be a Christian symbol of blindness.

butterfly lack of fixed purpose, restlessness, inconstancy (gypsy folklore). It was the Greek symbol for the psyche or soul, and the Christians also employed it as a symbol of the resurrection. The significance of its bursting from its chrysalis into glory, was, however, lost

insects (ctd.)

during the middle ages, when a more shallow symbolism became established and continues to the present day. Its modern symbolism is that of playfulness, fickleness and living in pleasure.

caterpillar trouble through secret enemies is predicted by this dream (gypsy folklore). Although ancient symbolists classified it with the butterfly as an emblem of the soul, modern interpreters regard it as the secret enemy, symbolized in the way it destroys leaves and vegetation.

cricket (the insect) a pleasant meeting of old friends is symbolized by this dream. Superstition holds this insect as a pleasant omen. Pliny mentions it as much esteemed among the ancient magicians.

fleas a dream of annoyance and discomfort (gypsy folklore). Probably the result of physical stimuli.

flies dreaming of flies predicts troublesome persons who will scandalize you (gypsy folklore).

gadflies a dream of trouble in store for the dreamer (gypsy folklore).

grasshopper a dream prognosticating poverty due to lack of energy on the part of the dreamer (Raphael). The symbol of improvidence.

hornet a dream of vexations (gypsy folklore). *See also* STING.

locusts a dream forecasting extravagance, misfortune and short-lived happiness (gypsy folklore).

maggots as is the case with dreams of INFECTIONS, ILLNESSES, insects etc, dreams of maggots point to some intuitive feeling that the dreamer has that something is not right; either something is causing mental disquiet, or some physical problem is requiring attention.

mosquitoes persecution from petty enemies (gypsy folklore).

moths a dream of moths denotes a love affair in which the dreamer will suffer betrayal (gypsy folklore). The proverbial moth and flame is symbolized in this dream.

wasps to dream of being stung by wasps, a dream denoting envious enemies (Artemidorus). *See also* STING.

insolvent if you dream that you are insolvent, you will not have to resort to this means to square yourself with the world, as your energy and pride will enable you to transact business in a fair way. But other worries may sorely afflict you.

To dream that others are insolvent, you will meet with honest men in your dealings, but by their frankness they may harm you. For a young woman, it means her sweetheart will be honest and thrifty, but vexatious discords may arise in her affairs.

intemperance to dream of being intemperate in the use of your intellectual forces, you will seek after foolish knowledge fail to benefit yourself, and give pain and displeasure to your friends.

If you are intemperate in love, or other passions, you will reap disease or loss of fortune and esteem. For a young woman to thus dream, she will lose a lover and incur the displeasure of close friends.

intercede to intercede for some one in your dreams, shows you will secure aid when you desire it most.

intermarry to dream of intermarrying, denotes quarrels and contentions which will precipitate you into trouble and loss.

interpreter to dream of an interpreter, denotes you will undertake affairs which will fail in profit.

intestine to dream of seeing intestines, signifies you are about to be visited by a grave calamity, which will remove some friend. To see your own intestines, denotes grave situations are closing around you; sickness of a nature to affect you in your daily communications with others threatens you. Probable loss, with much displeasure, is also denoted. If you think you lay them upon something, which turns out to be a radiator, and they begin to grow hot and make you very uncomfortable, and you ask others to assist you, and they refuse, it foretells unexpected calamity, which will probably come in the form of a desperate illness or a misfortune for which you will be censured by those formerly your friends. You may have trouble in extricating yourself from an unpromising predicament.

intoxication to dream of intoxication, denotes that you are cultivating your desires for illicit pleasures. *See* DRUNK.

inundation to dream of seeing cities or country submerged in dark, seething waters, denotes great misfortune and loss of life through some dreadful calamity.

To see human beings swept away in an inundation, portends bereavements and despair, making life gloomy and unprofitable.

To see a large area inundated with clear water, denotes profit and ease after seemingly hopeless struggles with fortune. *See* FOOD.

invalid to dream of invalids, is a sign of displeasing companions interfering with your interest. To think you are one, portends you are threatened with displeasing circumstances.

invective to dream of using invectives, warns you of passionate outbursts of anger, which may estrange you from close companions. To hear others using them, enemies are closing you in to apparent wrong and deceits.

inventor to dream of an inventor, foretells you will soon achieve some unique work which will add honour to your name. To dream that you are inventing something, or feel interested in some invention, denotes you will aspire to fortune and will be successful in your designs.

invisible an invisible presence, i.e. someone or something that cannot be seen but that is nevertheless active within the dream, is possibly symbolic of some influential authority figure.

invite to dream that you invite persons to visit you, denotes that some unpleasant event is near, and will cause worry and excitement in your otherwise pleasant surroundings.

If you are invited to make a visit, you will receive sad news.

For a woman to dream that she is invited to attend a party, she will have pleasant anticipations, but ill luck will mar them.

iron to dream of being hurt with iron signifies damage. To dream of trading in iron with strangers predicts losses and misfortune (Artemidorus).

ironing to dream of ironing, denotes domestic comforts and orderly business.

If a woman dreams that she burns her hands while ironing, it foretells she will have illness or jealousy to disturb her peace. If she scorches the clothes, she will have a rival who will cause her much displeasure and suspicions. If the irons seem too cold, she will lack affection in her home.

island an island may be a symbol of loneliness or a feeling of isolation on the part of the dreamer, or it may be interpreted as a desire to cut oneself off from others. A third possible interpretation of the appearance of an island in a dream is that the island represents the unborn child, and the water surrounding the island stands for the amniotic fluid in which the foetus floats. In gypsy folklore it is a dream predicting isolation and loneliness.

I

itch to see persons with the itch, and you endeavour to escape contact, you will stand in fear of distressing results when your endeavours will bring pleasant success.

If you dream you have the itch yourself, you will be harshly used, and will defend yourself by incriminating others. For a young woman to have this dream, omens she will fall into dissolute companionship.

To dream that you itch, denotes unpleasant avocations.

ivory this dream predicts abundance and success (gypsy folklore).

ivy a dream of strong trust and friendship (gypsy folklore). Ivy is a symbol of the Trinity and of the triple creative power, also of loyalty and friendship.

J

jackal *see* ANIMALS.

jackdaw *see* BIRDS.

jail if you dream of being confined in a jail, you will be prevented from carrying forward some profitable work by the intervention of envious people; but if you escape from the jail, you will enjoy a season of favourable business.

To see others in jail, you will be urged to grant privileges to persons whom you believe to be unworthy.

For a young woman to dream that her lover is in jail, she will be disappointed in his character, as he will prove a deceiver.

jailer dreams of IMPRISONMENT are symbolic of restrictions to the freedom of the individual. Therefore, a person appearing in the role of a jailer in a dream will stand for the source of that restriction. This is by no means necessarily another person; it may be the attitudes or inhibitions of the dreamer himself or herself. *See also* ENCLOSURE and CAPTIVE.

jam to dream of eating jam, if pure, denotes pleasant surprises and journeys.

To dream of making jam, foretells to a woman a happy home and appreciative friends.

janitor to dream of a janitor, denotes bad management and disobedient children. Unworthy servants will annoy you.

To look for a janitor and fail to find him, petty annoyances will disturb your otherwise placid existence. If you find him, you will have pleasant associations with strangers, and your affairs will have no hindrances.

January to dream of this month, denotes you will be afflicted with unloved companions or children.

jar to dream of empty jars, denotes impoverishment and distress.

To see them full, you will be successful.

If you buy jars, your success will be precarious and your burden will be heavy.

To see broken jars, distressing sickness or deep disappointment awaits you.

jasmine a dream of true love and success (gypsy folklore); a poetic symbol.

jasper to dream of seeing jasper, is a happy omen, bringing success and love. For a young woman to lose a jasper, is a sign of disagreement with her lover.

jaundice a dream of sickness and poverty (gypsy folklore).

javelin to dream of defending yourself with a javelin, your most private affairs will be searched into to establish claims of dishonesty, and you will prove your innocence after much wrangling.

If you are pierced by a javelin, enemies will succeed in giving you trouble.

To see others carrying javelins, your interests are threatened.

jaws to dream of seeing heavy, misshapen jaws, denotes disagreements, and ill feeling will be shown between friends.

If you dream that you are in the jaws of a wild beast, enemies will work injury to your affairs and happiness. This is a vexatious and perplexing dream.

If your own jaws ache with pain, you will be exposed to climatic changes, and malaria may cause you loss in health and finances.

jay-bird to dream of a jay-bird, foretells pleasant visits from friends and interesting gossips.

To catch a jay-bird, denotes pleasant, though unfruitful, tasks.

To see a dead jay-bird, denotes domestic unhappiness and many vicissitudes.

jealousy to dream that you are jealous of your wife, denotes the influence of enemies and narrow-minded persons. If jealous of your sweetheart, you will seek to displace a rival.

If a woman dreams that she is jealous of her husband, she will find many shocking incidents to vex and make her happiness a travesty.

If a young woman is jealous of her lover, she will find that he is more favourably impressed with the charms of some other woman than herself.

If men and women are jealous over common affairs, they will meet many unpleasant worries in the discharge of every-day business.

jelly to dream of eating jelly, many pleasant interruptions will take place.

For a woman to dream of making jelly, signifies she will enjoy pleasant reunions with friends.

jessamine to dream of jessamine, denotes you are approximating some exquisite pleasure, but which will be fleeting.

jester to dream of a jester, foretells you will ignore important things in looking after silly affairs.

jewellery to dream of broken jewellery, denotes keen disappointment in attaining one's highest desires.

If the jewellery be cankered, trusted friends will fail you, and business cares will be on you.

jewels jewels or *treasure* appearing in a dream are unlikely to represent material fortune of any kind. They are more likely to stand for that which the dreamer holds to be valuable in life in a non-material sense, for example, moral values, freedom of thought and creativity, family or romantic love.

To find treasure is a dream of success (gypsy folklore). One of the few dreams involving material gain that is not a dream of CONTRARY MEANING, the reason probably lies in the fact that treasure and its discovery so frequently figures as the traditional reward of virtue in fairy stories and in mythology. *See also* GEM.

jig to dance a jig, denotes cheerful occupations and light pleasures.

To see your sweetheart dancing a jig, your companion will be possessed with a merry and hopeful disposition.

To see ballet girls dancing a jig, you will engage in undignified amusements and follow low desires.

jockey to dream of a jockey, omens you will appreciate a gift from an unexpected source. For a young woman to dream that she associates with a jockey, or has one for a lover, indicates she will win a husband out of her station. To see one thrown from a horse, signifies you will be called on for aid by strangers.

jolly to dream that you feel jolly and are enjoying the merriment of companions, you will realise pleasure from the good behaviour of children and have satisfying results in business. If there comes the least rift in the merriment, worry will intermingle with the success of the future.

journey most obviously, dream journeys can represent the 'journey of life', or a particular stage in life, such as childhood or marriage. Thus a journey that is particularly hard will reflect a difficult period in life. To dream of passing through difficult territory and emerging into easy terrain can reflect a change for the better in life and the overcoming of past obstacles. Those who dream of losing their way and feel frightened and bewildered on their journey are perhaps lacking direction in their lives, or may feel that events are taking such a turn as to leave them without control.

aeroplane journeys may stand for a swift transition between one part of the dreamer's life and another.

bicycle can refer to a difficult phase of life that has to be overcome.

boat the extent of difficulty experienced in a dream of travelling by water can reflect the extent to which boundaries have arisen in the dreamers life. Sailing over smooth water predicts prosperity; rough water indicates misfortune. If the boat is a small one this is said to predict sudden wealth (Raphael).

car can be a symbol of desire or sexuality. There should be particular importance placed on whether the dreamer is driving or being driven, since this is a reflection on the dreamer's sense of independence.

train the way in which the dreamer is travelling may indicate the individual's energy, sexual or otherwise. For men the dream generally has a sexual content especially (using that old Freudian cliché) if the train enters a tunnel, for women it may express a desire for more power. *See also* RAILWAY.

uphill to travel uphill denotes advancement with difficulty.

wood travelling through a wood is a dream of trouble and hindrances.

joy to dream that you feel joy over any event, denotes harmony among friends.

jubilee to dream of a jubilee, denotes many pleasurable enterprises in which you will be a participant. For a young woman, this is a favourable dream, pointing to matrimony and increase of temporal blessings.

To dream of a religious jubilee, denotes close but comfortable environments.

judge and jury these are often symbolic of the way in which we judge ourselves and our own actions; alternatively, they can represent the influences that have shaped our personal morality. To dream of coming before a judge indicates malice, persecution, etc (gypsy folklore). This interpretation probably stems from the gypsy's experience of injustice and prejudice regarding their way of life.

judgement day to dream of the judgement day, foretells that you will accomplish some well-planned work, if you appear resigned and hopeful of escaping punishment. Otherwise, your work will prove a failure.

For a young woman to appear before the judgement bar and hear the verdict of 'Guilty', denotes that she will cause much distress among her friends by her selfish and unbecoming conduct. If she sees the dead rising, and all the earth solemnly and fearfully awaiting the end, there will be much struggling for her, and her friends will refuse her aid. It is also a forerunner of unpleasant gossip, and scandal is threatened. Business may assume hopeless aspects.

jug if you dream of jugs well filled with transparent liquids, your welfare is being considered by more than yourself. Many true friends will unite to please and profit you. If the jugs are empty, your conduct will estrange you from friends and station.

Broken jugs, indicate sickness and failures in employment.

If you drink wine from a jug, you will enjoy robust health and find pleasure in all circles. Optimistic views will possess you.

To take an unpleasant drink from a jug, disappointment and disgust will follow pleasant anticipations.

July to dream of this month, denotes you will be depressed with gloomy outlooks, but, as suddenly, your spirits will rebound to unimagined pleasure and good fortune.

jump a jump from one place to another may be interpreted as a chance that has been taken or that would be worthwhile taking in life. A failed jump represents either a fear of not succeeding in something or the realization that one has made an error in life.

jumping-jack to dream of a jumping-jack, denotes that idleness and trivial pastimes will occupy your thoughts to the exclusion of serious and sustaining plans.

June to dream of June, foretells unusual gains in all undertakings.

For a woman to think that vegetation is decaying, or that a drouth is devastating the land, she will have sorrow and loss which will be lasting in its effects.

juniper to dream of felling a juniper tree indicates good luck; eating juniper berries warns against unwise associations.

justice a good dream (gypsy folklore).

K

kaleidoscopes working before you in a dream, portend swift changes with little of favourable promise in them.

kangaroo *see* ANIMALS.

katydids to dream of hearing katydids, is a prognostic of misfortune and unusual dependence on others. If any sick person ask you what they are, foretells there will be surprising events in your present and future.

For a woman to see them, signifies she will have a quarrelsome husband or lover.

keg to dream of a keg, denotes you will have a struggle to throw off oppression. Broken ones, indicate separation from family or friends.

kerbstone to dream of stepping on a kerbstone, denotes your rapid rise in business circles, and that you will be held in high esteem by your friends and the public.

For lovers to dream of stepping together on a curb, denotes an early marriage and consequent fidelity; but if in your dream you step or fall from a kerbstone your fortunes will be reversed.

kettle a bright kettle denotes success in everyday life (Raphael). Its symbolism would derive from denoting the gypsy way of life.

key a key can indicate the solution to a problem, that which opens up the door to success. Alternatively, it may be that which has been keeping repressed emotions locked up within the dreamer. A third possible meaning for a key in a dream is sexual, the key possibly standing for the penis, and the keyhole representing the vagina. Also a dream of coldness and hindrances to travellers. Fortunate for managers of other people's affairs; to dream of giving a key augurs marriage; to receive one, honour and confidence; many keys denote wealth; to lose keys denotes anger and misfortune (gypsy folklore). A talisman of power, sagacity and foresight. The key is a Chinese symbol of prudence.

keyhole to dream that you spy upon others through a keyhole, you will damage some person by disclosing confidence. If you catch others peeping through a keyhole, you will have false friends delving into your private matters to advance themselves over you.

To dream that you cannot find the keyhole, you will unconsciously injure a friend.

kid to dream of a kid, denotes you will not be over-scrupulous in your morals or pleasures. You will be likely to bring grief to some loving heart.

kidnap a generally ill-omened dream. A dream of one's own kidnap is a warning to the dreamer to beware. To dream of perpetrating a kidnap is also a warning against others.

kidneys to dream about your kidneys, foretells you are threatened with a serious illness, or there will be trouble in marriage relations for you.

If they act too freely, you will be a party to some racy intrigue. If they refuse to perform their work, there will be a sensation, and to your detriment. If you eat kidney-stew, some officious person will cause you disgust in some secret lover affair.

killing to dream of killing someone is unlikely to mean that you wish anybody any real harm. It is more likely that the person who is being killed in the dream is a symbol for some aspect of the dreamer's self that he wishes to repress, change or eradicate. Thus, dreams of killing may indicate a feeling of self-loathing.

To dream of being killed may point to some factor in the dreamer's life that is in some way stifling the dreamer or making him or her feel helpless. *See also* MURDER and TYPICAL DREAMS.

king to dream of a king, you are struggling with your might, and ambition is your master.

To dream that you are crowned king, you will rise above your comrades and co-workers.

If you are censured by a king, you will be reproved for a neglected duty.

For a young woman to be in the presence of a king, she will marry a man whom she will fear. To receive favours from a king, she will rise to exalted positions and be congenially wedded.

kiss a kiss in a dream may be seen in general as an acknowledgement or acceptance of something. Thus, a dream of kissing somebody goodbye can be read as the acknowledgement of the need for some sort of transition in the waking life of the dreamer.

To kiss a relative in a dream denotes treason; a stranger, a speedy journey; the earth, humiliation; the hand of a person, friendship, good fortune; the face of a stranger, rashness followed by success (gypsy folklore).

kitchen *see* HOUSE.

kite a dream predicting elevation in life; should the string break this predicts sudden downfall (Raphael). This dream may well express a wish to escape or to better oneself.

kitten *see* ANIMALS.

knapsack to see a knapsack while dreaming, denotes you will find your greatest pleasure away from the associations of friends. For a woman to see an old dilapidated one, means poverty and disagreeableness for her.

knave to dream of being a knave signifies wealth; to be connected with them, lawsuits (Artemidorus).

knee *see* BODY.

kneeling *see* ACTIONS.

knife a knife in a dream is very possibly a sign of aggression on the part of the dreamer, a desire to inflict pain, although not necessarily physical pain, on somebody. A knife that is used against someone but with no effect may reflect feelings of powerlessness or inadequacy in the dreamer.

In certain contexts, a knife may represent the male libido or aggressive sexual feelings. An unfortunate dream, bright sharp knives connote enemies.

knife grinder to dream of a knife grinder, foretells robbery. For a woman, this omens unhappy unions and much drudgery.

knight in armour a dream of peril to come (gypsy folklore).

knitting a dream denoting wicked talk or gossip (gypsy folklore). The domestic occupations of women frequently bear this meaning.

knocker to dream of using a knocker, foretells you will be forced to ask aid and counsel of others.

knocking to hear knocking in your dreams, denotes that tidings of a grave nature will soon be received by you. If you are awakened by the knocking, the news will affect you the more seriously.

knots knots can be read as problems with which the dreamer is struggling in waking life. There may be a confusion of emotions concerning some aspect of the dreamer's life. A dream of embarrassment and perplexity (gypsy folklore); 'a knotty problem,' etc. The knot is a Chinese symbol of longevity and luck.

Krishna to see Krishna in your dreams, denotes that your greatest joy will be in pursuit of occult knowledge, and you will school yourself to the taunts of friends, and cultivate a philosophical bearing toward life and sorrow.

L

label to dream of a label, foretells you will let an enemy see the inside of your private affairs, and will suffer from the negligence.

laboratory to dream of being in a laboratory, denotes great energies wasted in unfruitful enterprises when you might succeed in some more practical business.

If you think yourself an alchemist, and try to discover a process to turn other things into gold, you will entertain far-reaching and interesting projects, but you will fail to reach the apex of your ambition. Wealth will prove a myth, and the woman you love will hold a false position towards you.

labour to dream that you watch domestic animals labouring under heavy burdens, denotes that you will be prosperous, but unjust to your servants, or those employed by you.

To see men toiling, signifies profitable work, and robust health. To labour yourself, denotes favourable outlook for any new enterprise, and bountiful crops if the dreamer is interested in farming.

labourer a dream denoting happiness, increase of fortune, etc (gypsy folklore). The labourer is symbolic of frugality and prudence.

labyrinth if you dream of a labyrinth, you will find yourself entangled in intricate and perplexing business conditions, and your wife will make the home environment intolerable; children and sweethearts will prove ill-tempered and unattractive.

If you are in a labyrinth of night or darkness, it foretells passing, but agonising sickness and trouble.

A labyrinth of green vines and timbers, denotes unexpected happiness from what was seemingly a cause for loss and despair.

In a network, or labyrinth of railroads, assures you of long and tedious journeys. Interesting people will be met, but no financial success will aid you on these journeys.

laces to wear them in a dream forecasts disappointment in some new garments (gypsy folklore).

ladder the ladder may represent a path in life that the dreamer is about to take. Climbing a ladder in a dream suggests that the dreamer is aware that there are hazards that have to be faced if goals in life are to be attained. Occasionally, a ladder may have sexual significance as a metaphor for an erection. This is also said to be a dream of advancement; to ascend denotes elevation; to descend predicts a downfall (Artemidorus).

ladle to see a ladle in your dreams, denotes you will be fortunate in the selection of a companion. Children will prove sources of happiness. If the ladle is broken or unclean, you will have a grievous loss.

lagoon to dream of a lagoon, denotes that you will be drawn into a whirlpool of doubt and confusion through misapplication of your intelligence.

lake *see* BROOK.

lambs *see* ANIMALS.

lame for a woman to dream of seeing anyone lame, foretells that her pleasures and hopes will be unfruitful and disappointing.

lament to dream that you bitterly lament the loss of friends, or property, signifies great struggles and much distress, from which will spring causes for joy and personal gain.

To lament the loss of relatives, denotes sickness or disappointments, which will bring you into closer harmony with companions, and will result in brighter prospects for the future.

lamp to carry a bright one denotes success and this is an especially favourable dream for lovers. A dim lamp denotes sickness; a light that goes out or is extinguished denotes death; or at least danger (Raphael). In ancient symbolism the lamp or flame represented the vital spark of life. Truth, righteousness and illumination are symbolized by the lamp in scriptural art.

lamp-post to see a lamp-post in your dreams, some stranger will prove your staunchest friend in time of pressing need.

To fall against a lamp-post, you will have deception to overcome, or enemies will ensnare you.

To see a lamp-post across your path, you will have much adversity in your life.

lance a dream of trouble and tragedy (Raphael). The lance is a phallic symbol and therefore this is an erotic dream (Jung). The lance was a Christian symbol of martyrdom and a Greek symbol of the god Mars.

land to dream of land, when it appears fertile, omens good; but if sterile and rocky, failure and despondency is prognosticated.

To see land from the ocean, denotes that vast avenues of prosperity and happiness will disclose themselves to you.

landau to dream that you ride in a landau, with your friend or sweetheart, denotes that incidents of a light, but pleasant character will pass in rapid succession through your life.

If the vehicle is overturned, then pleasure will abruptly turn into woe.

lantern to dream of carrying one on a dark night foretells riches. To stumble while carrying the lantern denotes trouble. If the light is darkened or extinguished then poverty is predicted (Artemidorus). Lanterns can symbolize leadership and it is the Christian symbol of piety and truth. The tarot gives it as a symbol of wisdom. ;

lap to dream of sitting on some person's lap, denotes pleasant security from vexing engagements. If a young woman dreams that she is holding a person on her lap, she will be exposed to unfavourable criticism.

To see a serpent in her lap, foretells she is threatened with humiliation at the hands of enemies. If she sees a cat in her lap, she will be endangered by a seductive enemy.

lap-dog to dream of a lap-dog, foretells you will be succoured by friends in some approaching dilemma If it be thin and ill-looking, there will be distressing occurrences to detract from your prospects.

lap-robe to dream of a lap-robe, indicates suspicious engagements will place you under the surveillance of enemies or friends.

To lose one, your actions will be condemned by enemies to injure your affairs.

lard to dream of lard, signifies a rise in fortune will soon gratify you. For a woman to find her hand in melted lard, foretells her disappointment in attempting to rise in social circles.

lark *see* BIRDS.

latch to dream of a latch, denotes you will meet urgent appeals for aid, to which you will respond unkindly. To see a broken latch, foretells disagreements with your dearest friend. Sickness is also foretold in this dream.

Latin to dream of studying this language, denotes victory and distinction in your efforts to sustain your opinion on subjects of grave interest to the public welfare.

laudanum to dream that you take laudanum, signifies weakness of your own; and that you will have a tendency to be unduly influenced by others. You should cultivate determination.

To prevent others from taking this drug, indicates that you will be the means of conveying great joy and good to people.

To see your lover taking laudanum through disappointment, signifies unhappy affairs and the loss of a friend.

To give it, slight ailments will attack some member of your domestic circle.

laughing to dream that you laugh and feel cheerful, means success in your undertakings, and bright companions socially.

Laughing immoderately at some weird object, denotes disappointment and lack of harmony in your surroundings.

To hear the happy laughter of children, means joy and health to the dreamer.

To laugh at the discomfiture of others, denotes that you will wilfully injure your friends to gratify your own selfish desires.

To hear mocking laughter, denotes illness and disappointing affairs.

laundry to dream of laundering clothes, denotes struggles, but a final victory in winning fortune. If the clothes are done satisfactorily, then your endeavours will bring complete happiness. If they come out the reverse, your fortune will fail to procure pleasure.

To see pretty girls at this work, you will seek pleasure out of your rank.

If a laundryman calls at your house, you are in danger of sickness, or of losing something very valuable.

To see laundry wagons, portends rivalry and contention.

laurel a dream betokening victory and pleasure (Raphael); symbol of victory.

law, lawyers a dream forecasting heavy business losses. After having this dream be careful about entering into bargains or contracts (Raphael).

lawns to dream of walking upon well-kept lawns, denotes occasions for joy and great prosperity.

To join a merry party upon a lawn, denotes many secular amusements, and business engagements will be successfully carried on.

For a young woman to wait upon a green lawn for the coming of a friend or lover, denotes that her most ardent wishes concerning wealth and marriage will be gratified. If the grass be dead and the lawn marshy, quarrels and separation may be expected.

To see serpents crawling in the grass before you, betrayal and cruel insinuations will fill you with despair.

lazy to dream of feeling lazy, or acting so, denotes you will make a mistake in the formation of enterprises, and will suffer keen disappointment.

For a young woman to think her lover is lazy, foretells she will have bad luck in securing admiration. Her actions will discourage men who mean marriage.

lead to dream of lead, foretells poor success in any engagement.

A lead mine, indicates that your friends will look with suspicion on your money making. Your sweetheart will surprise you with her deceit and ill temper.

To dream of lead ore, foretells distress and accidents. Business will assume a gloomy cast.

To hunt for lead, denotes discontentment, and a constant changing of employment.

To melt lead, foretells that by impatience you will bring failure upon yourself and others.

leaking to dream of seeing a leak in anything, is usually significant of loss and vexations.

leaping for a young woman to dream of leaping over an obstruction, denotes that she will gain her desires after much struggling and opposition.

learning to dream of learning, denotes that you will take great interest in acquiring knowledge, and if you are economical of your time, you will advance far into the literary world.

To enter halls, or places of learning, denotes rise from obscurity, and finance will be a congenial adherent.

To see learned men, foretells that your companions will be interesting and prominent.

For a woman to dream that she is associated in any way with learned people, she will be ambitious and excel in her endeavours to rise into prominence.

leather to dream of leather, denotes successful business and favourable engagements with women.

You will go into lucky speculations if you dream that you are dressed in leather.

Ornaments of leather, denotes faithfulness in love and to the home.

Piles of leather, denotes fortune and happiness.

To deal in leather, signifies no change in the disposition of your engagements is necessary for successful accumulation of wealth.

leaves TREES covered with fresh leaves signify success in business. Blossoms and FRUITS among leaves are a dream of marriage. Withered leaves signify losses and bad crops (Raphael).

ledger to dream of keeping a ledger, you will have perplexities and disappointing conditions to combat.

To dream that you make wrong entries on your ledger, you will have small disputes and a slight loss will befall you.

To put a ledger into a safe, you will be able to protect your rights under adverse circumstances.

To get your ledger misplaced, your interests will go awry through neglect of duty.

To dream that your ledger gets destroyed by fire, you will suffer through the carelessness of friends.

To dream that you have a woman to keep your ledger, you will lose money trying to combine pleasure with business.

For a young woman to dream of ledgers, denotes she will have a solid business man to make her a proposal of marriage.

To dream that your ledger has worthless accounts, denotes bad management and losses; but if the accounts are good, then your business will assume improved conditions.

leeches *see* ANIMALS.

leers *see* ONIONS.

leeward to dream of sailing leeward, denotes to the sailor a prosperous and merry voyage. To others, a pleasant journey.

legislature to dream that you are a member of a legislature, foretells you will be vain of your possessions and will treat members of your family unkindly. You will have no real advancement.

legs if you dream of admiring well-shaped feminine legs, you will lose your judgement, and act very silly over some fair charmer.

To see misshapen legs, denotes unprofitable occupations and ill-tempered comrades.

A wounded leg, foretells losses and agonising attacks of malaria.

To dream that you have a wooden leg, denotes that you will bemean yourself in a false way to your friends.

If ulcers are on your legs, it signifies a drain on your income to aid others.

To dream that you have three, or more, legs, indicates that more enterprises are planned in your imagination than will ever benefit you.

If you can't use your legs, it portends poverty.

To have a leg amputated, you will lose valued friends, and the home influence will render life unbearable.

For a young woman to admire her own legs, denotes vanity, and she will be repulsed by the man she admires. If she has hairy legs, she will dominate her husband.

If your own legs are clean and well shaped, it denotes a happy future and devoted friends.

lemonade if you drink lemonade in a dream, you will concur with others in signifying some entertainment as a niggardly device to raise funds for the personal enjoyment of others at your expense.

lemons to dream of seeing lemons on their native trees among rich foliage, denotes jealousy toward some beloved object, but demonstrations will convince you of the absurdity of the charge.

To eat lemons, foretells humiliation and disappointments.

Green lemons, denotes sickness and contagion.

To see shrivelled lemons, denotes divorce, if married, and separation, to lovers.

lending to dream that you are lending money, foretells difficulties in meeting payments of debts and unpleasant influence in private. To lend other articles, denotes impoverishment through generosity. To refuse to lend things, you will be awake to your interests and keep the respect of friends. For others to offer to lend you articles, or money, denotes prosperity and close friendships.

lentil if you dream of lentils, it denotes quarrels and unhealthy surroundings. For a young woman, this dream portends dissatisfaction with her lover, but parental advice will cause her to accept the inevitable.

leopard *see* ANIMALS.

leper a dream of shame and infamy, it also predicts illness (gypsy folklore).

letter letters may be symbols of intuitive feelings; an unopened letter would therefore represent that the dreamer is 'not listening to his heart'. Opening letters represents the achievement of greater self-awareness.

In certain contexts, an unopened letter may be interpreted as either virginity (protected) or sexual immaturity, or sexual awareness that has yet to be aroused. To write or receive them, good news (gypsy folklore).

letter-carrier if you dream of a letter-carrier coming with your letters, you will soon receive news of an unwelcome and an unpleasant character. To hear his whistle, denotes the unexpected arrival of a visitor. If he passes without your mail, disappointment and sadness will befall you. If you give him letters to mail, you will suffer injury through envy or jealousy. To converse with a letter-carrier, you will implicate yourself in some scandalous proceedings.

letter-file to see a letter-file in your dreams, is significant of important news, which will cause you an irksome journey. For a woman, this dream implies distressful news and unfaithful friends.

lettuce *see* GRASS.

liar to dream of being called one denotes wealth by questionable means (gypsy folklore).

library to dream of being in a library shows success through wisdom and learning (gypsy folklore).

lice a dream of lice contains much waking worry and distress. It often implies offensive ailments. Lice on stock, foretells famine and loss. To have lice on your body, denotes that you will conduct yourself unpleasantly with your acquaintances. To dream of catching lice, foretells sickness, and that you will cultivate morbidity.

license to dream of a license, is an omen of disputes and loss. Married women will exasperate your cheerfulness. For a woman to see a marriage license, foretells that she will soon enter unpleasant bonds, which will humiliate her pride.

lifeboat a dream predicting success at the last moment (Raphael).

life-insurance man to see life-insurance men in a dream, means that you are soon to meet a stranger who will contribute to your business interests, and change in your home life is foreshadowed, as interests will be mutual.

If they appear distorted or unnatural, the dream is more unfortunate than good.

light to dream of being aboard ship and of seeing a light far off assures one of his or her desires.

To dream of holding a burning light in the hands is a good sign, especially to the young, signifying accomplishment of designs, honours and good will to all persons. A light in the hands of another foretells the discovery of mischief and the punishment of the offender.

lighthouse a dream warning of a danger ahead and the possibility of a mistake in judgement (Raphael). Freudians see this symbol as having a strong sexual significance.

lightning a portentous dream of war and trouble (gypsy folklore).

lightning-rod to see a lightning-rod, denotes that threatened destruction to some cherished work will confront you. To see one change into a serpent, foretells enemies will succeed in their schemes against you. If the lightning strikes one, there will be an accident or sudden news to give you sorrow.

If you are having one put up, it is a warning to beware how you begin a new enterprise, as you will likely be overtaken by disappointment.

To have them taken down, you will change your plans and thereby further your interests. To see many lightning rods, indicates a variety of misfortunes.

lilies a symbol of innocence, chastity and purity. To dream of lilies promises happiness through virtue (Raphael).

lily of the valley a dream of humility.

water lilies signify regeneration and purification.

lotus a symbol of new birth and of immortality.

tiger lilies, a dream of the temptation of wealth (gypsy folklore).

lime to dream of lime, foretells that disaster will prostrate you for a time, but you will revive to greater and richer prosperity than before.

lime-kiln to dream of a lime-kiln, foretells the immediate future holds no favour for speculations in love or business

limes to dream of eating limes, foretells continued sickness and adverse straits.

limping a dream of limping predicts misfortune and shame (Artemidorus).

linen to dream of being dressed in clean linen denotes glad tidings; soiled linen, poverty, imprisonment, disappointment, etc.

linseed oil to see linseed oil in your dreams, denotes your impetuous extravagance will be checked by the kindly interference of a friend.

lion *see* ANIMALS.

lips to dream of thick, unsightly lips, signifies disagreeable encounters, hasty decision, and ill temper in the marriage relation.

Full, sweet, cherry lips, indicates harmony and affluence. To a lover, it augurs reciprocation in love, and fidelity.

Thin lips, signifies mastery of the most intricate subjects.

Sore, or swollen lips, denotes privations and unhealthy desires.

liquor to dream of buying liquor, denotes selfish usurpation of property upon which you have no legal claim If you sell it, you will be criticised for niggardly benevolence.

To drink some, you will come into doubtful possession of wealth, but your generosity will draw around you convivial friends, and women will seek to entrance and hold you.

To see liquor in barrels, denotes prosperity, but unfavourable tendency toward making home pleasant.

If in bottles, fortune will appear in a very tangible form.

For a woman to dream of handling, or drinking liquor, foretells for her a happy Bohemian kind of existence. She will be good-natured but shallow minded. To treat others, she will be generous to rivals, and the indifference of lovers or husband will not seriously offset her pleasures or contentment.

liver to dream of a disordered liver, denotes a querulous person will be your mate, and fault-finding will occupy her time, and disquiet will fill your hours.

To dream of eating liver, indicates that some deceitful person has installed himself in the affection of your sweetheart.

lizard *see* ANIMALS.

load a dream of care and toil, to succeed in carrying it signifies the triumph over difficulties (gypsy folklore).

loaves to dream of seeing loaves foretells want (gypsy folklore). Evidently a desire or need is assumed as the latent content of this dream.

lobster *see* ANIMALS.

lock a dream foretelling difficulty in the attainment of your desire (gypsy folklore).

locket if a young woman dreams that her lover places a locket around her neck, she will be the recipient of many beautiful offerings, and will soon be wedded, and lovely children will crown her life. If she should lose a locket, death will throw sadness into her life.

If a lover dreams that his sweetheart returns his locket, he will confront disappointing issues. The woman he loves will worry him and conduct herself in a displeasing way toward him.

If a woman dreams that she breaks a locket, she will have a

changeable and unstable husband, who will dislike constancy in any form, be it business or affection,

lockjaw to dream that you have lockjaw, signifies there is trouble ahead for you, as some person is going to betray your confidence. For a woman to see others with lockjaw, foretells her friends will unconsciously detract from her happiness by assigning her unpleasant tasks. If stock have it, you will lose a friend.

locomotive *see* JOURNEY.

locusts *see* INSECTS.

lodger for a woman to dream that she has lodgers, foretells she will be burdened with unpleasant secrets. If one goes away without paying his bills, she will have unexpected trouble with men. For one to pay his bill, omens favour and accumulation of money.

logs to dream of cleaving logs portends a visit from strangers (Artemidorus).

looking glass dreaming of looking in a looking glass or mirror, to married people signifies children. To the young looking in a mirror denotes sweethearts or is an expression of vanity. To see oneself in water forecasts the dreamer's death or that of a friend (Artemidorus). This dream can be directly traced through ancestral memory back to the legends of mythology.

looking to dream of looking from high places, out of windows, or in a well denotes ambition, imagination and confused desires.

loom to dream of standing by and seeing a loom operated by a stranger, denotes much vexation and useless irritation from the talkativeness of those about you. Some disappointment with happy expectations are coupled with this dream.

To see good-looking women attending the loom, denotes unqualified success to those in love. It predicts congenial pursuits to the married. It denotes you are drawing closer together in taste.

For a woman to dream of weaving on an old-time loom, signifies that she will have a thrifty husband and beautiful children will fill her life with happy solicitations.

To see an idle loom, denotes a sulky and stubborn person, who will cause you much anxious care.

Lord's Prayer to dream of repeating the Lord's Prayer, foretells that you are threatened with secret foes and will need the alliance and the support of friends to tide you over difficulties.

To hear others repeat it, denotes the danger of some friend.

loss dreams of losing things may reflect some sense of loss that the dreamer is feeling; for example, childhood may be now a thing of the past, or a love affair may be over.

In some cases the dream may indicate that a good opportunity may be, or already has been, missed.

For a woman to dream of losing her *wedding-ring* denotes little love for her husband. If she finds it again, the love is not wholly dead. For a man to lose his *shoes*, signifies reproaches (gypsy folklore).

lost dreaming of being lost indicates a certain sense of confusion in the dreamer's mind, a lack of direction in life, or mixed feelings towards a particular person or situation.

lottery to dream of a lottery, and that you are taking great interest in the drawing, you will engage in some worthless enterprise, which will cause you to make an unpropitious journey. If you hold the lucky number, you will gain in a speculation which will perplex and give you much anxiety.

To see others winning in a lottery, denotes convivialities and amusements, bringing many friends together.

If you lose in a lottery, you will be the victim of designing persons. Gloomy depressions in your affairs will result.

For a young woman to dream of a lottery in any way, denotes that her careless way of doing things will bring her disappointment, and a husband who will not be altogether reliable or constant.

To dream of a lottery, denotes you will have unfavourable friendships in business. Your love affairs will produce temporary pleasure.

louse to dream of a louse, foretells that you will have uneasy feelings regarding your health, and an enemy will give you exasperating vexation. *See* LICE.

love all emotions that are felt in dreams are genuine emotions. What has to be decided is whether the love that is felt in the dream is a compensation for that which is deficient in waking life, i.e. wish fulfilment or a reflection of something that the dreamer feels in waking life yet has not acknowledged. To dream of unsuccessful love is a dream of CONTRARY MEANING, you will marry and be happy. To dream that friends love you foretells prosperity in all things. To dream of being with your lover foretells a speedy marriage (Raphael).

lovely dreaming of lovely things, brings favour to all persons connected with you.

For a lover to dream that his sweetheart is lovely of person and character, foretells for him a speedy and favourable marriage.

If through the vista of dreams you see your own fair loveliness, fate bids you, with a gleaming light, awake to happiness.

lozenges to dream of lozenges, foretells success in small matters. For a woman to eat or throw them away, foretells her life will be harassed by little spites from the envious.

lucky to dream that you are lucky is a dream of CONTRARY MEANING, of misfortune (Raphael).

luggage luggage in dreams may be interpreted as 'emotional baggage', i.e. thoughts and feelings that the dreamer carries about and cannot, or will not, let go of.

lumber to dream of lumber, denotes many difficult tasks and but little remuneration or pleasure.

To see piles of lumber burning, indicates profit from an unexpected source.

To dream of sawing lumber, denotes unwise transactions and unhappiness.

lust, amorousness to dream you are amorous, warns you against personal desires and pleasures, as they are threatening to engulf you in scandal.

For a young woman it portends illicit engagements, unless she chooses staid and moral companions. For a married woman, it foreshadows discontent and desire for pleasure outside the home.

To see others amorous, foretells that you will be persuaded to neglect your moral obligations. To see animals thus, denotes you will engage in degrading pleasures with fast men or women.

lute delightful company, happiness, success (gypsy folklore).

luxury to dream that you are surrounded by luxury, indicates much wealth, but dissipation and love of self will reduce your income.

For a poor woman to dream that she enjoys much luxury, denotes an early change in her circumstances.

lying down *see* ACTIONS.

lying in bed *see* FURNITURE.

lying to dream of lying is bad except for players and those who practice it professionally (gypsy folklore).

A dream of lying may be spurred by a dishonest action, or one which is out of character in waking life.

lynx *see* ANIMALS.

lyre to dream of listening to the music of a lyre, foretells chaste pleasures and congenial companionship. Business will run smoothly.

For a young woman to dream of playing on one, denotes that she will enjoy the undivided affection of a worthy man.

M

macaroni to dream of eating macaroni, denotes small losses. To see it in large quantities, denotes that you will save money by the strictest economy. For a young woman, this dream means that a stranger will enter her life.

mace to dream of mace is good, for mace comforts the heart (Artemidorus).

machine machines can be interpreted as that which drives the individual, both in a physical sense (the heart, brain, hormones, etc) and also in a psychological sense (the wishes, desires and emotions which motivate the individual).

mad dog to dream of seeing a mad dog, denotes that enemies will make scurrilous attacks upon you and your friends, but if you succeed in killing the dog, you will overcome adverse opinions and prosper greatly in a financial way.

madness to dream of being mad, shows trouble ahead for the dreamer. Sickness, by which you will lose property, is threatened.

To see others suffering under this malady, denotes inconstancy of friends and gloomy ending of bright expectations.

For a young woman to dream of madness, foretells disappointment in marriage and wealth.

madstone to see a madstone applied to a wound from the fangs of some mad animal, denotes that you will endeavour, to the limits of your energy, to shield self from the machinations of enemies, which will soon envelop you with the pall of dishonourable defeat.

maggots *see* INSECTS.

magician a dream predicting unexpected events, surprises (gypsy folklore).

magistrate to dream of a magistrate, foretells that you will be harassed with threats of law suits and losses in your business.

magnet a dream warning you to resist the snares that are across your path. To see a magnet denotes that you are planning to fascinate some other person (Raphael).

magnet to dream of a magnet, denotes you will make favourable opportunities for your own advancement in a material way. For a young woman to think a magnet is attracting her, is an omen of happy changes in her family.

magnifying-glass to look through a magnifying-glass in your dreams, means failure to accomplish your work in a satisfactory manner. For a woman to think she owns one, foretells she will encourage the attention of persons who will ignore her later.

magpie *see* BIRDS.

malice to dream that someone bears you malice denotes a sudden advancement to an important position (gypsy folklore).

mallet to dream of a mallet, denotes you will meet unkind treatment from friends on account of your ill health. Disorder in the home is indicated.

mallows to dream of eating mallows signifies exemption from trouble, as this herb soothes skin and digestive irritations (Artem-idorus). This is an unusually clear example of the folklore from which symbols and symbolism in dreams have been derived.

malt to dream of malt, betokens a pleasant existence and riches that will advance your station.

To dream of taking malted drinks, denotes that you will interest yourself in some dangerous affair, but will reap much benefit therefrom.

man to dream of a man, if handsome, well formed and supple, denotes that you will enjoy life vastly and come into rich possessions. If he is misshapen and sour-visaged, you will meet disappointments and many perplexities will involve you.

For a woman to dream of a handsome man, she is likely to have distinction offered her. If he is ugly, she will experience trouble through some one whom she considers a friend.

manners to dream of seeing ugly-mannered persons, denotes failure to carry out undertakings through the disagreeableness of a person connected with the affair.

If you meet people with affable manners, you will be pleasantly surprised by affairs of moment with you taking a favourable turn.

man-of-war to dream of a man-of-war, denotes long journeys and separation from country and friends, dissension in political affairs is portended.

If she is damaged, foreign elements will work damage to home interests.

If she is sailing upon rough seas, trouble with foreign powers may endanger private affairs.

mansion to dream that you are in a mansion where there is a haunted chamber, denotes sudden misfortune in the midst of contentment.

To dream of being in a mansion, indicates for you wealthy possessions.

To see a mansion from distant points, foretells future advancement.

manslaughter for a woman to dream that she sees, or is in any way connected with, manslaughter, denotes that she will be desperately scared lest her name be coupled with some scandalous sensation. *See* MURDER.

mantilla to dream of seeing a mantilla, denotes an unwise enterprise which will bring you into unfavourable notice.

manufactory to dream of a large manufactory, denotes unusual activity in business circles. *See* FACTORY.

mantle *see* CLOAK.

manure to dream of seeing manure, is a favourable omen. Much good will follow the dream. Farmers especially will feel a rise in fortune.

manuscript to dream of manuscript in an unfinished state, forebodes disappointment. If finished and clearly written, great hopes will be realised.

If you are at work on manuscript, you will have many fears for some cherished hope, but if you keep the blurs out of your work you will succeed in your undertakings. If it is rejected by the publishers, you will be hopeless for a time, but eventually your most sanguine desires will become a reality.

If you lose it, you will be subjected to disappointment.

If you see it burn, some work of your own will bring you profit and much elevation.

map to dream of examining a map denotes that you will leave your native land (gypsy folklore).

maple a dream of comfort and a happy life (gypsy folklore). The national emblem of Canada, indicating goodness, service, etc.

marble to dream of a marble quarry, denotes that you life will be a financial success, but that your social surroundings will be devoid of affection.

To dream of polishing marble, you will come into a pleasing inheritance.

To see it broken, you will fall into disfavour among your associates by defying all moral codes.

march to dream of marching to the strains of music, indicates that you are ambitious to become a soldier or a public official, but you should consider all things well before making final decision.

For women to dream of seeing men marching, foretells their inclination for men in public positions. They should be careful of their reputations, should they be thrown much with men.

To dream of the month of March, portends disappointing returns in business, and some woman will be suspicious of your honesty.

mare see ANIMALS.

marigolds these are the symbol of the constant lover, happy marriage, advancement, and riches (Raphael). It is called the flower of flame or light, and is also used to break the spells of enchantment.

mariner a dream denoting voyages (gypsy folklore).

market see FAIR.

marmalade to dream of eating marmalade, denotes sickness and much dissatisfaction

For a young woman to dream of making it, denotes unhappy domestic associations.

marmot to dream of seeing a marmot, denotes that sly enemies are approaching you in the shape of fair women.

For a young woman to dream of a marmot, foretells that temptation will beset her in the future.

marriage a dream invariably auguring sickness, death, etc. In the case of a single person, a dream of marriage may be wish-fulfilment, but it can also be an exploration of one's feelings towards marriage, or a safe experiment with the concept.

Symbolically, marriage may represent the 'marriage' of two different, yet coexistent, parts of the self, such as the conscious and the unconscious, or the impulsive and the considerate. It could also mean the marriage between two personality attributes, such as gentleness and courage.

Mars an unfortunate dream forecasting quarrels at home and abroad (gypsy folklore).

marsh to dream of walking in a marshy country signifies a troubled life. SWAMPS denote sorrows and difficulties. To escape them, future comfort. A dream of trying to plough a marsh denotes misery in spite of work (gypsy folklore).

martyr a dream of honour and public approbation (gypsy folklore).

mask a mask is the face that the dreamer presents to the world; the secret or undiscovered aspects of his personality hide behind this.

A mask can also be a face that the individual adopts when coping with certain situations; thus, a soldier in battle will adopt the warrior mask. This is not his 'everyday' face, but, given the situation that is being faced, a genuine one.

mason to dream that you see a mason plying his trade, denotes a rise in your circumstances and a more congenial social atmosphere will surround you.

If you dream of seeing a band of the order of masons in full regalia, it denotes that you will have others beside yourself to protect and keep from the evils of life.

masquerade to attend one is a dream of deceptive pleasure (gypsy folklore).

mast to dream of seeing the masts of ships, denotes long and pleasant voyages, the making of many new friends, and the gaining of new possessions.

To see the masts of wrecked ships, denotes sudden changes in your circumstances which will necessitate giving over anticipated pleasures.

If a sailor dreams of a mast, he will soon sail on an eventful trip.

master to dream that you have a master, is a sign of incompetence on your part to command others, and you will do better work under the leadership of some strong-willed person.

If you are a master, and command many people under you, you will excel in judgement in the fine points of life, and will hold high positions and possess much wealth.

mastiff *see* ANIMALS.

mat to dream that a door mat has been stolen forecasts that someone will try to enter your house (Raphael).

match to dream of matches, denotes prosperity and change when least expected.

To strike a match in the dark, unexpected news and fortune is foreboded.

matting to dream of matting, foretells pleasant prospects and cheerful news from the absent. If it is old or torn, you will have vexing things come before you.

mattress a mattress may represent feelings of comfort and security or a relaxed approach, either to life in general or to a particular situation. Mattresses can also function in dreams much the same way as beds, in that they may represent the dreamer's life as he or she has created it (the bed he has made to lie on). *See also* FURNITURE.

mausoleum to dream of a mausoleum, indicates the sickness, death, or trouble of some prominent friend.

To find yourself inside a mausoleum, foretells your own illness.

may bugs to dream of May bugs, denotes an ill-tempered companion where a congenial one was expected.

may to dream of the month of May, denotes prosperous times, and pleasure for the young.

To dream that nature appears freakish, denotes sudden sorrow and disappointment clouding pleasure.

maypole a dream denoting love and lovers (gypsy folklore) The maypole dance and festival had its origin in pagan sex-worship and Freudians would still regard it to be an erotic symbol.

meadow to dream of walking through pleasant meadows portends happiness (gypsy folklore).

meals to dream of meals, denotes that you will let trifling matters interfere with momentous affairs and business engagements.

measles to dream that you have measles, denotes much worry, and anxious care will interfere with your business affairs.

To dream that others have this disease, denotes that you will be troubled over the condition of others.

meat for a woman to dream of raw meat, denotes that she will meet with much discouragement in accomplishing her aims. If she sees cooked meat, it denotes that others will obtain the object for which she will strive.

mechanic to dream of a mechanic, denotes change in your dwelling place and a more active business. Advancement in wages usually follows after seeing mechanics at work on machinery.

medal to dream of receiving medals for good conduct denotes depravity and loss of character (Raphael). This may be a wish dream arising from having a guilty conscience.

medicine to dream of taking it with difficulty is a dream of physical distress.

melancholy to dream that you feel melancholy over any event, is a sign of disappointment in what was thought to be favourable undertakings.

To dream that you see others melancholy, denotes unpleasant interruption in affairs. To lovers, it brings separation.

melon *see* FRUIT.

memorandum to dream that you make memoranda, denotes that you will engage in an unprofitable business, and much worry will result for you.

To see others making a memorandum, signifies that some person will worry you with appeals for aid.

To lose your memorandum, you will experience a slight loss in trade.

To find a memorandum, you will assume new duties that will cause much pleasure to others.

memorial to dream of a memorial, signifies there will be occasion for you to show patient kindness, as trouble and sickness threatens your relatives.

memory given that we spend so much time dreaming every night, it must be accepted that the great majority of our dreams are forgotten. This is not due to any failure on our part. A combination of circumstances conspires to erase most dreams from our minds. If time has passed between dreaming and waking, the mind may not be sufficiently focused to remember it. Some dreams are confusing and, therefore, difficult to recall with any degree of accuracy. Some dreams are simply too disturbing for the dreamer to confront in waking life and are consequently repressed by the subconscious.

menagerie to dream of visiting a menagerie, denotes various troubles.

mendicant for a woman to dream of mendicants, she will meet with disagreeable interference in her plans for betterment and enjoyment.

mending to dream of mending soiled garments, denotes that you will undertake to right a wrong at an inopportune moment; but if the garment be clean, you will be successful in adding to your fortune.

For a young woman to dream of mending, foretells that she will be a systematic help to her husband.

menstruation a man who dreams of menstruation may be exploring his more creative and productive aspects.

A woman who has ceased to menstruate but who dreams of menstruation may be having difficulties coming to terms with ageing and loss of fertility. *See also* BODY; WOUND.

mercury to dream of mercury, is significant of unhappy changes through the constant oppression of enemies. For a woman to be suffering from mercurial poison, foretells she will be deserted by and separated from her family.

merry to dream being merry, or in merry company, denotes that pleasant events will engage you for a time, and affairs will assume profitable shapes.

meshes to dream of being entangled in the meshes of a net, or other like constructions, denotes that enemies will oppress you in time of seeming prosperity. To a young woman, this dream foretells that her environments will bring her into evil and consequent abandonment. If she succeeds in disengaging herself from the meshes, she will narrowly escape slander.

message to dream of receiving a message, denotes that changes will take place in your affairs.

To dream of sending a message, denotes that you will be placed in unpleasant situations.

metamorphose to dream of seeing anything metamorphose, denotes that sudden changes will take place in your life, for good or bad, as the metamorphose was pleasant or frightful.

mice *see* ANIMALS.

microscope to dream of a microscope, denotes you will experience failure or small returns in your enterprises.

midwife a dream denoting the revelation of secrets.

mile-post to dream you see or pass a mile-post, foretells that you will be assailed by doubtful fears in business or love. To see one down, portends accidents are threatening to give disorder to your affairs.

milk to drink milk in a dream denotes joy. To sell it, is a prediction of disappointment in love. To dream of milking a cow predicts abundance and good fortune (gypsy folklore).

A sexual interpretation of a dream about milk is that the milk represents semen and that it reflects the sexual desire of the male dreamer. Milk can also reflect a subconscious desire to return to the breast of the mother, or to another important female figure in the dreamer's life.

milking to dream of milking, and it flows in great streams from the udder, while the cow is restless and threatening, signifies you will see great opportunities withheld from you, but which will result in final favour for you.

mill a dream that denotes happiness and riches (gypsy folklore).

mill-dam to dream that you see clear water pouring over a mill-dam, foretells pleasant enterprises, either of a business or social nature. If the water is muddy or impure, you will meet with losses, and troubles will arise where pleasure was anticipated.

If the dam is dry, your business will assume shrunken proportions.

miller to see a miller in your dreams, signifies your surroundings will grow more hopeful. For a woman to dream of a miller failing in an attempt to start his mill, foretells she will be disappointed in her lover's wealth, as she will think him in comfortable circumstances.

mine to dream of being in a mine, denotes failure in affairs.

To own a mine, denotes future wealth. *See* COAL MINE, COLLIERY.

mineral to dream of minerals, denotes your present unpromising outlook will grow directly brighter. To walk over mineral land, signifies distress, from which you will escape and be bettered in your surroundings.

mineral water to dream of drinking mineral water, foretells fortune will favour your efforts, and you will enjoy your opportunities to satisfy your cravings for certain pleasures.

mining to see mining in your dreams, denotes that an enemy is seeking your ruin by bringing up past immoralities in your life. You will be likely to make unpleasant journeys, if you stand near the mine.

If you dream of hunting for mines, you will engage in worthless pursuits.

minister to dream of seeing a minister, denotes unfortunate changes and unpleasant journeys.

To hear a minister exhort, foretells that some designing person will influence you to evil.

To dream that you are a minister, denotes that you will usurp another's rights. *See* PREACHER and PRIEST.

mink to dream of a mink, denotes you will have sly enemies to overcome. If you kill one, you will win your desires. For a young woman to dream that she is partial to mink furs, she will find protection and love in some person who will be inordinately jealous.

minuet to dream of seeing the minuet danced, signifies a pleasant existence with congenial companions.

To dance it yourself, good fortune and domestic joys are foretold.

mire to dream of going through mire, indicates that your dearest wishes and plans will receive a temporary check by the intervention of unusual changes in your surroundings.

mirror *see* LOOKING GLASS.

miser like all dreams pertaining to money or hoards, this is unfavourable (gypsy folklore).

mist to dream that you are enveloped in a mist, denotes uncertain fortunes and domestic unhappiness. If the mist clears away, your troubles will be of short duration. To see others in a mist, you will profit by the misfortune of others.

mistletoe a dream of fortune and health (gypsy folklore). The legends attached to the plant justify this symbolism.

mocking-bird to see or hear a mocking-bird, signifies you will be invited to go on a pleasant visit to friends, and your affairs will move along smoothly and prosperously. For a woman to see a wounded or dead one, her disagreement with a friend or lover is signified.

models to dream of a model, foretells your social affairs will deplete your purse, and quarrels and regrets will follow. For a young woman to dream that she is a model or seeking to be one, foretells she will be entangled in a love affair which will give her trouble through the selfishness of a friend.

molasses to dream of molasses, is a sign that some one is going to extend you pleasant hospitality, and, through its acceptance, you will meet agreeable and fortunate surprises. To eat it, foretells that you will be discouraged and disappointed in love. To have it smeared on your clothing, denotes you will have disagreeable offers of marriage, and probably losses in business.

moles to dream of moles, indicates secret enemies.

To dream of catching a mole, you will overcome any opposition and rise to prominence.

To see moles, or such blemishes, on the person, indicates illness and quarrels.

money money represents things that the dreamer regards as valuable. It can also symbolize power and sex.

monk *see* ABBOT.

monkeys *see* ANIMALS.

monster a monster almost always represents FEAR in a dream. This may be fear the dreamer has of something within him or herself, such as an obsession or an overriding passion, or it may be fear of something that one does not understand properly, such as love or death. *See also* GIANT; OGRE.

moon the moon may represent that which the dreamer believes to be unattainable, or a desire for romance. The many characteristics of the moon are said to have the following mystic interpretations:

a brilliant moon this dream is said to predict love and good health to a wife, to a husband, increase in wealth.

a new moon advancement in business.

waning predicts the death of a great man.

a halo around the moon denotes pardon and deliverance through a female.

a red moon this dream predicts imminent voyages and pilgrimages.

a dull moon this predicts death or illness to wife, sister or female relative. It may also foretell perilous journeys, especially by sea, brain fever or eye trouble.

an obscure moon becoming bright is a prediction of profit to a woman and joy to a man. If the moon goes from *clearness to obscurity*, loss, sadness and misfortune are predicted.

two moons denote increase in rank and dignity.

When a beautiful woman dreams of the moon, the dream forecasts high standing, dignity and admiration. To thieves, murderers, etc, it denotes justice. To invalids it denotes danger of death or shipwreck. For a young girl or widow to dream of a full, dazzling moon, the prognostication is marriage; to a married woman it predicts the birth of a beautiful daughter and to a man it signifies the birth of a son.

morgue to dream that you visit a morgue searching for some one, denotes that you will be shocked by news of the death of a relative or friend.

To see many corpses there, much sorrow and trouble will come under your notice.

morning glory a hopeful, happy dream (gypsy folklore). A symbol of the resurrection (Smith).

Morocco to see morocco in your dreams, foretells that you will receive substantial aid from unexpected sources. Your love will be rewarded by faithfulness.

morose if you find yourself morose in dreams, you will awake to find the world, as far as you are concerned, going fearfully wrong.

To see others morose, portends unpleasant occupations and unpleasant companions.

mortgage to dream that you give a mortgage on your property, denotes that you are threatened with financial upheavals, which will throw you into embarrassing positions.

To take, or hold one, against others, is ominous of adequate wealth to liquidate your obligations.

To find yourself reading or examining mortgages, denotes great possibilities before you of love or gain.

To lose a mortgage, if it cannot be found again, implies loss and worry.

mortification to dream that you feel mortified over any deed committed by yourself, is a sign that you will be placed in an unenviable position before those to whom you most wish to appear honourable and just. Financial conditions will fall low.

To see mortified flesh, denotes disastrous enterprises and disappointment in love.

Moses to dream that you see Moses, means personal gain and a connubial alliance which will be a source of sweet congratulation to yourself.

mosquitoes *see* INSECTS.

moss a dream signifying the acquisition and hoarding of money (gypsy folklore).

mother to dream of your mother (living) denotes joy; if she is dead, sorrow (gypsy folklore). *See also* TYPICAL DREAMS.

mother-in-law to dream of your mother-in-law, denotes there will be pleasant reconciliation for you after some serious disagreement.

If a woman dreams of a dispute with her mother-in-law, she will find that quarrelsome and unfeeling people will give her annoyance.

moths *see* INSECTS.

mountain mountains can be construed as obstacles in one's path, difficulties that loom large ahead. A dream of heaviness, fear and trouble (Artemidorus). *See also* TYPICAL DREAMS.

mourning to dream that you wear mourning, omens ill luck and unhappiness.

If others wear it, there will be disturbing influences among your friends causing you unexpected dissatisfaction and loss. To lovers, this dream foretells misunderstanding and probable separation.

mouse *see* ANIMALS.

mouse-trap to see a mouse-trap in dreams, signifies your need to be careful of character, as wary persons have designs upon you.

To see it full of mice, you will likely fall into the hands of enemies.

To set a trap, you will artfully devise means to overcome your opponents. *See* MICE.

moustache to dream that you have a moustache, denotes that your egotism and effrontery will cause you a poor inheritance in worldly goods, and you will betray women to their sorrow.

If a woman dreams of admiring a moustache, her virtue is in danger, and she should be mindful of her conduct.

If a man dreams that he has his moustache shaved, he will try to turn from evil companions and pleasures, and seek to reinstate himself in former positions of honour.

mouth *see* BODY.

mud dreams of mud, accompanied by feelings of repulsion, suggest guilt feelings on the part of the dreamer, or a deep-seated belief that something is 'dirty' in sexual terms. Feeling 'soiled' by mud in a dream may suggest that the dreamer is suffering from depression, while dreaming of sinking in mud or QUICKSAND might suggest suppressed feelings of powerlessness or despair in the dreamer's waking life.

When diving the future, to dream of being covered with mud denotes possible slander (gypsy folklore). *See also* DIGGING; EXCREMENT; QUAGMIRE.

muff to dream of wearing a muff, denotes that you will be well provided for against the vicissitudes of fortune.

For a lover to see his sweetheart wearing a muff, denotes that a worthier man will usurp his place in her affections.

mulberry-tree a dream of increase of wealth, of abundance of goods (Artemidorus). A symbol of prosperity in Persia and Italy.

mule *see* ANIMALS.

murder committing murder, or desiring to commit murder, in a dream points to the expression in dream life of strong feelings that are repressed in waking life. This is often sexual desire but may also be emotions that the dreamer is unable to express satisfactorily. *See also* TYPICAL DREAMS.

muscle to dream of seeing your muscle well developed, you will have strange encounters with enemies, but you will succeed in surmounting their evil works, and gain fortune.

If they are shrunken, your inability to succeed in your affairs is portended. For a woman, this dream is prophetic of toil and hardships.

museum to dream of a museum, denotes you will pass through many and varied scenes in striving for what appears your rightful position. You will acquire useful knowledge, which will stand you in better light than if you had pursued the usual course to learning. If the museum is distasteful, you will have many causes for vexation.

mushrooms to dream of eating them denotes danger of death or personal sickness to the dreamer (gypsy folklore). Evidently an anxiety dream, expressed in the doubt of the mushrooms.

music the playing of music in a dream suggests self-expression. Thus, the person who dreams that he or she can suddenly play beautiful music on an instrument may be fulfilling a waking desire to be able to give vent to certain feelings or to use his or her creative talents.

A dream of ravishing music signifies sudden and delightful news. Harsh sounds denote the contrary (Artemidorus).

musical instruments to see musical instruments, denotes anticipated pleasures.

If they are broken, the pleasure will be marred by uncongenial companionship. For a young woman, this dream foretells for her the power to make her life what she will.

musk to dream of musk, foretells unexpected occasions of joy, and lovers will agree and cease to be unfaithful.

mussels to dream of water mussels, denotes small fortune, but contentment and domestic enjoyment.

mustard to see mustard growing, and green, foretells success and joy to the farmer, and to the seafaring it prognosticates wealth.

To eat mustard seed and feel the burning in your mouth, denotes that you will repent bitterly some hasty action, which has caused you to suffer.

To dream of eating green mustard cooked, indicates the lavish waste of fortune, and mental strain.

For a young woman to eat newly grown mustard, foretells that she will sacrifice wealth for personal desires.

mute to converse with a mute in your dreams, foretells that unusual crosses in your life will fit you for higher positions, which will be tendered you.

To dream that you are a mute, portends calamities and unjust persecution.

myrrh to see myrrh in a dream, signifies your investments will give satisfaction. For a young woman to dream of myrrh, brings a pleasing surprise to her in the way of a new and wealthy acquaintance.

myrtle to see myrtle in foliage and bloom in your dream, denotes that your desires will be gratified, and pleasures will possess you.

For a young woman to dream of wearing a sprig of myrtle, foretells to her an early marriage with a well-to do and intelligent man.

mystery to find yourself bewildered by some mysterious event, denotes that strangers will harass you with their troubles and claim your aid. It warns you also of neglected duties, for which you feel much aversion. Business will wind you into unpleasant complications.

To find yourself studying the mysteries of creation, denotes that a change will take place in your life, throwing you into a higher atmosphere of research and learning, and thus advancing you nearer the attainment of true pleasure and fortune.

N

nails to see nails in your dreams, indicates much toil and small recompense.

To deal in nails, shows that you will engage in honourable work, even if it be lowly.

To see rusty or broken nails, indicates sickness and failure in business.

naked a dream of sickness, poverty, affront, fatigue. Invariably ominous according to older interpreters. Modern students, however, attribute to it a totally different significance; holding it in some instances as a wish dream, in others as an erotic dream and again as a dream symbolizing freedom from social restraint. The theory of the subconscious and its warnings, etc, is, however, in accord with the older school, for the dream of nakedness might readily originate in fear, especially with women who habitually devote a large amount of thought to clothes. *See also* TYPICAL DREAMS.

napkin to dream of a napkin, foretells convivial entertainment in which you will figure prominently. For a woman to dream of soiled napkins, foretells that humiliating affairs will thrust themselves upon her.

navy to dream of the navy, denotes victorious struggles with unsightly obstacles, and the promise of voyages and tours of recreation. If in your dream you seem frightened or disconcerted, you will have strange obstacles to overcome before you reach fortune. A dilapidated navy is an indication of unfortunate friendships in business or love.

nearsighted to dream that you are nearsighted, signifies embarrassing failure and unexpected visits from unwelcome persons. For a young woman, this dream foretells unexpected rivalry.

To dream that your sweetheart is nearsighted, denotes that she will disappoint you.

neck a dream of power, honour, riches. Imperfections or ailments of the neck, however, predict sickness (Artemidorus).

necklace a dream of riches and honour. If you break the necklace it predicts misfortune (gypsy folklore).

necromancer to dream of a necromancer and his arts, denotes that you are threatened with strange acquaintances who will influence you for evil.

nectar a dream of drinking nectar predicts riches, honour and a long life (gypsy folklore). Nectar was the drink of the ancient gods and this is the source of the symbolism.

need a dream of need denotes wealth in store (gypsy folklore). The shrewd interpreter might easily infer that the anxiety that roused the dream would give birth to the frugality or thrift that tend to accumulate wealth.

needles a dream of disputes and quarrels (gypsy folklore).

neighbour to see your neighbours in your dreams, denotes many profitable hours will be lost in useless strife and gossip. If they appear sad, or angry, it foretells dissension and quarrels.

nephew to dream of your nephew, denotes you are soon to come into a pleasing competency, if he is handsome and well looking; otherwise, there will be disappointment and discomfort for you.

nest if the nest is full of eggs it is a dream predicting profit, domestic happiness or success in love. A nest with broken eggs, or dead birds reflects distress and desolation, and a feeling of failure and hoplessness.

net to dream of being entangled in a net denotes worry and a powerful enemy who is attempting to ensnare you (gypsy folklore).

nettles to dream of stinging yourself denotes striving to attain desire. In youth it predicts love that will risk all.

new year to dream of the new year, signifies prosperity and connubial anticipations. If you contemplate the new year in weariness, engagement will be entered into inauspiciously.

news to hear good news in a dream, denotes that you will be fortunate in affairs, and have harmonious companions; but if the news be bad, contrary conditions will exist.

newspaper reporter if in your dreams you unwillingly see them, you will be annoyed with small talk, and perhaps quarrels of a low character.

If you are a newspaper reporter in your dreams, there will be a varied course of travel offered you, though you may experience unpleasant situations, yet there will be some honour and gain attached.

newspaper to dream of buying and selling newspapers denotes hard work and small profit. To read one indicates deception (gypsy folklore).

niece for a woman to dream of her niece, foretells she will have unexpected trials and much useless worry in the near future.

night to be suddenly overtaken by night refers to the sudden appearance of an rival. To walk on a dark night denotes grief, disappointment and loss. It is ominous to dream of night-birds, with the exception of the nightingale, which denotes joyful news to the dreamer. If the dreamer is a married woman, she will have children who will be great singers (Artemidorus). It is said that Jenny Lind's mother dreamed of a nightingale. *See also* TIME.

nightgown to dream of wearing a nightgown denotes an honourable career. To dream of tearing the nightgown signifies that you feel that you have commited a hasty action (gypsy folklore).

nightingale *see* NIGHT.

nightmares the content of a nightmare comes second in importance to the fear that the dreamer necessarily feels while having the nightmare. That is to say that any interpretation of the nightmare has to acknowledge first that the fear is genuine and that it will be reflected in some way in the dreamer's waking thoughts. If the source of this fear in waking life can be pinpointed, (fear of death, fear of one's sexuality, etc) then the interpretation of the other elements of the nightmare will be more straightforward.

nine *see* NUMBERS.

ninepins to dream that you play ninepins, denotes that you are foolishly wasting your energy and opportunities. You should be careful in the selection of companions. All phases of this dream are bad.

nobility to dream of fraternizing with the nobility, signifies social downfall (gypsy folklore).

noise if you hear a strange noise in your dream, unfavourable news is presaged. If the noise awakes you, there will be a sudden change in your affairs.

noodles to dream of noodles, denotes an abnormal appetite and desires. There is little good in this dream.

nose *see* BODY.

notary to dream of a notary, is a prediction of unsatisfied desires, and probable lawsuits. For a woman to associate with a notary, foretells she will rashly risk her reputation, in gratification of foolish pleasure.

November to dream of November, augers a season of indifferent success in all affairs.

numbers numbers in dreams can be meaningful in relation to the person who is dreaming; for example, two may be significant to a person who has two children. Numbers are also imbued with a more general symbolism.

one may mean unity, wholeness, or the self. In some cases it may be a symbol for the phallus, or represent the male.

two can mean balance between two things, a complementary relationship, two alternatives that are open, or two things that are in opposition.

three may symbolize the genitals of the male, the threesome of two parents and child, or the Holy Trinity.

four may stand for stability and the status quo, the four seasons and the four elements being an essential part of the world as we know it to be.

five represents the human body—five fingers, five toes, five senses, the combination of head, arms and legs.

six is associated with balance, and occasionally sex.

seven represents spirituality or something that is sacred.

eight is symbolic of death and rebirth or resurrection.

nine is a symbol of pregnancy.

ten is a symbol of male and female as one.

twelve is a symbol of time or the whole year.

twenty-four is a symbol of the cycle of night and day.

zero may be a symbol for the female.

numbness a dream implying futile labour and discouragement.

nun *see* ABBOT.

nuptial for a woman to dream of her nuptials, she will soon enter upon new engagements, which will afford her distinction, pleasure, and harmony. S*ee* MARRIAGE.

nurse a nurse is a symbol of caring, a dream of being tended by a nurse may be compensation for love that is felt to be lacking in waking life. The caring or nurturing may occasionally have sexual significance. To dream of a nurse denotes sickness, sorrow and trouble (gypsy folklore).

nursing for a woman to dream of nursing her baby, denotes pleasant employment.

For a young woman to dream of nursing a baby, foretells that she will occupy positions of honour and trust.

For a man to dream of seeing his wife nurse their baby, denotes harmony in his pursuits.

nut trees to see nut TREES and to crack and eat their FRUIT signifies riches gathered at great pains. Hidden nuts denote the discovery of treasure (Artemidorus).

nutmeg to dream of eating one is a dream of sickness. To grate one is an indication of victory despite obstacles (gypsy folklore).

nuts if the kernels are well-filled this is a dream of riches, happiness and honours. Shrivelled kernels denote disappointment (gypsy folklore).

nymph to see nymphs bathing in clear water, denotes that passionate desires will find an ecstatic realisation. Convivial entertainment will enchant you.

To see them out of their sphere, denotes disappointment with the world.

For a young woman to see them bathing, denotes that she will have great favour and pleasure, but they will not rest strictly within the moral code. To dream that she impersonates a nymph, is a sign that she is using her attractions for selfish purposes, and thus the undoing of men.

O

oak to dream of seeing a forest of oaks, signifies great prosperity in all conditions of life.

To see an oak full of acorns, denotes increase and promotion.

If blasted oak, it denotes sudden and shocking surprises.

For sweethearts to dream of oaks, denotes that they will soon begin life together under favourable circumstances.

oar a dream that predicts a long life, riches, happiness (Artemidorus). The symbol of strength, longevity, etc. To dream of losing an oar is said to refer to the death of the dreamer's father, mother or someone to whom he or she looks for protection (gypsy folklore).

oasis an oasis in a dream may symbolize something, particularly an emotion, that has been missing in the dreamer's life and without which he or she feels barren.

oath whenever you take an oath in your dreams, prepare for dissension and altercations on waking.

oatmeal to dream of eating oatmeal, signifies the enjoyment of worthily earned fortune.

For a young woman to dream of preparing it for the table, denotes that she will soon preside over the destiny of others.

oats a dream denoting success, to each after his own desire (gypsy folklore). Agricultural symbols are invariably auspicious.

obedience to dream that you render obedience to another, foretells for you a common place, a pleasant but uneventful period of life.

If others are obedient to you, it shows that you will command fortune and high esteem.

obelisk a dream of fame and wealth, of honours to be conferred (gypsy folklore).

obituary to dream of writing an obituary, denotes that unpleasant and discordant duties will devolve upon you.

If you read one, news of a distracting nature will soon reach you.

obligation to dream of obligating yourself in any incident, denotes

261

that you will be fretted and worried by the thoughtless complaints of others.

If others obligate themselves to you, it portends that you will win the regard of acquaintances and friends.

obscurity to dream that the SUN is obscured denotes damage to the reputation; to dream that the MOON is obscured affects the life in a lesser degree (gypsy folklore).

observatory to dream of viewing the heavens and beautiful landscapes from an observatory, denotes your swift elevation to prominent positions and places of trust.

For a young woman this dream signals the realisation of the highest earthly joys. If the heavens are clouded, your highest aims will miss materialisation.

obstacles obstacles that the dreamer encounters in dream life will be reflected by inhibitions, uncertainties or restrictions in waking life.

Confronting an obstacle in a dream may point to a need for the dreamer to overcome a fear in waking life.

occultist to dream that you listen to the teachings of an occultist, denotes that you will strive to elevate others to a higher plane of justice and forbearance. If you accept his views, you will find honest delight by keeping your mind and person above material frivolities and pleasures.

ocean the ocean was the ancient symbol of life. In a dream a calm ocean indicates good, a stormy one ill and a smooth ocean denotes accomplishment in love and in life. *See also* WATER.

October to imagine you are in October is ominous of gratifying success in your undertakings. You will also make new acquaintances which will ripen into lasting friendships.

oculist a dream denoting some fault to repair, some evil or injury to confess (gypsy folklore). To dream of consulting an oculist, denotes that you will be dissatisfied with your progress in life, and will use artificial means of advancement.

odd-fellow to dream of this order, signifies that you will have sincere friends, and misfortune will touch you but lightly.

To join this order, foretells that you will win distinction and conjugal bliss.

odour to dream of inhaling sweet odours, is a sign of a beautiful woman ministering to your daily life, and successful financiering.

To smell disgusting odours, foretells unpleasant disagreements and unreliable servants.

offence to dream of being offended, denotes that errors will be detected in your conduct, which will cause you inward rage while attempting to justify yourself. To give offence, predicts for you many struggles before reaching your aims.

For a young woman to give, or take offence, signifies that she will regret hasty conclusions, and disobedience to parents or guardian.

offerings and vows to the gods signify a desire to return to virtue and divine love (gypsy folklore).

office to be deposed from office is a dream auguring ill, and if the dreamer be sick it presages death (Artemidorus).

offspring to dream of your own offspring, denotes cheerfulness and the merry voices of neighbours and children.

To see the offspring of domestic animals, denotes increase in prosperity.

ogre dreams of encounters with ogres will often be an expression of the dreamer's attitudes to authority, or perhaps a father figure. *See also* GIANT and MONSTER.

oil dreaming of oil may indicate a need to 'lubricate' a relationship in order to keep it running along smoothly, whether by adopting peacekeeping tactics in a difference of opinion or by suppressing one's own feelings in order to keep things on an even keel.

oilcloth to dream of oilcloth is a warning that you will meet coldness and treachery.

To deal in it, denotes uncertain speculations.

ointment a dream of illness (gypsy folklore).

old age a dream denoting wisdom (gypsy folklore).

old woman a fortunate dream. To dream of courting and marrying an old woman is also fortunate, but you will also have criticism from some quarters (Artemidorus).

olive *see* FRUIT.

olive tree peace, delight, dignity and the attainment of desire (Artemidorus).

omelette to see omelette being served in your dream, warns you of flattery and deceit, which is about to be used against you.

To eat it, shows that you will be imposed upon by some one seemingly worthy of your confidence.

omnibus to dream that you are being drawn through the streets in an omnibus, foretells misunderstandings with friends, and unwise promises will be made by you.

one *see* NUMBERS.

one-eyed to see one-eyed creatures in your dreams, is portentous of an overwhelming intimation of secret intriguing against your fortune and happiness.

onions dreaming of onions denotes luck both good and bad. To eat onions predicts receiving money, discovery of lost or stolen articles or a faithful but hasty sweetheart. Also attacks from thieves and failure of crops. To gather onions, joyful news, recovery from illness and a speedy removal (Artemidorus).

opal a dream of deceitful security (gypsy folklore). The bad luck attributed to the gem coincides with the interpretation.

opera to dream of attending an opera, denotes that you will be entertained by congenial friends, and find that your immediate affairs will be favourable.

opium to dream of opium, signifies strangers will obstruct your chances of improving your fortune, by sly and seductive means.

opulence for a young woman to dream that she lives in fairy like opulence, denotes that she will be deceived, and will live for a time in luxurious ease and splendour, to find later that she is mated with shame and poverty. When young women dream that they are enjoying solid and real wealth and comforts, they will always wake to find some real pleasure, but when abnormal or fairy-like dreams of luxury and joy seem to encompass them, their waking moments will be filled with disappointments; as the dreams are warnings, super-induced by their practicality being supplanted by their excitable imagination and lazy desires, which should be overcome with energy, and the replacing of practicality on her base. No young woman should fill her mind with idle day dreams, but energetically strive to carry forward noble ideals and thoughts, and promising and helpful dreams will come to her while she restores physical energies in sleep. *See* WEALTH.

oranges *see* FRUIT.

orang-utan to dream of an orang-utan, denotes that some person is falsely using your influence to further selfish schemes. For a young woman, it portends an unfaithful lover.

orator being under the spell of an orator's eloquence, denotes that you will heed the voice of flattery to your own detriment, as you will be persuaded into offering aid to unworthy people.

If a young woman falls in love with an orator, it is proof that in her loves she will be affected by outward show.

orchards dreaming of orchards in FRUIT denotes abundance. If there are fountains in the orchard this refers to pleasure and great wit. Barren trees in an orchard bear a contrary meaning (Artemidorus).

orchestra an orchestra playing harmoniously is indicative of the elements in the waking life of the dreamer working together to create a satisfying and harmonious whole. More specifically, it can be a sign of a contented relationship with oneself.

organ the sound of a church organ augurs happiness and prosperity (Raphael).

organist to see an organist in your dreams, denotes a friend will cause you much inconvenience from hasty action. For a young woman to dream that she is an organist, foretells she will be so exacting in her love that she will be threatened with desertion.

ornament a dream denoting want and extreme poverty as a result of extravagance (Raphael).

orphan condoling with orphans in a dream, means that the unhappy cares of others will touch your sympathies and cause you to sacrifice much personal enjoyment.

If the orphans be related to you, new duties will come into your life, causing estrangement from friends ant from some person held above mere friendly liking.

ostrich *see* BIRDS.

otter *see* ANIMALS.

ottoman dreams in which you find yourself luxuriously reposing upon an ottoman, discussing the intricacies of love with your sweetheart, foretells that envious rivals will seek to defame you in the eyes of your affianced, and a hasty marriage will be advised.

ouija board to dream of working on an ouija board, foretells the miscarriage of plans and unlucky partnerships. To fail to work, one is ominous of complications, caused by substituting pleasure for business. If it writes fluently, you may expect fortunate results from some well-planned enterprise.

oven an oven may represent pregnancy or the womb. It may also represent one's ability to change as one grows and develops.

overalls for a woman to dream that she sees a man wearing overalls, she will be deceived as to the real character of her lover. If a wife, she will be deceived in her husband's frequent absence, and the real cause will create suspicions of his fidelity.

overboard to fall overboard from a sailing vessel denotes poverty, imprisonment and sickness (Raphael). This is a dream reflecting anxiety.

overcoat to dream of an overcoat, denotes you will suffer from contrariness, exhibited by others. To borrow one, foretells you will be unfortunate through mistakes made by strangers. If you see or are wearing a handsome new overcoat, you will be exceedingly fortunate in realising your wishes.

owl *see* BIRDS.

oxen *see* ANIMALS.

oyster shells *see* ANIMALS.

oysters *see* ANIMALS.

P

pacify to endeavour to pacify suffering ones, denotes that you will be loved for your sweetness of disposition. To a young woman, this dream is one of promise of a devoted husband or friends.

Pacifying the anger of others, denotes that you will labour for the advancement of others.

If a lover dreams of soothing the jealous suspicions of his sweetheart, he will find that his love will be unfortunately placed.

packet to dream of seeing a packet coming in, foretells that some pleasant recreation is in store for you.

To see one going out, you will experience slight losses and disappointments.

packing packing in a dream indicates a desire that the dreamer has for a change of some sort, getting away from old circumstances and emotions, possibly fulfilling a need for freedom. Dreaming that one is having difficulty in making up one's mind what to pack, or finding it hard to close and fasten the suitcase, would therefore indicate that the dreamer is as yet mentally unprepared for the changes that lie in store.

padlock a padlock denotes mysteries to be solved (gypsy folklore). It is also a Christian symbol of silence.

page to see a page, denotes that you will contract a hasty union with one unsuited to you. You will fail to control your romantic impulses.

If a young woman dreams she acts as a page, it denotes that she is likely to participate in some foolish escapade.

pagoda to see a pagoda in your dreams, denotes that you will soon go on a long desired journey.

If a young woman finds herself in a pagoda with her sweetheart, many unforeseen events will transpire before her union is legalised. An empty one, warns her of separation from her lover.

pail to dream of full pails of milk, is a sign of fair prospects and pleasant associations.

An empty pail is a sign of famine, or bad crops.

For a young woman to be carrying a pail, denotes household employment.

pain to dream that you are in pain, will make sure of your own unhappiness. This dream foretells useless regrets over some trivial transaction.

To see others in pain, warns you that you are making mistakes in your life.

painting a dream of painting a house denotes sickness in the family, but thrift and luck in business. To paint beautiful landscapes denotes poverty and false hopes (gypsy folklore).

palace a good dream foretelling wealth and dignity (gypsy folklore)

palisade to dream of the palisades, denotes that you will alter well-formed plans to please strangers, and by so doing, you will impair your own interests.

pall to dream of a body being borne to the grave foretells that the dreamer will attend a wedding.

pall-bearer to dream of a pall-bearer, indicates some enemy will provoke your ill feeling, by constant attacks on your integrity. If you see a pall-bearer, you will antagonise worthy institutions, and make yourself obnoxious to friends.

pallet to dream of a pallet, denotes that you will suffer temporary uneasiness over your love affairs. For a young woman, it is a sign of a jealous rival.

palm a dream foretelling success and prosperity. To a married woman it refers to children, to a single woman it is a prediction of marriage (Artemidorus). The palm is the Christian emblem of victory.

palm tree a dream foreshadowing great joy (gypsy folklore). The sacred tree of lower Egypt, also the Tree of Life (Egyptian). The Scriptural symbol for the righteous and godly.

palmistry for a young woman to dream of palmistry, foretells she will be the object of suspicion.

If she has her palms read, she will have many friends of the opposite sex, but her own sex will condemn her. If she reads others' hands, she will gain distinction by her intelligent bearing. If a minister's hand, she will need friends, even in her elevation.

palsy to dream that you are afflicted with palsy, denotes that you are making unstable contracts.

To see your friend so afflicted, there will be uncertainty as to his faithfulness and sickness, too, may enter your home.

For lovers to dream that their sweethearts have palsy, signifies that dissatisfaction over some question will mar their happiness.

pancake to dream of eating pancakes, denotes that you will have excellent success in all enterprises undertaken at this time.

To cook them, denotes that you will be economical and thrifty in your home.

pane of glass to dream that you handle a pane of glass, denotes that you are dealing in uncertainties. If you break it, your failure will be accentuated.

To talk to a person through a pane of glass, denotes that there are obstacles in your immediate future, and they will cause you no slight inconvenience.

panic panic felt by dreaming will have its origin in something in the dreamer's life that is causing similar feelings that need to be dealt with. *See also* FEAR.

panorama to dream of a panorama, denotes that you will change your occupation or residence. You should curb your inclinations for change of scene and friends.

pansy this dream foretells of a constant sweetheart, but also great poverty. The pansy is the emblem of remembrance and kind thought.

panther *see* ANIMALS.

pantomime a dream denoting living among deceitful persons (gypsy folklore).

paper writing paper that has not been written on may represent things that have gone unsaid or feelings that have not been expressed by the dreamer.

Wrapping paper can be construed, in certain contexts, as either the dreamer's protection against the world, or the persona he or she adopts to show to the world. To dream of white paper denotes innocence. If the paper is written on then deception is a possibility. To dream of printed paper denotes good fortune (gypsy folklore).

parables to dream of parables, denotes that you will be undecided as to the best course to pursue in dissenting to some business complication. To the lover, or young woman, this is a prophecy of misunderstandings and disloyalty.

paradise a good dream to each according to his desire and calling (Raphael).

paralysis dreams of paralysis may be a reflection of the way in which the dreamer is feeling in waking life—unable to function properly, helpless, etc. They may, however, in a semi-wakened state, merely be a subconscious acknowledgement of the fact that while the individual is dreaming, the major muscle groups are rendered inactive. Can be a dream denoting the approach of illness (gypsy folklore).

parasol to dream of a parasol, denotes, for married people, illicit enjoyments.

If a young woman has this dream, she will engage in many flirtations, some of which will cause her interesting disturbances, lest her lover find out her inclinations. *See* UMBRELLA.

parcel parcels and packages can be interpreted in a similar fashion to LETTERs. An unopened parcel or package is indicative of feelings yet to be explored or self-knowledge yet to be acquired.

pardon to dream that you are endeavouring to gain pardon for an offence which you never committed, denotes that you will be troubled, and seemingly with cause, over your affairs, but it will finally appear that it was for your advancement. If offence was committed, you will realise embarrassment in affairs.

To receive pardon, you will prosper after a series of misfortunes.

parents parents in dreams rarely represent real parents, rather the male and female aspects of the dreamer's nature, i.e. the man and woman who are within everybody.

A dream of warning, especially if the parents are dead. If you have been foolish their visit is to rebuke and to warn you of danger (Raphael). It may be a dream inspired by a guilty conscience, expressed through the symbolism of the subconsciousness.

park to walk through a park, health and happiness (Raphael). The difference in the symbolism of the park and that of GROVES and FORESTS is due to the difference in the ages to which they belonged respectively, the park being a medieval institution, while the grove dates to denote antiquity.

parrot *see* BIRDS.

parsley to dream of parsley, denotes hard-earned success, usually the surroundings of the dreamer are healthful and lively.

To eat parsley, is a sign of good health, but the care of a large family will be your portion.

parsnips to see or eat parsnips, is a favourable omen of successful business or trade, but love will take on unfavourable and gloomy aspects.

parting to dream of parting with friends and companions, denotes that many little vexations will come into your daily life.

If you part with enemies, it is a sign of success in love and business.

partner to dream of seeing your business partner with a basket of crockery on his back, and, letting it fall, gets it mixed with other crockery, denotes your business will sustain a loss through the indiscriminate dealings of your partner. If you reprimand him for it, you will, to some extent, recover the loss.

partnership to dream of forming a partnership with a man, denotes uncertain and fluctuating money affairs. If your partner be a woman, you will engage in some enterprise which you will endeavour to keep hidden from friends.

To dissolve an unpleasant partnership, denotes that things will arrange themselves agreeable to your desires; but if the partnership was pleasant, there will be disquieting news and disagreeable turns in your affairs.

partridges *see* BIRDS.

party to dream of an unknown party of men assaulting you for your money or valuables, denotes that you will have enemies banded together against you. If you escape uninjured, you will overcome any opposition, either in business or love.

To dream of attending a party of any kind for pleasure, you will find that life has much good, unless the party is an inharmonious one.

passenger to dream that you see passengers coming in with their luggage, denotes improvement in your surroundings. If they are leaving you will lose an opportunity of gaining some desired property. If you are one of the passengers leaving home, you will be dissatisfied with your present living and will seek to change it.

passing bell to dream of hearing the bell that was once rung to announce a passing funeral denotes the illness of the dreamer or of a near relative (Raphael).

password to dream of a password, foretells you will have influential aid in some slight trouble soon to attack you. For a woman to dream that she has given away the password, signifies she will endanger her own standing through seeking frivolous or illicit desires.

past we may dream of people and things from our past in order to try to recreate the way in which we felt at that time, or alternatively, in order to work out unresolved inner conflicts about those times and to express emotions that have been previously repressed.

pasteboard to dream of pasteboard, denotes that unfaithful friends will deceive you concerning important matters. To cut pasteboard, you will throw aside difficulties in your struggle to reach eminent positions.

pastry to dream of pastry, denotes that you will be deceived by some artful person. To eat it, implies heartfelt friendships. If a young woman dreams that she is cooking it, she will fail to deceive others as to her real intentions.

patches for a woman to dream of patching her husband's or her children's garments is an excellent prediction of wellbeing and riches (Raphael). Frugality and thrift are invariably recorded as happy omens.

patent medicine to dream that you resort to patent medicine in your search for health, denotes that you will use desperate measures in advancing your fortune, but you will succeed, to the disappointment of the envious.

To see or manufacture patent medicines, you will rise from obscurity to positions above your highest imaginings.

patent to dream of securing a patent, denotes that you will be careful and painstaking with any task you set about to accomplish. If you fail in securing your patent, you will suffer failure for the reason that you are engaging in enterprises for which you have no ability.

If you buy one, you will have occasion to make a tiresome and fruitless journey.

To see one, you will suffer unpleasantness from illness.

path a difficult, narrow, treacherous or winding path will point to troubles in waking life. A smooth, well-trodden path will indicate that the dreamer is adopting a 'safe' approach to life, following in the footsteps of others perhaps.

paunch to see a large paunch, denotes wealth and the total absence of refinement.

To see a shrivelled paunch, foretells illness and reverses.

pauper to dream that you are a pauper, implies unpleasant happenings for you.

To see paupers, denotes that there will be a call upon your generosity.

pebbles for a young woman to dream of a pebble-strewn walk, she will be vexed with many rivals and find that there are others with charms that attract besides her own. She who dreams of pebbles is selfish and should cultivate leniency towards others' faults.

pawnbroker a dream of poverty, losses and disappointments (gypsy folklore).

peaches *see* FRUIT.

peacock *see* BIRDS.

pearls a dream of tears (gypsy folklore). The jewel is also symbolic of weeping, especially to brides.

pears *see* FRUIT.

peas a dream denoting success in business (Artemidorus).

pecans to dream of eating this appetising nut, you will see one of your dearest plans come to full fruition, and seeming failure prove a prosperous source of gain.

To see them growing among leaves, signifies a long, peaceful existence. Failure in love or business will follow in proportion as the pecan is decayed.

If they are difficult to crack and the fruit is small, you will succeed after much trouble and expense, but returns will be meagre.

pelican to dream of a pelican, denotes a mingling of disappointments with successes.

To catch one, you will be able to overcome disappointing influences.

To kill one, denotes that you will cruelly set aside the rights of others.

To see them flying, you are threatened with changes, which will impress you with ideas of uncertainty as to good.

pen pencil pens and pencils are means of communication. Occasionally, a pen or a pencil may act as a dream metaphor for the male sexual organ.

Dreaming of a pen is said to predict adversity and loss to a business man (gypsy folklore). Probably derived from the idea that knowledge interfered with the accomplishment of business.

penalties to dream that you have penalties imposed upon you, foretells that you will have duties that will rile you and find you rebellious.

To pay a penalty, denotes sickness and financial loss. To escape the payment, you will be victor in some contest.

pencil to dream of pencils, denotes favourable occupations. For a young woman to write with one, foretells she will be fortunate in marriage, if she does not rub out words; in that case, she will be disappointed in her lover.

penis *see* BODY.

penitentiary to dream of a penitentiary, denotes you will have engagements which will, unfortunately, result in your loss. To be an inmate of one, foretells discontent in the home and failing business. To escape from one, you will overcome difficult obstacles.

penny to dream of pennies, denotes unsatisfactory pursuits. Business will suffer, and lovers and friends will complain of the smallness of affection. To lose them, signifies small deference and failures. To find them, denotes that prospects will advance to your improvement. To count pennies, foretells that you will be business-like and economical.

pension to dream of drawing a pension, foretells that you will be aided in your labours by friends.

To fail in your application for a pension, denotes that you will lose in an undertaking and suffer the loss of friendships.

people *see* CROWD.

pepper a dream denoting truthfulness to the verge of irritation (gypsy folklore).

peppermint to dream of peppermint, denotes pleasant entertainment and interesting affairs.

To see it growing, denotes that you will participate in some pleasure in which there will be a dash of romance.

To enjoy drinks in which there is an effusion of peppermint, denotes that you will enjoy assignations with some attractive and fascinating person. To a young woman, this dream warns her against seductive pleasures.

performing *see* ACTING.

perfume to compound petals and to distribute perfume among friends is a dream predicting agreeable news. To receive perfume as a gift denotes news in accordance with whether the scent is agreeable or otherwise.

perspiration to dream that you are in a perspiration, foretells that you will come out of some difficulty, which has caused much gossip, with new honours.

pest or **pestilence** a dream threatening sickness and misfortune (gypsy folklore).

pets dreams of puppies or kittens may not so much reflect a woman's desire to own a cute baby animal as to have a child of her own. To dream of having one denotes protection by friends. *See also* ANIMALS.

petticoat a dream of trouble and sorrow (Raphael).

pewter to dream of pewter, foretells straitened circumstances.

phantom to dream that a phantom pursues you, foretells strange and disquieting experiences.

To see a phantom fleeing from you, foretells that trouble will assume smaller proportions. *See* GHOST.

pheasants *see* BIRDS.

phoenix a dream of renewed health and vigour (gypsy folklore). The symbol of immortality, resurrection, the soul.

phosphorus to dream of seeing phosphorus, is indicative of evanescent joys. For a young woman, it foretells a brilliant but brief success with admirers.

photographs photographs are images; a photograph of the past in a dream represents the dreamer's image of the past, while a photo of the dreamer him or herself will represent the dreamer's self-image.

A dream warning you to make a final settlement of your affairs (gypsy folklore). *See also* IMAGES.

physician for a young woman to dream of a physician, denotes that she is sacrificing her beauty in engaging in frivolous pastimes. If she is sick and thus dreams, she will have sickness or worry, but will soon overcome them, unless the physician appears very anxious, and then her trials may increase, ending in loss and sorrow.

piano to dream of seeing a piano, denotes some joyful occasion.

To hear sweet and voluptuous harmony from a piano, signals success and health. If discordant music is being played, you will have many exasperating matters to consider. Sad and plaintive music, foretells sorrowful tidings.

To find your piano broken and out of tune, portends dissatisfaction with your own accomplishments and disappointment in the failure of your friends or children to win honours.

To see an old-fashioned piano, denotes that you have, in trying moments, neglected the advice and opportunities of the past, and are warned not to do so again.

For a young woman to dream that she is executing difficult, but entrancing music, she will succeed in winning an indifferent friend to be a most devoted and loyal lover.

pickaxe a warning of coming evil, perhaps destruction by fire (gypsy folklore).

pickles to dream of pickles, denotes that you will follow worthless pursuits if you fail to call energy and judgement to your aid.

For a young woman to dream of eating pickles, foretells an unambitious career.

To dream of pickles, denotes vexation in love, but final triumph.

For a young woman to dream that she is eating them, or is hungry for them, foretells she will find many rivals, and will be overcome unless she is careful of her private affairs. Impure pickles, indicate disappointing engagements and love quarrels.

pickpocket to dream of a pickpocket, foretells some enemy will succeed in harassing and causing you loss. For a young woman to have her pocket picked, denotes she will be the object of some person's envy and spite, and may lose the regard of a friend through these evil machinations, unless she keeps her own counsel. If she picks others' pockets, she will incur the displeasure of a companion by her coarse behaviour.

picnic to dream of attending a picnic, foreshadows success and real enjoyment.

Dreams of picnics, bring undivided happiness to the young.

Storms, or any interfering elements at a picnic, implies the temporary displacement of assured profit and pleasure in love or business.

pictures a dream of falsehood and deceit (Raphael).

pier to stand upon a pier in your dream, denotes that you will be brave in your battle for recognition in prosperity's realm, and that you will be admitted to the highest posts of honour.

If you strive to reach a pier and fail, you will lose the distinction you most coveted.

pies to dream of making pies augurs joy and profit (gypsy folklore).

pig *see* ANIMALS.

pigeons *see* BIRDS.

pilgrim to dream of pilgrims, denotes that you will go on an extended journey, leaving home and its dearest objects in the mistaken idea that it must be thus for their good.

To dream that you are a pilgrim, portends struggles with poverty and unsympathetic companions.

For a young woman to dream that a pilgrim approaches her, she will fall an easy dupe to deceit. If he leaves her, she will awaken to her weakness of character and strive to strengthen independent thought.

pill we take medicine because we believe it is doing us good and not because we like the taste. Similarly, dreaming of swallowing pills would indicate that the dreamer is doing something in waking life not because he or she wishes to do it but because he or she feels it to be necessary, either good for the dreamer, or a good thing to do in a moral sense.

This is a dream forecasting sickness (gypsy folklore). This interpretation is attributable to sensory stimuli, and to subconscious knowledge of a physical condition.

pillow a dream prognosticating death (gypsy folklore). The pillow is a Christian symbol of eternal rest. It was used as a symbol of power and placed with the dead in order to enable them to lift their heads.

pilot a dream of a pilot is one of safety and protection (gypsy folklore).

pimple to dream of your flesh being full of pimples, denotes worry over trifles.

To see others with pimples on them, signifies that you will be troubled with illness and complaints from others.

For a woman to dream that her beauty is marred by pimples, her conduct in home or social circles will be criticised by friends and acquaintances. You may have small annoyances to follow this dream.

pincers a dream of persecution and injustice (gypsy folklore). In Christian symbolism pincers represent martyrdom.

pine cone a happy dream auguring health (gypsy folklore). The pine cone is the symbol of life, abundance and power.

pine tree to see a pine tree in your dream signifies idleness and remissness (Artemidorus). This tree was especially dedicated to Dionysius, hence the interpretation after the passing of the Greek Gods.

pineapples *see* FRUIT.

pins this dream signifies contradiction and discussion of trivial matters (gypsy folklore). Sharp or pointed instruments usually have an unpleasant interpretation.

pipe a dream of a pipe is one of peace and tranquillity (gypsy folklore). The symbolism of the 'Pipe of Peace' is probably derived from the American Indian.

pirate to be captured by a pirate may symbolize threat and a feeling of loss of control to the dreamer. For a woman it may signify that she thinks her partner has too much control in her life. To a girl this dream predicts marriage to a foreigner; to a man it signifies travel in strange lands (Raphael). *See also* PLANK.

pistol *see* GUN.

pit a dream forecasting the decline of business, possible descent to want and distress. To fall into a pit denotes misfortune and tragedy (Raphael).

pitcher to dream of carrying a pitcher is a dream of failure. To dream of dropping or breaking it predicts disaster, death (gypsy folklore).

pitchfork an evil dream except to farmers, to whom it predicts wealth through toil (gypsy folklore). The pitchfork is a symbol of Satan in Christian art.

place the place in which the dream scenario plays out will do much to reflect the dreamer's state of mind or mood in real life.

plague to dream of a plague raging, denotes disappointing returns in business, and your wife or lover will lead you a wretched existence.

If you are afflicted with the plague, you will keep your business out of embarrassment with the greatest manoeuvring. If you are trying to escape it, some trouble, which looks impenetrable, is pursuing you.

plain for a young woman to dream of crossing a plain, denotes that she will be fortunately situated, if the grasses are green and luxuriant; if they are arid, or the grass is dead, she will have much discomfort and loneliness. *See* PRAIRIE.

plane to dream that you use a plane, denotes that your liberality and successful efforts will be highly commended.

To see carpenters using their planes, denotes that you will progress smoothly in your undertakings.

To dream of seeing planes, denotes congeniality and even success.

A love of the real, and not the false, is portended by this dream.

planets a dream denoting joyful tidings (gypsy folklore). Probably derived from the Biblical description of the birth of Christ.

plank to walk a plank in your dream forewarns you of treachery (gypsy folklore). *See also* PIRATES.

plants *see* FLOWERS.

plaster to dream of seeing walls plainly plastered, denotes that success will come, but it will not be stable.

To have plaster fall upon you, denotes unmitigated disasters and disclosure.

To see plasterers at work, denotes that you will have a sufficient competency to live above penury.

plate for a woman to dream of plates, denotes that she will practise economy and win a worthy husband. If already married, she will retain her husband's love and respect by the wise ordering of his household. *See* DISHES.

play for a young woman to dream that she attends a play, foretells that she will be courted by a genial friend, and will marry to further her prospects and pleasure seeking. If there is trouble in getting to and from the play, or discordant and hideous scenes, she will be confronted with many displeasing surprises.

pleasure to dream of pleasure, denotes gain and personal enjoyment.

plough to dream of a plough, signifies unusual success, and affairs will reach a pleasing culmination.

To see persons ploughing, denotes activity and advancement in knowledge and fortune.

For a young woman to see her lover ploughing, indicates that she will have a noble and wealthy husband. Her joys will be deep and lasting.

To plough yourself, denotes rapid increase in property and joys.

ploughing ploughing is generally seen as a symbol of sexual intercourse, the preparing of fertile ground, the sowing of the seed, etc.

plums *see* FRUIT.

pocket to dream of your pocket, is a sign of evil demonstrations against you.

pocketbook to find a pocketbook filled with bills and money in your dreams, you will be quite lucky, gaining in nearly every instance your desire. If empty, you will be disappointed in some big hope.

If you lose your pocketbook, you will unfortunately disagree with your best friend, and thereby lose much comfort and real gain.

poison to feel that you are poisoned in a dream, denotes that some painful influence will immediately reach you.

If you seek to use poison on others, you will be guilty of base thoughts, or the world will go wrong for you.

For a young woman to dream that she endeavours to rid herself of a rival in this way, she will be likely to have a deal of trouble in securing a lover.

To throw the poison away, denotes that by sheer force you will overcome unsatisfactory conditions.

To handle poison, or see others with it, signifies that unpleasantness will surround you.

To dream that your relatives or children are poisoned, you will receive injury from unsuspected sources.

If an enemy or rival is poisoned, you will overcome obstacles.

To recover from the effects of poison, indicates that you will succeed after worry.

To take strychnine or other poisonous medicine under the advice of a physician, denotes that you will undertake some affair fraught with danger.

poker to dream of seeing a red hot poker, or fighting with one, signifies that you will meet trouble with combative energy.

To play at poker, warns you against evil company; and young women, especially, will lose their moral distinctiveness if they find themselves engaged in this game.

polar bears in dreams, are prognostic of deceit, as misfortune will approach you in a seeming fair aspect. Your bitterest enemies will wear the garb of friendship. Rivals will try to supersede you.

To see the skin of one, denotes that you will successfully overcome any opposition. *See* BEAR, ANIMALS.

pole star a dream of loyalty and devotion (gypsy folklore). The universal emblem of stability.

pole the most obvious interpretation of a pole or anything similar in shape that appears in a dream is a sexual one, i.e. that the pole represents the male organ.

pole-cat to dream of a pole-cat, signifies salacious scandals.

To inhale the odour of a pole-cat on your clothes, or otherwise smell one, you will find that your conduct will be considered rude, and your affairs will prove unsatisfactory.

To kill one, denotes that you will overcome formidable obstacles.

police to a decent person this dream denotes honours (Raphael).

polishing to dream of polishing any article, high attainments will place you in enviable positions.

politician to dream of a politician, denotes displeasing companionships, and incidences where you will lose time and means.

If you engage in political wrangling, it portends that misunderstandings and ill feeling will be shown you by friends.

For a young woman to dream of taking interest in politics, warns her against designing duplicity,

polka to dream of dancing the polka, denotes pleasant occupations. *See* DANCING.

pomegranate *see* FRUIT.

pond *see* BROOK.

pony to see ponies in your dreams, signifies moderate speculations will be rewarded with success.

pool *see* WATER.

poor to dream that you, or any of your friends, appear to be poor, is significant of worry and losses.

poor-house to see a poor-house in your dream, denotes you have unfaithful friends, who will care for you only as they can use your money and belongings.

popcorn a dream of eating popcorn augurs a pleasant surprise.

Popcorn is associated with movie-going and could symbolise a desire for fame in the dreamer.

Pope any dream in which you see the Pope, without speaking to him, warns you of servitude. You will bow to the will of some master, even to that of women.

To speak to the Pope, denotes that certain high honours are in store for you. To see the Pope looking sad or displeased, warns you against vice or sorrow of some kind.

poplar to dream of a green poplar denotes fulfilled hopes, if withered it denotes disappointment (gypsy folklore). It was once held sacred to Heracles. Afterwards it symbolized the Holy Rood of the Christians.

poppy a dream denoting illness to the sleeper or tidings of illness to loved ones (gypsy folklore). An interpretation evidently derived from the use of the poppy in the manufacture of opium, rather than from the symbolism of the blossoms.

porcelain to dream of porcelain, signifies you will have favourable opportunities of progressing in your affairs. To see it broken or soiled, denotes mistakes will be made which will cause grave offence.

porch to dream of a porch, denotes that you will engage a new undertakings, and the future will be full of uncertainties.

If a young woman dreams that she is with her lover on a porch, implies her doubts of some one's intentions.

To dream that you build a porch, you will assume new duties.

porcupine *see* ANIMALS.

pork if you eat pork in your dreams, you will encounter real trouble, but if you only see pork, you will come out of a conflict victoriously. *See* BACON.

porpoise a dream of joy and happiness (Artemidorus).

porridge to dream of porridge, denotes pleasant love-making will furnish you interesting recreation from absorbing study and planning for future progression.

porter seeing a porter in a dream, denotes decided bad luck and eventful happenings.

To imagine yourself a porter, denotes humble circumstances.

To hire one, you will be able to enjoy whatever success comes to you.

To discharge one, signifies that disagreeable charges will be preferred against you.

portfolio a dream bespeaking mysteries, things hidden from sight (gypsy folklore).

portrait a dream forecasting long life to the person represented, especially if the portrait is painted on wood. To receive or to give a portrait away signifies treason (gypsy folklore).

position one's position in a dream, in particular in relation to other people in the dream, will be significant in terms of one's position in life, i.e. how one sees oneself in relation to the world, not only to position, but also to time, morality and beliefs.

closeness either stands for intimacy, someone the dreamer feels close to, or an idea or value that he or she holds dear.

distance denotes something from which the dreamer feels remote. This may be an unachievable aim or a set of beliefs from which he or she feels detached.

height dreaming that one is above something or someone, looking down upon them, may indicate the dreamer's feeling of moral or intellectual superiority. It might also mean that the dreamer feels he or she has 'risen above' certain difficulties in life.

looking up where the individual dreams of being at a lower level, looking up at things or people, these things or people may represent higher ideals to which the dreamer aspires, or, in some contexts, an authority, a superior being or a God. *See also* HEIGHT.

in front/behind generally speaking, things that lie behind the dreamer may be interpreted as things or ideas of the past which have now been left behind. What lies in front of the dreamer is, therefore, the future.

postage to dream of postage stamps, denotes system and remuneration in business.

If you try to use cancelled stamps, you will fall into disrepute.

To receive stamps, signifies a rapid rise to distinction.

To see torn stamps, denotes that there are obstacles in your way.

postman to dream of a postman, denotes that hasty news will more frequently be of a distressing nature than otherwise. *See* LETTER CARRIER.

post-office to dream of a post-office, is a sign of unpleasant tidings. and ill luck generally.

pot to dream of a pot, foretells that unimportant events will work you vexation. For a young woman to see a boiling pot, omens busy employment of pleasant and social duties. To see a broken or rusty one, implies that keen disappointment will be experienced by you.

potatoes to dream of digging potatoes predicts success and profit. If, however, there are only a few or they are very small, this denotes failure (gypsy folklore).

potter to dream of a potter, denotes constant employment, with satisfactory results. For a young woman to see a potter, foretells she will enjoy pleasant engagements.

potter's field to see a potter's field in your dreams, denotes you will have poverty and misery to distress you. For a young woman to walk through a potter's field with her lover, she will give up the one she loves in the hope of mercenary gain.

poultice to dream that one is applied to any part of the body implies trouble to that particular organ or limb (gypsy folklore).

poultry to see dressed poultry in a dream, foretells extravagant habits will reduce your security in money matters. For a young woman to dream that she is chasing live poultry, foretells she will devote valuable time to frivolous pleasure.

poverty a dream of CONTRARY MEANING to the poor, but ill for the rich or for those who use eloquent speech (Artemidorus).

powder to see powder in your dreams, denotes unscrupulous people are dealing with you. You may detect them through watchfulness.

prairie to dream of a prairie, denotes that you will enjoy ease, and even luxury and unobstructed progress.

An undulating prairie, covered with growing grasses and flowers, signifies joyous happenings.

A barren prairie, represents loss and sadness through the absence of friends. To be lost on one, is a sign of sadness and ill luck.

prayer to dream of saying prayers, or seeing others doing so, foretells you will be threatened with failure, which will take strenuous efforts to avert.

preacher to dream of a preacher, denotes that your ways are not above reproach, and your affairs will not move evenly.

To dream that you are a preacher, foretells for you losses in business, and distasteful amusements will jar upon you.

To hear preaching, implies that you will undergo misfortune.

To argue with a preacher, you will lose in some contest.

To see one walk away from you, denotes that your affairs will move with new energy. If he looks sorrowful, reproaches will fall heavily upon you.

To see a long-haired preacher, denotes that you are shortly to have disputes with overbearing and egotistical people.

precipice dreaming of standing at the top of a precipice suggests fear of 'taking the plunge', i.e. fear of failure.

Falling off the edge of a precipice may be either a feeling of loss of control in waking life, or a symbol of death or what is not understood. Being trapped at the bottom of a precipice in a dream would suggest that the dreamer feels helpless and trapped in his or her present situation. *See also* ABYSS; TYPICAL DREAMS.

pregnancy for a woman to dream that she is pregnant, can signify that she has plans; that a project that has been on her mind is about to come to fruition.

From folklore, for a virgin, this dream omens scandal and adversity. If a woman is really pregnant and has this dream, it prognosticates a safe delivery and swift recovery of strength.

presents presents in dreams may represent affection in real life. *See also* GIFTS.

priest *see* ABBOT.

primroses a dream boding sickness, sorrow, death (Raphael).

printer to see a printer in your dreams, is a warning of poverty, if you neglect to practice economy and cultivate energy. For a woman to dream that her lover or associate is a printer, foretells she will fail to please her parents in the selection of a close friend.

printing office to be in a printing office in dreams, denotes that slander and contumely will threaten you

To run a printing office is indicative of hard luck.

For a young woman to dream that her sweetheart is connected with a printing office, denotes that she will have a lover who is unable to lavish money or time upon her, and she will not be sensible enough to see why he is so stingy.

prison a dream of CONTRARY MEANING denoting happiness, hope, etc (Raphael). Evidently many of these interpretations trace their derivation to the days of the early Christians when persecution and humiliation were borne with joy and hope. *See also* IMPRISONMENT, JAIL.

privacy to dream that your privacy suffers intrusion, foretells you will have overbearing people to worry you. For a woman, this dream warns her to look carefully after private affairs. If she intrudes on the privacy of her husband or lover, she will disabuse some one's confidence, if not careful of her conversation.

prize dreaming of receiving a prize may indicate a wish for recognition in the waking life of the dreamer.

prize fight to see a prize fight in your dreams, denotes your affairs will give you trouble in controlling them.

prize fighter for a young woman to see a prize fighter, foretells she will have pleasure in fast society, and will give her friends much concern about her reputation.

procession to see one in a dream denotes happiness and joy to come (gypsy folklore).

profanation misery and future misfortune are herein denoted (gypsy folklore).

profits to dream of profits, brings success in your immediate future.

promenade to dream of promenading, foretells that you will engage in energetic and profitable pursuits.

To see others promenading, signifies that you will have rivals in your pursuits.

property to dream that you own vast property, denotes that you will be successful in affairs, and gain friendships.

prostitution dreams of prostitution are generally indicative of some sexual need. A man who dreams of being with a prostitute may be seeking pure sexual gratification, without the need for emotional attachment. If the feeling of the dream is one of disgust, the man may want to express some aspect of his sexuality about which he feels ashamed.

Women who dream of prostitution may feel guilty about sex, or may have sexual needs that are not being met because they are being repressed.

prunes *see* FRUIT.

public house to dream of keeping a public house denotes extremes financially. To dream of drinking in one denotes sickness, poverty or imprisonment for debt (gypsy folklore).

publican to dream of a publican, denotes that you will have your sympathies aroused by some one in a desperate condition, and you will diminish your own gain for his advancement. To a young woman, this dream brings a worthy lover; but because of his homeliness she will trample on his feelings unnecessarily.

publisher to dream of a publisher, foretells long journeys and aspirations to the literary craft.

If a woman dreams that her husband is a publisher, she will be jealous of more than one woman of his acquaintance, and spicy scenes will ensue.

For a publisher to reject your manuscript, denotes that you will suffer disappointment at the miscarriage of cherished designs. If he accepts it, you will rejoice in the full fruition of your hopes. If he loses it, you will suffer evil at the hands of strangers.

puddings to dream of puddings, denotes small returns from large investments, if you only see it.

To eat it, is proof that your affairs will be disappointing.

For a young woman to cook, or otherwise prepare a pudding, denotes that her lover will be sensual and worldly minded, and if she marries him, she will see her love and fortune vanish.

puddles a dream denoting undesirable acquaintances who will get the dreamer into trouble (gypsy folklore).

pulpit to dream of a pulpit, denotes sorrow and vexation.

To dream that you are in a pulpit, foretells sickness, and unsatisfactory results in business or trades of any character.

pulse to dream of your pulse, is warning to look after your affairs and health with close care, as both are taking on debilitating conditions.

To dream of feeling the pulse of another, signifies that you are committing depredations in Pleasure's domain.

pump to see a pump in a dream, denotes that energy and faithfulness to business will produce desired riches, good health also is usually betokened by this dream.

To see a broken pump, signifies that the means of advancing in life will be absorbed by family cares. To the married and the unmarried, it intimates blasted energies.

If you work a pump, your life will be filled with pleasure and profitable undertakings.

pumpkin to dream of a pumpkin predicts that the dreamer will have admirers. To eat one signifies indisposition (gypsy folklore).

punch to dream of drinking the concoction called punch, denotes that you will prefer selfish pleasures to honourable distinction and morality.

To dream that you are punching any person with a club or fist, denotes quarrels and recriminations.

punishment the person who dreams of dire punishments and retribution may well suffer from attacks of conscience in waking life, especially if his or her way of life is at odds with the set of morals he or she was brought up with.

pup to dream of pups, denotes that you will entertain the innocent and hapless, and thereby enjoy pleasure. The dream also shows that friendships will grow stronger, and fortune will increase if the pups are healthful and well formed, and vice versa if they are lean and filthy. *see* DOGS and HOUND PUPS.

purchases to dream of purchases usually augurs profit and advancement with pleasure.

purity of the air the dream of pure air is supposedly lucky. Of a dream of bad air, the reverse may be said (gypsy folklore).

purse the purse is a symbol of the female genitalia. The interpretation of a dream of one will depend very much on how it is viewed by the dreamer. This dream may express feelings concerning loss of femininity or anxiety over possible infertility or the approach of the menopause.

To find a full purse is said to be a prediction of happiness; to dream of losing one denotes sickness (gypsy folklore).

putty to dream of working in putty, denotes that hazardous chances will be taken with fortune.

If you put in a window-pane with putty, you will seek fortune with poor results.

pyramid a dream of grandeur and wealth. To be on top of one predicts great achievement (gypsy folklore).

Q

quacking to dream of something (not necessarily a duck) quacking denotes that you are tired and exasperated by a lot of talking that has been going on around you recently.

quadrille to dream of dancing a quadrille, foretells that some pleasant engagement will occupy your time. *See* DANCING.

quagmire to fall into one predicts impassable barriers (Artemidorus). *See also* MUD and QUICKSAND.

quail *see* BIRDS.

Quaker to dream of a Quaker, denotes that you will have faithful friends and fair business. If you are one, you will deport yourself honourably toward an enemy.

For a young woman to attend a Quaker meeting, portends that she will by her modest manners win a faithful husband who will provide well for her household.

quarantine to dream of being in quarantine, denotes that you will be placed in a disagreeable position by the malicious intriguing of enemies.

quarrel dreams about quarrelling or fighting mostly indicate that the dreamer is going through an inner struggle of some kind.

The mystical view is that this is a dream of the contrary, to quarrel in a dream means to make love (Raphael).

quarry to dream of falling down a quarry denotes sudden illness (gypsy folklore).

quartet to dream of a quartet, and you are playing or singing, denotes favourable affairs, jolly companions, and good times.

To see or hear a quartet, foretells that you will aspire to something beyond you.

quay a dream that promises protection (gypsy folklore).

quayside departures from a quayside are indicative of change in the life of the dreamer. One who dreams of taking leave at a quayside will very possibly be embarking on a significantly different stage in life.

Farewells at the quayside are acknowledgements of old ways and of thoughts being left behind. *See also* JOURNEY.

queen to behold a king or a queen in a dream predicts joy, honour and prosperity (Artemidorus).

question to ask questions in a dream signifies good luck. If the dreamer is asked questions he or she is unable to answer, then this this signifies ill fortune.

quicksands a dream warning you of temptations and weaknesses of which you are unaware (Raphael).

Alternatively, you may be feeling trapped or frustrated by something. *See also* MUD; QUAGMIRE.

quicksilver a dream denoting changes, vicissitudes and restlessness (gypsy folklore).

quills to dream of quills, denotes to the literary inclined a season of success.

To dream of them as ornaments, signifies a rushing trade, and some remuneration.

For a young woman to be putting a quill on her hat, denotes that she will attempt many conquests, and her success will depend upon her charms.

quilts to dream of quilts, foretells pleasant and comfortable circumstances. For a young woman, this dream foretells that her practical and wise business-like ways will advance her into the favourable esteem of a man who will seek her for a wife.

If the quilts are clean, but having holes in them, she will win a husband who appreciates her worth, but he will not be the one most desired by her for a companion. If the quilts are soiled, she will bear evidence of carelessness in her dress and manners, and thus fail to secure a very upright husband.

quinine to dream of quinine, denotes you will soon be possessed of great happiness, though your prospects for much wealth may be meagre. To take some, foretells improvement in health and energy. You will also make new friends, who will lend you commercial aid.

quinsy to dream of being afflicted with this disease, denotes discouraging employment.

To see others with it, sickness will cause you much anxiety.

quoits to play at quoits in dreams, foretells low engagements and loss of good employment. To lose, portends of distressing conditions.

R

rabbit *see* ANIMALS.

race dreaming of taking part in a race suggests a sense of competitiveness, an awareness of one's position in life and, depending on the dream, either acknowledgement that one might not succeed or a sense of achievement at this particular stage in life. Sometimes a race might indicate a particular rivalry in the dreamer's life.

A good dream to well persons, to the sick a speedy termination to the race of life is denoted (Artemidorus).

rack to dream of a rack, denotes the uncertainty of the outcome of some engagement which gives you much anxious thought.

racket to dream of a racket, denotes that you will be foiled in some anticipated pleasure. For a young woman, this dream is ominous of disappointment in not being able to participate in some amusement that has engaged her attention.

racoon *see* ANIMALS.

radio this is generally a symbol for communication or, in some cases, intuition, i.e. an ability to pick up feelings 'in the air'.

radish to dream of seeing a bed of radishes growing, is an omen of good luck. Your friends will be unusually kind, and your business will prosper.

If you eat them, you will suffer slightly through the thoughtlessness of some one near to you.

To see radishes, or plant them, denotes that your anticipations will be happily realised.

raffle a dream of doubt and uncertainty (gypsy folklore).

raft a warning of danger from which you will be delivered (gypsy folklore).

rage to be in a rage and scolding and tearing up things generally, while dreaming, signifies quarrels, and injury to your friends.

To see others in a rage, is a sign of unfavourable conditions for business, and unhappiness in social life.

For a young woman to see her lover in a rage, denotes that there will be some discordant note in their love, and misunderstandings will naturally occur.

rags a dream of CONTRARY MEANING predicting success (gypsy folklore).

railing to dream of seeing railings, denotes that some person is trying to obstruct your pathway in love or business.

To dream of holding on to a railing, foretells that some desperate chance will be taken by you to obtain some object upon which you have set your heart. It may be of love, or of a more material form.

railway a dream that is generally symbolic of the dreamer's journey through life, denoting change (gypsy folklore). *See also* JOURNEY and PATH.

rain dreams of torrential rain may point to feelings of depression or may indicate a cleansing process of some sort, i.e. a 'washing away' of guilt feelings or sadness, or a flood of long-repressed emotion.

The rain may have a refreshing quality to it and therefore represent some much needed change in the dreamer's life or spiritual wellbeing.

Rain is said to predict trouble, heavy, or not, according to state of the rain in the dream (Raphael). *See also* DELUGE.

rainbow in general this is a good sign for the future, or a sign denoting a change in the dreamer's present condition. A rainbow in the East denotes benefits to the poor and the sick. In the West it is a good omen for the rich but not for the poor. A rainbow overhead denotes a change in fortune, although this might mean a change for the worse. A rainbow on the right is a good sign, on the left, bad, judging right and left according to the sun. Wherever it appears it is thought to bring good fortune to those who are in poverty and suffering affliction by changing the air (Artemidorus).

raisins to dream of eating raisins, implies that discouragement will darken your hopes when they seem about to be realised.

raking a dream of success (Raphael).

ram *see* ANIMALS.

ramble to dream that you are rambling through the country, denotes that you will be oppressed with sadness, and the separation from friends, but your worldly surroundings will be all that one could desire. For a young woman, this dream promises a comfortable home, but early bereavement.

ramrod to dream of a ramrod, denotes unfortunate adventures. You will have cause for grief. For a young woman to see one bent or broken, foretells that a dear friend or lover will fail her.

ransom to dream that a ransom is made for you, you will find that you are deceived and worked for money on all sides. For a young woman, this is prognostic of evil, unless some one pays the ransom and relieves her.

rape dreams of rape do not necessarily point to a fear of being raped (or of raping), nor do they point to desires on the dreamer's part. Rape is essentially violence, intrusion and abuse of power; dreams of rape are more likely to be exploring the dreamer's feelings in relation to these concepts rather than in relation to the rape itself.

rapids to imagine that you are being carried over rapids in a dream, denotes that you will suffer appalling loss from the neglect of duty and the courting of seductive pleasures.

raspberries *see* FRUIT.

rats *see* ANIMALS.

rattan cane to dream of a rattan cane, foretells that you will depend largely upon the judgement of others, and you should cultivate independence in planning and executing your own affairs.

rattle to dream of seeing a baby play with its rattle, omens peaceful contentment in the home, and enterprises will be honourable and full of gain. To a young woman, it augurs an early marriage and tender cares of her own.

To give a baby a rattle, denotes unfortunate investments.

rat-trap to dream of falling into a rat-trap, denotes that you will be victimised and robbed of some valuable object.

To see an empty one, foretells the absence of slander or competition.

A broken one, denotes that you will be rid of unpleasant associations.

To set one, you will be made aware of the designs of enemies, but the warning will enable you to outwit them.

raven *see* BIRDS.

razor to dream of a razor, portends disagreements and contentions over troubles.

To cut yourself with one, denotes that you will be unlucky in some deal which you are about to make.

Fighting with a razor, foretells disappointing business, and that some one will keep you harassed almost beyond endurance.

reading to dream of reading romance indicates joy; to dream of reading serious books, wisdom (Artemidorus).

reapers to dream of seeing reapers busy at work at their task, denotes prosperity and contentment. If they appear to be going through dried stubble, there will be a lack of good crops, and business will consequently fall off.

To see idle ones, denotes that some discouraging event will come in the midst of prosperity.

To see a broken reaping machine, signifies loss of employment, or disappointment in trades.

reception to dream of attending a reception, denotes that you will have pleasant engagements. Confusion at a reception will work you disquietude.

recurring dreams it is quite common for people to begin having a certain dream fairly early on in life and then to continue having dreams that, even if they are not the same, are very similar in many ways, several times over a period of many years. The recurrence of dreams points to the recurrence of certain sorts of situations or emotions in the dreamer's waking life. The dreamer's reaction to, or way of coping with, the situation or emotion has altered little over the years and so the dream relating to the situation or emotion has remained, in essence, the same. When the dreamer matures or changes and ceases to react in this way then the dream will no longer occur or will be very different.

red *see* COLOURS.

reeds to dream of seeing them near the WATER warns you to be decisive if you want to succeed (gypsy folklore). The scriptural metaphor uses them to symbolize weakness.

reflection you see yourself in a reflection, and so a reflection in a dream is the view that the dreamer holds of him or herself, i.e. it is his or her own self-image.

refrigerator refrigerators chill things, preserve them and keep them static. Perhaps something is holding the dreamer in a kind of stasis. Perhaps this preservation is a good thing, perhaps not. The cold could be symbolic too of cold emotions.

From folklore, to see an oldfashioned ice box in your dreams, portends that your selfishness will offend and injure someone who endeavours to gain an honest livelihood.

register to dream that some one registers your name at a hotel for you, denotes you will undertake some work which will be finished by others.

If you register under an assumed name, you will engage in some guilty enterprise which will give you much uneasiness of mind.

reindeer *see* ANIMALS.

relics this dream comes as a warning to guard your valuables (gypsy folklore).

religion any individual, whether religious or not, may dream of religious figures or religious imagery. The appearance of a religious figure, of God even, need not be related to religion in any way. For example, God may represent a figure of authority whom the dreamer respects deeply. Religious imagery may merely indicate that the dreamer needs to turn inwards more and to get in touch with the spiritual side of him or herself. *See also* GOD.

rent to dream that you rent a house, is a sign that you will enter into new contracts, which will prove profitable.

To fail to rent out property, denotes that there will be much inactivity in business.

To pay rent, signifies that your financial interest will be satisfactory.

If you can't pay your rent, it is unlucky for you, as you will see a falling off in trade, and social pleasures will be of little benefit.

reprieve to be under sentence in a dream and receive a reprieve, foretells that you will overcome some difficulty which is causing you anxiety.

For a young woman to dream that her lover has been reprieved, denotes that she will soon hear of some good luck befalling him, which will be of vital interest to her.

reptile a reptile is a symbol of anger, quarrels and bitterness. If a single woman has this dream it denotes a false lover.

rescue a dream forecasting a rise in the world, and the possible establishment of a successful business (gypsy folklore).

resign to dream that you resign any position, signifies that you will unfortunately embark in new enterprises.

To hear of others resigning, denotes that you will have unpleasant tidings.

resurrection to dream that you are resurrected from the dead, you will have some great vexation, but will eventually gain your desires. To see others resurrected, denotes unfortunate troubles will be lightened by the thoughtfulness of friends

resuscitate to dream that you are being resuscitated, denotes that you will have heavy losses, but will eventually regain more than you lose, and happiness will attend you.

To resuscitate another, you will form new friendships, which will give you prominence and pleasure.

revelation to dream of a revelation, if it be of a pleasant nature, you may expect a bright outlook, either in business or love; but if the revelation be gloomy you will have many discouraging features to overcome.

revenge to dream of taking revenge predicts a bed of sickness for the dreamer (Raphael).

revival to dream you attend a religious revival, foretells family disturbances and unprofitable engagements.

If you take a part in it, you will incur the displeasure of friends by your contrary ways.

revolver for a young woman to dream that she sees her sweetheart with a revolver, denotes that she will have a serious disagreement with some friend, and probably separation from her lover. *See* PISTOL, FIREARMS.

rheumatism to feel rheumatism attacking you in a dream, foretells unexpected delay in the accomplishment of plans.

To see others so afflicted brings disappointments.

rhinestones to dream of rhinestones, denotes pleasures and favours of short duration. For a young woman to dream that a rhinestone proves to be a diamond, foretells she will be surprised to find that some insignificant act on her part will result in good fortune.

rhinoceros to dream that you see a rhinoceros, foretells you will have a great loss threatening you, and that you will have secret troubles. To kill one, shows that you will bravely overcome obstacles.

rhubarb to dream of rhubarb growing, denotes that pleasant entertainment will occupy your time for a while.

To cook it, foretells spirited arguments in which you will lose a friend.

To eat it, denotes dissatisfaction with present employment.

rib to dream of seeing ribs, denotes poverty and misery.

ribbon seeing ribbons floating from the costume of any person in your dreams, indicates you will have gay and pleasant companions, and practical cares will not trouble you greatly.

For a young woman to dream of decorating herself with ribbons, she will soon have a desirable offer of marriage, but frivolity may cause her to make a mistake. If she sees other girls wearing ribbons, she will encounter rivalry in her endeavours to secure a husband. If she buys them, she will have a pleasant and easy place in life. If she feels angry or displeased about them, she will find that some other woman is dividing her honours and pleasures with her in her social realm.

rice to dream of eating rice denotes abundance of instruction (Artemidorus). Certain legends and traditions of Western Europe associate rice with wisdom because sages were said to live upon it, such as the yogis of India, etc.

riches a dream of CONTRARY MEANING (gypsy folklore).

riddles to dream that you are trying to solve riddles, denotes you will engage in some enterprise which will try your patience and employ your money.

The import of riddles is confusion and dissatisfaction.

riding a dream of good fortune (Raphael). A dream of a galloping horse is an erotic one (Freud, Jung).

riding school to attend a riding school, foretells some friend will act falsely by you, but you will throw off the vexing influence occasioned by it.

ring for a woman to dream that her wedding ring breaks denotes the death of her husband. If the ring presses her finger the dream forecasts the illness of her husband or of someone in his family. To dream that someone draws a ring on the dreamer's finger denotes marriage (Raphael). In all times the ring has been held as an amulet of affection and of home, its suggestion in a dream is therefore obvious. *See also* LOSS.

ringworm to dream of having ringworm appear on you, you will have a slight illness, and some exasperating difficulty in the near future.

To see them on others, beggars and appeals for charity will beset you.

riot to dream of riots, foretells disappointing affairs.

To see a friend killed in a riot, you will have bad luck in all undertakings, and the death, or some serious illness, of some person will cause you distress.

rising to dream of rising to high positions, denotes that study and advancement will bring you desired wealth.

If you find yourself rising high into the air, you will come into unexpected riches and pleasures, but you are warned to be careful of your engagements, or you may incur displeasing prominence.

rival to dream you have a rival, is a sign that you will be slow in asserting your rights, and will lose favour with people of prominence.

For a young woman, this dream is a warning to cherish the love she already holds, as she might unfortunately make a mistake in seeking other bonds.

If you find that a rival has outwitted you, it signifies that you will be negligent in your business, and that you love personal ease to your detriment.

If you imagine that you are the successful rival, it is good for your advancement, and you will find congeniality in your choice of a companion.

river to see a broad, rapid and muddy river is a dream denoting difficulties. Calm and clear water predicts happiness and prosperity (Raphael). The river is usually taken as a symbol of human life and represented as smooth or turbulent according to the nature of the occurrences. *See also* WATER.

road *see* PATH.

roast to see or eat roast in a dream, is an omen of domestic infelicity and secret treachery.

robin *see* BIRDS.

rock a rock may represent stability, 'down-to-earthness', or simply what is real. Rocks are symbols of impassable obstacles (gypsy folklore).

rocket to dream of a rocket denotes a momentary triumph. The symbolism here may well have been derived from the old proverb of 'going up like a rocket and coming down like a stick.' *See also* TORPEDO.

rocking-chairs seen in dreams, bring friendly intercourse and contentment with any environment.

To see a mother, wife, or sweetheart in a rocking chair, is ominous of the sweetest joys that earth affords.

To see vacant rocking-chairs, forebodes bereavement or estrangement. The dreamer will surely merit misfortune in some form.

rod a dream of sadness (gypsy folklore). Dreaming of a rod or any other similar object may have significance as an erotic symbol, denoting the penis (Freud).

rogue to see or think yourself a rogue, foretells you are about to commit some indiscretion which will give your friends uneasiness of mind. You are likely to suffer from a passing malady.

For a woman to think her husband or lover is a rogue, foretells she will be painfully distressed over neglect shown her by a friend.

rogue's gallery to dream that you are in a rogue's gallery, foretells you will be associated with people who will fail to appreciate you. To see your own picture, you will be overawed by a tormenting enemy.

Roman candle to see Roman candles while dreaming, is a sign of speedy attainment of coveted pleasures and positions.

To imagine that you have a loaded candle and find it empty, denotes that you will be disappointed with the possession of some object which you have long striven to obtain.

roof a dream indicating command and dignity (gypsy folklore).

roof corner to see a person dressed in mourning sitting on a roof corner, foretells there will be unexpected and dismal failures in your business. Affairs will appear unfavourable in love.

rook *see* BIRDS.

rooster to dream of a rooster, foretells that you will be very successful and rise to prominence, but you will allow yourself to become conceited over your fortunate rise. To see roosters fighting, foretells altercations and rivals. S*ee* CHICKENS, BIRDS.

root to dream of eating them denotes mental disorder (gypsy folklore).

rope depending upon the context of the dream, a rope may represent the umbilical cord, one's attachment to someone close, e.g. one's mother, or it may represent a restriction to the dreamer or the dreamer's own inhibitions in waking life. To dream of being led by ropes warns you against making any contracts with others (gypsy folklore).

rosebush to see a rosebush in foliage but no blossoms, denotes prosperous circumstances are enclosing you. To see a dead rosebush, foretells misfortune and sickness for you or relatives.

rosemary to see it in a dream is a good sign. To smell it, however, is an augury of death (gypsy folklore).

roses in season this is a dream of happiness; dead, wilted, or out of season a dream of trouble and poverty (gypsy folklore).

rosette to wear or see rosettes on others while in dreams, is significant of frivolous waste of time; though you will experience the thrills of pleasure, they will bring disappointments.

rouge a dream of treason and deceit (Raphael).

roundabout to dream of seeing a roundabout, denotes that you will struggle unsuccessfully to advance in fortune or love.

rowing a dream of success unless the boat is upset, in which case it is bad (Raphael).

rubber to dream of being clothed in rubber garments, is a sign that you will have honours conferred upon you because of your steady and unchanging stand of purity and morality. If the garments are ragged or torn, you should be cautious in your conduct, as scandal is ready to attack your reputation.

To dream of using "rubber" as a slang term, foretells that you will be easy to please in your choice of pleasure and companions.

If you find that your limbs will stretch like rubber, it is a sign that illness is threatening you, and you are likely to use deceit in your wooing and business.

To dream of rubber goods, denotes that your affairs will be conducted on a secret basis, and your friends will fail to understand your conduct in many instances.

rubbish to dream of rubbish, denotes that you will badly manage your affairs.

ruby to dream of a ruby, foretells you will be lucky in speculations of business or love. For a woman to lose one, is a sign of approaching indifference of her lover.

rudder to dream of a rudder, you will soon make a pleasant journey to foreign lands, and new friendships will be formed. A broken rudder, augurs disappointment and sickness.

ruins a dream of CONTRARY MEANING denoting unexpected gains (gypsy folklore).

rum to dream of drinking rum, foretells that you will have wealth, but will lack moral refinement, as you will lean to gross pleasures.

running *see* ACTIONS.

running sore *see* ABSCESS.

rupture to dream that you are ruptured, denotes you will have physical disorders or disagreeable contentions. If it be others you see in this condition, you will be in danger of irreconcilable quarrels.

rust dreaming of rust is an indication of destruction of property (gypsy folklore).

rye bread to see or eat rye bread in your dreams, foretells you will have a cheerful and well-appointed home.

rye to see it growing is a dream of triumph over enemies.

S

saber a dream of triumph over enemies (gypsy folklore). An erotic dream (Freud). *See also* WEAPONS.

sable to be in a room hung with sable is a dream which was said to predict the death of a close friend (Artemidorus).

sack a sack or bag is most commonly a symbol for the womb in a dream.

saddle to dream of saddles, foretells news of a pleasant nature, also unannounced visitors. You are also, probably, to take a trip which will prove advantageous.

safe to dream of seeing a safe, denotes security from discouraging affairs of business and love.

To be trying to unlock a safe, you will be worried over the failure of your plans not reaching quick maturity.

To find a safe empty, denotes trouble.

saffron seen in a dream warns you that you are entertaining false hopes, as bitter enemies are interfering secretly with your plans for the future.

To drink a tea made from saffron, foretells that you will have quarrels and alienation in your family.

sage to dream of the herb sage is a prediction of honour and advancement (Raphael).

sailboat *see* BOAT.

sailing *see* JOURNEY.

sailor a sailor warns of a dangerous sea voyage (Raphael).

salad to dream of eating salad, foretells sickness and disagreeable people around you.

For a young woman to dream of making it, is a sign that her lover will be changeable and quarrelsome.

salamander *see* ANIMALS.

salmon *see* ANIMALS.

salt salt is what gives the dreamer's life its flavour, the dreamer's attitudes to situations encountered, the feelings sparked off through interaction with others, the influence and moods of those who surround the dreamer in daily life. Wisdom is here foretold (gypsy folklore). Salt is the symbol of wisdom and wit.

saltpetre to dream of saltpetre, denotes change in your living will add loss to some unconquerable grief.

salve to dream of salve, denotes you will prosper under adverse circumstances and convert enemies into friends.

samples to dream of receiving merchandise samples, denotes improvement in your business. For a travelling man to lose his samples, implies he will find himself embarrassed in business affairs, or in trouble through love engagements. For a woman to dream that she is examining samples sent her, denotes she will have chances to vary her amusements.

sand dreams of walking on sand, particularly deep, soft sand or sand dunes, reflect feelings of insecurity on the part of the dreamer.

Sanskrit to dream of Sanskrit, denotes that you will estrange yourself from friends in order to investigate hidden subjects, taking up those occupying the minds of cultured and progressive thinkers.

sapphire to dream of sapphire, is ominous of fortunate gain, and to woman, a wise selection in a lover.

sardines to eat sardines in a dream, foretells that distressing events will come unexpectedly upon you.

For a young woman to dream of putting them on the table, denotes that she will be worried with the attentions of a person who is distasteful to her.

sardonyx to dream of sardonyx, signifies gloomy surroundings will be cleared away by your energetic overthrow of poverty. For a woman, this dream denotes an increase in her possessions, unless she loses or throws them away, then it might imply a disregard of opportunities to improve her condition.

sash to dream of wearing a sash, foretells that you will seek to retain the affections of a flirtatious person.

For a young woman to buy one, she will be faithful to her lover, and win esteem by her frank, womanly ways.

Satan to dream of Satan, foretells that you will have some dangerous adventures, and you will be forced to use strategy to keep up honourable appearances.

To dream that you kill him, foretells that you will desert wicked or immoral companions to live upon a higher plane.

If he comes to you under the guise of literature, it should be heeded as a warning against promiscuous friendships, and especially flatterers.

If he comes in the shape of wealth or power, you will fail to use your influence for harmony, or the elevation of others.

If he takes the form of music, you are likely to go down before his wiles.

If in the form of a fair woman, you will probably crush every kindly feeling you may have for the caresses of this moral monstrosity.

To feel that you are trying to shield yourself from Satan, denotes that you will endeavour to throw off the bondage of selfish pleasure, and seek to give others their best deserts. *See* DEVIL.

satin a dream of joy and profit, etc (gypsy folklore).

satyr a dream of lechery and lewdness (gypsy folklore).

sausage to dream of making sausage, denotes that you will be successful in many undertakings.

To eat them, you will have a humble, but pleasant home.

saw to dream that you use a hand-saw, indicates an energetic and busy time, and cheerful home life.

To see big saws in machinery, foretells that you will superintend a big enterprise, and the same will yield fair returns. For a woman, this dream denotes that she will be esteemed, and her counsels will be heeded.

To dream of rusty or broken saws, denotes failure and accidents.

To lose a saw, you will engage in affairs which will culminate in disaster.

To hear the buzz of a saw, indicates thrift and prosperity.

To find a rusty saw, denotes that you will probably restore your fortune.

To carry a saw on your back, foretells that you will carry large, but profitable, responsibilities.

sawdust to dream of sawdust, signifies that grievous mistakes will cause you distress and quarrelling in your home.

scabbard to dream of a scabbard, denotes some misunderstanding will be amicably settled. If you wonder where your scabbard can be, you will have overpowering difficulties to meet.

scaffold *see* GALLOWS.

scald-head to see any one with a scald-head in your dreams, there will be uneasiness felt over the sickness or absence of some one near to you.

If you dream that your own head is thus afflicted, you are in danger of personal illness or accidents.

scalding to dream of being scalded, portends that distressing incidents will blot out pleasurable anticipations.

scales to dream of weighing on scales, portends that justice will temper your conduct, and you will see your prosperity widening.

For a young woman to weigh her lover, the indications are that she will find him of solid worth, and faithfulness will balance her love.

scandal for a young woman to dream that she discussed a scandal, foretells that she will confer favours, which should be sacred, to some one who will deceive her into believing that he is honourably inclined. Marriage rarely follows swiftly after dreaming of scandal.

scandal to dream that you are an object of scandal, denotes that you are not particular to select good and true companions, but rather enjoy having fast men and women contribute to your pleasure. Trade and business of any character will suffer dullness after this dream.

scarcity to dream of scarcity, foretells sorrow in the household and failing affairs.

scarecrow a dream denoting dishonest friends (gypsy folklore).

scarlet fever to dream of scarlet fever, foretells you are in danger of sickness, or in the power of an enemy. To dream a relative dies suddenly with it, foretells you will be overcome by villainous treachery.

sceptre to imagine in your dreams that you wield a sceptre, foretells that you will be chosen by friends to positions of trust, and you will not disappoint their estimate of your ability.

To dream that others wield the sceptre over you, denotes that you will seek employment under the supervision of others, rather than exert your energies to act for yourself.

school in dreams, school represents the values and restrictions that we impose on our own lives as a result of early experience.

To dream of attending school and being unable to learn shows an undertaking that the dreamer does not understand (Artemidorus). *See also* EXAMS; TYPICAL DREAMS.

school teacher to dream of a school teacher, denotes you are likely to enjoy learning and amusements in a quiet way. If you are one, you are likely to reach desired success in literary and other works.

scissors a dream forecasting marriage for a young girl, but it is a bad omen for a married woman (gypsy folklore). An erotic dream (Jung).

scorpions *see* ANIMALS.

scrap-book to dream of a scrap-book, denotes disagreeable acquaintances will shortly be made.

scratch a dream forecasting an accident (gypsy folklore).

scratch head to dream that you scratch your head, denotes strangers will annoy you by their flattering attentions, which you will feel are only shown to win favours from you.

screech-owl to dream that you hear the shrill startling notes of the screech-owl, denotes that you will be shocked with news of the desperate illness, or death of some dear friend.

screw to dream of seeing screws, denotes that tedious tasks must be performed, and peevishness in companions must be combated. It also denotes that you must be economical and painstaking.

scroll this dream forecasts the revelation of secret things.

sculptor to dream of a sculptor, foretells you will change from your present position to one less lucrative, but more distinguished.

For a woman to dream that her husband or lover is a sculptor, foretells she will enjoy favours from men of high position.

scum to dream of scum, signifies disappointment will be experienced by you over social defeats.

scythe the loss of a friend through death (gypsy folklore). The scythe was the medieval emblem of death.

sea foam for a woman to dream of sea foam, foretells that indiscriminate and demoralising pleasures will distract her from the paths of rectitude. If she wears a bridal veil of sea foam, she will engulf herself in material pleasure to the exclusion of true refinement and innate modesty. She will be likely to cause sorrow to some of those dear to her, through their inability to gratify her ambition.

sea placid and smooth denotes happiness; rough and turbulent, sorrow (gypsy folklore). *See also* WATER.

seal to dream that you see seals, denotes that you are striving for a place above your power to maintain.

Dreams of seals usually show that the dreamer has high aspirations and discontent will harass him into struggles to advance his position.

seamstress to see a seamstress in a dream, portends you will be deterred from making pleasant visits by unexpected luck.

seaport to dream of visiting a seaport, denotes that you will have opportunities of travelling and acquiring knowledge, but there will be some who will object to your anticipated tours.

searching dreams of searching might indicate some feeling of loss in waking life, a loved one, perhaps, or one's childhood. Alternatively, it can indicate a search for a new path in life, that is, a new start. To dream of searching, but not finding, may show either that what is lost is lost forever or that the dreamer has some apprehension about finding what he or she is looking for.

seat to think, in a dream, that some one has taken your seat, denotes you will be tormented by people calling on you for aid. To give a woman your seat, implies your yielding to some fair one's artfulness.

secret order to dream of any secret order, denotes a sensitive and excited organism, and the owner should cultivate practical and unselfish ideas and they may soon have opportunities for honest pleasures, and desired literary distinctions.

There is a vision of selfish and designing friendships for one who joins a secret order.

Young women should heed the counsel of their guardians, lest they fall into discreditable habits after this dream.

If a young woman meets the head of the order, she should oppose with energy and moral rectitude against allurements that are set brilliantly and prominently before those of her sex. For her to think her mother has joined the order, and she is using her best efforts to have her mother repudiate her vows, denotes that she will be full of love for her parents, yet will wring their hearts with anguish by thoughtless disobedience.

To see or hear that the leader is dead, foretells severe strains, and trials will eventually end in comparative good.

seducer for a young woman to dream of being seduced, foretells that she will be easily influenced by showy persons.

For a man to dream that he has seduced a girl, is a warning for him to be on his guard, as there are those who will falsely accuse him. If his sweetheart appears shocked or angry under these proposals, he will find that the woman he loves is above reproach. If she consents, he is being used for her pecuniary pleasures.

seed seeds may simply represent parts of the human reproductive process, the sperm or egg. Alternatively, much like acorns, seeds can symbolize potential, either in people or situations.

To sow seed in a dream is said to predict the foundation of future wealth, joy, and health (gypsy folklore).

seeing seeing is the sense that all sighted people predominantly use in their dreams, although their eyes are not functioning as they do in waking life.

The imagery and impressions that a dream leaves us with are translated into their sensory equivalents, and sight is the most common of these. Thus, our dreams offer us a panorama through which we can gain greater insight into aspects of our lives and our inner selves. Seeing things in dreams will offer the chance for the dreamer to see him or herself in a clearer light in real life.

sentinel a dream of personal security (gypsy folklore).

sentry to dream of a sentry, denotes that you will have kind protectors, and your life will be smoothly conducted.

seraglio feebleness of disposition and inactivity are here indicated (gypsy folklore).

seraphim a dream of spiritual exaltation, piety (gypsy folklore).

serenade to hear a serenade in your dream, you will have pleasant news from absent friends, and your anticipations will not fail you.

If you are one of the serenaders, there are many delightful things in your future.

serpent a dream of temptation and of evil (gypsy folklore). Obviously the dream interpreters of modern times have accepted the Christian and Jewish symbolism, rather than that of more remote antiquity. Freud and Jung, however, revert to more primitive times and interpret this as an erotic dream. Raphael interprets the serpent dream as one of 'a deadly enemy bent on your ruin; to kill one denotes success over your enemy'. The serpent was the ancient Egyptian symbol of wisdom and of the sun. Curled in a circle it represented time without end; twisted around a staff, it denoted health. 'More subtle thou art than any beast of the field.' (Bible). *See also* REPTILE; SNAKE.

servants to dream of having servants symbolizes having secret enemies. To hear them talk denotes scandal and suspicion.

seven *see* NUMBERS.

sewing to dream of sewing on new garments, foretells that domestic peace will crown your wishes.

sex sex is a basic force that drives all humans. The human race needs to procreate in order to survive. Being a basic, primitive urge, it has come, through time, to be seen as somehow 'at odds' with the rational side of human beings. Animals are primitive, human beings have reasoning. Consequently, humans have imposed upon themselves certain restraints concerning sexual behaviour. These restraints are not universally the same, and it is true to say that for many people, their conditioning concerning sexual behaviour through family, religious authority, etc, may be completely at odds with his or her desires. Thus, sexual desires have to be sublimated in waking life.

The dream world is a safe place for the dreamer to explore feelings that he or she may feel prevented from expressing in waking life. Thus it can act as a release for sexual tension. Dreams of sex, or dreams in which sexual symbols occur (and there are many), can, if interpreted properly, offer considerable insight to the dreamer.

It must be added, however, that overtly sexual dreams can disturb some people and fill them with such feelings of guilt and revulsion that they try to sublimate the dreams themselves, instead of using the dream as a simple release or tool for building greater self-awareness.

shakers to dream of seeing members of the sect called Shakers in a dream, denotes that you will change in your business, and feel coldness growing towards your sweetheart.

If you imagine you belong to them, you will unexpectedly renounce all former ties, and seek new pleasures in distant localities.

Shakespeare to dream of Shakespeare, denotes that unhappiness and despondency will work much anxiety to momentous affairs, and love will be stripped of passion's fever.

To read Shakespeare's works, denotes that you will unalterably attach yourself to literary accomplishments.

shaking hands for a young woman to dream that she shakes hands with some prominent ruler, foretells she will be surrounded with pleasures and distinction from strangers. If she avails herself of the opportunity, she will stand in high favour with friends. If she finds she must reach up to shake hands, she will find rivalry and opposition. If she has on gloves, she will overcome these obstacles.

To shake hands with those beneath you, denotes you will be loved and honoured for your kindness and benevolence. If you think you or they have soiled hands, you will find enemies among seeming friends.

For a young woman to dream of shaking hands with a decrepit old man, foretells she will find trouble where amusement was sought.

shame, embarrassment for anyone to dream that they are ashamed, denotes that some unfriendly person will take advantage of ignorance to place them in a compromising situation.

shampoo to dream of seeing shampooing going on, denotes that you will engage in undignified affairs to please others.

To have your own head shampooed, you will soon make a secret trip, in which you will have much enjoyment, if you succeed in keeping the real purport from your family or friends.

shamrock the shamrock denotes good health and longevity, some say a journey by water (gypsy folklore).

shanty to dream of a shanty, denotes that you will leave home in the quest of health. This also warns you of decreasing prosperity.

shark *see* ANIMALS.

shave to merely contemplate getting a shave, in your dream, denotes you will plan for the successful development of enterprises, but will fail to generate energy sufficient to succeed.

shaving to dream that you are being shaved, portends that you will let impostors defraud you.

To shave yourself, foretells that you will govern your own business and dictate to your household, notwithstanding that the presence of a shrew may cause you quarrels.

If your face appears smooth, you will enjoy quiet, and your conduct will hot be questioned by your companions. If old and rough, there will be many squalls or, the matrimonial sea.

If your razor is dull and pulls your face, you will give your friends cause to criticise your private life.

If your beard seems grey, you will be absolutely devoid of any sense of justice to those having claims upon you.

If a woman dreams of being shaved, she is afraid that she is becoming too masculine, or too unattractive, and wishes to change that.

shawl to dream of a shawl, denotes that some one will offer you flattery and favour.

To lose your shawl, foretells sorrow and discomfort. A young woman is in danger of being jilted by a good-looking man, after this dream.

shears to see shears in your dream, denotes that you will become miserly and disagreeable in your dealings.

To see them broken, you will lose friends and standing by your eccentric demeanour.

sheaves a favourable dream (gypsy folklore).

sheep *see* ANIMALS.

sheet iron to see sheet iron in your dream, denotes you are unfortunately listening to the admonition of others. To walk on it, signifies distasteful engagements.

shellfish *see* ANIMALS.

shells to walk among and gather shells in your dream, denotes extravagance. Pleasure will leave you naught but exasperating regrets and memories. *see* MUSSELS , ANIMALS.

shelter to dream of seeking shelter against rain denotes secret trouble. To fly from a storm indicates evil to come; to find shelter predicts misery and despair. To have shelter refused predicts eventual triumph and joy (gypsy folklore). Here the interpretation is easily traceable to early Christian persecution, when shelter and food were refused to the elect.

shelves to see empty shelves in dreams, indicates losses and consequent gloom.

Full shelves, augurs happy contentment through the fulfilment of hope and exertions.

shepherd to dream of being a shepherd is a dream denoting great piety and charity (gypsy folklore). Jesus Christ was called the 'Good Shepherd' giving the symbolism here.

sheriff to dream of seeing a sheriff, denotes that you will suffer great uneasiness over the uncertain changes which loom up before you.

To imagine that you are elected sheriff or feel interested in the office, denotes that you will participate in some affair which will afford you neither profit nor honour.

To escape arrest, you will be able to further engage in illicit affairs. *See* BAILIFF and POLICE.

ship a dream of hopes and plans, fulfilled according to the fate of the dreamer in question (gypsy folklore). Also the Christian symbol of hope, etc. *See also* BOAT and JOURNEY.

shipwreck a shipwreck is a symbol of abandoned hopes and misfortunes. To see others shipwrecked in your dream denotes that you will rise above them (gypsy folklore).

shirt a torn shirt denotes slander; to tear it yourself is a symbol of indiscretion. A whole and good shirt is a dream of success (gypsy folklore).

shirt-studs to dream of shirt-studs, foretells you will struggle to humour your pride, and will usually be successful. If they are diamonds, and the centre one is larger than the others, you will enjoy wealth, or have an easy time, surrounded by congenial friends.

shoemaker to dream of a shoemaker predicts a life of toil and difficulty (gypsy folklore).

shoes to dream of wearing a new pair of shoes denotes many JOURNEYS. To travel without shoes means comfort and honour as you pass through life (Raphael). *See also* LOSS.

shooting a shooting in a dream may be a metaphor for sexual assault. To shoot a bird augurs completion of purpose; to shoot and miss is ominous. To shoot a bird of prey forecasts triumph over enemies (Raphael). *See also* KILLING and WEAPONS.

shop to dream of a shop, denotes that you will be opposed in every attempt you make for advancement by scheming and jealous friends. *see* STORE.

shot to dream that you are shot, and are feeling the sensations of dying, denotes that you are to meet unexpected abuse from the ill feelings of friends, but if you escape death by waking, you will be fully reconciled with them later on.

To dream that a preacher shoots you, signifies that you will be annoyed by some friend advancing views condemnatory to those entertained by yourself.

shotgun to dream of a shotgun, foretells domestic troubles and worry with children and servants.

To shoot both barrels of a double-barrelled shotgun, foretells that you will meet such exasperating and unfeeling attention in your private and public life that suave manners giving way under the strain and your righteous wrath will be justifiable.

shoulder to dream of seeing naked shoulders, foretells that happy changes will make you look upon the world in a different light than formerly.

To see your own shoulders appearing thin, denotes that you will depend upon the caprices of others for entertainment and pleasure.

shovel to see a shovel in a dream, signifies laborious but noble work will be undertaken.

A broken or old one, implies frustration of hopes.

shower *see* RAIN.

shrew to dream of a shrew, foretells that you will have a task to keep some friend in a cheerful frame of mind, and that you will unfit yourself for the experiences of everyday existence.

shrimp *see* ANIMALS.

shrinking dreaming of shrinking is perhaps an expression of feelings of insignificance or humility.

shroud to dream of a shroud, denotes sickness and its attendant distress and anxiety, coupled with the machinations of the evil-minded and false friends. Business will threaten decline after this dream.

To see shrouded corpses, denotes a multitude of misfortunes.

To see a shroud removed from a corpse, denotes that quarrels will result in alienation.

shrubs love and happiness are augured by this dream (gypsy folklore).

sibyl to consult a sibyl denotes deception and ill-founded fears; to dream of being one forecasts the disclosure of future events (gypsy folklore).

sickness to dream of being sick denotes illness or imprisonment. To dream of attending the sick denotes joy and virtue.

side to dream of seeing only the side of any object, denotes that some person is going to treat your honest proposals with indifference.

To dream that your side pains you, there will be vexations in your affairs that will gall your endurance.

To dream that you have a fleshy, healthy side, you will be successful in courtship and business.

siege to dream of being involved in a seige denotes a feeling of attack and a desire for protection. For a young woman to dream that she is in a siege, and sees cavalry around her, denotes that she will have serious drawbacks to enjoyments, but will surmount them finally, and receive much pleasure and profit from seeming disappointments.

sieve a dream of waste and want (gypsy folklore).

sigh to dream that you are sighing over any trouble or sad event, denotes that you will have unexpected sadness, but some redeeming brightness in your season of trouble.

To hear the sighing of others, foretells that the misconduct of dear friends will oppress you with a weight of gloom.

silk to be clad in silk predicts honour. To dream of trading in silk is a prediction of profit (Artemidorus).

silkworm if you dream of a silkworm, you will engage in a very profitable work, which will also place you in a prominent position.

To see them dead, or cutting through their cocoons, is a sign of reverses and trying times.

silver a dream auguring unsuspected revelation (gypsy folklore). Silver is the emblem of knowledge.

singing this is a dream of CONTRARY MEANING that it is a dream of lamentation. To sing yourself signifies your own trouble, to hear others sing denotes distress among friends (Raphael).

single for married persons to dream that they are single, foretells that their union will not be harmonious, and constant despondency will confront them.

sinking *see* WATER.

Siren domestic difficulties are denoted by a dream of the mythological sea nymphs the Sirens (gypsy folklore). The symbolism is derived from the Greek myth that the singing of the Sirens lured sailors to their deaths on the rocks they inhabited.

six *see* NUMBERS.

skate to dream that you are skating on ice, foretells that you are in danger of losing employment, or valuable articles. If you break through the ice, you will have unworthy friends to counsel you.

To see others skating, foretells that disagreeable people will connect your name in scandal with some person who admires you.

To see skates, denotes discord among your associates.

To see young people skating on roller skates, foretells that you will enjoy good health, and feel enthusiastic over the pleasures you are able to contribute to others.

skeleton a dream of horror and fright (gypsy folklore). *See also* FEAR.

skull a dream denoting penance (gypsy folklore). Here the symbolism is obviously Christian.

sky to see the sky clear and blue denotes health and prosperity; cloudy, troubles in proportion to the clouds (gypsy folklore).

slander to dream that you are slandered, is a sign of your untruthful dealings with ignorance. If you slander anyone, you will feel the loss of friends through selfishness.

slander to dream that you are the subject of slander, denotes that your interests will suffer at the hands of evil-minded gossips. For a young woman, it warns her to be careful of her conduct, as her movements are being critically observed by persons who claim to be her friends.

slang to use slang in a dream augurs pleasure followed by regret (gypsy folklore).

slaughter-house to dream of a slaughter-house, denotes that you will be feared more than loved by your sweetheart or mistress. If the dream denotes your work situation your business will possible have some problems and ther may be gossip involved. *See* BUTCHER.

slave to dream of seeing a slave punished denotes arbitrary injustice of which you will be the victim (gypsy folklore).

sleep to dream of sleeping on clean, fresh beds, denotes peace and favour from those whom you love.

To sleep in unnatural resting places, foretells sickness and broken engagements.

To sleep beside a little child, betokens domestic joys and reciprocated love.

To see others sleeping, you will overcome all opposition in your pursuit for woman's favour.

To dream of sleeping with a repulsive person or object, warns you that your love will wane before that of your sweetheart, and you will suffer for your escapades.

For a young woman to dream of sleeping with her lover or some fascinating object, warns her against yielding herself a willing victim to his charms.

sleepwalking *see* SOMNAMBULIST.

sleigh to see a sleigh in your dreams, foretells you will fail in some love adventure, and incur the displeasure of a friend. To ride in one, foretells injudicious engagements will be entered into by you.

sliding a dream of success. To fall, however, connotes misfortune. To be tripped denotes an enemy (Raphael). *See also* TYPICAL DREAMS.

slighted to dream of slighting any person or friend, denotes that you will fail to find happiness, as you will cultivate a morose and repellent bearing.

If you are slighted, you will have cause to bemoan your unfortunate position.

slight-of-hand to dream of practising slight-of-hand, or seeing others doing so, signifies you will be placed in a position where your energy and power of planning will be called into strenuous play to extricate yourself.

slippers to dream of slippers, warns you that you are about to perform an unfortunate alliance or intrigue. You are likely to find favour with a married person which will result in trouble, if not scandal.

To dream that your slippers are much admired, foretells that you will be involved in a flirtation, which will suggest disgrace.

smallpox to see people with smallpox in your dream, denotes unexpected and shocking sickness, and probably contagion. You will meet failure in accomplishing your designs.

smoke a dream indicating false glory (gypsy folklore).

snail *see* ANIMALS.

snake *see* SERPENT and ANIMALS.

sneeze to dream that you sneeze, denotes that hasty tidings will cause you to change your plans.

To see or hear others sneeze, some people will bore you with visits.

snouts to dream of snouts, foretells dangerous seasons for you.

Enemies are surrounding you, and difficulties will be numerous.

snow a dream of prosperity. A snow storm, however, foretells difficulties from which the dreamer will escape (gypsy folklore).

snuff to dream of snuff, signifies your enemies are seducing the confidence of your friends. For a woman to use it in her dreams, foretells complications which will involve her separation from a favoured friend.

soap a dream of transient worries (gypsy folklore).

socialist to see a socialist in your dreams, your unenvied position among friends and acquaintances is predicted. Your affairs will be neglected for other imaginary duties.

sold to dream that you have sold anything, denotes that unfavourable business will worry you.

soldiers a soldier may be an expression of the discipline, or lack of it, in the dreamer's life. Abandonment of present employment is predicted in this dream.

somnambulist (sleep walker) to imagine while dreaming that you are a somnambulist, portends that you will unwittingly consent to some agreement of plans which will bring you anxiety or ill fortune.

son to dream of your son, if you have one, as being handsome and dutiful, foretells that he will afford you proud satisfaction, and will aspire to high honours. If he is maimed, or suffering from illness or accident, this symbolizes trouble ahead.

If you dream your son has come into danger, and hear his cries, it is a sign of deep grief, loss and sickness. If he is rescued, the threatened danger will pass.

soot if you see soot in your dreams, it means that you will meet with ill success in your affairs. Lovers will be quarrelsome and hard to please.

sorcerer to dream of a sorcerer, foretells your ambitions will undergo strange disappointments and change.

sores to dream of seeing sores, denotes that illness will cause you loss and mental distress.

To dress a sore, foretells that your personal wishes and desires will give place to the pleasure of others.

To dream of an infant having a deep sore so that you can see the bone, denotes that distressing and annoying incidents will detract from your plans, and children will be threatened with contagion.

To dream of sores on yourself, portends early decay of health and impaired mentality. Sickness and unsatisfactory business will follow this dream.

soul to dream of seeing your soul leaving your body, signifies you are in danger of sacrificing yourself to useless designs, which will dwarf your sense of honour and cause you to become mercenary and uncharitable.

For an artist to see his soul in another, foretells he will gain distinction if he applies himself to his work and leaves off sentimental roles.

To imagine another's soul is in you, denotes you will derive solace and benefit from some stranger who is yet to come into your life.

For a young woman musician to dream that she sees another young woman on the stage clothed in sheer robes, and imagining it is her own soul in the other person, denotes she will be out-rivalled in some great undertaking.

To dream that you are discussing the immortality of your soul, denotes you will improve opportunities which will aid you in gaining desired knowledge and pleasure of intercourse with intellectual people.

soup to dream of soup, is a forerunner of good tidings and comfort.

To see others taking soup, foretells that you will have many good chances to marry.

For a young woman to make soup, signifies that she will not be compelled to do menial work in her household, as she will marry a wealthy man.

To drink oyster soup made of sweet milk, there will be quarrels with some bad luck, but reconciliation will follow.

sovereign to dream that you are a sovereign is a dream of CONTRARY MEANING indicating disgrace (gypsy folklore).

sowing to dream that you are sowing seed, foretells to the farmer fruitful promises, if he sows in new ploughed soil.

To see others sowing, much business activity is portended, which will bring gain to all.

spade to dream of a spade is a dream signifying futile toil.

sparrows *see* BIRDS.

spear a dream of suffering at the hands of enemies (gypsy). A symbol of the Passion, the spear was also worshipped as the emblem of the god Mars. Freud attributes an erotic meaning to this dream. *See also* WEAPONS.

spectacles to dream of wearing them denotes disgrace and low spirits (gypsy folklore).

spice a sad dream (gypsy folklore). A symbol of the passion and death of Christ.

spiders *see* ANIMALS.

spider-web to see spider-webs, denotes pleasant associations and fortunate ventures.

spinning this dream denotes many worries.

spirit or spectre to see spirits in a dream, denotes that some unexpected trouble will confront you. If they are white-robed, the health of your nearest friend is threatened, or some business speculation will be disapproving. If they are robed in black, you will meet with treachery and unfaithfulness.

If a spirit speaks, there is some evil near you, which you might avert if you would listen to the counsels of judgement.

To dream that you hear spirits knocking on doors or walls, denotes that trouble will arise unexpectedly.

To see them moving draperies, or moving behind them, is a warning to hold control over your feelings, as you are likely to commit indiscretions. Quarrels are also threatened.

To see the spirit of your friend floating in your room, foretells disappointment and insecurity.

To hear music supposedly coming from spirits, denotes unfavourable changes and sadness in the household.

spitoon to see a spitoon in a dream, signifies that an unworthy attachment will be formed by you, and that your work will be neglected.

To spit in one, foretells that reflections will be cast upon your conduct.

spitting to dream of spitting, denotes unhappy terminations of seemingly auspicious undertakings. For some one to spit on you, foretells disagreements and alienation of affections.

spleen to dream of spleen, denotes that you will have a misunderstanding with some party who will injure you.

splendour to dream that you live in splendour, denotes that you will succeed to elevations, and will reside in a different state to the one you now occupy.

To see others thus living, signifies pleasure derived from the interest that friends take in your welfare.

splinter to dream of splinters sticking into your flesh, denotes that you will have many vexations from members of your family or from jealous rivals.

If while you are visiting you stick a splinter in your foot, you will soon make, or receive, a visit which will prove extremely unpleasant. Your affairs will go slightly wrong through your continued neglect.

sponges seen in a dream, denote that deception is being practised upon you.

To use one in erasing, you will be the victim of folly.

spools of thread a dream of serious worries (gypsy folklore).

spoons to see, or use, spoons in a dream, denotes favourable signs of advancement. Domestic affairs will afford contentment.

To think a spoon is lost, denotes that you will be suspicious of wrong doing.

To steal one, is a sign that you will deserve censure for your contemptible meanness in your home.

To dream of broken or soiled spoons, signifies loss and trouble.

spring good fortune and success (gypsy folklore).

spur to dream of wearing spurs, denotes that you will engage in some unpleasant controversy.

To see others with them on, foretells that enmity is working you trouble.

spy to dream that spies are harassing you, denotes dangerous quarrels and uneasiness.

To dream that you are a spy, denotes that you will make unfortunate ventures.

spy-glass to dream that you are looking through a spy-glass, denotes that changes will soon occur to your disadvantage.

To see a broken or imperfect one, foretells unhappy dissension and loss of friends.

squall to dream of squalls, foretells disappointing business and unhappiness.

squinting to dream that you see some person with squinting eyes, denotes that you will be annoyed with unpleasant people.

For a man to dream that his sweetheart, or some good-looking girl, squints her eyes at him, foretells that he is threatened with loss by seeking the favours of women. For a young woman to have this dream about men, she will be in danger of losing her fair reputation.

squirrel to dream of seeing squirrels, denotes that pleasant friends will soon visit you. You will see advancement in your business also.

To kill a squirrel, denotes that you will be unfriendly and disliked.

To pet one, signifies family joy.

To see a dog chasing one, foretells disagreements and unpleasantness among friends.

stable to dream of a stable, is a sign of fortune and advantageous surroundings.

To see a stable burning denotes successful changes, or it may be seen in actual life.

staff a dream of pilgrimage and journeys (gypsy folklore). Dreaming of a staff may also have a sexual significance.

stag *see* ANIMALS.

stage driver to dream of a stage driver, signifies you will go on a strange journey in quest of fortune and happiness.

stain to see stain on your hands, or clothing, while dreaming, foretells that trouble over small matters will assail you.

To see a stain on the garments of others, or on their flesh, foretells that some person will betray you.

stairs to dream of passing up a stairs, foretells good fortune and much happiness.

If you fall down stairs, you will be the object of hatred and envy.

To walk down, you will be unlucky in your affairs, and your love-making will be unfavourable.

To see broad, handsome stairs, foretells approaching riches and honours.

To see others going down stairs, denotes that unpleasant conditions will take the place of pleasure.

To sit on stair steps, denotes a gradual rise in fortune and delight.

stall to dream of a stall, denotes impossible results from some enterprise will be expected by you.

stallion to dream of a stallion, foretells prosperous conditions are approaching you, in which you will hold a position which will confer honour upon you. To dream you ride a fine stallion, denotes you will rise to position and affluence in a phenomenal way; however, your success will warp your morality and sense of justice. To see one with the rabies, foretells that wealthy surroundings will cause you to assume arrogance, which will be distasteful to your friends, and your pleasures will be deceitful.

stammer to dream that you stammer in your conversation, denotes that worry and illness will threaten your enjoyment. To hear others stammer, foretells that unfriendly persons will delight in annoying you and giving you needless worry.

standard-bearer to dream that you are a standard-bearer, denotes that your occupation will be pleasant, but varied.

To see others acting as standard-bearers, foretells that you will be jealous and envious of some friend.

stars *see* PLANETS.

starving a dream of CONTRARY MEANING auguring success and plenty (gypsy folklore).

statues to see statues in dreams, signifies estrangement from a loved one. Lack of energy will cause you disappointment in realising wishes.

stealing to dream of stealing, or of seeing others commit this act, foretells bad luck and loss of character.

To be accused of stealing, denotes that you will be misunderstood in some affair, and suffer therefrom, but you will eventually find that this will bring you favour.

To accuse others, denotes that you will treat some person with hasty inconsideration.

steeple to see a steeple rising from a church, is a harbinger of sickness and reverses.

A broken one, points to death in your circle, or friends.

To climb a steeple, foretells that you will have serious difficulties, but will surmount them.

To fall from one, denotes losses in trade and ill health.

steps to walk up steps is a dream auguring success in love, a happy marriage and a rise in life (Raphael).

step-sister to dream of a step-sister, denotes you will have unavoidable care and annoyance upon you.

stethoscope to dream of a stethoscope, foretells calamity to your hopes and enterprises. There will be troubles and recriminations in love.

sticks if you dream of seeing a dense smoke ascending from a pile of sticks, it denotes that enemies are bearing down upon you, but if the sticks are burning brightly, you will escape from all unpleasant complications and enjoy great prosperity.

If you walk on burning sticks, you will be injured by the unwise actions of friends. If you succeed in walking on them without being burned, you will have a miraculous rise in prospects.

To dream of seeing sticks piled up to burn you at the stake, signifies that you are threatened with loss, but if you escape, you will enjoy a long and prosperous life.

sticks to dream of sticks, is an unlucky omen.

stiffness someone who dreams of feeling stiff or being unable to move with any flexibility may, in waking life, be taking an attitude of inflexibleness about some situation.

stillborn to dream of a stillborn infant, denotes that some distressing incident will come before your notice.

stilts to dream of walking on stilts, denotes that your fortune is in an insecure condition.

To fall from them, or feel them break beneath you, you will be pre-cipitated into embarrassments by trusting your affairs to the care of others.

sting a dream of a sting by a BEE, WASP or HORNET denotes injury by a wicked person (Raphael).

stockings to dream of stockings is a dream of distress and trouble. Holes warn you to guard your conduct (gypsy folklore).

stone mason to see stone masons at work while dreaming, foretells disappointment.

To dream that you are a stone mason, portends that your labours will be unfruitful, and your companions will be dull and uncongenial.

stone to see stones in your dreams, foretells numberless perplexities and failures.

To walk among rocks, or stones, omens that an uneven and rough pathway will be yours for at least a while.

To make deals in ore-bearing rock lands, you will be successful in business after many lines have been tried. If you fail to profit by the deal, you will have disappointments. If anxiety is greatly felt in clos-ing the trade, you will succeed in buying or selling something that will prove profitable to you.

Small stones or pebbles, implies that little worries and vexations will irritate you.

If you throw a stone, you will have cause to admonish a person.

If you design to throw a pebble or stone at some belligerent per-son, it denotes that some evil feared by you will pass because of your untiring attention to right principles.

storage battery to dream of a storage battery, opportune specula-tions will return you handsome gains.

store to dream of a store filled with merchandise, foretells prosperity and advancement.

An empty one, denotes failure of efforts and quarrels.

To dream that your store is burning, is a sign of renewed activity in business and pleasure.

If you find yourself in a department store, it foretells that much pleasure will be derived from various sources of profit.

To sell goods in one, your advancement will be accelerated by your energy and the efforts of friends.

To dream that you sell a pair of soiled, grey cotton gloves to a woman, foretells that your opinion of women will place you in hazardous positions. If a woman has this dream, her preference for some one of the male sex will not be appreciated very much by him.

stork *see* BIRDS.

storm heavy misfortunes which will vanish (gypsy folklore).

stranger to see a stranger is a dream of honour and success.

straw misfortune, lack of money (gypsy folklore).

strawberries *see* FRUIT.

stream *see* BROOK, RIVER and WATER.

street to dream that you are walking in a street, foretells ill luck and worries. You will almost despair of reaching the goal you have set up in your aspirations.

To be in a familiar street in a distant city, and it appears dark, you will make a journey soon, which will not afford the profit or pleasure contemplated. If the street is brilliantly lighted, you will engage in pleasure, which will quickly pass, leaving no comfort.

To pass down a street and feel alarmed lest a thug attack you, denotes that you are venturing upon dangerous ground in advancing your pleasure or business.

street-poster to dream that you are a street-poster, denotes that you will undertake some unpleasant and unprofitable work.

To see street-posters at work, foretells disagreeable news.

struggling with a burglar or in a dangerous place is a dream of the attainment of honour. The struggle to obtain mastery denotes recovery from illness, to dream of being overcome in a struggle forecasts that the subject may be near to death (gypsy folklore).

stumble if you stumble in a dream while walking or running, you will meet with disfavour, and obstructions will bar your path to success, but you will eventually surmount them, if you do not fall.

stumps to dream of a stump, foretells you are to have reverses and will depart from your usual mode of living. To see fields of stumps, signifies you will be unable to defend yourself from the encroachments of adversity. To dig or pull them up, is a sign that you will extricate yourself from the environment of poverty by throwing off sentiment and pride and meeting the realities of life with a determination to overcome whatever opposition you may meet.

success a dream of CONTRARY MEANING signifying failure (gypsy folklore).

suckle to see the young taking suckle, denotes contentment and favourable conditions for success is unfolding to you.

suffocating to dream that you are suffocating, denotes that you will experience deep sorrow and mortification at the conduct of some one you love. You should be careful of your health after this dream.

sugar to dream of swallowing a quantity of sugar denotes that privation is about to beset you (gypsy folklore).

suicide a dream denoting misfortunes brought about by yourself (gypsy folklore). It is not a prediction of your own oncoming death but, as with many dreams of death, it signifies a change, this time in the way that you lead you life.

sulphur a dream of purification (gypsy folklore). Medieval physicians thought sulphur the greatest disinfectant and purifier.

sun to see the sun is a dream of success. The sun rising denotes good news. A setting sun is bad, while for the sun to be overcast foretells troubles and changes (gypsy folklore). The sun is the invariable symbol of light and wisdom, and can represent warm feelings about something or towards someone.

sundial a dream denoting wasted time (gypsy folklore).

sunshade to dream of seeing young girls carrying sunshades, foretells prosperity and exquisite delights.

A broken one, foretells sickness and death to the young.

surgeon to dream of a surgeon, denotes you are threatened by enemies who are close to you in business. For a young woman, this dream promises a serious illness from which she will experience great inconvenience.

surgical instruments to see surgical instruments in a dream, foretells dissatisfaction will be felt by you at the indiscreet manner a friend manifests toward you.

surroundings the surroundings in which a dream is seen to be played out are often reflections of the dreamer's feelings. Thus, a sombre and dreary setting is likely to indicate depressed feelings on the dreamer's part, while bright colours will reflect feelings of happiness and contentment. A dream of cold surroundings, with snow and ice perhaps, can reflect emotional or attitudinal coldness, and a dream of a warm, safe environment will indicate that the dreamer feels secure and content.

swallow *see* BIRDS.

swamp to dream of getting into a swamp foretells vexations through lack of money. *See also* MARSH.

swan *see* BIRDS.

swearing to dream of swearing, denotes some unpleasant obstructions in business. A lover will have cause to suspect the faithfulness of his affianced after this dream.

To dream that you are swearing before your family, denotes that disagreements will soon be brought about by your disloyal conduct.

sweeping to dream of sweeping, denotes that you will gain favour in the eyes of your husband, and children will find pleasure in the home.

If you think the floors need sweeping, and you from some cause neglect them, there will be distresses and bitter disappointments awaiting you in the approaching days.

To servants, sweeping is a sign of disagreements and suspicion of the intentions of others.

sweet taste to dream of any kind of a sweet taste in your mouth, denotes you will be praised for your pleasing conversation and calm demeanour in a time of commotion and distress.

To dream that you are trying to get rid of a sweet taste, foretells that you will oppress and deride your friends, and will incur their displeasure.

sweetheart to dream that he or she is well and smiling denotes purity and constancy. If your sweetheart is pale or ailing, the reverse is the case (Raphael).

swelling to dream that you see yourself swollen, denotes that you will amass fortune, but your egotism will interfere with your enjoyment.

To see others swollen, foretells that advancement will meet with envious obstructions.

swimming with the head above water, success; the head under water, denotes misfortune; to sink forecasts ruin (Raphael). *See also* TYPICAL DREAMS.

Swiss cheese to dream of Swiss cheese, foretells that you will come into possession of substantial property, and healthful amusements will be enjoyed.

switch to dream of a switch, foretells changes and misfortune.

A broken switch, foretells disgrace and trouble.

To dream of a railroad switch, denotes that travel will cause you much loss and inconvenience.

To dream of a switch, signifies you will meet discouragement in momentous affairs.

sword to wear one is a dream denoting authority; to be cut with one, humiliation (gypsy folklore). *See also* WEAPONS.

sybil to dream of a sybil, foretells that you will enjoy assignations and other demoralising pleasures.

sycamore this dream signifies marriage to a single person, but jealousy to the wedded (gypsy folklore). In Eastern lands it symbolized the tree of life.

symphony to dream of symphonies, heralds delightful occupations. *see* MUSIC.

synagogue to dream of a synagogue, foretells that you have enemies powerfully barricading your entrance into fortune's realms. If you climb to the top on the outside, you will overcome oppositions and be successful.

If you read the Hebrew inscription on a synagogue, you will meet disaster, but will eventually rebuild your fortunes with renewed splendour. *see* CHURCH.

syringe to dream of a syringe, denotes that false alarm of the gravity of a relative's condition will reach you. To see a broken one, foretells you are approaching a period of ill health or worry over slight mistakes in business.

T

table to see one denotes sensual pleasures, to break one in your dream predicts a removal (gypsy folklore).

tablet a dream forecasting amazing events (gypsy folklore).

tack a dream of quarrels and enmity (gypsy folklore).

tadpole to dream of tadpoles, foretells uncertain speculation will bring cause for uneasiness in business. For a young woman to see them in clear water, foretells she will form a relation with a wealthy but immoral man.

tail to dream of seeing only the tail of a beast, unusual annoyance is indicated where pleasures seemed assured.

To cut off the tail of an animal, denotes that you will suffer misfortune by your own carelessness.

To dream that you have the tail of a beast grown on you, denotes that your evil ways will cause you untold distress, and strange events will cause you perplexity.

tailor to dream of a tailor, denotes that worries will arise on account of some journey to be made. To have a misunderstanding with one, shows that you will be disappointed in the outcome of some scheme. For one to take your measure, denotes that you will have quarrels and disagreements.

talisman to dream that you wear a talisman, implies you will have pleasant companions and enjoy favours from the rich. For a young woman to dream her lover gives her one, denotes she will obtain her wishes concerning marriage.

talking talking in a dream may represent a deeper form of communication than talking in daily life.

Sometimes people dream that they try to talk but cannot manage to get the words out, or find that all they can do is babble meaninglessly. This indicates that the dreamer is unable to express some feeling in waking life, or that he or she feels emotionally cut off from other people, misunderstood and frustrated.

tallow to dream of tallow, forebodes that your possessions of love and wealth will quickly vanish.

tamarind a dream of this tree denotes rain or news and trouble through a woman (gypsy folklore).

tambourine a dream of good luck (gypsy folklore). The gypsy instrument at festivals.

tank to dream of an oil tank, foretells you will be prosperous and satisfied beyond your expectations. To see a leaking tank, denotes loss of money.

To dream of an army tank denotes a fear of being attacked or a desire to destroy something.

tannery to dream of a tannery, denotes contagion and other illness. Loss in trade is portended.

To dream that you are a tanner, denotes that you will have to engage in work which is not to your taste, but there will be others dependent upon you.

To buy leather from a tannery, foretells that you will be successful in your undertakings, but will not make many friends.

tape to dream of tape, denotes your work will be wearisome and unprofitable. For a woman to buy it, foretells she will find misfortune laying oppression upon her.

tapestry to dream of seeing rich tapestry, foretells that luxurious living will be to your liking, and if the tapestries are not worn or ragged, you will be able to gratify your inclinations.

If a young woman dreams that her rooms are hung with tapestry, she will soon wed some one who is rich and above her in standing.

tapeworm to dream you see a tapeworm, or have one, denotes disagreeable prospects for health or for pleasure.

tar dreaming of tar denotes travels by water. If tar is found on the hands, this denotes a difficulty (gypsy folklore).

tar to dream that you see or travel on a tar macadam road, is significant of pleasant journeys, from which you will derive much benefit. For young people, this dream foretells noble aspirations.

tarantula to see a tarantula in your dream, signifies enemies are about to overwhelm you with loss. To kill one, denotes you will be successful after much ill-luck.

target to dream of a target, foretells you will have some affair demanding your attention from other more pleasant ones. For a young woman to think she is a target, denotes her reputation is in danger through the envy of friendly associates.

tassels a dream denoting delight (gypsy folklore).

tattoo to see your body appearing tattooed, foretells that some difficulty will cause you to make a long and tedious absence from your home.

To see tattoos on others, foretells that strange loves will make you an object of jealousy.

To dream you are a tattooist, is a sign that you will estrange yourself from friends because of your fancy for some strange experience.

taxes to dream that you pay your taxes, foretells you will succeed in destroying evil influences rising around you. If others pay them, you will be forced to ask aid of friends. If you are unable to pay them, you will be unfortunate in experiments you are making.

tea a dream denoting encumbered finances (gypsy folklore).

teacups to dream of teacups, foretells that affairs of enjoyment will be attended by you. For a woman to break or see them broken, omens her pleasure and good fortune will be marred by a sudden trouble. To drink wine from one, foretells fortune and pleasure will be combined in the near future.

teapot augurs new friendships (gypsy folklore).

tears a dream of CONTRARY MEANING denoting joy (gypsy folklore).

teasing to dream of teasing denotes trouble and sickness. To dream of being teased denotes good news (gypsy folklore).

teeth *see* BODY and TYPICAL DREAMS.

telegram you will go on a very long journey after dreaming of a telegram (gypsy folklore).

telephones telephones, and what is done with them in a dream, will reflect the dreamer's feelings about how he or she is able or unable to communicate his or her emotions to other people in waking life.

telescope to dream of a telescope, portends unfavourable seasons for love and domestic affairs, and business will be changeable and uncertain.

To look at planets and stars through one, portends for you journeys which will afford you much pleasure, but later cause you much financial loss.

To see a broken telescope, or one not in use, signifies that matters will go out of the ordinary with you, and trouble may be expected.

tempest *see* STORM.

temple *see* CHURCH.

temptation to dream that you are surrounded by temptations, denotes that you will be involved in some trouble with an envious person who is trying to displace you in the confidence of friends. If you resist them, you will be successful in some affair in which you have much opposition.

ten *see* NUMBERS.

tenant for a landlord to see his tenant in a dream, denotes he will have business trouble and vexation. To imagine you are a tenant, foretells you will suffer loss in experiments of a business character. If a tenant pays you money, you will be successful in some engagements.

tenpins if you dream at playing at tenpins, you will doubtless soon engage in some affair which will bring discredit upon your name, and you will lose your money and true friendship.

To see others engaged in this dream, foretells that you will find pleasure in frivolous people and likely lose employment.

For a young woman to play a successful game of tenpins, is an omen of light pleasures, but sorrow will attend her later.

tent denotes war or a quarrel close at hand (gypsy folklore).

terror to dream that you feel terror at any object or happening, denotes that disappointments and loss will envelope you.

To see others in terror, means that unhappiness of friends will seriously affect you.

tests dreaming of tests may be a reflection of the dreamer's awareness of being judged by his or her actions in daily life. They may also be general stress-induced anxiety dreams. *See also* EXAMS and TYPICAL DREAMS.

text to dream of hearing a minister reading his text, denotes that quarrels will lead to separation with some friend.

To dream that you are in a dispute about a text, foretells unfortunate adventures for you.

If you try to recall a text, you will meet with unexpected difficulties.

If you are repeating and pondering over one, you will have great obstacles to overcome if you gain your desires.

thatch to dream that you thatch a roof with any quickly, perishable material, denotes that sorrow and discomfort will surround you.

If you find that a roof which you have thatched with straw is leaking, there will be threatening of danger, but by your rightly directed energy they may be averted.

thaw to dream of seeing ice thawing, foretells that some affair which has caused you much worry will soon give you profit and pleasure.

To see the ground thawing after a long freeze, foretells prosperous circumstances.

theatre to dream of being at a theatre, denotes that you will have much pleasure in the company of new friends. Your affairs will be satisfactory after this dream. If you are one of the players, your pleasures will be of short duration.

If you attend a vaudeville theatre, you are in danger of losing property through silly pleasures. If it is a grand opera, you will succeed in you wishes and aspirations.

If you applaud and laugh at a theatre, you will sacrifice duty to the gratification of fancy.

To dream of trying to escape from one during a fire or other excitement, foretells that you will engage in some enterprise, which will be hazardous.

thermometer a dream denoting fever or some sudden change in the temperature (gypsy folklore).

thicket *see* HEDGE.

thief to dream of being a thief and that you are pursued by officers, is a sign that you will meet reverses in business, and your social relations will be unpleasant. If you pursue or capture a thief, you will overcome your enemies. *See* STEALING.

thighs to dream of their being broken or injured implies an accident or death in a foreign country (gypsy folklore).

thimble a dream denoting a vain search for work (gypsy folklore).

thirst to quench a thirst with clear water denotes sleep and contentment. To drink tepid or foul water is an indication of feelings of discomfort lasting through the night (gypsy folklore).

thistle to mow thistles denotes insolence, to be pricked by one forecasts vexation (gypsy folklore).

thorns a dream denoting grief, care and difficulties (gypsy folklore). Thorns are symbols of the Christian Passion.

thread a dream denoting mysterious intrigues. To unravel the thread denotes the discovery of a secret. A dream of gold thread denotes success through intrigue; silver thread indicates that this intrigue is frustrated (gypsy folklore).

three *see* NUMBERS.

threshing to dream of threshing grain, denotes great advancement in business and happiness among families. But if there is an abundance of straw and little grain, unsuccessful enterprises will be undertaken.

To break down or have an accident while threshing, you will have some great sorrow in the midst of prosperity.

throat *see* BODY; TYPICAL DREAMS.

throne a dream connoting credit, renown and honour (gypsy folklore).

thumb to dream of seeing a thumb, foretells that you will be the favourite of artful persons and uncertain fortune.

If you are suffering from a sore thumb, you will lose in business, and your companions will prove disagreeable. To dream that you have no thumb, implies destitution and loneliness. If it seems unnaturally small, you will enjoy pleasure for a time. If abnormally large, your success will be rapid and brilliant.

A soiled thumb indicates gratification of loose desires. If the thumb has a very long nail, you are liable to fall into evil through seeking strange pleasures.

thunder *see* LIGHTNING.

tickle to dream of being tickled, denotes insistent worries and illness.

If you tickle others, you will throw away much enjoyment through weakness and folly.

ticks to dream you see ticks crawling on your flesh, is a sign of impoverished circumstances and ill health. Hasty journeys to sick beds may be made.

To mash a tick on you, denotes that you will be annoyed by treacherous enemies.

To see in your dreams large ticks on stock, enemies are endeavouring to get possession of your property by foul means.

tide to watch the tide is a dream of sorrow (gypsy folklore). *See also* WATER.

tiger *see* ANIMALS.

till to dream of seeing money and valuables in a till, foretells coming success. Your love affairs will be exceedingly favourable. An empty one, denotes disappointed expectations.

timber to see timber in your dreams, is an augury of prosperous times and peaceful surroundings.

If the timber appears dead, there are great disappointments for you. *See* FOREST.

time time can do strange things in dreams. We can find ourselves as an adult among the people and places of our childhood, and we can leap from one apparent time zone to another without disturbing the continuity of the dream. Certain times of day, however, are thought to have certain meanings within the world of dreams.

afternoon/evening may represent the later years of life.

daylight/daytime may represent the conscious self.

morning may represent childhood.

night its blackness may represent that which is unknown, perhaps that which lies in the future. According to the mood of the dream, night may represent a time of fear, or a time of peace and rest.

tinker a dream denoting trouble with neighbours (gypsy folklore).

tipsy to dream that you are tipsy, denotes that you will cultivate a jovial disposition, and the cares of life will make no serious inroads into your conscience.

To see others tipsy, shows that you are careless as to the demeanour of your associates. To see it withered, denotes that she will miss happiness through careless conduct.

toad *see* ANIMALS.

toadstool a dream denoting sudden elevation (gypsy folklore). Interpretation derived from their growth of a single night.

tobacco a dream denoting sensual pleasure (gypsy folklore).

toddy to dream of taking a toddy, foretells interesting events will soon change your plan of living.

toil dreaming of toil, rude labour, drawing water, etc, denotes servitude to the rich and profit to the poor (gypsy folklore).

tomato to dream of eating a tomato denotes happiness of a short duration (gypsy folklore). For many years the tomato was thought to be poisonous and was considered dangerous to eat.

Eating a tomato also has a certain sexual imagery so this dream may denote erotic feelings.

tomb a dream of marriage, the more handsome the tomb the more brilliant the alliance (gypsy folklore).

tongue to dream of seeing your own tongue, denotes that you will be looked upon with disfavour by your acquaintances.

To see the tongue of another, foretells that scandal will vilify you.

To dream that your tongue is affected in any way, denotes that your carelessness in talking will get you into trouble.

tools tools can often be interpreted as representing the male sexual organ in dreams. In certain contexts, when a tool is being used as a weapon, this may indicate hidden feelings of aggression, perhaps of a sexual nature.

toothless to dream that you are toothless, denotes your inability to advance your interests, and ill health will cast gloom over your prospects.

To see others toothless, foretells that enemies are trying in vain to calumniate you.

tooth-picks to dream of tooth-picks, foretells that small anxieties, and spites will harass you unnecessarily if you give them your attention.

If you use one, you will be a party to a friend's injury.

topaz to see topaz in a dream, signifies Fortune will be liberal in her favours, and you will have very pleasing companions. For a woman to lose topaz ornaments, foretells she will be injured by jealous friends who court her position. To receive one from another beside a relative, foretells an interesting love affair will occupy her attention.

tops to dream of a top, denotes that you will be involved in frivolous difficulties.

To see one spinning, foretells that you will waste your means in childish pleasures.

To see a top, foretells indiscriminate friendships will involve you in difficulty.

torches *see* FIRE, CANDLES etc.

tornado if you dream that you are in a tornado, you will be filled with disappointment and perplexity over the miscarriage of studied plans for swift attainment of fortune.

torpedo a dream foretelling a shocking discovery (gypsy folklore). The obvious Freudian interpretation of a torpedo in a dream is that it is a phallic symbol. *See also* ROCKET.

torrent to wade in one, sorrows, adversity; to be caught in one, danger of lawsuits (gypsy folklore).

tortoise *see* ANIMALS.

torture to dream of being tortured, denotes that you will undergo disappointment and grief through the machination of false friends.

If you are torturing others, you will fail to carry out well-laid plans for increasing your fortune.

If you are trying to alleviate the torture of others, you will succeed after a struggle in business and love.

touching touching can indicate satisfactory communication with others. Feeling oneself being touched may represent conscious awareness. Trying not to touch or be touched by somebody may indicate anger and perhaps a desire to detach oneself from him or her.

tourist to dream that you are a tourist, denotes that you will engage in some pleasurable affair which will take you away from your usual residence.

To see tourists, indicates brisk but unsettled business and anxiety in love.

tower most obviously, a tower in a dream may have a phallic meaning; alternatively, it can reflect feelings of aloofness or of isolation.

To ascend a tower signifies a reversal of fortune (gypsy folklore). Interpretation corresponds with the aversion of the Hebrews for towers, an example of which is instanced in the story of the Tower of Babel.

toys to see toys in dreams, foretells family joys, if whole and new, but if broken, death will rend your heart with sorrow.

To see children at play with toys, marriage of a happy nature is indicated.

To give away toys in your dreams, foretells you will be ignored in a social way by your acquaintances.

trade to dream of trading, denotes fair success in your enterprise. If you fail, trouble and annoyances will overtake you.

tragedy to dream of a tragedy, foretells misunderstandings and grievous disappointments.

To dream that you are implicated in a tragedy, portends that a calamity will plunge you into sorrow and peril.

train journey *see* JOURNEY.

train, missing a *see* TYPICAL DREAMS.

traitor to see a traitor in your dream, foretells you will have enemies working to despoil you. If some one calls you one, or if you imagine yourself one, there will be unfavourable prospects of pleasure for you.

transfiguration to dream of the transfiguration, foretells that your faith in man's own nearness to God will raise you above trifling opinions, and elevate you to a worthy position, in which capacity you will be able to promote the well being of the ignorant and persecuted.

To see yourself transfigured, you will stand high in the esteem of honest and prominent men.

trap a dream of losses through law and lawsuits (gypsy folklore).

trap door to see someone emerging from a trap door is a dream of a secret divulged. To dream of one shut down denotes mystery and hidden treasures (gypsy folklore).

travelling *see* JOURNEY.

tray to see trays in your dream, denotes your wealth will be foolishly wasted, and surprises of unpleasant nature will shock you. If the trays seem to be filled with valuables, surprises will come in the shape of good fortune.

treasure *see* JEWELS.

tree the tree can be understood to represent all aspects of our life. It is a manifestation of our growth and of where we are coming from. The roots represent our roots, and the branches represent the different aspects of our personalities and our direction in life. Its buds and new leaves represent new life; both that of future generations, and new life in the sense of spiritual renewal. *Falling leaves* are symbolic of that which is cast off from us, the things that we leave behind as we progress through life. The FRUIT of the tree stands for what we have created in life; our achievements, our children and our own selves can all be seen as our 'fruit'. The flowers of the tree may be seen as the human ability to procreate, or more specifically, female fertility. The bark is our protectiveness towards ourselves. The growth of the tree is a mirror for the growth of our bodies and spirits, and for the energy or life force that is necessary for that growth.

A dead tree seen in a dream may represent the death of a person, or the passing of something in your life. *See also* FLOWER, FRUIT.

trench a dream denoting siege and triumph over resistance.

triangle a dream concerning objects of respect and adoration (gypsy folklore).

tripe to see tripe in a dream, means sickness and danger.

To eat tripe, denotes that you will be disappointed in some serious matter.

triplets to dream of seeing triplets, foretells success in affairs where failure was feared.

For a man to dream that his wife has them, signifies a pleasant termination to some affair which has been long in dispute.

To hear newly-born triplets crying, signifies disagreements which will be hastily reconciled to your pleasure.

For a young woman to dream that she has triplets, denotes that she will suffer loss and disappointment in love, but will succeed to wealth.

tripod a dream of unveiling the future, of uncertainty (gypsy folklore). Obviously derived from the tripod upon which the oracles were seated when forecasting.

trophy to see trophies in a dream, signifies some pleasure or fortune will come to you through the endeavours of mere acquaintances. For a woman to give away a trophy, implies doubtful pleasures and fortune.

trousers to dream of trousers, foretells that you will be tempted to dishonourable deeds.

If you put them on wrong side out, you will find that a fascination is fastening its hold upon you.

trout *see* ANIMALS.

trowel to dream of a trowel, denotes you will experience reaction in unfavourable business, and will vanquish poverty. To see one rusty or broken, unavoidable ill luck is fast approaching you.

trumpet to blow a trumpet denotes triumph over enemies. To hear one denotes coming trouble (Raphael). Invariably the symbol of triumph.

trunk if the trunk is full it shows economy. If it is empty it denotes extravagance (Raphael).

truss to see a truss in your dream, your ill health and unfortunate business engagements are predicted.

trusts to dream of trusts, foretells indifferent success in trade or law.

If you imagine you are a member of a trust, you will be successful in designs of a speculative nature.

tub always a bad dream. If the tub is filled with water it denotes evil. If it is empty it predicts misfortune (Raphael).

tumble *see* FALLING.

tunnel to dream of crawling through a tunnel may indicate a subconscious wish for 'rebirth' of some sort, i.e. a fresh start. This tunnel symbolizes the birth canal.

A tunnel may also, in certain contexts, be interpreted as a passageway or a positive route from one phase of life to another. The transition or journey may not always be easy, but there is a 'light at the end of the tunnel' to motivate the dreamer.

turf to dream of a racing turf, signifies that you will have pleasure and wealth at your command, but your morals will be questioned by your most intimate friends.

To see a green turf, indicates that interesting affairs will hold your attention.

turkey *see* BIRDS.

Turkish baths to dream of taking a Turkish bath, foretells that you will seek health far from your home and friends, but you will have much pleasurable enjoyment

To see others take a Turkish bath, signifies that pleasant companions will occupy your attention.

turning *see* ACTIONS.

turnips a field of riches. To the lover, a faithful sweetheart (gypsy folklore).

turpentine to dream of turpentine, foretells your near future holds unprofitable and discouraging engagements. For a woman to dream that she binds turpentine to the wound of another, shows she will gain friendships and favour through her benevolent acts.

turquoise to dream of a turquoise, foretells you are soon to realise some desire which will greatly please your relatives. For a woman to have one stolen, foretells she will meet with crosses in love. If she comes by it dishonestly, she must suffer for yielding to hasty susceptibility in love.

turtle dove *see* BIRDS.

turtle *see tortoise*, ANIMALS.

tweezers to see tweezers in a dream, denotes uncomfortable situations will fill you with discontent, and your companions will abuse you.

twelve, twenty-four, two *see* NUMBERS.

twine to see twine in your dream, warns you that your business is assuming complications which will be hard to overcome. *See* THREAD.

twins to dream of seeing twins, foretells security in business, and faithful and loving contentment in the home. If they are sickly, it signifies that you will have disappointment and grief.

type to see type in a dream, portends unpleasant transactions with friends. For a woman to clean type, foretells she will make fortunate speculations which will bring love and fortune.

typhoid to dream that you are affected with this malady, is a warning to beware of enemies, and look well to your health. If you dream that there is an epidemic of typhoid, there will be depressions in business, and usual good health will undergo disagreeable changes.

typical dreams some dreams are universal. They are common to all races and conditions of people and are accepted by physiologists, psychologists, seers and scientists, to be alike in their frequency of recurrence and of having a certain similarity of content.

The number of typical dreams is necessarily limited; the following list comprises the most universally recognised: FLYING, FALLING, SWIMMING or floating, levitation, NAKEDNESS, standing upon the edge of a precipice, dreams of dead persons, of the death of relatives, losing a tooth or having one drawn, return to schooldays, dreaming of lakes, rivers, etc, dreams of burglars, dreams of climbing.

To the dreams given above Freud adds dreams of missing a train and of the anxiety attendant upon school examinations. He distinguishes four typical erotic dreams: passing through narrow alleys; passing through suites of rooms; being pursued by wild animals, horses, bulls, etc; and being threatened with knives, daggers, etc.

The interpretations of these dreams and their attributed origins are given below.

flying Havelock Ellis termed this as the most usual of the typical dreams. He traces to it the day of man's first transcendent, heavenward thought. It derives its symbolism from the legend of Icarus; the story of the winged feet of Mercury, the tutelary god of the dream. St Jerome and the happy pagan bishop Synesius attributed it to God's grace. According to *Ellis*, the origin of this dream is physical; it is due to the rhythmic rising and falling of the sleeper's respiratory organs—with the possibility of a snore! In substantiation of this view he instances cases of persons who have drawn near the brink of death, and having lost consciousness, have had the sensation of flying, as though the soul were taking flight. *Freud* attributes this dream to erotic sources, with the possibility of several different interpretations. The flying dream may have its origin in a childhood desire to be freed from conventionality and restraint. He says that this dream is invariably characterized by a keen sense of delight and freedom. *Christians* and theosophists construe this dream as a corroboration of their belief in the flight of the spirit. The *gypsy* interpretation of flying is as a fortunate dream. *Raphael*, on the contrary, qualifies it thus: 'To dream of flying denotes that you will escape many difficulties and dangers. If you dream that you are trying to fly very high you will aspire to a position that you will never reach and for which you are not qualified.' To servants it means liberty, to the poor it is a dream of riches. To fly very high from the earth without wings signifies fear and danger, as also to fly over the houses and through the streets and forlorn ways signifies trouble and sedition.

hovering, gliding, ascending or rising and falling are attributed generally to the same sources as the dream of flying. *Ellis*, however, adds that as a rule the falling dream comes at the end of a flying dream and that being usually accompanied by fear, it presupposes an organic origin, for example a circulatory or nervous trouble, even apoplexy or epilepsy. Another physical reason for this dream could be that on falling asleep the dreamer does not feel that he is supported by the bed, and that therefore he has the sensation of being in the air, i.e., unsupported. *Freud* attributes it to eroticism, as in the case of the flying dream, but adds that in woman it frequently has its origin in the fear of a moral downfall. He classifies it as a typical, sexual dream of fear. *Raphael* interprets this dream as foretelling the loss of a sweetheart; to a sailor it augurs shipwreck. *Gypsy* folklore tells that it symbolizes losses and crosses, unless the dreamer should pick himself up afterwards, in which case this dream foretells changes and movings.

swimming dreams of swimming are generally attributed to the respiration, but *Ellis* qualifies this by adding that they are sometimes due to certain sensations on the skin. *Freud* holds it to be an erotic dream associated with childhood memories. *Raphael*'s supernatural interpretation of swimming with the head up is a prediction of success in business and in love affairs. Swimming with the head under water in this dream implies trouble and unpleasant news. If you are swimming in dirty water it predicts slander and malice, and if you dream of sinking ruin will follow.

nakedness and being insufficiently clad Freud and Ellis agree that this dream is usually caused by the perception felt in sleep when one has thrown off the covers and is exposed. Freud divides this dream into two varieties, one in which the dreamer is indifferent to his or her condition and perhaps is a reflection of the desire to abandon restraint, and the other in which the dreamer is overwhelmed with shame perhaps reflecting sexual guilt. The *supernatural* interpretation is a prediction of a disgrace or embarrassment. To the *gypsy* interpreters it predicts sickness poverty and general misfortune.

dream of the death of parents or of dead persons here *Freud* takes a rather extreme view and classifies this as a wish dream. He subdivides it under two headings, the dream in which the dreamer is unmoved and the dream in which he or she is grieved. The dream without attendant grief is not a typical dream, in that it is used to symbolize another wish, i.e. it is not the direct desire that someone should die but is a deeper reference to something that the dreamer wants to end. The dream attended by expressions of grief, however deep, is an expression of a desire they feel or have felt at some time in the past, that they want to get rid of the person who died in the dream. Freud gives an example of a woman who dreamed that her siblings suddenly grew wings and flew up into the sky. Of course, he says, the lady wished all her relatives dead or she would not have had this dream. *Other interpretations* might take the less controversial view of this dream and translate it as reflecting the dreamer's feelings of sorrow and trouble.

falling out of teeth this dream can be attributed to dental irritation or to people who grind their teeth in their sleep. The *Freudian* school would define it as an erotic dream, a dream reflecting feelings of sexual insecurity or immaturity. *Oneirocritics* agree that it forecasts heavy sorrows. *Raphael* expresses the general view that to dream that your teeth are very loose predicts personal illness. If one or all come out it denotes an imminent death.

return to school days it is generally thought to be caused by a cramped position of the body or the limbs, suggesting the restraint of a school desk. This dream is often an indication that the dreamer lacks confidence at work or in a relationship.

the examination dream the recollection of the feeling of not being properly prepared for something, whether it is an exam or not, is common to everyone. The exam dream reflects the feeling of being put under pressure either at work or in a relationship and is not restricted to students.

the dream of missing a train here *Freud* classifies this as a 'consolation dream' directed against a fear, or the fear of dying. The sexual symbolism of the train may also give the interpretation that the dreamer feels sexually inadequate in some way, or unable to cope with a certain relationship. *Ellis*, on the other hand, attributes dreams of trains and railroads to the physical cause of having a headache. This dream may indicate physical or mental exhaustion in the dreamer, resentment of missed opportunities or indicate an inability to cope with his or her present life. With a few exceptions the mystical interpreters agree that to see oneself in a railroad train indicates either a change of residence or a long journey. A few hold this dream to mean the visit of a friend from a distance.

climbing a hill, sweating, drawing heavy loads, etc, these dreams might have the physical cause of pulmonary, respiratory or cardiac troubles, manifesting themselves in sleep through the subconscious before the waking mind has recognized them. The dream of climbing indicates ambition. The analysis depends on how the dreamer progresses. If progress is difficult then there is some obstacle in the way of that ambition.

burglars breaking into the house is attributed to sounds in the environment which become exaggerated by the dream consciousness. Freud, however, traces this dream to erotic sources. The fear of loss or a reflection of feelings of invaded privacy. *Raphael* declares that to dream of burglars and to overcome them signifies victory over enemies. To be defeated by the burglars signifies proportionate misfortune.

standing upon the brink of a precipice might be caused by lying diagonally across the bed with the feet extended beyond the edge. It is a dream reflecting an unconscious fear. *Artemidorus* and *Raphael* construe this as a dream of warning. This symbolism can be applied to a psychoanalytic approach too. The dreamer may have an extremely difficult task ahead of him or her causing significant worry, or the precipice may symbolize a choice that has to be made.

lakes, springs, etc Freud suspects dreams of lakes to be of erotic origin, while *Raphael* says that to dream of a glassy lake denotes prosperity and future happiness. A muddy lake, on the contrary, is supposed to represent loss and heavy cares.

murder the dream of committing murder, while not precisely typical in that it lacks unanimity as to its fundamental source, is nevertheless sufficiently universal to merit mention among the typical dreams. *Freud* attributes the dream of murder to the suppressed wish of the dreamer. Other writers claim that the dream is due to the innate wickedness of the human heart when freed from conventional restraint. Dreaming of committing a murder could be an expression of anger, and of being the victim of a murder reflects feelings of insecurity and victimization.

u

ugly to dream that you are ugly, denotes that you will have a difficulty with your sweetheart, and your prospects will assume a depressed shade.

If a young woman thinks herself ugly, she will conduct herself offensively toward her lover, which will probably cause a break in their pleasant associations.

ulcer it was thought that to dream of having an ulcer denoted good health into old age (gypsy folklore). The symbolism is attributable to the idea that ulcers, boils, etc, clear the system. *See also* ABSCESS.

umbrella a dream denoting a sheltered and peaceful life (gypsy folklore). An Eastern symbol of distinction.

uncle or **aunt** a dream denoting family quarrels (gypsy folklore). The symbolism is evidently attributable to the proverbial wicked uncle and guardian.

underground dreams of being underground may indicate a deep exploration of ourselves, or may point to a need to look more closely at the inner self.

Something buried underground may represent a secret, or an aspect of the self that is either repressed or hidden from the rest of the world.

undertaker as a dream of CONTRARY MEANING this forecasts a wedding (gypsy folklore).

underwear *see* CLOTHES.

undressing a dream of undressing suggests the revelation of something that has been kept hidden, or a 'baring of the soul'. Thus it may suggest the giving of oneself in a certain sense, either sexual or spiritual. Undressing may express a desire to be free of constrictions in one's life. *See also* TYPICAL DREAMS.

unfortunate to dream that you are unfortunate, is significant of loss to yourself, and trouble for others.

unguent to use, a dream of profit (gypsy folklore).

unicorn a dream of righteousness (gypsy folklore). The symbolism derives from the unicorn as an ancient emblem of purity.

uniform a dream of glory, valour and celebrity (gypsy folklore).

universal dreams *see* TYPICAL DREAMS.

unknown to dream of meeting unknown persons, foretells change for good, or bad as the person is good looking, or ugly, or deformed.

To feel that you are unknown, denotes that strange things will cast a shadow of ill luck over you.

uphill *see* JOURNEY.

urgent to dream that you are supporting an urgent petition, is a sign that you will engage in some affair which will need fine financiering to carry it through successfully.

urinal to dream of a urinal, disorder will predominate in your home.

urine to dream of seeing urine, denotes ill health will make you disagreeable and unpleasant with your friends.

To dream that you are urinating, is an omen of bad luck, and trying seasons to love.

urn a dream of death (gypsy folklore).

usher *see* BRIDE.

usurer to find yourself a usurer in your dreams, foretells that you will be treated with coldness by your associates, and your business will decline to your consternation.

If others are usurers, you will discard some former friend on account of treachery.

usurper to dream that you are a usurper, foretells you will have trouble in establishing a good title to property.

If others are trying to usurp your rights, there will be a struggle between you and your competitors, but you will eventually win.

For a young woman to have this dream, she will be a party to a spicy rivalry, in which she will win.

V

vaccinate to dream of being vaccinated, foretells that your susceptibility to female charms will be played upon to your sorrow.

To dream that others are vaccinated, shows you will fail to find
contentment where it is sought, and your affairs will suffer decline in
consequence.

For a young woman to be vaccinated on her leg, foreshadows her
undoing through treachery.

vagabond sudden journeys or changes from place to place (gypsy
folklore). *See also* TINKER and GYPSY.

vagina *see* BODY.

valentine to dream that you are sending valentines, foretells that you
will lose opportunities of enriching yourself.

For a young woman to receive one, denotes that she will marry a
weak, but ardent lover against the counsels of her guardians.

valet concealed, domestic enemy (gypsy folklore).

valise filled it denotes abundance; empty, misery.

valley to dream of walking in a pleasant valley denotes sickness
(Raphael). An interpretation in conformity with the modern theory
of physical stimuli, and attributing hills, valleys, mountains, etc, to
sensations in various parts of the body. Mountains and valleys might
also be interpreted as representing the various curves of the body.

vampire images of vampires appearing in dreams may be provoked
by Hallowe'en or scary films but not necessarily so. Dreaming of being attacked by a vampire suggests a feeling of being drained by another's dependency, or being weakened by another person's stronger
will. Also a dream warning against thieves and other insidious persons (gypsy folklore).

vanishing something that vanishes in a dream may be something or
someone that has gone from dreamer's life, or it may be a lost opportunity. To dream of vanishing oneself may be an exploration of
the idea of death, or due to poor self-image.

vapour bath to dream of a vapour bath, you will have fretful people for companions, unless you dream of emerging from one, and then you will find that your cares will be temporary.

varnishing to dream of varnishing anything, denotes that you will seek to win distinction by fraudulent means.

To see others varnishing, foretells that you are threatened with danger from the endeavour of friends to add to their own possessions.

vase labour is signified by this dream (Raphael).

vat to see a vat in your dreams, foretells anguish and suffering from the hands of cruel persons, into which you have unwittingly fallen.

Vatican to dream of the Vatican, signifies unexpected favours will fall within your grasp. You will form the acquaintance of distinguished people, if you see royal personages speaking to the Pope.

vault to dream of a vault, denotes bereavement and other misfortune. To see a vault for valuables, signifies your fortune will surprise many, as your circumstances will appear to be meagre. To see the doors of a vault open, implies loss and treachery of people whom you trust.

vegetables to dream of eating them denotes sickness (Raphael). Dreaming of vegetables may also be an indication that you think your life is dull.

vehicle to ride in a vehicle while dreaming, foretells threatened loss, or illness.

To be thrown from one, foretells hasty and unpleasant news. To see a broken one, signals failure in important affairs.

To buy one, you will reinstate yourself in your former position. To sell one, denotes unfavourable change in affairs.

veil a dream of modesty (gypsy folklore). The veil is a symbol of hidden things (Tarot). Even now, in many cultures the veil is still a symbol of the submission of woman to man.

veins a dream of trouble and of sorrows (gypsy folklore).

velvet a dream of velvet signifies honour and riches (Artemidorus).

veneer to dream that you are veneering, denotes that you will systematically deceive your friends, your speculations will be of a misleading nature.

ventriloquist to dream of a ventriloquist, denotes that some treasonable affair is going to prove detrimental to your interest.

If you think yourself one, you will not conduct yourself honourably towards people who trust you.

For a young woman to dream she is mystified by the voice of a ventriloquist, foretells that she will be deceived into illicit adventures.

veranda to dream of being on a veranda, denotes that you are to be successful in some affair which is giving you anxiety.

For a young woman to be with her lover on a veranda, denotes her early and happy marriage.

To see an old veranda, denotes the decline of hopes, and disappointment in business and love.

vermin a dream denoting sickness (gypsy folklore). A typical dream in alcohol addicts. *See also rats*, ANIMALS.

vertigo to dream that you have vertigo, foretells you will have loss in domestic happiness, and your affairs will be under gloomy outlooks.

vessels to dream of vessels, denotes labour and activity.

vexed if you are vexed in your dreams, you will find many worries scattered through your early awakening.

If you think some person is vexed with you, it is a sign that you will not shortly reconcile some slight misunderstanding.

viands to see viands or *delicacies* in a dream denotes idleness. If you eat them this denotes sickness (gypsy folklore).

vicar to dream of a vicar, foretells that you will do foolish things while furious with jealousy and envy.

For a young woman to dream she marries a vicar, foretells that she will fail to awake reciprocal affection in the man she desires, and will live a spinster, or marry to keep from being one.

vice to dream that you are favouring any vice, signifies you are about to endanger your reputation, by letting evil persuasions entice you.

If you see others indulging in vice, some ill fortune will engulf the interest of some relative or associate.

victim to dream that you are the victim of any scheme, foretells that you will be oppressed and over-powered by your enemies. Your family relations will also be strained.

To victimise others, denotes that you will amass wealth dishonourably and prefer illicit relations, to the sorrow of your companions.

victory a victory over rivals is a dream of success (Raphael).

village *see* CITY.

villagers a dream denoting carefree gaiety (gypsy folklore).

vine to dream of vines, is propitious of success and happiness. Good health is in store for those who see flowering vines. If they are dead, you will fail in some momentous enterprise.

To see poisonous vines, foretells that you will be the victim of a plausible scheme and you will impair your health.

vinegar to dream of drinking vinegar signifies sickness (Artemidorus). This dream may be due to sensory stimuli, acidity, etc.

vines *see* FRUIT.

violence to dream of violence from one from whom you had a right to expect kindness denotes success, promotion because this is a dream of CONTRARY MEANING (Raphael).

violets a ream of violets in season is a dream of success. Out of season they signify lawsuits. Double violets are a symbol of extreme happiness or of pain (gypsy folklore).

violin a dream of social pleasures (gypsy folklore).

viper *see* ANIMALS.

virgin to dream of a virgin, denotes that you will have comparative luck in your speculations. For a married woman to dream that she is a virgin, foretells that she will suffer remorse over her past, and the future will hold no promise of better things.

For a young woman to dream that she is no longer a virgin, foretells that she will run great risk of losing her reputation by being indiscreet with her male friends.

For a man to dream of illicit association with a virgin, denotes that he will fail to accomplish an enterprise, and much worry will be caused him by the appeals of people. His aspirations will be foiled through unwarranted associations.

vision to see a vision of a person in a vision or dream is said to denote the death of that person. If the vision is of a place, this denotes disappointment and illusion (gypsy folklore).

visit if you visit in your dreams, you will shortly have some pleasant occasion in your life.

If your visit is unpleasant, your enjoyment will be marred by the action of malicious persons.

For a friend to visit you, denotes that news of a favourable nature will soon reach you. If the friend appears sad and travel-worn, there will be a note of displeasure growing out of the visit, or other slight disappointments may follow. If she is dressed in black or white and looks pale or ghastly, serious illness or accidents are predicted.

vitriol if you see vitriol in your dreams, it is a token of some innocent person being censured by you.

To throw it on people, shows you will bear malice towards parties who seek to favour you.

For a young woman to have a jealous rival throw it in her face, foretells that she will be the innocent object of some person's hatred. This dream for a business man, denotes enemies and much persecution.

voices a dream of merry voices connotes distress and weeping. A dream of wailing voices is one of CONTRARY MEANING signifying joy and merriment (gypsy folklore). To hear your name called in a dream by strange voices, denotes that your business will fall into a precarious state, and that strangers may lend you assistance, or you may fail to meet your obligations.

To hear the voice of a friend or relative, denotes the desperate illness of some one of them, and may be death; in the latter case you may be called upon to stand as guardian over some one, in governing whom you should use much discretion.

Lovers hearing the voice of their affianced should heed the warning. If they have been negligent in attention they should make amends. Otherwise they may suffer separation from misunderstanding.

To hear the voice of the dead may be a warning of your own serious illness or some business worry from bad judgement may ensue. The voice is an echo thrown back from the future on the subjective mind, taking the sound of your ancestor's voice from coming in contact with that part of your ancestor which remains with you. A certain portion of mind matter remains the same in lines of family descent.

volcano the dream of a volcano denotes family quarrels, disturbances and fights (gypsy folklore).

vomit to dream of vomiting, is a sign that you will be afflicted with a malady which will threaten invalidism, or you will be connected with a racy scandal.

To see others vomiting, denotes that you will be made aware of the false pretences of persons who are trying to engage your aid.

For a woman to dream that she vomits a chicken, and it hops off, denotes she will be disappointed in some pleasure by the illness of some relative. Unfavourable business and discontent are also predicted.

If it is blood you vomit, you will find illness a hurried and unexpected visitor. You will be cast down with gloomy foreboding, and children and domesticity in general will ally to work you discomfort.

vote if you dream of casting a vote on any measure, you will be engulfed in a commotion which will affect your community.

To vote fraudulently, foretells that your dishonesty will overcome your better inclinations.

voucher to dream of vouchers, foretells that patient toil will defeat idle scheming to arrest fortune from you.

To sign one, denotes that you have the aid and confidence of those around you, despite the evil workings of enemies.

To lose one, signifies that you will have a struggle for your rights with relatives.

vow if a vow is broken, the dream denotes misfortune. If the vow is fulfilled this signifies success (gypsy folklore).

voyage *see* JOURNEY.

vulture *see* BIRDS.

W

wadding if seen in a dream, brings consolation to the sorrowing, and indifference to unfriendly criticism.

wading for a girl to dream of wading in clear water denotes a speedy marriage. If she is bathing in muddy water then she is to become involved in an illicit encounter (Raphael).

wafer if seen in a dream, purports an encounter with enemies. To eat one, suggests impoverished fortune.

For a young woman to bake them, denotes that she will be tormented and distressed by fears of remaining in the unmarried state.

wager to dream of making a wager, signifies that you will resort to dishonest means to forward your schemes.

If you lose a wager, you will sustain injury from base connections with those out of your social sphere.

To win one, reinstates you in favour with fortune.

If you are not able to put up a wager, you will be discouraged and prostrated by the adverseness of circumstances.

wages if received in dreams, brings unlooked for good to persons engaging in new enterprises.

To pay out wages, denotes that you will be confounded by dissatisfaction.

To have your wages reduced, warns you of unfriendly interest that is being taken against you.

An increase of wages, suggests unusual profit in any undertaking.

wagon to dream of a wagon, denotes that you will be unhappily mated, and many troubles will prematurely age you.

To drive one down a hill, is ominous of proceedings which will fill you with disquiet, and will cause you loss.

To drive one up hill, improves your worldly affairs.

To drive a heavily loaded wagon, denotes that duty will hold you in a moral position, despite your efforts to throw her off.

To drive into muddy water, is a gruesome prognostication, bringing you into a vortex of unhappiness and fearful foreboding.

To see a covered wagon, foretells that you will be encompassed by mysterious treachery, which will retard your advancement.

For a young woman to dream that she drives a wagon near a dangerous embankment, portends that she will be driven into an illicit entanglement, which will fill her with terror, lest she be openly discovered and ostracised. If she drives across a clear stream of water, she will enjoy adventure without bringing opprobrium upon herself.

wagtail to see a wagtail in a dream, foretells that you will be the victim of unpleasant gossip, and your affairs will develop unmistakable loss.

waif to dream of a waif, denotes personal difficulties, and especial ill-luck in business.

wail a wail falling upon your ear while in the midst of a dream, brings fearful news of disaster and woe.

For a young woman to hear a wail, foretells that she will be deserted and left alone in distress, and perchance disgrace.

waist and shirt-waist to dream of a round full waist, denotes that you will be favoured by an agreeable dispensation of fortune.

A small, unnatural waist, foretells displeasing success and recriminating disputes.

For a young woman to dream of a nice, ready-made shirt-waist, denotes that she will win admiration through her ingenuity and pleasing manners.

To dream that her shirt-waist is torn, she will be censured for her illicit engagements. If she is trying on a shirt-waist, she will encounter rivalry in love, but if she succeeds in adjusting the waist to her person, she will successfully combat the rivalry and win the object of her love.

waiter to dream of a waiter, signifies you will be pleasantly entertained by a friend. To see one cross or disorderly, means offensive people will thrust themselves upon your hospitality.

wake to dream of attending a wake denotes scandalous assertions (gypsy folklore).

walking dreaming of walking in the dirt symbolizes sickness. Walking in the night denotes trouble (gypsy folklore). Walking through

WATER is said to symbolize grief. The difficulty experienced by the dreamer in walking through water is a subconscious expression of a difficulty in life. It may be that they are unable to fulfil an aspiration or ambition, or it may be an expression of a difficulty in communicating with someone.

walking stick to see a walking stick in a dream, foretells you will enter into contracts without proper deliberation, and will consequently suffer reverses. If you use one in walking, you will be dependent upon the advice of others. To admire handsome ones, you will entrust your interest to others, but they will be faithful.

wall just as walls are built in real life to offer protection from the elements or from other people, so the wall in a dream can be read as a defensive image. It stands for the attitudes and postures we may adopt to protect ourselves and our feelings and the face we present to the world when we are sceptical. A wall that surrounds the dreamer may represent a feeling of being 'well-defended', i.e. a feeling of security.

To dream of a wall as an impassable barrier denotes difficulties in the family. Narrow walls are an indication of danger; to ascend without injury denotes success (Raphael). *See also* HOUSE.

wallet to see wallets in a dream, foretells burdens of a pleasant nature will await your discretion as to assuming them. An old or soiled one, implies unfavourable results from your labours.

walnuts to see or eat them, a sign of trouble and difficulty (Artemidorus).

walrus *see* ANIMALS.

waltz a dream denoting wasted time (gypsy folklore).

want to dream that you are in want, denotes that you have unfortunately ignored the realities of life, and chased folly to her stronghold of sorrow and adversity.

If you find yourself contented in a state of want, you will bear the misfortune which threatens you with heroism, and will see the clouds of misery disperse.

To relieve want, signifies that you will be esteemed for your disinterested kindness, but you will feel no pleasure in well doing.

war a dream warning of danger of persecution (gypsy folklore).

warbling of BIRDS, assured success (gypsy folklore).

wardrobe *see* FURNITURE.

warehouse dreaming of a warehouse denotes success and accumulation of possessions through frugality and saving (gypsy folklore).

warrant to dream that a warrant is being served on you, denotes that you will engage in some important work which will give you great uneasiness as to its standing and profits.

To see a warrant served on some one else, there will be danger of your actions bringing you into fatal quarrels or misunderstandings. You are likely to be justly indignant with the wantonness of some friend.

warts if you are troubled with warts on your person, in dreams, you will be unable to successfully parry the thrusts made at your honour.

To see them leaving your hands, foretells that you will overcome disagreeable obstructions to fortune.

To see them on others, shows that you have bitter enemies near you. If you doctor them, you will struggle with energy to ward off threatened danger to you and yours.

washboard to see a washboard in your dreams, is indicative of embarrassment. If you see a woman using one, it predicts that you will let women rob you of energy and fortune.

A broken one, portends that you will come to grief and disgraceful deeds through fast living.

wash-bowl to dream of a wash-bowl, signifies that new cares will interest you, and afford much enjoyment to others.

To bathe your face and hands in a bowl of clear water, denotes that you will soon consummate passionate wishes which will bind you closely to some one who interested you, but before passion enveloped you.

If the bowl is soiled, or broken, you will rue an illicit engagement, which will give others pain, and afford you small pleasure.

washer woman seen in dreams, represents infidelity and a strange adventure. For the business man, or farmer, this dream indicates expanding trade and fine crops. For a woman to dream that she is a washer woman, denotes that she will throw decorum aside in her persistent effort to hold the illegal favour of men.

washing *see* WATER.

wasps *see* INSECTS and STING.

waste to dream of wandering through waste places, foreshadows doubt and failure, where promise of success was bright before you. To dream of wasting your fortune, denotes you will be unpleasantly encumbered with domestic cares.

watch a good dream denoting success (gypsy folklore).

watchman loss through theft, a dream of warning (gypsy folklore).

water lily to dream of a water lily, or to see them growing, foretells there will be a close commingling of prosperity and sorrow or bereavement.

water mill a favourable dream (gypsy folklore).

water water is essential to life and, therefore, inevitably has a certain importance in dreams.

Dreaming of the SEA may indicate an awareness of the depth of our unconsciousness, the subconscious knowledge that our inner selves go much deeper than our immediate awareness.

The vastness of the sea or the OCEAN reflects the huge realm of the unconscious. Surging waves in a dream may indicate a feeling in the dreamer of the life energies that flow within, the unknown forces between will and action, for example.

Waves, and the ebb and flow of the tide, may represent the ebb and flow of human emotions, from negative to positive and back again.

Images of SWIMMING in a deep pool may represent a regressive wish on the part of the dreamer with the pool symbolizing the amniotic fluid within the womb. Consequently, to dream of coming out of a pool of water may be indicative of a new start in life, or a wish for such a thing.

To dream of DROWNING, if FEAR is present, may indicate a fear of death; to dream of simply sinking underwater, without any feelings of an unpleasant nature, may indicate either a wish to explore one's unconscious in more depth, or an exploration of the idea of death.

Images of *washing* in a dream may indicate a desire for moral or spiritual cleansing, or a feeling that one has been cleansed of a particular feeling or emotion. To dream of washing oneself denotes good health after an illness or a change for the better (gypsy folklore). *See also* FOUNTAIN; WALKING.

water-bearer, water-carrier always a good dream (gypsy folklore). To see water-carriers passing in your dreams, denotes that your prospects will be favourable in fortune, and love will prove no laggard in your chase for pleasure.

If you think you are a water-carrier, you will rise above your present position.

waterfall to dream of a waterfall, foretells that you will secure your wildest desire, and fortune will be exceedingly favourable to your progress.

watermelon *see* FRUIT.

waves *see* WATER.

wax a dream denoting an unstable character, doubt on the part of the dreamer (gypsy folklore). *See also* BEES.

wax candle *see* CANDLE.

wax taper to dream of lighting wax tapers, denotes that some pleasing occurrence will bring you into association with friends long absent.

To blow them out, signals disappointing times, and sickness will forestall expected opportunities of meeting distinguished friends.

way to dream you lose your way, warns you to disabuse your mind of lucky speculations, as your enterprises threaten failure unless you are painstaking in your management of affairs.

wealth a dream of CONTRARY MEANING forecasting sickness, even death (gypsy folklore).

weapons weapons are generally symbols of aggression, either sexual, emotional or physical. The situation and the type of weapon may give a clue as to the nature of the aggression (for example, a GUN or a *cannon* may be symbols for the phallus; the discharge of these weapons representing EJACULATION). *See also* KNIFE and AGGRESSION.

weasel *see* ANIMALS.

weather if the weather is good this is a dream denoting deceptive security. *See also* STORM.

weathercock denotes fickle friends (Artemidorus).

weaving a dream of weaving denotes success in trade (Raphael).

web to dream of webs, foretells deceitful friends will work you loss and displeasure. If the web is non-elastic, you will remain firm in withstanding the attacks of the envious persons who are seeking to obtain favours from you.

wedding clothes to see wedding clothes, signifies you will participate in pleasing works and will meet new friends. To see them soiled or in disorder, foretells you will lose close relations with some much-admired person.

wedding dreams of a wedding in which the dreamer is the bride or the groom may be wish-fulfilment. Alternatively, a wedding may indicate a close spiritual or emotional tie, in other words, 'a marriage of two minds'. This may be a dream of CONTRARY MEANING denoting a FUNERAL. If the dreamer is ill, his own death is denoted (gypsy folklore).

wedding ring *see* LOSS.

wedge to dream of a wedge, denotes you will have trouble in some business arrangements which will be the cause of your separation from relatives.

Separation of lovers or friends may also be implied.

wedlock to dream that you are in the bonds of an unwelcome wedlock, denotes you will be unfortunately implicated in a disagreeable affair.

For a young woman to dream that she is dissatisfied with wedlock, foretells her inclinations will persuade her into scandalous escapades.

For a married woman to dream of her wedding day, warns her to fortify her strength and feelings against disappointment and grief. She will also be involved in secret quarrels and jealousies. For a woman to imagine she is pleased and securely cared for in wedlock, is a propitious dream.

weeding a dream of health, wealth and happiness (Raphael).

weeds a dream of much labour and small benefit (gypsy folklore).

weeping a dream of CONTRARY MEANING denoting joy (gypsy folklore).

weevil to dream of weevils, portends loss in trade and falseness in love.

weighing to dream of weighing, denotes that you are approaching a prosperous period, and if you set yourself determinedly toward success you will victoriously reap the full fruition of your labours.

To weigh others, you will be able to subordinate them to your interest.

For a young woman to weigh with her lover, foretells that he will be ready at all times to comply with her demands.

welcome to dream that you receive a warm welcome into any society, foretells that you will become distinguished among your acquaintances and will have deference shown you by strangers. Your fortune will approximate anticipation.

To accord others welcome, denotes your congeniality and warm nature will be your passport into pleasures, or any other desired place.

well to dream that you are employed in a well, foretells that you will succumb to adversity through your misapplied energies. You will let strange elements direct your course.

To fall into a well, signifies that overwhelming despair will possess you. For one to cave in, promises that enemies' schemes will overthrow your own.

To see an empty well, denotes you will be robbed of fortune if you allow strangers to share your confidence.

To see one with a pump in it, shows you will have opportunities to advance your prospects.

To dream of an artesian well, foretells that your splendid resources will gain you admittance into the realms of knowledge and pleasure.

To draw water from a well, denotes the fulfilment of ardent desires. If the water is impure, there will be unpleasantness.

Welsh rarebits to dream of preparing or eating Welsh rarebits, denotes that your affairs will assume a complicated state, owing to your attention being absorbed by artful women and enjoyment of neutral fancies.

wet nurse to dream that you are a wet nurse, denotes that you will have the care of the aged, or little children.

For a woman to dream that she is a wet nurse, signifies that she will depend on her own labours for sustenance.

wet to dream that you are wet, denotes that a possible pleasure may involve you in loss and disease. You are warned to avoid the blandishments of seemingly well-meaning people.

For a young woman to dream that she is soaking wet, portends that she will be disgracefully implicated in some affair with a married man.

whale *see* ANIMALS.

whalebone to see or work with whalebone in your dreams, you still form an alliance which will afford you solid benefit.

wharf to dream of a wharf denotes assurance of safety (gypsy folklore).

wheat a dream denoting great wealth (gypsy folklore).

wheel the wheel may be an image of the life cycle, the continuum of birth, life and death. It may also represent one's fortune, like the spin of the roulette wheel. The wheel is a symbol of eternity, and therefore a happy dream (gypsy folklore).

whetstone to dream of a whetstone, is significant of sharp worries and close attention is needed in your own affairs, if you avoid difficulties.

You are likely to be forced into an uncomfortable journey.

whip to dream of whipping an ANIMAL denotes sorrow to you; to dream of being whipped is said to predict an imminent scandal (gypsy folklore). The whip was a symbol of martyrdom.

whirlpool a dream warning you of danger, physical or otherwise (gypsy folklore). The dreams of whirling or of being whirled are readily attributable to physical causes, headaches, vertigo, etc.

whirlwind heavy troubles (gypsy folklore). For physical causes *see* WHIRLPOOL.

whisky to dream of whisky in bottles, denotes that you will be careful of your interests, protecting them with energy and watchfulness, thereby adding to their proportion.

To drink it alone, foretells that you will sacrifice your friends to your selfishness.

To destroy whisky, you will lose your friends by your ungenerous conduct.

Whisky is not fraught with much good. Disappointment in some form will likely appear.

To see or drink it, is to strive and reach a desired object after many disappointments. If you only see it, you will never obtain the result hoped and worked for.

whisper to dream of whispering or hearing a whisper denotes scandal (gypsy folklore).

whistle to hear a whistle in your dream, denotes that you will be shocked by some sad intelligence, which will change your plans laid for innocent pleasure.

To dream that you are whistling, foretells a merry occasion in which you expect to figure largely. This dream for a young woman indicates indiscreet conduct and failure to obtain wishes is foretold.

white lead to dream of white lead, denotes relatives or children are in danger because of your carelessness. Prosperity will be chary of favour.

white moth to dream of a white moth, foretells unavoidable sickness, though you will be tempted to accuse yourself or some other with wrong-doing, which you think causes the complaint. For a woman to see one flying around in the room at night, forebodes unrequited wishes and disposition which will effect the enjoyment of other people. To see a moth flying and finally settling upon something, or disappearing totally, foreshadows death of friends or relatives.

white *see* COLOURS.

whitewash to dream that you are whitewashing, foretells that you will seek to reinstate yourself with friends by ridding yourself of offensive habits and companions.

For a young woman, this dream is significant of well-laid plans to deceive others and gain back her lover who has been estranged by her insinuating bearing toward him.

widowhood a dream of CONTRARY MEANING denoting satisfaction and joy (gypsy folklore).

wife to a woman this dream predicts that she will never be a wife; to a man this predicts his wife's illness and recovery (gypsy folklore).

wig a dream warning the dreamer of peril ahead (gypsy folklore). A dream of a wig may reflect a subconscious insecurity about one's appearance, or it may symbolize something that the dreamer wants to hide.

wild man to see a wild man in your dream, denotes that enemies will openly oppose you in your enterprises. To think you are one foretells you will be unlucky in following out your designs.

wild to dream that you are running about wild, foretells that you will sustain a serious fall or accident.

To see others doing so, denotes unfavourable prospects will cause you worry and excitement.

wildcat *see* ANIMALS.

wilderness a warning that the dreamer's friends will prove false and that he must rely on his own judgements (gypsy folklore).

will to dream of making your own will denotes depression. To dream of another making a will denotes a wish to profit from the industry of someone else.

willow a dream of sorrow and grief (gypsy folklore). Old English writers associate this plant with graves and mourning.

wind the wind is thought to represent the motivating forces and external influences that 'blow' us along in life, as distinct from conscious wishes and desires.

A moderate breeze is a dream of joyful tidings. Strong winds predict arguments in love and in all matters (gypsy folklore).

windmill changes for the better (gypsy folklore).

window to sit at one forecasts slanderous reports. To set a light in one symbolizes knowledge (gypsy folklore), deriving from the window being an ancient symbol of knowledge.

wine to dream of drinking, health, wealth, etc (gypsy folklore). To dream of drinking in moderation might well imply strength and refreshment through sensory stimuli. Some dream interpreters translate this as a forecast of the dreamer's marriage.

wine-cellar to dream of a wine-cellar, foretells superior amusements or pleasure will come in your way, to be disposed of at your bidding.

wine-glass to dream of a wine-glass, foretells that a disappointment will affect you seriously, as you will fail to see anything pleasing until shocked into the realisation of trouble.

wings to dream of having wings was thought to forecast your own death, or that of the person to whom they are attached (gypsy folklore). Wings were the symbol of immortality and evoke images of angels.

Dreaming of having wings could simply be the expression of a wish to be more independent, or of escaping an unpleasant situation.

winter to dream of winter, is a prognostication of ill-health and dreary prospects for the favourable progress of fortune. After this dream your efforts will not yield satisfactory results.

wire a dream denoting loss of liberty. Gold wire denotes utter poverty, while iron wire was thought to symbolize drunkenness (gypsy folklore).

wisdom to dream you are possessed of wisdom, signifies your spirit will be brave under trying circumstances, and you will be able to overcome these trials and rise to prosperous living. If you think you lack wisdom, it implies you are wasting your native talents.

witch to dream of witches, denotes that you, with others, will seek adventures which will afford hilarious enjoyment, but it will eventually rebound to your mortification. Business will suffer prostration if witches advance upon you, home affairs may be disappointing.

witchcraft misfortune to the dreamer and his family (gypsy folklore). This interpretation may have been made for the possible purpose of inspiring an awe of the black art.

witness to dream that you bear witness against others, signifies you will have great oppression through slight causes. If others bear witness against you, you will be compelled to refuse favours to friends in order to protect your own interest. If you are a witness for a guilty person, you will be implicated in a shameful affair.

wizard to dream of a wizard, denotes you are going to have a big family, which will cause you much inconvenience as well as displeasure. For young people, this dream implies loss and broken engagements.

wolf *see lion*, ANIMALS.

womb dreams of returning to the womb or dreams that contain symbols that may represent such a desire suggest either the dreamer's desire to be free of a sense of responsibility, to cease to be answerable for his or her actions, or the dreamer's desire for a sense of security that he or she feels is lacking in waking life.

women to dream of women, foreshadows intrigue.

To argue with one, foretells that you will be outwitted and foiled.

To see a dark-haired woman with blue eyes and a pug nose, definitely determines your withdrawal from a race in which you stood a showing for victory. If she has brown eyes and a Roman nose, you will be cajoled into a dangerous speculation. If she has auburn hair with this combination, it adds to your perplexity and anxiety. If she is a blonde, you will find that all your engagements will be pleasant and favourable to your inclinations.

wood *see* JOURNEY.

wooden shoe to dream of a wooden shoe, is significant of lonely wanderings and penniless circumstances. Those in love will suffer from unfaithfulness.

wood-pile to dream of a wood-pile, denotes unsatisfactory business and misunderstandings in love.

wool to buy or to sell wool is a dream of prosperity and abundance (gypsy folklore).

work to be tired from work is a dream of sickness. To see men at work denotes success in business. To work with the right hand signifies good fortune and with the left embarrassment (gypsy folklore).

workhouse to dream of being in one denotes a legacy (gypsy folklore).

workman to dream of a workman, denotes you are soon to lose money by useless travels. For a woman, this dream brings pleasant trips, though unexpected ones.

workshop a dream of thrift and wealth (gypsy folklore).

worms *see* ANIMALS.

wormwood a dream predicting bitter trials (gypsy folklore). Because of its taste and medicinal effect wormwood was an ancient symbol of bitterness.

wound a person who dreams of being wounded may have had some experience in the past from which he or she has not yet recovered mentally. A man who dreams of severe injury may have a fear of CASTRATION. Women may dream of MENSTRUATION as a wound, or the wound may represent loss of virginity (about which she possibly has negative feelings). Wounds may also represent emotional distress.

wrapping paper *see* PAPER.

wreath a dream of triumph (gypsy folklore). The symbolism derives from the wreath being a pagan emblem of triumph.

wreck a dream of a wreck denotes misfortunes to come (gypsy folklore).

wrinkles to dream of seeing wrinkles in your own face promises that you will live to a great age (Raphael).

wrist *see* BODY.

writing paper *see* PAPER.

writing writing is mostly a symbol for communication. A promise of surprise through a letter (gypsy folklore). *See also* TALKING.

y

yacht to see a yacht in clear, smooth water denotes success. If the yacht is at sail in stormy seas, the reverse is signified.

yard stick to dream of a yard stick, foretells much anxiety will possess you, though your affairs assume unusual activity.

yarn a dream denoting inheritance and powerful friends (gypsy folklore).

yawning if you dream that you are yawning it is a warning to beware of surprises (gypsy folklore).

yearn to feel in a dream that you are yearning for the presence of anyone, denotes that you will soon hear comforting tidings from your absent friends.

For a young woman to think her lover is yearning for her, she will have the pleasure of soon hearing some one making a long-wished-for proposal. If she lets him know that she is yearning for him, she will be left alone and her longings will grow apace.

yeast a dream symbolizing the stirring of discontent (gypsy folklore).

yellow bird to see a yellow bird flitting about in your dreams, foretells that some great event will cast a sickening fear of the future around you. To see it sick or dead, foretells that you will suffer for another's wild folly.

yew tree a dream of this tree denotes honour and great wealth (gypsy folklore). The yew was a sacred tree amongst the Romans and the early Britons, who prized it especially in the manufacture of bows.

yield to dream you yield to another's wishes, denotes that you will throw away by weak indecision a great opportunity to elevate yourself.

If others yield to you, exclusive privileges will be accorded you and you will be elevated above your associates.

To receive poor yield for your labours, you may expect cares and worries.

yoke to dream of wearing a yoke denotes anger (gypsy folklore).

young to dream of becoming youthful denotes a faithful and loving partner or spouse.

Yule log to dream of a Yule log, foretells that your joyous anticipations will be realised by your attendance at great festivities.

Z

zebra *see* ANIMALS.

zenith to dream of the zenith, foretells elaborate prosperity, and your choice of suitors will be successful.

zephyr inconstancy is predicted by this dream (gypsy folklore). A symbol of lightness and fickleness.

zero a dream denoting a rise to the apex of power and fortune (gypsy folklore). *See also* NUMBERS.

zinc a dream connoting the distrust of friends (gypsy folklore).

zither a message from a lover is augured by this dream.

zodiac to dream of the twelve signs of the zodiac shows a great traveller, and predicts a voyage around the world (gypsy folklore).

zoo dreams of a zoo in which all the ANIMALS are contented and in which the mood is obviously optimistic, may indicate a desire, that the dreamer may not have expressed in waking life, to exist within the confines of a family unit or similar setup.

Dreams of a more unpleasant nature, where the animals are distressed, would indicate unhappiness in the dreamer and a deep

Appendix

Adler, Alfred (1870–1937) Austrian psychiatrist and an associate of
FREUD, although he rejected Freud's emphasis on sexuality. He
founded a school of psychoanalysis based on the individual's quest
to overcome feelings of inadequacy (the 'inferiority complex'). His
main works were *The Practice and Theory of Individual Psychology* (1923),
and *Understanding Human Nature* (1927).

Artemidorus Daldianus *or* **Ephesius** (c. 120 AD) compiler of a
five-volume dream book, *Oneirocritica*, which some say forms the basis of the mystical side of dream interpretation today. He differenti-
ates between the dreams of kings and commoners, and universal
and individual interpretation. Dreams which represent something
as happening to the individual who dreams them, show that they
have a personal significance. If the dream relates to another it will
concern him alone.

Ellis, Henry Havelock (1859–1939) English physician and writer
on the psychology of sex. He wrote *Studies in the Psychology of Sex*
(1897–1928), the first objective study of the subject of sexual capacity which caused great controversy at the time.

Freud, Sigmund (1856–1939) Austrian neurologist and founder of
the psychoanalytic movement. He worked with Austrian neurologist
Josef Breuer (1842–1925) in using hypnosis to find the cause of hys-
terical illness. His work with Jean Martin Charcot (1825–1893) led
to the development of 'free association' instead of hypnosis and together they sought to perfect the psychoanalytic method.

Freud's revolutionary theories on psychosexual behaviour, and in
particular infantile sexuality, caused controversy and lost him many
friends and colleagues. Despite this he published *Die Traumdeutung*
(1900) (The Interpretation of Dreams). This developed his theory,
that neuroses are caused by repressed sexual urges, to apply to the
content of dreams. Dream symbols are the disguised representation
of forbidden sexual desires.

Alfred ADLER and Carl JUNG were like-minded colleagues of Freud's, involved in the founding of the Psychoanalytical Association, but both broke with Freud to develop their own theories on psychoanalysis. Freud developed his psychosexual theory further to describe the structure of the subconscious mind into three parts: id, ego, and superego.

His work is viewed as flawed and restricting by modern psychologists, but Freud's contribution to psychoanalysis was revolutionary in that he made the establishment consider that there could be non-physiological explanations for disordered behaviour. He died of cancer in 1939.

Jung, Carl Gustav (1875–1961) Swiss psychiatrist and follower of FREUD until 1913 with the publication of his book *The Psychology of the Unconscious* where Jung proposed ideas that were radically different from Freud's. He started a school of analytical psychology that combined Freudianism with humanistic psychology. Jung regarded the libido as part of our general biological function. Jung also emphasized the importance of the 'collective unconscious' as well as the personal conscience that Freud stressed. He catalogued various personality types; the most important of which were the 'introvert' and 'extrovert' types. Jung also wrote at length on religious symbolism and the meaning of life.

Laing, Ronald David (1927–1989) Scottish existential psychiatrist, and writer of *The Divided Self* (1960). His ideas on the approach to mental health were revolutionary. Rather than trying to cure the patient of their symptoms Laing proposed that psychiatrist and patient should accept that having a mental illness, such as schizophrenia, is a unique and positive experience. His writing later led him into the field of existential philosophy and also poetry.

latent content the latent content of dreams is the presumed meaning behind the MANIFEST CONTENT.

manifest content the manifest content of the dream is the actual apparent content of the dream, which acts symbolically to represent the LATENT CONTENT.

oneirocriticism a term, now out of use, meaning the interpretation of dreams.

oneiromancy another archaism meaning divination by the content of dreams.

Raphael (*1795–1832*) pen name of Robert Cross Smith, an astrologer and oneiromantic of the nineteenth century who published, amongst other several books on astrology and the mysteries, a *Royal Book of Dreams, 1830*. This he claimed to have unearthed in the form of an ancient manuscript and in it he gives an explanation of geomancy and the art of dream interpretation.

Dream Diary

Waking notes

If you wish to analyse your dreams, perhaps the most useful thing you can do is keep a dream diary. It is almost impossible to remember the details of a dream as the day goes on, so a vital thing to be able to do upon waking from a dream is to quickly note what you can remember of it. Do not try to recall every small detail of the dream, just record the strong images and sensations that come to you. You can then go back to sleep, and rest assured that you can analyse and interpret the dream at your leisure later in the day, with the help of this book if you need it.

Do you wish to try to analyse the present or the future?

Well ... that's up to you. How confident do you feel in your psychic abilities? Some say that we all have psychic abilities, and yet that in most people these powers lie dormant, waiting to be awoken. But such powers need practice like any other human talent. Divination via dreams, for example as part of the Native American vision quest, requires great preparation: the choosing of a sacred place, fasting, praying and enforced solitude. We recomend that before you place your faith in predicting the future by your dreams you should con-sider how dedicated you are to enhancing your psychic abilities! We recommend that you read *Spells and Psychic Powers* by Soraya if you are interested in enhancing your psychic skills.

Interpreting the present, you will find, is somewhat easier! Draw upon your own interpretation of your dream symbols above all other interpretations. It it you and you alone who holds the key to what these symbols mean to you.

Dream Diary

Date:

Dream:

Location/surroundings

People/animals

Symbols

Emotions/feelings: _____

_____

_____

_____

_____

_____

_____

Interpretation: _____

_____

_____

_____

_____

_____

_____

_____

_____

_____

_____

_____

_____

_____

_____

_____

_____

DREAMS
and
DESTINY

ASTROLOGY &
HOROSCOPES

Introduction

History

Astrology is an ancient craft that has its origin in the mists of time. It is impossible to place accurately the beginnings, but one thing that is certain is that astrology began as a subject intimately combined with astronomy. Its history is therefore the history of astronomy until the two subjects parted company, a split that essentially began when Nicolai Copernicus (1473–1543) published his book *De revolutionibus*. In this book he postulated that, contrary to earlier thinking in which the earth was the centre of the solar system, the Sun actually formed the focus about which all the planets orbited.

It is thought that there was some study of these subjects five to six thousand years ago when Chaldean priests made maps of the skies. The Chaldeans were the most ancient of the Babylonian peoples. It was believed that heavenly bodies exerted influence upon man and whatever could not be ascribed to man must be due to actions of the gods or the deities of the planets. Subsequent study of the solar system began as pure observation because records and other data for calculation simply did not exist.

The Egyptian and Greek civilizations gave much to the theories and practice of astrology, although much remained unwritten. It is said that the Chaldeans instructed the priests of the Pharaohs in astrology, and monuments exist that show a working knowledge of the subject. This was around 400–350 BC. A little earlier, in Greece around the beginning of the sixth century BC, the philosopher Thales (*c.*643–*c.*546 BC) studied astronomy and astrology as did Pythagoras (569–470 BC) who was credited by Copernicus as the person who developed the theory that the earth and other planets revolved around the Sun.

There were many other Greek students, notably: Plato; Hippocrates, who combined astrology with medical diagnosis; Hipparchus, the founder of observational astronomy, who in 134 BC discovered a new star; and Claudius Ptolemaeus (100–178 AD). Ptolemy wrote the *Almagest*, which is a star catalogue of just over a thousand stars, and also a consideration of the motion of the Moon and the planets. He also wrote the *Tetrabiblos*, the earliest surviving book on astrology.

In Rome and the extended empire at this time, astrology was held in very high regard, and great faith was placed in the work and advice of astrologers who were appointed to the Emperors. The Moon was considered particularly influential and can be found depicted on many of their coins. Among the many Romans active in this field were Porphyry (232–304 AD), who is said to have developed the house method, and Julius Maternus (around 300 AD), who wrote a number of books on astrology.

From about 500 AD Arabs became the prime movers in science and philosophy, but by the early Middle Ages (the thirteenth century) interest was rekindled in Europe, at which time astrology had been divided into three distinct fields: *natural* or *mundane* astrology, which is prominent in forecasting national events, weather, etc; *horary* astrology, used to answer a question through the use of a chart drawn up for the actual time of asking; and *judicial* astrology, in which the fortune of an individual is determined by using a birth chart.

The fifteenth and sixteenth centuries in Europe saw the rise of several famous names, including the Polish astronomer Copernicus. Although Copernicus concurred with the views of Pythagoras, he could not prove the theory, and many attribute the real establishment of the principle (i.e. that the planets orbit the Sun) to Johannes Kepler (1571–1630), the German astronomer. The medieval precursor of chemistry was alchemy, and one famous practitioner was Phillipus Aureolus Paracelsus (1493–1541), who also had some astrological leanings. He believed that the Sun, planets and stars influenced people, whether for good or evil. From this era also came Nostradamus (1503–1566). Michael Nostradamus has become one of the most famous of astrologists and prophets, and he also studied medicine. Almost from the outset it was thought that medical knowledge must, by necessity, include an understanding of astrology.

The work of the Dane Tycho Brahe (1546–1601) could, in some respects, be considered a watershed in the study of astrology/astronomy. Brahe became an observer of the heavens and in so doing was recognized as the most accurate since Hipparchus, centuries before. He prepared tables, designed instruments and studied the motion of the planets, particularly Mars, and it was this initial work that led Kepler to formulate his famous laws of planetary motion. Kepler was assistant to Brahe when the latter moved to Prague following the death of his patron,

King Frederick. Kepler's work proved to be pivotal in advancing the understanding of astronomy. Kepler compared the work of Ptolemy, Copernicus and Tycho Brahe to produce three laws:

1 The orbit of each planet is an ellipse with the Sun at one of the foci (an ellipse has two foci.)
2 A line drawn from a planet to the Sun sweeps out equal areas in equal times.
3 The squares of the sidereal periods (time taken to orbit the Sun, measured relative to the stars) are proportional to the cubes of the mean distances from the Sun.

Kepler believed that the stars exerted an influence upon events and that astrology could predict the most mundane of happenings. During the sixteenth and seventeenth centuries there were many famous names who combined astrology with astronomy, mathematics or, commonly, medicine. These included the Italian physicist Galileo Galilei, a French professor of mathematics and doctor of medicine, Jean Morin, an Italian monk and mathematician, Placidus de Tito, and in England, William Lilly, who became famous as a practitioner of horary astrology and accurately predicted the Great Fire of London in 1666.

The poet John Dryden used astrology in predicting numerous events in his own life and the lives of his sons, including both their deaths. Following Dryden's own death in 1700, although not because of it, astrological practice declined on the continent but flourished in England. This influence extended to France at the start of the nineteenth century, where a sound scientific basis to the subject was sought.

William Allan (1800–1917), otherwise known as Alan Leo, was considered by many to be the father of modern astrology. He lectured widely throughout England and edited a magazine called *Modern Astrology*. He was also a professional astrologer and a prolific author on the subject, writing 30 books. In 1915 he founded the Astrological Lodge of London. Although the war years were disruptive to the study and practice of astrology, a large following was developed in North America. However, continental Europe suffered during the Second World War as Hitler's forces caused wholesale destruction, and Hitler himself, unhappy with adverse astrological predictions, destroyed books and records and incarcerated unfortunate practitioners.

Today astrology holds interest for many people, and growing numbers are becoming fascinated by its study. However, there is a dichotomy between astrology and astronomy.

The Solar System

The early visualizations of the heavens and the stars showed the Earth at the centre of a large revolving sphere. It was thought that the stars seen in the sky were somehow fastened onto the inner surface of this sphere. The stars that appeared to revolve around the Earth but did not move in relation to each other were called the 'fixed stars'. Among the many fixed stars there are some in particular that have certain characteristics and that can be used in astrological charts. For example, Regulus (or Alpha Leonis) is the brightest star in the constellation of Leo and signifies pride, good luck and success.

From early times it was noted that while many stars remained fixed, five in particular did not, and these wandered about the sky. These were the planets of the solar system because at that time not all eight remaining planets (other than Earth) had been identified. The discovery of Uranus, Neptune and Pluto followed the invention of the telescope, and Uranus was the first planet so observed, in 1781.

For the purposes of astrology, the Sun, which is actually a star, is considered as a planet. It is approximately 150 million kilometres from Earth and has a diameter of 1.4 million kilometres. Energy is generated in the core, from nuclear fusion, where the temperature is about fifteen million degrees.

The planets

The Moon is a satellite of Earth but for convenience is also treated as a planet. It orbits the Earth roughly every 27 days, and the same face is always kept towards Earth, lit by light reflected from the Sun. The Moon seems to change size—the process known as waxing and waning—and it is called 'new' when it is situated between the Earth and the Sun and, because it is not illuminated, cannot be seen. The full Moon occurs about 14 days later, when the full face is totally illuminated.

Planets with their orbits between the Sun and the Earth's orbit are called 'inferior'. There are two planets in this category, Mercury and Venus. Mercury is the smallest planet in the solar system and takes 88

Earth days to complete one orbit, rotating slowly on its axis, and taking 58 Earth days for one revolution. Its elliptical orbit is eccentric, varying in distance from the Sun from 47 to 70 million kilometres.

Venus is the brightest planet seen from Earth and is known as the morning or evening star. It is about 108 million kilometres from the Sun and has a diameter similar to Earth's, at 12,300 kilometres. Venus spins very slowly on its axis, and a day is equivalent to 24.3 Earth days, and a year is 225 days. It is unusual in being the only planet to revolve in the opposite direction to the path of its orbit.

The remaining planets, from Mars to Pluto, are called the 'superior planets', being on the distant side of Earth from the Sun. Mars takes about 687 Earth days to complete an orbit, and a day is just a fraction longer than one Earth day. The surface is solid and mainly red in colour because of the type of rock. There are many surface features, some of which are attributed to the action of water, although none is found there now. Mars is sometimes a dominant feature of the night sky, particularly when it occasionally approaches nearer to Earth, and it has from ancient times exerted considerable fascination.

Jupiter is the largest and heaviest planet in the solar system and has a diameter of 142,800 kilometres. The planet gives out more energy than it receives from the Sun and must therefore have an internal energy source. It is due, in part, to this that the atmosphere is seen to be in steady movement. Parallel bands of colour are seen, but a particularly noticeable feature is the Great Red Spot, which is thought to be an enormous storm, larger than Earth, coloured red because of the presence of phosphorus. The magnetic field of Jupiter is thousands of times stronger than Earth's, and radio waves emanate from the planet. Jupiter has 18 satellites, or moons, of which four are called the 'Galilean satellites'—Io, Europa, Ganymede and Callisto—because they were first seen by Galileo in 1610. There are three other groups of satellites, of which the innermost contains Adastrea, Amalthea, Metis and Thebe.

The next planet out from the Sun is Saturn, the second largest in the solar system. It has a diameter of 120,800 kilometres and the orbit takes 29 Earth years at a distance of 1507 million kilometres from the Sun. Because of its rapid rotation, Saturn is flattened at the poles with a consequent bulging at its equator. A day lasts for a little over 10 hours, and the surface temperature is -170 degrees Celsius. The most obvious and interesting feature of Saturn is its rings, which consist of ice, dust and rock debris, and some of which may have derived from the break-up of a satellite. The rings are about a quarter of a million kilometres across, and there are three main ones but hundreds of smaller ones.

Saturn also has 24 satellites, or moons, of which Titan is the largest with a diameter of 5200 kilometres (larger than Mercury). Some moons were discovered by the Voyager spacecraft in 1989, including Atlas, Calypso and Prometheus.

The planets Mercury through to Saturn were all known to astrologers and astronomers for many years. The remaining planets, Uranus, Neptune and Pluto, were discovered only in modern times, after the advent of the telescope. These are therefore often called the 'modern planets' by astrologers.

Uranus is 50,080 kilometres in diameter and a day lasts 17 hours while a year is equivalent to 84 Earth years. Because of its tilted axis, some parts of the planet's surface are in light for about 40 years and then in darkness for the remainder of its year. Uranus was discovered by William Herschel in 1781 but was something of a mystery until 1986 and the approach of Voyager. It has a faint ring system and 15 moons, some of which are very small indeed (less than 50 kilometres in diameter).

Neptune was discovered in 1846, but its existence was earlier correctly postulated because of observed irregularities in the orbit of Uranus. It takes 165 Earth years to complete an orbit and is almost 4.5 billion kilometres from the Sun. It is 17 times the mass of Earth and has a diameter at its equator of 48,600 kilometres. There are three rings and eight known satellites, the largest of which, Titan, is similar in size to the Earth's Moon.

Pluto, the smallest and most distant planet from the Sun, had its existence predicted because of its effect on the orbits of Neptune and Uranus and was finally discovered in 1930, although little is known about it. A day is equivalent to almost seven days on Earth, and a year is nearly 249 Earth years. Pluto has a very wide elliptical orbit, which brings it closest to the Sun (its *perihelion*) once in each orbit. Because of its great distance from the Sun (7.4 billion kilometres at its maximum), the surface temperature is very low, about -230 degrees Celcius. In 1979, one small moon, called Charon, was discovered, but since it is about one quarter the size of Pluto itself, the two act almost as a double planet system.

A few technicalities

As has been mentioned, the orbits of the planets are elliptical rather than circular, and there is a degree of eccentricity as well. When viewed from Earth, this combination of factors produces what may appear to be peculiar effects. For example, planets may move around the sky, slow and then appear to move backwards for a time. This apparent backward motion is called *retrograde motion* and is simply caused by the Earth moving more quickly through its orbit in comparison to another planet. It *seems* as though the planet being observed is moving backwards, but in reality it is moving forwards, albeit in the line of sight at a slower rate. It is similar to a fast train moving alongside a slow train, which makes the latter appear to be moving backwards. In astronomical tables R denotes retrograde while D marks a return to direct motion.

Another astronomical parameter used in astrology is that of conjunctions. A *conjunction* is when two or more planets (including the Sun of course) are in a line when viewed from Earth. On occasion, Earth, Venus and the Sun will all be in a straight line. If Venus is between Earth and the Sun it is called an 'inferior conjunction'. If, however, Venus is on the other side of the Sun from Earth, it is a 'superior conjunction'. The same applies to Mercury. *Opposition* is when, for example, Earth lies between the Sun and Mars; then Mars is in opposition. Opposition is when one of the superior planets (all except Mercury, Venus and, of course, Earth) is opposite the Sun in the sky, i.e. making an angle of 180 degrees when viewed from Earth (*see* figure on opposite page).

Of vital significance to the correct interpretive study of astrology are a number of parameters that enable the relative positions of planets to be fixed. These include the three great circles, one of which is the ecliptic, and the Zodiac. (A great circle is essentially any circle projected onto the celestial sphere whose plane passes through the centre of the Earth.) The horizon and celestial equator (the Earth's equator projected outward onto the celestial sphere) form two great circles, and the ecliptic is the third. The *ecliptic* is the path that the Sun apparently forms in the heavens. Of course the Earth orbits the Sun, but it seems from Earth to mark out a path that lies at an angle to the celestial equator. This means that the two lines cross twice, at the vernal and autumn equinoxes, otherwise known as the March equinox (or

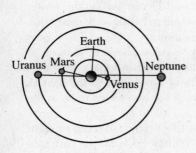

Conjunction

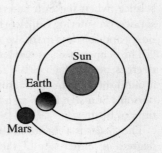

Mars in opposition to the sun

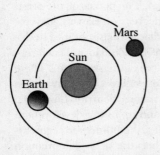

Mars in superior conjunction

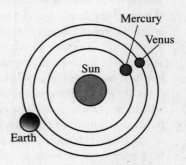

Mercury and Venus in superior conjunction

Conjunctions

first point of the sign Aries) and September equinox (or first point of the sign Libra). (*See* figure on previous page)

The two points at which the ecliptic is farthest from the celestial equator are called the solstices, and these occur in June for the summer solstice (when the Sun enters Cancer) and December for the winter solstice (on entering Capricorn). In the southern hemisphere these equinoxes and solstices mark the reverse situation.

The ecliptic itself is divided into twelve equal divisions, each of 30 degrees, one for each of the Zodiac signs. As the Sun apparently moves around the Earth, it goes from one sign of the Zodiac to the next. A person's Sun sign is the sign before which the Sun seems to be at the time of birth.

The *Zodiac* is a 'band' in the heavens that extends to seven or eight degrees on either side of the ecliptic. Within this band, or path, are contained the apparent movements of the planets, except Pluto. The solar system can be considered as a relatively planar feature, and within this plane the Earth revolves around the Sun. The planes of the orbits of all the other planets are within seven degrees of Earth's, save for Pluto, which is nearer 17 degrees. The Zodiac is then split into twelve segments of 30 degrees, one for each sign of the Zodiac and each represented by a particular star constellation (*see* figure opposite). These signs are essentially a means of naming the sections of the sky within which the planets move. The constellation names, Scorpio, Libra, etc, have no significance although they are bound up in the development of the subject. It should be noted that today, the 30-degree segments no longer coincide with the constellation because of a phenomenon called *precession of the equinoxes*. Precession results in the Earth's axis of rotation not remaining in the same position but forming a cone shape traced out in space. It is due to the gravitational pulls of the Sun and Moon producing a turning force, or torque. This occurs only because the Earth bulges at the equator—a perfect sphere would not be affected. The Earth takes almost 26,000 years (known as the Great Year) to sweep out the cone, and in astrology the point Aries 0 degrees (the First Point of Aries), where the celestial equator cuts the ecliptic, moves with time. Because of precession, the equator crossing-point moves around the ecliptic, and now the First Point of Aries (the vernal equinox of astronomy) lies in the constellation of Pisces and is soon to move into Aquarius. The 30 degrees along the ecliptic that is Aries remains

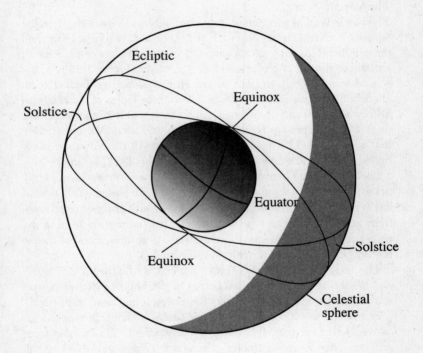

The ecliptic and the celestial sphere

the 30 degrees counted from the vernal equinox, although that equinox is farther back each year (this is, therefore, retrograde motion). Aries has been considered the first sign from hundreds of years BC, when it was believed that the Earth had a birthday.

The Great Year

The Great Year, as mentioned, is divided into twelve periods when the equinox is taken to be against each of the constellations that lie around the ecliptic. This is by no means an accurate division or placement, and the beginning of each period, or age, cannot be fixed easily as the constellations overlap and vary in size. However, each age is taken to be about 2000 years, and by tracing the characteristics of each age in history a pattern can be constructed. From available historical details, the last 2000 years are typified as Piscean and the 2000 years before that as Taurean. This links with the precession of the equinoxes mentioned earlier, and so the next period will be the *Age of Aquarius*.

Each age of the Great Year identified this far has certain characteristics associated with the sign. The *Age of Leo* began about 10000 BC and has as its animal representative the lion, with which are connected creativity and regality. The Sun is its planet. It is interesting to note the early attempts at art, by way of prehistoric cave paintings, and of course the vital importance of the Sun in those times.

The *Age of Cancer* (8000–6000 BC) is associated with the traits of home and family. At this time human beings began building dwellings, and some carvings symbolizing fertility have been found from this period.

From 6000 to 4000 BC was the *Age of Gemini*, which represents a sign of intellectual capacity. It is thought that writing began in some form during this Age, hence communication, a further characteristic of Gemini, became important. Civilization developed apace with cuneiform writing by the end of the Age, and it is possible that human beings had begun to travel and explore.

The *Age of Taurus* followed, from 4000 to 2000 BC, and there are numerous instances that relate to the Taurean features of solidity and security with beauty. These traits are seen in the Egyptian dynasties and the worship of the bull, and in the enormous and ornate temples and the pyramids.

The next age is that of *Aries* (2000 BC–0 AD). Aggressive and assertive qualities are associated with Aries, as are physical fitness and supremacy.

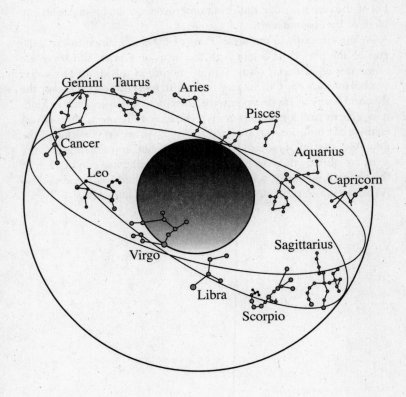

The Constellations

These are balanced by courage and also harmony. All these characteristics are well exemplified by the Greeks, who dominated in battle and architecture and yet created the first democratic government. The symbol of the ram found an outlet in numerous ways, including as an emblem of the Roman army.

We are currently in the *Age of Pisces* (0–2000 AD), albeit towards the end of the period. It began with the birth of Christ, and there are numerous connections to the sign of the fish at this time. The secret symbol for the early Christians was the fish, Jesus was called *Ichthus*, the fish, and many of his disciples were fishermen. Qualities such as kindness, charity and forgiveness are typical, as is selflessness, although an element of confusion can also be discerned. We are on the brink of the new Age, that of *Aquarius* (2000–4000 AD), but in many respects the signs are already there to be seen. Aquarian influence can be seen in the strong presence of science and technology and space travel. Also Aquarian is a sense of detachment and of being impersonal.

Signs and Symbols

Zodiac symbols

Each sign of the Zodiac has a particular graphical representation, called a glyph, which relates to an animal or something similar. The same applies to the planets, and these symbols are used , with others, in constructing an astrological chart.

Symbol	Sign	Representation	Name
♈	Aries	the ram's horns	The Ram
♉	Taurus	the bull's head	The Bull
♊	Gemini	two children	The Twins
♋	Cancer	the breasts	The Crab
♌	Leo	the heart, or the lion's tail	The Lion

Symbol	Sign	Representation	Name
♍	Virgo	the female genitalia	The Virgin
♎	Libra	a pair of scales	The Balance
♏	Scorpio	the male genitalia	The Scorpion
♐	Sagittarius	the Centaur's arrow	The Archer
♑	Capricorn	a goat's head and fish's tail	The Goat
♒	Aquarius	waves of water or air	The Water-bearer
♓	Pisces	two fish	The Fishes

Planet symbols

The glyphs of the planets are as follows:

Planet	Symbol
Sun	☉
Moon	☾
Mercury	☿
Venus	♀
Mars	♂
Jupiter	♃
Saturn	♄
Uranus	♅
Neptune	♆
Pluto	♇

These planetary symbols are all made up of essentially the same elements, the cross, half-circle and circle, all in different combinations. These pictorial representations are linked with the very early days of human beings, when communication was achieved using such graphical methods. As such, these elements each have a particular significance:

—the circle represents eternity, something without end, the spirit;

—a dot inside a circle represents the spirit or power beginning to come out;

—the cross represents the material world;

—and the semicircle stands for the soul.

The Signs of the Zodiac

Names from the depths of history

The signs appear to have got their names from the depths of history and prehistory, and do not necessarily concur with their astronomical counterparts, the constellations. In some civilizations, the signs were attributed to parts of the body. The likeliest race to have adopted this were the Greeks, who also linked the signs to various plants.

Aries	—	the head
Libra	—	the kidneys
Taurus	—	the throat
Scorpio	—	genitalia
Gemini	—	hands and arms
Sagittarius	—	hips and thighs
Cancer	—	the breasts
Capricorn	—	the knee
Leo	—	the heart
Aquarius	—	calf and ankle
Virgo	—	the intestines
Pisces	—	the feet

Below are given the main features of the signs of the Zodiac, and these will be followed later by a fuller description of the character and personal details associated with the various sun signs, i.e. when the Sun passes through each of the signs as it appears to move on the ecliptic.

Aries

The astrological new year occurs around 21 March, when the Sun enters Aries, and this new aspect is mirrored in typical Arian traits of energy, keenness and enthusiasm. The Arian can be something of a pioneer and thus somewhat self-centred with a selfish streak. Aries is the most personal of the signs.

Taurus

Taureans seek and reflect stability, security, and are generally practical with a possessive side to their character. Risks will be taken only if they are absolutely essential, and even then it will be only after a great deal of careful thought. In general Taureans are trustworthy and pleasant and yet unenterprising, which in some may lead to them become a little boring.

Gemini

This third sign of the Zodiac is that of the heavenly twins, which, not surprisingly, can surface as a certain duality, which in a negative sense may result in someone being two-faced. Geminians are intelligent, quick of mind, versatile, and are often good communicators. If the dual nature is too strongly negative then it may lead to a lack of achievement through being over-committed and trying to do too many things at once.

Cancer

Changeable, sympathetic, kind, hard on the outside but easily hurt or offended, emotional and devoted—a home and family builder. These are all Cancerian traits and paint an essentially sensitive picture but with the strengths of devotion and faithfulness. Intellectually, Cancerians are very intuitive and have a strong imagination. If these traits are over-stressed or misused, it can lead to restlessness and over-worry.

Leo

Leo is the only sign ruled by the Sun and, like the lion, so-called king of the beasts, the Leonian can be regal, dignified and magnanimous. They are faithful, trusting but strong-willed, with fixed principles and ideas, and yet if carried too far this may result in bossiness. Similarly, someone may become snobbish, conceited and domineering.

Virgo

Virgoans are typically worker types; they dislike a leading role in anything, and yet they are intellectually very capable, although with a tendency to worry. In work and at home they pay attention to detail with precision and clarity. Closeness to others may be avoided, resulting in the perception among others of Virgoans keeping to themselves, which in turn may be misinterpreted as inhospitality.

Libra

This seventh sign of the Zodiac is opposite to Aries, which makes Librans interested in relating to a partner. As such they tend to be companionable, tactful and like to be in pleasant surroundings. Librans are often unfairly dubbed as lazy. They may also have a tendency to be quite aggressive. A Libran may be of the type who sits on the fence over an issue and, seeing both sides of an argument, may be impossibly indecisive.

Scorpio

This sign is one of intense energy, with deep, passionate feelings about the object of their attention, be it a person or an issue. Scorpions can be passionate, but in excess this can result in resentment, jealousy and even hatred. However, they can equally be warm and charming, and their virtues become apparent when dealing with real life rather than more trivial matters.

Sagittarius

In the earlier days of astrology, Sagittarius was always represented by a man joined to a horse, signifying the duality of the sign—a combination of strength and intelligence. Sagittarians are often intellectuals with a thirst for a challenge and an ability of body and mind to match. Taken to extremes, these traits can mean restlessness, carelessness, extravagance and a tendency to 'horseplay'.

Capricorn

Capricornians tend to be practical, ambitious and caring, and they often possess an excellent sense of humour. In personal relationships caution is their watchword but once decided they will make good partners. Capricornians are also traditionalists and excel in routine work or in organizational capacities. On the negative side, they may become too mean and stern, and caution may turn into selfishness.

Aquarius

Aquarians are typically independent and individualistic, and also friendly. Indeed, friendships once formed tend to be faithful, although contact with others can be rather impersonal. The freedom required by an Aquarian makes them paradoxical when it comes to love. However, the enquiring mind and originality is seen to good effect in pursuit of art or working in science and technology. An excess of Aquarian traits produces someone who is rebellious, tactless and eccentric.

Pisces

The last sign of the Zodiac, Pisces, is typified by a sensitivity that may border on the inhibited unless encouraged. Pisceans can be inspired and highly intuitive, although this may be clouded by mood swings, from elation to depression. Kindness is a common trait, and there is often a strong spiritual faith. In excess, Piscean characteristics may result in muddled thinking, weakness of character and excessive worry.

Groups of the Zodiac and Rulings

The twelve signs of the Zodiac are traditionally subdivided into a number of groups. The members of each group share certain characteristics that in terms of chart interpretation provide additional information rather than primary details.

The first grouping is the *triplicities*, otherwise known as the elements, and consists of the signs for fire, earth, air and water. Aries, Leo and Sagittarius are the *fire triplicity*. This sign is represented by a keenness and enthusiasm and a tendency literally to burn with excitement. Often more sensitive people will be considered slow and dealt with impatiently. While people with the fire sign may be lively and exuberant, their fault will often be that they are too lively. However, such tendencies are likely to be offset, to some extent, by features elsewhere in a chart.

The *earth triplicity* contains Taurus, Virgo and Capricorn and, as might be expected, people with this sign are 'down to earth', although the earth sign is not totally dominant. However, the beneficial aspects include practicality and caution, and although considered dull by livelier people, there is a reassuring solidity and trustworthiness about people with this sign.

Gemini, Libra and Aquarius form the *air triplicity*, and communication is one of the key attributes. An 'ideas person' would have this sign prominent in his or her chart, but a potential fault can be that schemes and ideas occupy too much time at the expense of productivity. In addition, such people can be dismissive of sensitivity or caution in others.

The final triplicity is that of *water*, and it contains Cancer, Scorpio and Pisces. Such people are naturally sensitive and intuitive, and often inspired, while also emotional and protective. Such people tend to be cautious of those with strong personalities, and their own faults may result from being too emotional.

It is often the case that people who have a shared strength in these signs will be compatible. Reference to the elements produces obvious attractions:

Fire — air fans flames while water puts them out and earth smothers.
Earth — water refreshes it while air and fire dry it out.
Air — fire responds to air, while earth and water restrict it.
Water — earth holds it, but air and fire diminish it.

The *quadruplicities* (otherwise known as qualities) form the second grouping. The signs of the Zodiac are divided into three groups of four. The three qualities are 'cardinal', 'fixed' and 'mutable'. Aries, Libra, Cancer and Capricorn are of the *cardinal quadruplicity*. People with this sign dominant in their chart are outgoing and tend to lead. Taurus, Scorpio, Leo and Aquarius are of the *fixed quadruplicity*, which implies stability and a resistance to change. The *mutable quadruplicity* includes the remaining signs, Gemini, Sagittarius, Virgo and Pisces, and all have an adaptability.

The third grouping is into positive and negative (otherwise known as masculine and feminine). In essence these are descriptive rather than definitive terms and equate in a general sense to being self-expressive or extrovert (positive) on the one hand and receptive or introvert on the other.

Taking into account the three groupings, the Zodiac signs are as follows:

Aries	fire, cardinal, masculine
Taurus	earth, fixed, feminine
Gemini	air, mutable, masculine
Cancer	water, cardinal, feminine
Leo	fire, fixed, masculine
Virgo	earth, mutable, feminine
Libra	air, cardinal, masculine
Scorpio	water, fixed, feminine
Sagittarius	fire, mutable, masculine
Capricorn	earth, cardinal, feminine
Aquarius	air, fixed, masculine
Pisces	water, mutable, feminine

When interpreting charts, another useful link between signs is *polarity*. This is the relationship between a sign and the opposite sign across the Zodiac. Thus, on a circular display of the twelve signs, Aries is opposite Libra, Cancer opposite Capricorn, Taurus opposite Scorpio, etc. The signs thus opposed do not, however, have opposite tendencies; rather, the polar signs complement each other.

It will be helpful to consider a few other definitions and some lines and angles that are critical in the construction of a chart. The *ascendant* is defined as the degree of a sign (or the ecliptic) that is rising above the horizon at an individual's birth and marks the junction of the first sign. This is essentially the beginning for any astrological chart construction and interpretation, and after calculation is marked on the chart, working clockwise upwards from the horizon line, which runs east-west across the chart. The ascendant can only be constructed if a birth time is known. The ascendant indicates the beginning of the personality and how an individual faces the world—his or her true self. There are many other factors that may lessen the influence of the ascendant sign, but if some characteristic comes out of a chart that reinforces one linked to the ascendant, then it will be a very significant trait.

The *descendant* is the point opposite to the ascendant, at 180 degrees to it, and is always the cusp, or junction, of the seventh house. Although it may often be left out of charts, the descendant is meant to indicate the sort of partner, friends, etc, with whom one associates and feels comfortable.

The *midheaven* is often abbreviated to MC, from the Latin *medium coeli*. At the time when one particular sign of the Zodiac is appearing over the horizon (the ascendant) there will inevitably be another sign that is at its greatest height. This sign is then said to culminate at the upper meridian of the appropriate place—in brief, the midheaven is the intersection of the meridian with the ecliptic at birth. Midheaven relates to the career of an individual and the way in which it is pursued. It can also provide a general indication of aims and intentions and the type of partner that may be sought. The point opposite to the midheaven is the *imum coeli* and is connected to the subject's origins, his or her early and late life, and parental/domestic circumstances. The *imum coeli*, or IC, is sometimes referred to as the nadir, but strictly speaking this is incorrect. The nadir is actually a point in the heavens that is directly opposite the zenith, which itself is a point in the heavens directly over any place.

Influence of the planets

Every sign of the Zodiac has what is called a *ruling planet*, which is the planet that rules the ascendant sign. From the list below, it can be seen that if someone has Pisces rising, the ruling planet will be Neptune.

Each planet rules one sign, save for Venus and Mercury, which each rule two. Of course, before William Herschel discovered Uranus in 1781 there were only seven planets (including the Sun and Moon) and therefore three further planets ruled two signs; Saturn ruled Aquarius in addition to Capricorn, Jupiter ruled Pisces in addition to Sagittarius, and Mars ruled Scorpio in addition to Aries. There are also a number of planets that are termed personal. The *personal planets* are the Sun and Moon (which are always personal), the planet that rules the ascendant sign (called the chart ruler). The Sun ruler is the planet that rules the Sun sign, and the planet that rules the sign occupied by the Moon is called the Moon ruler.

These different rulings were established a long time ago. There are additional features and weightings given to the rulings, known as *exaltation, detriment* and *fall*. Each planet is exalted when it is in a particular sign from which it works well and with which there is a notable similarity, resulting in more significance being attributed to it in an interpretation. The exaltations are also listed below:

Planet	Ruling in	Exalted in	Detrimental in	Fall
Sun	Leo	Aries	Aquarius	Libra
Moon	Cancer	Taurus	Capricorn	Scorpio
Mercury	Gemini	Virgo and Virgo	Sagittarius	Pisces
Venus	Taurus	Pisces and Libra	Aries	Virgo
Mars	Aries	Capricorn	Libra	Cancer
Jupiter	Sagittarius	Cancer	Gemini	Capricorn
Saturn	Capricorn	Libra	Cancer	Aries
Uranus	Aquarius	Scorpio	Leo	Taurus
Neptune	Pisces	Leo	Virgo	Aquarius
Pluto	Scorpio	Virgo	Taurus	Pisces

The ruling planets and relationships

Opposing the ruling sign of the Zodiac, each planet also has a sign of detriment. In this the planet is said to be debilitated. Finally, in this section comes the sign opposite to exaltation, which is called the fall sign. This is the sign opposite to the sign of exaltation and, is where the planet is thought to be weak. (*See* list on the previous page).

The Houses of the Chart

The astrological chart is divided into houses—in effect this is a way of subdividing the space around the Earth. There are numerous such systems, which have been devised over the years and which fall into three groups: the Equal House System; the Quadrant System; and a variation on these systems.

The *Equal House System* is one of the oldest and after a period of disuse is now back in favour. The ecliptic is divided into twelve equal parts, and the houses are marked by great circles that meet at the poles of the ecliptic and start by going through the degree of the ecliptic ascending over the horizon, and then through every point 30 degrees farther around.

The main *Quadrant Systems* are called after the people who developed them, for example, Campanus, Regromontanus and Placidus, and appeared in the thirteenth, fourteenth and fifteenth centuries respectively. The system of Placidus was used almost exclusively until the early 1950s because it was the only system with published reference tables. It was, however, the only system that did not utilize great circles as the boundaries of the houses.

The final system, a variation, includes the system of Porphyry, which has its origins in antiquity. This is based on the Quadrant System, producing four unequal divisions that are then equally divided into three.

The Equal House System is probably the simplest to use, and in it each house has a certain relevance or significance, affecting a particular aspect of life. The first six houses are concerned with a personal application while the last six apply more to one's dealings with other people and matters outside the home and family. There follows an expanded though not comprehensive description of each house, stipulating the association of house with sign and planet and the resulting meanings. In this context, the planets stand for the provision of an impetus; the signs show how and where that impetus or motivation is to be used; and the houses indicate in which aspect of life the result will be seen.

The first house

This house is associated with Aries and the planet Mars, and because it includes the ascendant, or rising sign, is the most important house of the birth chart. This house refers to the person, which may include such factors as physical characteristics, nature, health, ego and so on. Planets within eight degrees of the ascendant will strongly affect all aspects of the person, including behaviour.

The second house

The second house is associated with Taurus and the planet Venus, and is concerned with the possessions and feelings of the person. As such, this house reflects attitudes to money, and since money and love are intimately entwined, this aspect will be of relevance when interpreting a chart. The second house is also concerned with priorities and the growth of things.

The third house

This is the house of Gemini and the planet Mercury, which not surprisingly means a concern for siblings and also neighbours. Other matters of a local nature, such as schooling, local travel and everyday matters of business, fall under this house. Mental attitude, also falls into the third house, meaning that many important patterns of behaviour, can be considered here. Decisions such as where to live and personal environment are typical examples. All aspects of communication also fall within this house. For anyone who is lost as to what decision to take, a positive influence from the third house will help him or her.

The fourth house

The sign of Cancer and the Moon are associated with the fourth house. The key concerns of this house are the home itself, home circumstances and the family, and caring for someone or something. The mother, or a mother figure, is a particularly strong feature of this house. The concept of the home and the protective enclosing also has analogy with the womb and the grave—thus, the beginning and end of life are also concerns.

The fifth house

This house is very different from the fourth, and the association of Leo and the Sun makes it the house of pleasure and creativity. This includes all such aspects, whether they be related to art, authors, games, gambling, and other leisure pursuits. Moving into the more personal sphere, the fifth house also accounts for lovers and love affairs, probably on a superficial level rather than a lasting, deep relationship. The other personal manifestation of creativity, that of producing children, and parents' feelings about children and procreation, fall under the rule of this house.

The sixth house

The sixth house is the last that impinges upon the person and personal acts, behaviour and relationships. Its sign is Virgo and the planet is Mercury. This is a very functional house, referring as it does to work of a routine nature, health and similar matters. The work may be in the work place, hence it also relates to employers, or at home in the daily round of chores. The concern of health also includes diet, and this house will help to assess the need and timing for a change.

The seventh house

The last six houses refer to the wider influences of one's life and to outward application. Libra and the planet Venus are associated with the seventh house, and the fundamental concern is with relationships with others. This house concerns commitment in partnership and can reflect the likely type of partner sought. It can also relate to the establishment of a business or the employment of new people, from the viewpoint of personal interaction. Because this house encompasses dealings with others, it can also include hostility and conflict.

The eighth house

This house, the opposite of the second, is associated with Scorpio and Pluto, and refers to possessions gained through others, whether as gifts or legacies. In fact, all financial matters fall within this house. It is also the house of birth and death, or alternatively beginnings and endings.

Deep relationships, including those of a sexual nature, are dealt with, as are matters of the occult and the afterlife.

The ninth house

The ninth house, the house of Sagittarius and Jupiter, is from the opposite of the third, which is concerned with neighbours and matters local. The ninth focuses upon travel to foreign countries and extensive study, and also has been called the house of dreams. Longer-distance communication and matters such as the law and literature are covered by the ninth house. Indeed, all factors that potentially may increase one's experience or awareness are appropriate.

The tenth house

The tenth house is the opposite of the fourth house and looks outward to life in general, being concerned with hopes and ambitions and making one's way in life. It used to be called the house of the carer and the father, when perspectives and opportunities were more limited than today. As such this is the province of the long-term carer and also denotes responsibility in the context of the delegation, both giving and receiving. This house is pertinent when career changes are considered, and is associated with Capricorn and Saturn.

The eleventh house

The eleventh house is associated with Aquarius and Uranus. It is the house of acquaintances, social contacts and friends (but not close friends), and as such may encompass societies, clubs and similar groupings. It also provides an indication of whether a person looks favourably upon charitable causes and whether any activities in this direction are genuine or for the self—the house of social conscience in effect. It was called the house of hopes and wishes.

The twelfth house

The twelfth house, associated with Pisces and Neptune, is linked with things that are hidden, self-sacrifice, psychic matters and also matters of

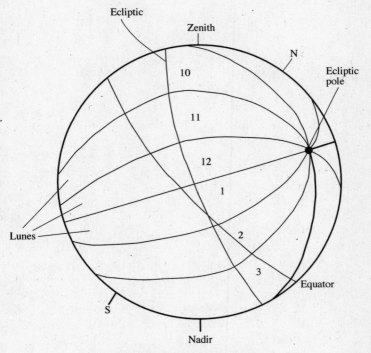

The Equal House System

an institutional nature. This last aspect may refer to hospitals or prisons, and as such may include the more serious illnesses. It can also shed light on problems of a psychological nature, reflected to some extent in its previous name—the house of sorrows.

The following section on Sun signs provides more information on personality, characteristics, associations and aspects of personal involvement and interaction.

Zodiac:
The Sun Signs in Detail

The cusps of the signs

One point should be carefully noted: the Sun enters each sign of the Zodiac on or about the 21st of each month, but it is still influenced to a certain extent by the attributes of the preceding sign, which do not fade away entirely until a week or so has elapsed. For this reason the pure and unmixed attributes of any sign are not manifested until about the 27th of the month. From that date the full force of the sign continues to be exerted until the Sun prepares to enter the next sign, which occurs about the 21st of the next month, and then, mingling with the influence of the new sign, gradually fades away and becomes extinguished in about a week, that is, about the 27th, when the new sign displays its full vigour.

This period—from about the 21st to the 27th of any month—in which the influences of two signs overlap and mingle, is known as the 'cusp' of the signs, and persons born at this time partake in a greater, or less, measure of the attributes of both signs. In estimating their character and fortune, both signs should be taken into account. For instance, a person who was born on September 25, a few days after the Sun has entered Libra, but with some of Virgo's influence still in force, is ruled by both Virgo and Libra, and the pages devoted to both of these signs should be consulted.

Aries

Dates

21 March to 20 April. The Sun enters the zodiacal sign Aries on approximately March 21 each year, remaining in this sign until about
April 20. For the first seven days or so of its occupancy it is still influenced by the gradually declining power of the preceding sign, Pisces;
so that persons born between March 21 and 27 are to some extent
ruled by Pisces, as well as by Aries.

Origin and glyph

The ram's horns, which may be traced back to Egypt.

Ruling planet and groupings

Mars; masculine, cardinal and fire.

Typical traits

Most people born under the sign of Aries (the Ram) are full of energy.
They often react like a battering ram, barging ahead with horns out and
head tucked under, with little regard for either themselves or others.

Arians often give the impression of being very self-confident. But do
not be fooled by appearances. They are really just as insecure as the
rest of us. They are simply much better than most people at covering it
up. Arians are almost as vain as they are brave. They love to be popular
and the centre of attention. And they spend a lot of time on their appearance.

Arians are no good at deceit or pretence. They are honest and direct
people, but they tend not to think before they speak or act. So they can
easily offend or hurt other people. Aries is known by astrologers as a
fiery and positive sign, and is aptly symbolized by the ram, an animal
of great courage and spirit. Aries is ruled by the planet Mars, and those
born during this period are notable for their action, energy and initiative. In life's battles they play the part of guides and leaders; they glory
in fighting and in surmounting difficulties, and their courage and self-
confidence make them pioneers in all kinds of enterprises.

Arians have several noticeable characteristics, such as courage, seemingly boundless energy, enthusiasm, initiative and enterprise, and a desire for adventure and travel. This means that when faced with a particular challenge, there is a tendency to rush in without heeding the consequences, and this can often cause problems. This impulsiveness is, of course, one of their less appealing traits, and it may also be accompanied by selfishness. This manifests itself in the need to accomplish set tasks and reach planned goals, although they tend to have the beneficial quality of being able to concentrate on the primary aim by removing anything that is unnecessary and of little importance. Competitiveness is never far from the surface for an Arian, no matter what aspect of life is involved.

Their aptitude for responsibility and command gains them an ascendancy over others, and they are never so happy or so well employed as when they are supervising or directing a difficult undertaking, and imparting some of their own boundless enthusiasm to their followers and employees. As an example, we will mention Sir John Franklin, the famous Arctic explorer, who was born on April 16, 1786—a man marked out by destiny to be a natural leader of others, and one whose guidance was followed without question to the remotest parts of the earth.

The ambition of persons ruled by Aries knows no bounds, nor does their ability to overcome obstacles. Therefore, provided their interest in their occupation is sustained, they are fated more than all other types to rise to the head of any affairs in which they may be actively concerned. They are, however, impatient and rather capricious, and are apt to lose interest in an undertaking that does not promise to engross all their activities. Moreover, they will not brook the slightest opposition or contradiction; having implicit faith in their own abilities and in the cause which they have espoused —whether it be right or wrong— they will impose their will upon others and override their opinions, and even when proved to be in the wrong they will seldom admit the fact.

Prince Bismarck; (born April 1, 1815), the 'man of blood and iron,' was ruled by Aries, and his autocratic, domineering and fearless character illustrates the truth of what has been stated.

The outstanding defects of Aries subjects are rashness and excessive self-confidence, which often bring about their ruin. Aries people are inclined to outstrip the bounds of discretion in every direction, and they seldom learn restraint from past disasters. By their excessive frankness and boldness of speech they frequently make themselves detested, and by their unwarranted optimism and temerity they bring misfortune upon themselves and others.

Though they are splendid organizers and have the ability to see far ahead, they seldom work according to fixed and well-laid plans; in fact, scheming and subtlety of any kind are foreign to them, and they prefer to be guided by their natural intuition and presence of mind rather than by rules and precedents or a matured course of action.

Aries subjects cannot be led or compelled; but they can easily be deceived or seduced. Having little guile or subtlety in their own make-up, they fail to recognize it in others. Thus they can be influenced by suggestions cunningly made, and are readily deceived by praise and flattery, often of the most gross and obvious kind. Then, inflated by conceit and arrogance, they can be made to view things in a distorted way, and may be impelled to a course of action which, of their accord, they would never have contemplated; whereas any open attempt to control or overrule them would be met with instant, and often violent, opposition. If an Aries subject is convinced that he or she has been deceived or made to appear a fool, his or her anger is terrible to behold and the deception is never forgotten, although at other times he or she is among the first to forgive injuries and slights.

The highest type of person born under Aries is a resolute idealist. He or she or she will fight to the bitter end in the cause that he or she holds dear, and will sacrifice everything for it, and opposition—even persecution—only makes the fire of his or her conviction burn the brighter.

Idealists of this type were William Booth, the founder of the Salvation Army, and Albert, king of the Belgians; both of them were born under the rule of Aries, and both suffered for convictions which they would not abandon.

Relationships and love

Subjects of Aries are not easy to get on with in married life, especially if their partner refuses to give way in everything, as he or she would be expected to do.

Moreover, they seem quite at a loss to understand the psychology of the other sex, and their want of tact often causes pain. But they will always rise in arms to defend their spouse and children from the attacks of other people, and they are assiduous in providing for their comfort. Aries folk often suffer acutely through their affections and feelings, though their intense pride impels them to appear unmoved. Women belonging to Aries often gain a distinct advantage, socially and financially, upon their marriage.

In personal relationships, Arians can be very passionate, and Aries men look for a strong partner. Arian women are equally demanding and often prefer a career to being at home, although the two can be combined. Providing there are no adverse influences elsewhere on a person's chart, Arians are faithful but there are those who are continually moving on to new relationships and challenges.

As parents Arians are, not unexpectedly, energetic and in the main will encourage their children in a variety of activities. It is all too easy, however, for the ebullience of the parent to overshadow the wishes of the child, and that can easily result in discord.

Arians are very faithful to their friends and are willing to do a lot for them. But they get very disappointed and cross if their efforts are not appreciated.

It is usually great fun having an Arian as a partner. He or she will be enthusiastic and very romantic. But it may prove difficult to hold on to an Arian, as they do not like being tied down. And they get bored very quickly and always like something new.

Arians don't mind having several partners at the same time. On the other hand they get furious and very jealous if their partners have the same idea.

Deep down, the Arian is pretty insecure, so if you are in love with one, you must remember that he or she has a great need to be reminded frequently of your love.

The most harmonious partnerships in friendship and marriage for Aries people are formed with those born between July 21 and August 21 and between November 21 and December 21.

Occupations

To satisfy the Arian character, an occupation ought to be challenging, with goals to aim for and with the opportunity to lead. Boring, routine jobs would not satisfy, but if that were the outcome then other activities would have to compensate. Large organizations with some freedom and a defined career structure, such as teaching, the police or the civil service, would be appropriate.

Natives of Aries excel in any occupation in which they can organize,

express themselves and give full rein to their abundant intellectual powers. Therefore, they do well as explorers and pioneers, soldiers, leaders
of reform and temperance movements, directors and heads of business concerns, political leaders, surgeons, nurses, editors, scientists, in-
ventors and innovators. If they are artistically gifted, they often achieve
fame as writers, painters and musicians. Raphael, the great Italian
painter, Swinburne, Wordsworth, and Hans Andersen were born under Aries, as also were Johann Sebastian Bach, René Descartes, and
William Harvey who discovered the circulation of the blood. All these
men were innovators in their various ways, men who refused to be
fettered by rules or custom.

Good advice
An obvious word of advice for the Arian is to try to be a little more
patient. And perhaps being a little more diplomatic would be a good
idea too.

Fire and earth compatibility
The fire signs are not very compatible with the earth signs. Every time
an Arian becomes enthusiastic about something, the Taureans and
Capricorns will be real party-poopers and try to bring the Arian down
to earth again. And if there is one thing an Arian cannot abide, it is
being contradicted and told that one's ideas are a load of rubbish.
   Of the three earth signs, Arians get on best with Virgo and worst
with Capricorn.

Fire and air compatibility
Whereas earth can smother a fire, air is necessary for it to burn and
flare up. So an Arian can get lots of encouragement for even the crazi-
est of ideas if he or she sticks to a Gemini or an Aquarian. On the
other hand they tend to lose contact with reality, so the ideas often
come to nothing.
   Of all the air signs, Arians get on worst with Librans.

Fire and water compatibility
Everyone knows that water puts out fire. So the combination of fire
and water is not very good. The sensitive Piscean or Cancerian cannot

understand the Arian person at all. And for his or her part, the Arian feels that water sign people are far too careful and considerate.

Of all the water signs, Arians get on best with Scorpions.

Health

Aries rules the head, brain and face, and its subjects are liable to suffer from ailments and accidents affecting these parts, such as headaches, concussion, apoplexy, disorders of the eyes, nose and skin of the face, as well as cuts, burns, bruises and other head wounds. The stomach and kidneys may also give trouble at times. In other respects, the health is usually good, owing to the strong vital force imparted by Aries and its ruler, Mars.

To attract good vibrations

Those who would obtain the utmost from life should endeavour to attract harmonious astrological vibrations. The native of Aries should wear, and be surrounded with, bright colours, especially bright green, pink and yellow; however, all shades of red are good. White is also fortunate, but should not be worn entirely unrelieved by any other colour.

Wider aspects

In their other pursuits, Arians import their eager approach, which in certain circumstances can be positively damaging, for example, knocks and bruises in the early years.

Taurus

Dates

21 April to 21 May. The Sun enters the zodiacal sign Taurus about April 21 every year, and remains in this sign until about May 21. For the first seven days or so of this period (until about April 27) the gradually lessening power of Aries continues to exert its influence, and all persons born between April 21 and 27 fall under the rule of Aries as well as under that of Taurus.

Origin and glyph

The bull's head, which has links with early civilizations in Egypt.

Ruling planet and groupings

Venus; feminine, fixed and earth.

Typical traits

Taureans rely upon stability and security, both in an emotional and financial context, but granted this they can be extremely reliable, patient and tenacious. They tend to be persistent, methodical and see things through to the end, and this can be reflected in their steady progress through life, including their career. Their lack of flexibility can often lead to resistance to change, even when it is for the better. However, when facing the challenge, they usually cope better than most. Taureans are practical people who dislike waste, and they tend to have high standards.

Taureans are usually very economical. This doesn't mean they are stingy, but they know how to handle their money and hate to have any debts. On the other hand they open both their hearts and wallets if one of their friends gets into trouble.

Taurus is an earthy sign and is symbolized by the bull, which represents nature and fertility. It is ruled by the beautiful and poetic planet Venus, and so it is not surprising that its subjects are usually distinguished by their love of beauty and harmony in every aspect of life, and by their intuition and sympathy with nature in all her moods. No matter how airy may be their flights of fancy, they never lose contact with the earth and terrestrial matters, and their imaginative and speculative powers are always tempered with sound common sense. This practical outlook is one of the leading traits of Taurus subjects; they are fond of work, and even those of the most refined type are not ashamed to work with their hands. They are particularly fond of gardening and any kind of labour connected with the earth and vegetation, but they are less successful in connection with animals.

Great pertinacity and fixity of purpose also characterizes the sons and daughters of Taurus. They will concentrate all their attention upon a single aim and refuse to be turned aside from their goal. They are usually of a happy and mild disposition and, though acutely sensitive of slights and rebuffs, are slow to anger. When thoroughly roused, however, the whole aspect of Taureans is completely altered, and they give way to furious and ungovernable wrath. Their unyielding determination does not desert them in anger, for they seldom forget an injury, and will fight their enemies unflinchingly to the bitter end. But they will have no part in trickery, deception and underhand dealings, which are quite foreign to their nature, so that all their battles are carried on in the open. As soon as an enemy shows signs of collapse, the Taurean is instantly sorry for him or her, and in this way frequently makes a fool of himself.

The receptive power of the Taurean mind is enormous; and natives of this sign are more powerfully affected by their associates and environment than are, perhaps, any other type of people. With their natural love of all that is harmonious and beautiful, they are deeply revolted by ugliness, squalor and strife and by coarse companions; and uncongenial surroundings of this kind reduce them to the lowest pitch of misery. On the other hand, they respond instantly to refined and sympathetic surroundings, when they give of their best. They make good and cheerful hosts, and are very successful socially—which is rather surprising, since their nature is usually retiring. Taureans have also a pronounced faculty for imposing their will upon others, which is probably another aspect of their strong intuitive powers.

Robespierre, whose birthday fell within the Taurus period, possessed this power of dominating his associates. It is seen in other types as well, especially in men of unusual intellect who have helped to mould the mind both of their contemporaries and their successors. Foremost among such is Shakespeare (born April 23, 1564), while others of this type include Joseph Addison, Alexander Pope, Machiavelli; Froude, William H. Prescott, Gibbon and Hume, the historians; Thomas Huxley and Edward Jenner, each of whom brought about a revolution in science; Herbert Spencer, the philosopher; and Robert Owen, the social reformer.

Natives of Taurus rarely have difficulty in attracting followers, either in business or for any kind of movement or project, but they should guard against being swayed by other people's advice instead of by their own good sense and intuition. They are often called upon to bear great responsibilities, which they do willingly and well, although not without becoming unduly worried.

Relationships and love

Subjects of Taurus have an intense love nature, which refuses to be satisfied with anything less than the entire affection of their marriage partner and friends. Being guided almost entirely by impulse, they frequently make disastrous mistakes in choosing a husband or wife. They demand perfection in their mate and are critical and exacting, as well as inclined to be unreasonably and violently jealous, but there is no malice behind their outbursts, which are only the natural result of the interplay between their strong physical nature and their acutely sensitive feelings. This makes them ardent and fascinating lovers, who know how to play at ill upon the emotions of their beloved as upon an instrument.

A good partnership is important to Taureans, and this means a happy harmonious partnership. Their need to put down roots can render them very good at making a home, as does the practical side of their character. They usually make good husbands and wives, and parents, but they may make the mistake of getting stuck in a rut.

Having established a good home, Taureans will probably consider children to be very important, and the parents will strive to make their children happy. Babies and toddlers can be slow to reach the obvious milestones such as walking, but in later childhood things need to be learnt only once. Discipline is important because Taureans are essentially traditional and look for rules and guidance.

Subjects of Taurus will find that their most harmonious affinities and friendships are formed with those born between August 21 and September 21 and between December 21 and January 21.

Good advice

Taureans are not very good at handling their emotions and can be lazy. They will put up with a lot just to avoid an argument. But when pushed too far they become really incensed. So they would do well to solve their conflicts straight away, even though that may present some awkward moments.

Earth and water compatibility

The earth is only productive if there is enough water. Similarly, the down-to-earth Taureans and the more emotional water sign people such as the Cancerians and Pisceans can enjoy fruitful relations. Both groups enjoy nature and seeing things grow and prosper.

Scorpions are the only water sign people that Taureans do not get on so well with.

Earth and air compatibility

These two signs are not very compatible. The practical, careful and down-to-earth Taureans find it hard to swallow the fanciful ideas that the Libran or the Aquarian dream up. Their common-sense attitude swiftly dismisses these ideas.

For their part, air sign people often find Taureans very boring. And they get frustrated by the time it takes for a Taurean to make up his or her mind.

They may be able to work together, when the combination of Taurean thoroughness and the lively imagination of air sign people strikes a balance.

Taureans get on best with Librans and worst with Aquarians.

Earth and fire compatibility

Earth and fire signs are not very compatible either. Fire sign people tend to get extremely enthusiastic about things, and cannot bear to come up against a killjoy, who keeps trying to bring them back down to earth.

For their part, Taureans cannot bear to be with people who keep wanting to change things all the time, and who also try to rush them because they think things are moving too slowly.

Occupations

Although Taureans do not like taking risks, they are ambitious. However, they are more likely to stay with a job than to chop and change, and will quite possibly remain in uninteresting employment because the income is well nigh guaranteed. Sure handling of money and financial affairs comes easily to Taureans, and many find careers in the financial sector.

Subjects of this earthy sign are suited to any occupation in which their imagination can have full scope. Being naturally musical and artistic, they make good composers, singers and musicians, as well as poets, novelists and painters. Apart from Shakespeare and others already mentioned, Robert Browning, Dante Gabriel Rossetti, Anthony Trollope, Sir James Barrie, Alphonse Daudet, J.M.W. Turner, J. L. Gérôme, Albrecht Dürer, Joseph Haydn and Sir Arthur Sullivan were all born under the rule of Taurus.

The lower types make good gardeners and agriculturists, builders and decorators, and are successful in almost any occupation that is practical and creative. Taurus subjects also excel in ministering to the wants of others and making them comfortable, and hence they make splendid physicians, nurses, matrons, housekeepers and cooks.

An outstanding example is Florence Nightingale, 'the Lady with the Lamp,' who was born on May 12, 1820. Taureans are also congenially employed as house and estate agents, florists, soldiers and government officials.

Health

The typical subject of Taurus is, like his or her prototype the bull, endowed with a vigorous constitution and splendid health. If there is a weak point, it is usually the throat or neck, and attacks of sore throat, tonsillitis and catarrh are likely. But the commonest complaints afflicting Taurus people are probably those arising from excess and indiscretions of diet. Music has a profound effect upon them, and when ill, tired or run down they are more quickly restored to health by good music and refined surroundings than by any other remedy.

To attract good vibrations

Taurus subjects can attune themselves to fortunate vibrations, which will make their life harmonious and successful, by surrounding themselves with all shades of blue and incorporating it in their clothes. Indigo, too, will be found restful and soothing, but red should be avoided, except, perhaps, the softest shades of rose. All colours should be subdued, for Taureans have little need of stimulants.

Wider aspects

Routine is vital, and change or uncertainty makes them uncomfortable. They enjoy leisure pursuits but must guard against becoming too lazy.

Gemini

Dates

22 May to 21 June. The Sun passes into the zodiacal sign of Gemini on approximately May 21, but this sign does not begin to exert its full and unalloyed power until about May 27, since for a week or so its influence is blended with that of the preceding sign, Taurus. Therefore, persons born between May 21 and 27 are also ruled in part by Taurus. Gemini continues in full force until about June 21.

Origin and glyph

Two children, from Castor and Pollux of Classical mythology, which are bright stars.

Ruling planet and groupings

Mercury; masculine, mutable and air.

Typical traits

These include such characteristics as liveliness, versatility and intelligence, but these are tempered to some degree by a nervous energy and a certain inconsistency at times. They are logical, ordered and very quick of mind, seeking variety in their lives, both at home and in their work. They tend to be good communicators but at times let their desire to communicate dominate all else. They can take in information very quickly if they are concentrating enough, but run the risk of knowing a little about a lot rather than grasping one topic in great depth. This is not necessarily a bad thing, of course.

They may seem to be nervous people, but that is largely because they are restless and inquisitive. They have to know everything, so they chatter to anyone who's around.

Geminis have vivid imaginations, and sometimes find it hard to distinguish between fantasy and reality. It is not because they really want to lie: they just can't help embroidering on the truth.

A Gemini will often seem to be two different people at the same time. Madly happy one minute, and unbearably sad the next. And then five minutes later he or she will have forgotten what the problem was.

In ancient days Gemini was symbolized by twin children—the Castor and Pollux of Roman mythology. Its astrological symbol consists of two columns united at the top and bottom, an apt illustration of the marked duality of mind and character displayed by those born under this sign. Gemini is known astrologically as an airy sign, and this again accords with the character of its subjects—subtle, intellectual, and versatile, but restless, undependable and diffuse.

The moral and intellectual make-up of a subject of Gemini is like a house divided against itself. This lack of unity is observable in all his or her actions, and often leads him or her into the most perplexing situations. Gemini is ruled by the restless planet Mercury, and a Gemini subject is truly 'mercurial' in everything, for he or she seems to be governed alternately by the attraction of two widely different poles. At one time he or she is full of ardour, energy and enthusiasm, with sparkling wit; but before long a sudden change occurs without any apparent cause, and he or she appears cold, lethargic and unresponsive. Gemini subjects are usually intelligent to a remarkable degree; their intellect penetrates rapidly to the root of any matter and strips it of difficulties, and thus they are extraordinarily apt at acquiring knowledge. But the interest soon wears off, and their attention wanders to something fresh and untried; and for this reason their knowledge, though covering a wide range of subjects, is, as mentioned before, seldom more than superficial.

In their relations with friends they are most undependable—at one moment affable and effusive, at another, so cold and unapproachable that the perplexed acquaintances are driven to conclude that unwittingly and unintentionally they must said something deeply offensive. But when next they meet the Gemini he or she is cordiality itself. However, when the mood suits them, the subjects of Gemini are remarkably good company, being exceptionally witty, merry, generous and—at least, to all appearances—sympathetic and considerate. Actually, however, this itself is only a passing whim or caprice, and they are only kind-hearted when it suits their mood of the moment.

Their nature being what it is, they crave change of scene and activity more than anything, and so are driven on by an insatiable thirst for travel and novelty. They are happy and successful travellers, being able to adapt themselves to any kind of circumstances and environment, though not for long will they make their home in one place, if they can avoid it. The famous African explorer, Sir H. M. Stanley, who was ruled by Gemini, is an outstanding example of this genius for travel.

Gemini people have very fair and unbiased critical faculties. They are able to look dispassionately at both sides of a question, and put themselves in the place of the other person. Their intentions are generally disinterested and honest, but are frequently spoiled by their lack of dependability.

They are often brilliantly clever, ingenious and inventive, and, given some fixity of purpose, there is no intellectual height to which they cannot climb, no depth of thought which they cannot sound. Among the striking instances of this superior Gemini type are Blaise Pascal, the great mathematician and philosopher, George Stephenson, of locomotive fame, Adam Smith, the economist, and William Pitt, who took the helm of State at the early age of twenty-four.

Gemini subjects are usually refined, possessing artistic tastes of a high order, and are gifted with wonderful tact. Their keen penetration extends to their fellow beings, and they are excellent judges of character and ability. Since they readily divine the character and intentions of an opponent, and as a result are able to use his or her own weapons against him or her, they nearly always triumph in an argument or a battle of wits.

Most Geminis find it difficult to be punctual, since they are always being distracted by new things which they want to investigate. So if you make a date with a Gemini, you should be prepared to wait quite a while before he or she turns up (if indeed they do actually turn up).

Geminis have a great sense of humour, and if you have a good story to tell, you can be sure of a rapt audience. But if you start a long explanation with lots of small details they are bound to interrupt you or become bored: they probably worked out the punch line ages ago and can't be bothered to listen to all your waffle.

Their inventiveness and love of change causes them forever to be devising ingenious schemes or launching moneymaking projects, but these are often abandoned before they have a chance of coming to fruition. The lower types make clever crooks and sharpers, who usually succeed in evading detection.

Relationships and love

The Geminian curiosity and versatility render relationships a little more prone than most to disruption or diversion. However, partnerships can last, particularly if the husband/wife finds an interesting companion with whom he or she can interact intellectually. Gemini women often marry men who can deal with domestic chores, as such women have no love of housework.

As parents, they can be lively and creative but sometimes over-critical. It is not uncommon for Geminians to make poor parents because they can be too impatient, too heavily involved in their own careers and over-competitive, seeking reflected glory in their children's achievements.

Geminis seldom make do with just one friend. They prefer a whole crowd, and they like friends with lots of different interests.

Because Geminis are so restless, they can sometimes hurt their friends' feelings. Just when you think you are having a nice chat together, a Gemini will get up and disappear. And a moment later you will see him or her in deep conversation with somebody else at the other end of the room. He or she didn't mean to hurt you, but someone happened to turn up who was more interesting than you at the time.

Geminis don't like to talk about their feelings. You could say they are ruled by their minds more than their hearts, and so unless you are really good friends, it can be difficult to get to know a Gemini properly.

You must be prepared to share your Gemini with hundreds of other people.

The uncertainty of the Gemini temperament does not favour lasting friendship, and is the cause of much friction in married life. Moreover, those ruled by this sign are given to fickleness in their affections; they may lead a double life or commit bigamy. They are little swayed by passion, and the only way to retain their fidelity is constantly to meet their varying moods in a fresh and unexpected manner. All forms of monotony are fatal to success when dealing with Gemini people.

It can be something of a trial to have a relationship with a Gemini, because it often seems like having two sweethearts at the same time. Two twins, but definitely not identical. On the contrary, they are very different.

One day your Gemini can be so tender, that you are quite sure of his or her love. Then the next time you are together, your Gemini is cross and grumpy and finds fault with everything you do. Your clothes are horrid and your opinions are stupid, everything is wrong. Then shortly afterwards all is forgiven and forgotten again.

The Geminis' restless nature also means that they seldom stick to one partner for very long. They love to flirt around, although never very seriously. As they find it difficult to reveal their feelings, they will tend to back off if you try to get too close to them or to gain their full confidence. If you still persist then you run the risk of losing your Gemini.

Those who can live with them most harmoniously are born between January 21 and February 21 and between September 21 and October 21.

Good advice

If you want to give Geminis some advice, tell them to slow down every now and then. But don't expect Geminis to crawl along like snails. They might also be advised to a spend a little more time with one pursuit, person or place before they go rushing off in search of something better.

Air and earth compatibility

People born under an air sign are seldom very happy together with an earth sign. They feel that the more contemplative Taurus or Virgo is too slow off the mark when the action starts.

On the other hand Gemini people do need to come down to earth occasionally when they get a bit too frivolous, and it does the earth sign good to 'get some air under their wings' now and then.

Of all the earth signs, Geminis seem to get on best with those born under the sign of Capricorn.

Air and fire compatibility

A Gemini is usually attracted by any idea, however crazy it may be. Leos and Arians are full of crazy ideas, so Geminis get on well with the fire signs.

However, when an air sign and a fire sign embark on a major project together, they can easily lose contact with reality. Their plans can flare up and fizzle out to nothing.

Of all the fire signs, Geminis get on best with Leos and Arians.

Air and water compatibility

As it is impossible to breathe under water, Geminis can feel suffocated by water people.

On the other hand, they have much to learn from one another. Water sign people are often very sensitive, and dealing with emotions is not one of the Gemini's strongest points. So perhaps a water sign person can teach the Gemini how to handle his or her emotions better.

Of all the water signs, Geminis get on best with Scorpions.

Occupations

Geminians are very good when dealing with money and can, therefore, be admirably suited to banking or accountancy. As might be expected, the ability to communicate and the lively personality mean they may also fit well into employment in some aspect of the media or advertising. The pitfalls inevitably are that attention to detail may be lacking and that there must be variety. Conversely, they handle pressure well and are good at handling several tasks at once.

Those born under Gemini are most profitably engaged in work calling for mental gifts above the ordinary, as well as tact, subtlety, good judgment, and quickness of wit. They make excellent writers, journalists, teachers, secretaries, lawyers, barristers, magistrates, and diplomats, and are often successful as clerks, financiers, stockbrokers, and surveyors. They are usually very happy in any occupation involving travelling and constant change of scene and interest. People of the Gemini type often display literary ability of a high order, among the many outstanding examples being Lord Lytton, Emerson, Thomas Moore, Pushkin, Walt Whitman, Thomas Hardy, Sir Edwin Arnold and Charles Kingsley.

Gemini people are incredibly inquisitive and always on the hunt for new things to explore. On the other hand they find it hard to be thorough and steady at work, because they are always on the lookout for something new.

Geminis rarely make long-term plans. They live for the moment, and don't think about tomorrow. The computer world is not a bad choice for a Gemini, both on the technical side as well as on the sales force.

Health

Gemini rules the shoulders, arms, hands and lungs, and its subjects may suffer from disorders and accidents to these parts. But their most common ailments are those affecting the nervous system (governed by Mercury, the ruler of Gemini). They are liable to nervous debility, nervous exhaustion, neuritis, mental strain and intense irritability, and their chief remedy lies in avoiding worry as much as possible.

To attract good vibrations

The colours most in harmony with Gemini are white, silver, yellow and light green. These should be worn on the person, and used freely in light furnishings and decorations.

Wider aspects:

Change and variety remain of paramount importance, whether in leisure pursuits or retirement. Individualism will dominate over group activities, which may become routine.

Cancer

Dates

22 June to 22 July. The Sun enters the zodiacal sign Cancer about June 22 each year, remaining therein until July 22. However, the power of Cancer is not fully exerted until about June 27, and people born between June 22 and 27 are also controlled to some extent by the gradually declining influence of Gemini, which should be taken into account when their character and fortune are being estimated.

Origin and glyph

The glyph represents the breasts; Cancer probably came from ancient Babylon.

Ruling planet and groupings

Moon; feminine, cardinal and water.

Typical traits

The protective nature of the Cancerian is the overriding aspect of the character, but it is tempered by a stubborn and often moody streak. Although they tend to be of the worrying type, Cancerians have a remarkably good intuition, and their instinctive reactions and decisions can usually be relied upon. There is, however, a changeability about Cancerians that manifests itself in several ways. They can rapidly adapt to pick up information, habits, etc, from others. It also means that they can be touchy and, like the crab, may be hiding a soft, easily hurt person beneath a seemingly hard shell.

The symbol of Cancer is the crab, a creature whose habits typify the timid, hesitant yet tenacious disposition of those born under this sign. Cancer is known by astrologers as a watery sign, and it is ruled by the negative and watery Moon. Therefore, it is not surprising that this negative quality is the chief characteristic of those born under Cancer; it can be observed in all their actions and habits of life, making them shy, timid and retiring, constantly anxious over trifles, intensely sensitive, hesitant, romantic, dreamy, but undemonstrative; their tenacity and powers of endurance are, however, little short of amazing. Having once committed themselves usually after much hesitation—to a definite course of action, they will pursue it resolutely until they have either achieved their goal or perished by the wayside. Of this type were Garibaldi, Mazzini, John Huss, and Calvin, all subjects of Cancer, and all notable for their fixity of purpose.

Few people are as sensitive as those born under Cancer. The least censure, criticism or lack of understanding is taken deeply to heart, but they respond with gratitude to appreciation and encouragement. However, they will not tolerate interference in their affairs or in any project which they have undertaken, preferring to shoulder all the labour and responsibility rather than allow any meddling on the part of others. In uncongenial surroundings, or when tried by much opposition or lack of success, they become morbid and introspective; but they shrink to the last from opening their hearts to others, and jealously keep their worries and grief to themselves.

People of the Cancer type are often dominated by a fear of the future and old age. This may lead them to hoard money, and to become selfish and niggardly. However, they rarely want for money in actual fact, although their business affairs may pass through trying periods. They are very unsuccessful as gamblers, and their wealth—which is often excessive—is usually the fruit of persistent hard work, coupled with shrewdness, economy and foresight. Among the many sons of Cancer who have accumulated vast riches in this way may be mentioned John D. Rockefeller, Cecil Rhodes and John Jacob Astor.

Cancer subjects have most retentive memories, and this gift is often useful to them in their work, whatever it may be. They have also a great respect for convention, and are deeply interested in everything that is old, sacred or historical. At the same time, the freshness of unspoilt nature appeals to them strongly, and they are never so happy as when wandering in the woods and fields, especially in the neighbourhood of water.

Lower types of the Cancer subject are usually found to be indolent, greedy, mean, intensely selfish, suspicious, morbidly sensitive, and keenly resentful of imaginary injuries and slights. The higher types, however, who are hard-working, peace-loving and devoted to their families, provide one of the most valuable elements in the community.

Cancer is very close to the moon. And the moods of a Cancerian alternate according to the phases of the moon. Cancerians are very moody and so you never know whether they are going to be happy and cheerful or down in the dumps.

Cancerians are very sensitive to any kind of criticism. And since they also have incredible memories, one has to be wary of offending them. For they will remember an offensive remark for years to come.

Cancerians love secrets but don't expect them to tell you theirs. They definitely don't like discussing their private lives, although they love to hear all about yours.

Relationships and love

Affection runs very deep in Cancer folk, though they seldom wear their heart on their sleeve, so that their lack of demonstrativeness is often taken for lack of sentiment. They are happiest when in the heart of their family, to whom they are intensely devoted, but if, as is frequently the case, they consider that they are not properly understood by those dear to them, they become miserable and dejected, and retire within themselves. Their love affairs and domestic life are often full of worries and difficulties, which, however, are usually overcome by their great pertinacity and patience.

If you look at a picture of a crayfish, it looks as though it is about to give you a tremendous hug. Its 'arms' are spread wide open, waiting for you to fall into them.

But it also has very strong claws and keeps a powerful grip on you once it has latched on.

And that is what it is like to have a Cancerian partner. Cancerians take love very seriously, and because they are so fond of their mothers, they look for someone they can attach themselves to with the same degree of intensity. Some people may find them too possessive and stifling.

On the other hand, if you have a Cancerian friend, you can be sure of their loyalty: they will not run off with someone else at the drop of a hat.

If you examine a crayfish closely, you will discover that it has a hard outer shell which protects a very soft animal underneath. Without this shell it would be easy prey for its enemies.

People born under the sign of Cancer are also like this. They are very soft and sensitive and easy to hurt.

Cancer

The caring nature of Cancerians makes them excellent at building a home and good at forming long-lasting partnerships. In general Cancerians like to look back in preference to forwards and commonly stay in the same house for a long period of time. A slightly negative aspect is that their protective nature can become excessive and turn into clinging, and they may be touchy and occasionally snap for no apparent reason.

The sensitive almost retiring aspect of the character can be seen quite early in life, and this may continue to the point that they become very shy at school; they may hide behind a shell. It is commonly the case that Cancerians will eye new social contacts somewhat warily, keeping them at arm's length. However, when they get to know each other better, firm friendships can develop.

Cancerians usually like their extended family within a reasonably short distance and are keen to help anyone who may need their support.

The Cancerian is a domestic animal, and does not have many friends outside the family. And because Cancerians are so touchy, they sometimes have difficulty in hanging on to their friends, who have to handle them with kid gloves.

You will not find Cancerian people quarrelling with their friends one minute and being best buddies the next. Or fighting with a friend on the way home from school and playing with him or her the same evening. They are fairly steadfast.

A Cancerian friend is a great help if you are unhappy. They are good listeners. And because they are so sensitive, they immediately sense what is the matter. In fact they may have guessed it even before you start to tell them.

Those born during the Cancer period will find their closest and most enduring friendships with people born between February 21 and March 21 and between October 21 and November 21.

Good advice

We have already pointed out the extreme sensitivity of Cancerians. But they really need to learn that not all the unpleasant things said are meant as an attack. They could equally well be meant as good advice.

They also need to think about what they say themselves, because they are not nearly always so sensitive when it comes to other people's feelings.

Water and air compatibility

The air signs, Gemini, Libra and Aquarius, can learn from the water signs, and vice versa. For instance, Cancerians find it hard to grasp that other people are not made or think the same way as themselves. The air signs are better at this. In return, water sign people can teach the air signs to handle their emotions better.

Water and air are quite compatible. But just as water can suffocate air, for you cannot breathe under water, a Cancerian may have an over-possessive and stifling effect on an air sign.

On the other hand, air can churn water into high seas and a surging storm. And this happens when a Gemini or Libra makes no allowances for the more sensitive Cancer. Then the Cancerian mood is also likely to become tempestuous.

Of all the air Signs, Cancerians usually find their best friends are Aquarians.

Water and earth compatibility

Water is essential for all growth on earth. People born under an earth sign usually get on well with Cancerians. One lot are down-to-earth and sensible, the other more emotional. So if they do not try to dominate each other, but respect each other's idiosyncrasies, they can derive much pleasure from each other's company.

A plant can wither and die from over-watering, and a relationship can also founder if a Cancerian gives free rein to his feelings without any consideration of the more down-to-earth Taurean, Virgo or Capricorn.

Taurus and Virgo are the earth signs that Cancer people usually get on best with.

Water and fire compatibility

These two signs are usually not very compatible. Cancer people just cannot cope with Arians or Leos who come charging in at top speed and want to carry out some half-baked plan straight away.

In return, fire sign people often get annoyed with Cancerians who they feel are too considerate of other people's opinions and concerned about not offending others.

Occupations

Those who are ruled by Cancer are generally successful in occupations of a public nature, or those in which they can serve large numbers of people. On this account, they make good government officials, politicians, caterers and hotel proprietors. They often instinctively follow occupations connected with liquids, such as those of publican, wine merchant, barmaid, laundry proprietor and hydraulic engineer.

Cancerians can turn their hand to most things, and their careful, intuitive approach can make them successful. They tend to work well with people and often adopt the role of mediator, where diplomacy is required. The caring professions (for example, medicine) are obviously well matched to the Cancer character, but teaching may also be suitable. Although business may prosper under a Cancerian, there is often a tendency, even a fear, to change, which may show itself as inflexibility.

They are happy when on the sea, and make good sailors and naval officers. Many famous sailors have been born under this sign, including Paul Jones and Admiral Farragut. Success in finance and 'big business' often rewards the subjects of Cancer, so long as their activities are free from gambling and speculation. The literary and musical professions, especially if these bring them before the public, are also well suited to their romantic and imaginative temperament.

Health

Cancer governs the chest, the stomach and the higher organs of digestion. The most common accidents to which Cancer subjects are liable are chest injuries and broken ribs, while their most frequent ailments are bronchitis, pulmonary tuberculosis, pneumonia, pleurisy, dropsy, rheumatism and all diseases of the stomach. They should always try to exercise prudence and restraint in regard to what they eat, for they are naturally inclined to indulge over-freely in the pleasures of the table, with consequent indigestion and biliousness. Overindulgence in alcohol should in particular be guarded against, for Cancer subjects are liable to develop into drunkards. Finally, they should do all in their power to resist worry, their most potent enemy.

To attract good vibrations

Emerald green and glistening white are the colours most in harmony with this sign, and people of the Cancer type should always make a point of using these colours lavishly in their dress and in the decoration of their home.

Wider aspects

Cancerians are extremely sensitive, and while outwardly they appear charming and friendly, they can be temperamental and subject to wide mood swings. In general they love change, and while travel appeals, home has the greatest attraction.

Leo

Dates

23 July to 23 August. The Sun enters the zodiacal sign of Leo on approximately July 23 each year, and remains therein until about August 21. But the full influence of this sign does not begin to exert itself until about July 27, being mingled until then with the gradually decreasing force of the preceding sign, Cancer. Therefore, people born on the cusp—between July 23 and 27—are also partly ruled by Cancer, and should study the influence of that sign as well.

Origin and glyph

It probably originated in ancient Egypt, from the constellation; the glyph resembles the lion's tail.

Ruling planet and groupings

Sun; masculine, fixed, fire.

Typical traits

Leonians tend to be generous, creative and yet proud individuals who nevertheless need to keep a tight rein on themselves to avoid becoming overbearing. The creative nature needs to find an outlet in whatever guise, and it is common for Leonians to become organizers, with confidence and energy, although beneath that they may be rather nervous. The possible risk is that Leonians may end up taking over and feel they always know best, so they must learn to listen to the views of other people. They can also display a temper, if only briefly, and are prone to panic if things go badly wrong. However, they generally regain control of the situation quickly. Their impatience and tendency to go over the top are countered by the abundance of their positive qualities.

Leo is a positive and fiery sign, ruled by the ardent, masculine and strongly magnetic Sun. It is symbolized by the lion, and the typical person born under this sign has much of the 'leonine' in his or her nature, including great courage, loyalty, energy, dignity, and a decided gift for leadership. Even his or her personal appearance is often leonine, for the purest and most representative types are distinguished by a tall, vigorous frame, broad back and shoulders, well-developed muscles, an erect carriage, a shock of yellow, golden or tawny hair, and a general appearance of pride and fearlessness.

Affection, sympathy and warmth of heart characterize people who are born under this sign. Their love embraces the whole of humanity, and their loyalty is such that they will defend their friends even to their own detriment, and will never desert one whose cause they have championed, unless disgusted by his or her treachery or deceit. Their nature is essentially so simple and noble that the least suggestion of guile or double-dealing is more hateful to them than anything, and is the only thing that can alienate their affection. They are utter strangers to fear, both physical and moral, and when roused are terrific fighters, but at the same time they will submit to a great deal of provocation before showing signs of anger. Then, no matter to what pitch of fury they may be wrought, they always fight fairly and according to the rules, and are invariably generous to a vanquished enemy.

Natives of Leo are direct and open in speech and the expression of opinions, but they are frequently tactless—for to them diplomacy savours of guile, which they detest. They are also inclined to be stern, severe and heavy in manner, even to those they love deeply, and are very quick-tempered when there is any suggestion of their honour or dignity being impugned.

Leos love to perform, and be the centre of attention all the time. If there is a boy trying to impress all the girls in the playground by balancing on the walls or doing something else to attract attention, then you can be pretty sure that he is a Leo.

Leos love flattery. And they lap up praise like a cat who has been given a bowl of cream. For they never doubt that people really mean it, and that they fully deserve it.

Leos are not the type to reflect on things. You can bet on it that the gentle boys, with whom you can sit and chat for hours, were definitely not born under the sign of Leo. On the other hand, Leos are often very generous and warm people.

Ask a Leo for a piece of advice, and you can be sure of his help. And don't be afraid to follow it. But do not try and return the favour, for good advice is something one dispenses to one's subjects, and as you know, a king has no superiors.

Leo

Leos do everything in the extreme. When Leos are on the go, there is a regular buzz of activity all around. But when they stop, they can be so incredibly lazy that they will not lift a finger and get everyone else to wait on them.

Their convictions usually become settled early in life, and are rarely changed or modified later; they are expressed dogmatically, even defiantly. The extreme Leo types are often very narrow-minded and bigoted.

Their ambition is great and their strength of will considerable, so that it is not surprising that they usually surmount all difficulties that lie between them and their goal. In obtaining their desires, they frequently appear ruthless; this is seldom the result of wanton cruelty, but springs from the belief that the few must be sacrificed for the ultimate good of the majority. Leo people are born to play the part of leaders, and they have the gift of inspiring rare devotion in those who believe in them. Striking instances of this type are the emperor Napoleon, Benito Mussolini, Cavour, and Simon Bolivar, all of whom were born under this sign.

In money matters Leo folk are usually favoured by fortune, and they may rise to the position of financial magnates; if they do, it will not be through trickery, but as a result of their own energy and natural gifts. They will wish to share their wealth with others, and will subscribe freely to charities, but at the same time will surround themselves with all the luxury and refinement that money can command; in the lower types, this will be manifested as vulgar ostentation. Indeed, a love of display characterizes all Leo subjects, and they have a marked predilection for all that flashes and glitters, especially gold, brass and bright metal objects, strong sunshine and brilliant colours.

The less highly developed Leo subjects may be boastful, vulgar and ostentatious, arrogant and tyrannical and possessed of a mania for popularity. They are usually absurdly sensitive on points of dignity, and may also be wasteful and recklessly extravagant.

Relationships and love

Being extremely affectionate themselves, Leo folk are ruled by affection, and they make the finest marriage partners, parents and friends— kind, loyal, and considerate. They can generally be ruled through their feelings (though not in any other way whatever), and they may be deceived or even led into doing wrong by playing on their sentiments. In love and marriage they make many errors and suffer deeply from them; they are prone to mistake pity and sympathy for love, and may realize their error when too late, but their natural generosity and forbearance often save their married life from shipwreck.

To their partners Leonians will be affectionate, but their strong will and urge to lead can make them rather domineering. However, they can be very sensitive, and criticism can cut deeply. As parents, Leonians understand and encourage their children and will do anything to ensure they are not unhappy. However, they are not over-compliant and often associate with traditional values when it comes to behaviour and education.

If you have fallen for a Leo man and you want to attract his attention, then you just have to flatter him and turn yourself into a willing audience.

In return you will get a real gentleman, who will protect you like a gallant knight and perform great deeds for your sake.

But you must realise that he is incredibly vain, and if you start offending him he will back off.

Of all the Sun signs, Leos are the first to start falling in love and to have sweethearts. And it is not all smooth sailing, because they are either up in the clouds or down in the dumps. And their mood can change a hundred times in the course of one day.

If you are a man who has fallen in love with a Leo woman, you will have to face a lot of competition. Leos are popular so if you have an inferiority complex you will have your work cut out to capture a Leo. Because a Leo woman knows just what she wants and won't settle for the first man who happens to come along.

And if you are the kind who likes to have your sweetheart sitting admiringly at your feet listening to you expanding on all your great ideas, then you would be well advised to find a woman who was not born under the sign of Leo.

Leos love to be in the centre of things and the constant focus of attention. So it is not always easy to have a Leo as a friend, since you must expect to stand on the sidelines. Many Leo girls choose to be friends with girls who are less pretty or less charming than themselves. So then there is little danger of the friend stealing any limelight from the vain Leo.

On the other hand you will never be bored with a Leo around.

Leo

Sometimes one gets the impression that a Leo never really grows up.

But Leo people are also very caring especially towards the weaker members of society. They may complain about being lumbered with everything, but they don't really mean it. Actually they rather enjoy shouldering the whole burden themselves.

And they are also very generous. If you are short of cash you can more or less depend on your Leo friend coming up with a loan.

Those born under Leo have the closest ties of affection with people whose birthdays occur between March 21 and April 21 and between November 21 and December 21.

Good advice

Even though Leo people may find it difficult, it would be a good idea if they occasionally took themselves less seriously.

Leos also tend to go the whole hog with things that interest them. It would be sometimes better both for them and those around them if they learned to take things more easily now and again.

Fire and earth compatibility

There is nothing more annoying than someone saying 'Stop making such a fuss' when you have taken out all the stops to convince them of your brilliant idea, or who just reacts to your grand plans with a derisive remark.

And as Leo people are the most vulnerable and vain of all the fire signs, they sometimes find it difficult to get on with earth signs, Taurus, Virgo and Capricorn. For the earth signs will try to bring the Leos back down to earth again, however enthusiastic they may be.

Of all the earth signs, Leos get on best with Capricorns.

Fire and air compatibility

Whereas earth sign people can suffocate a fire sign like Leo, the air signs fan their flames so they burn more strongly.

On the other hand, the two together tend to lose touch with reality. So if a Leo starts making great plans with a Gemini or a Libra, these often end up like castles in the air. Of the air signs Leos get on best with Librans.

Fire and water compatibility

People born under these signs find it hard to understand one another, so a Leo will rarely count a Cancerian or a Scorpio amongst his or her best friends.

Leos are always in too much of a hurry to make allowances for the water sign people, who they consider to be 'wet'. In return, water sign people think that Leos are too self-satisfied, egoistic and bombastic.

Of all the water signs, Leos get on best with Pisceans.

Occupations

Whatever their occupation or position, Leo individuals will work hard, in part because they are happier when they have people working for them. For many, luxury or glamour will appeal, and if they can achieve this through their employment then so much the better. As such, they may turn to acting, sport or working in the jewellery trade. They will often go for highly paid jobs, which they equate with status, but, equally, they make good employers, expecting the best of their employees but generous in return. Leo produces rulers, soldiers, statesmen, church dignitaries, and governors, leaders and managers of every kind. Financiers, 'captains of industry', bankers, jewellers, and goldsmiths are also born under its rays. On the artistic side, the Leonine love of colour, action and display may produce talent for the stage, literature and painting. Famous Leo subjects so gifted being Mary Anderson, the actress, Shelley, Southey, Sir Walter Scott, De Quincey, George Bernard Shaw, Alexandre Dumas, Fenelon, John Dryden, Izaak Walton, and Jean Baptiste Corot, the painter. The Leo type is not happy when in a subordinate position, and cannot bear to be ruled or given orders; but he or she makes an able, though exacting, employer or manager. You will discover that many actors are born under the sign of Leo.

Health

The vitality of Leo folk is boundless; they have the ability to absorb the vivifying power of the sun to the fullest extent, and sunlight, coupled with fresh air, is their finest tonic and restorative, But they should be careful not to indulge overmuch in violent exercise, for there is danger of the heart being strained or weakened. The heart, spine, back and eyes are the parts of the body most liable to disease or injury. Heart trouble, palpitation, angina, spinal disease, lumbago, meningitis, and disorders of the eyes are among the commonest complaints of the Leo type; but they hate to give way to sickness, and will put up an heroic fight before being prostrated. It is fatal for Leo people to be idle, since they then become morose and gloomy; and when in good health they should be constantly occupied with some interesting employment.

To attract good vibrations

Those born in the Leo period should wear all shades of gold, yellow and orange, while light green and white are also suitable. Gold, and all bright, glittering objects, such as polished brass or copper ornaments, will be found lucky and should be kept about the house.

Wider aspects

The Leonian is better leading rather than following and excels where generalities rather than attention to detail are accepted.

Virgo

Dates

24 August to 22 September. The Sun enters the zodiacal sign Virgo on approximately August 24 every year and leaves it on September 21. However, the influence of this sign does not begin to be fully exerted until about a week after the Sun's entry, being diluted by the force of the preceding sign, Leo. Therefore, persons born between August 24 and 27 are also partly ruled by Leo, and should consult the characteristics given by that sign as well.

Origin and glyph

The Egyptian goddess of grain (Nidaba) was probably the origin, and in old pictures the Virgin is shown bearing an ear of corn and holding a child; the glyph is the female genitalia.

Ruling planet and groupings

Mercury; feminine, mutable and earth.

Typical traits

Virgoans are traditionally shy and modest, hard-working and practical and yet, perhaps, rather dull. They have a well-developed tendency to criticize both themselves and others, and often allow this to go too far. If a positive tenor is applied to Virgoan traits, it results in someone who works hard, is sensible and intelligent, and very good at detailed tasks.

Being essentially a worker, Virgoans are not interested in taking the lead but more in completing a task to the best of their ability. There is a likelihood that Virgoans will be worriers, and they often worry about nothing at all, which can be misconstrued or counterproductive. However, their own positive qualities are the best tools to deal with such problems.

Virgo people are nearly always worried about something. They want everything to be in order, and they spend lots of time planning to ensure perfect results every time. They are incredibly conscientious and have such a tight check on things that for instance, they seldom have money problems.

It is not easy to criticise a Virgo, because they get terribly hurt. They find things hard enough as it is, because they feel that they never really live up to their own high standards.

Virgo people cannot get on with people who have sudden crazy whims. Don't expect your Virgo partner to get up in the middle of the night to make a lasagne just because you are hungry and can't sleep. They think that there is a time and place for everything.

The negative and earthy sign Virgo is associated with intellectual power, and subjects of Virgo are distinguished by the keenness of their wits and their remarkable discrimination. They are, perhaps, the most calm, level-headed and practical of all the twelve types, for they seldom allow a vestige of sentiment or affection to interfere with, or bias, their judgment or conduct. Indeed, it is probable that sentiment is very shallow in Virgo people, for even the superior types are notable for their selfishness. At the same time, these characteristics have a useful function to fulfil, for they act as a wholesome check upon the more impulsive and expansive types; and, by their critical judgment and cool reasoning ability, natives of Virgo help to avert many errors and catastrophes that would not be foreseen by more rash and emotional people until too late.

Virgo people are pliant and adaptable. They can readily vary their manner and behaviour to suit the company in which they find themselves; while their tactfulness may often amount to servility. But this is not the result of fear; it is usually part of a deliberate plan or scheme, carefully prepared beforehand, and with a definite end in view.

Virgo people are not usually acquisitive, but, should one born under this sign set his or her heart upon anything, he or she will stop at nothing to attain it, and, if he or she is of a lower type, he or she may display the most extraordinary cunning, hypocrisy and cold-blooded guile. Not even human life stands in the way of a person of the undeveloped Virgo type when once his or her mind has become fixed upon a definite aim. This type is also capable of displaying greater cruelty than any other; he or she can commit the most shocking injustices and barbarities in cold blood, and nothing will move him or her to pity when he or she is actuated by hatred or self-interest. Of this type were the emperor Caligula, Richelieu, Queen Elizabeth of England, and

Abdul Hamid, ex-sultan of Turkey, the 'Great Assassin', all of whom
were natives of Virgo.

Subjects of Virgo have the love of inquiry developed to the utmost;
they are never satisfied to take anything on trust, but must always find
out for themselves. Accordingly, under this sign many famous philoso-
phers, mathematicians, and scientific investigators have been born, including Baron Cuvier, John Locke, Tommaso Campanella, Comte de
Buffon, Baron von Humboldt, and the Marquis de Condorcet.

Generally Virgo people are modest and reserved; they shrink from
publicity, and will not talk readily about their own affairs, preferring to
criticize the actions of others and analyse their motives. They are lacking in enthusiasm, and show reluctance to fall in with the plans of
others or to assist them in any way. They are entirely individual and
quite lacking in camaraderie and the 'team spirit.' When pursuing their
own objects, which they do in a steadfast, practical and matter-of-fact
manner, they will listen noncommittally to the advice of others, but
will seldom act upon it.

Their lack of sentiment makes them very slow to anger, but they are
equally slow to forgive, and seldom compose a quarrel of their own
accord. But they can swallow resentment and put their pride in their
pocket when they consider it to be in their own interests to do so.

Virgo subjects are precise and methodical in all that they do, and
have a great respect for law, order and precedent and for the achievements of the past. They are fond of harmony and elegance, and their
taste is restrained and austere; but their imagination is decidedly limited, and is far exceeded by their reasoning powers. They are very fond
of reading, and are able to remember very clearly a great deal of what
they read and see.

The weaker varieties of this type are cunning, capricious and cruel
in the extreme, cynical, unduly critical, caustic in their speech and per-
petually finding fault. They are also snobbish, servile and excessively
selfish.

Relationships and love

Virgo subjects are well suited to married life, being dutiful, faithful and
proud of their family, though usually they are quite undemonstrative.
The happiness of their union may depend upon their ability to control
their proclivity for criticism and fault-finding.

Virgo

Virgoans are very loyal in relationships and fond of their family, although this love may not manifest itself openly but rather in private. They may be self-effacing or even devalue themselves by feeling unworthy. A more common fault would be to over-criticize, but in the main they are caring, sound partners.

A great deal of time and attention will be paid to the home to keep it nice, but care should be exercised so that standards are not kept too high.

Virgos are very considerate people, and therefore make good friends, especially if you have problems and need some consoling. They are also very perceptive and so you would do well to consider any advice they give you. It is probably quite sensible.

However, it can sometimes be a bit tiresome having a Virgan friend because they are so critical. He or she will pick at your wildest plans until you have been convinced that they are no good and you might as well drop them.

A positive Virgan trait is their sense of humour—but you can save your dirty jokes for other people.

If you are a woman who has fallen in love with a Virgo, do not expect him to stand serenading you outside the house every night.

On the other hand you can be almost certain that he will never forget your birthday, or make you wait for him under the clock for half an hour, just because he had to watch the end of a football match on TV. If he says he is coming at a certain time, he'll be there.

Virgo people are very touchy, so if you manage to get invited to his house, and you are asked to stay for dinner, do remember all your best table manners. Virgos are sticklers for that sort of thing. And if his mother should also happen to be a Virgo, she will like you instantly and consider you to be the ideal partner for her son if you polish off your food so your plate looks as though the dog has licked it clean—just as long as you don't lick it yourself!

Men who are trying to impress a Virgo woman should not let themselves be led to mistake the Virgo sense of humour for an interest in farting and belching competitions! Any attempt in that direction will meet with instant rejection. And you will not fare much better if you try telling the latest dirty jokes.

A Virgo man is not likely to succumb to the allure of the topless girl on the beach. He is more likely to offer her his jumper, thinking that she may be freezing.

However, many Virgo people love to flirt. And they are good at it. But that does not mean that you are destined for a long-term partnership. In fact, there is evidence to prove that more Virgos remain single than any of the other sun signs.

But if you do manage to hook a Virgo, which can be very difficult because they are so critical, then you can count on a very faithful and stable partner for life.

Their best affinities for marriage and friendship occur with those born between April 21 and May 21 and between December 21 and January 21.

Good advice

Virgos can drive others round the bend with their obsession for cleaning and perfection in everything. They really ought to remember that there are more important things in life than whether every nook and cranny is clean. And they should also stop worrying so much. Some even get quite sick from worry.

Earth and water compatibility

People born under a water sign are very emotional and therefore often get on well with the more down-to-earth Virgo. For the earth to bear fruit, it needs to be watered, but too much water will drown the plants. The relationship will founder if one of the parties becomes too dominating. Of all the water signs, Virgos find it hardest to get on with Pisceans.

Earth and air compatibility

These two signs are not very compatible. The practical, careful and down-to-earth Virgos cannot take the fanciful ideas that Geminis, Librans or Aquarians come up with. Their need for a few common sense details will smartly topple all those vague notions.

In return, the air signs consider Virgos rather boring, and think that they take too pragmatic a view of life, never wanting to have any fun.

They may be able to work together on the odd occasion when the practical common sense of the Virgo combines well with the lively imagination of air sign people. But they do not make for good partners in love.

Of all the air signs, Virgo people get on best with Aquarians.

Earth and fire compatibility

The fire signs are bursting with energy and enterprise. On the other hand Virgo people never undertake anything that has not been closely considered and planned down to the last detail.

These two signs usually find it hard to get on well. Virgo people do not understand how others can love new and exciting projects, and enjoy living at high speed. They prefer a routine and like any new project to be preceded by a thorough and detailed planning process.

Occupations

The critical and analytical faculties with which natives of Virgo are endowed make them well fitted to enter the law or politics. Among well-known lawyers, politicians, and statesmen born under Virgo were Sir Edward Marshall-Hall, Lord Oxford and Asquith, Bonar Law, Sir Charles Dilke, Lord Burleigh, Sir Robert Walpole, Richelieu, Colbert, Lafayette, Louis Kossuth, President Taft and President Diaz.

Virgo also favours the occupations of literary pursuits, music, and dramatic critic, editor, doctor, policeman and detective. Mercury, the ruler of Virgo, governs clerical work; therefore the professions of secretary, accountant, schoolmaster, printer and stationer are also indicated. The accuracy and precision of Virgo produce good chemists, engineers, watch and instrument makers and mechanics. Others become doctors, computer experts or psychologists. Whatever the job, their own cars will always be in top shape. It is a matter of course for everything to be spick and span.

As already mentioned, Virgoans are not particularly ambitious and therefore are happier when supervised at work. If attention to detail is required then they are very capable and proficient in problem-solving or working in science or medicine. Although they like to be appreciated, they are happier working as a member of a team. They have an incisive style, useful in the media and the teaching profession.

Health

Virgo rules the abdomen and intestines, and its subjects suffer most commonly from dysentery, colic, diarrhoea, constipation, in digestion and debility. As a general rule, their health is good, though they are prone to worry causelessly over themselves, and to resort to all kinds of patent medicines and quack remedies. A morbid craving for drink or drugs may be experienced, and should be eradicated forthwith.

To attract good vibrations

In order to draw to themselves the right kind of magnetism, those born under Virgo should wear and be surrounded with pale blue, pale gold and yellow. Jade green will also be harmonious, for it is the colour of Mercury.

Wider aspects

There is a desire for purity, perfection and happiness, which, provided that their self-esteem is strong enough, is attainable through application of their own qualities.

Libra

Dates

23 September to 23 October. The Sun enters Libra on September 23, and leaves this sign on approximately October 23. Since the full power of Libra is not exerted until about September 27, when the decreasing influence of Virgo finally ceases, persons born between September 23 and 27 are also partly ruled by Virgo, and they should consult the attributes given by that sign as well.

Origin and glyph

The element of the scales may have several origins, possibly from their use in weighing harvests; the glyph is similar to a yoke.

Ruling planet and groupings

Venus; masculine, cardinal and air.

Typical traits

Librans are true to their origin—they are always trying to achieve a balance, whether between views, negotiating parties, or in their own environment. In many instances, because they prefer not to take one side or the other, they sit in the middle, and this indecision can be their greatest fault. Turned to positive effect, by combining their desire to balance with their undoubted charm, Librans make fine 'diplomats' and can often settle an argument to everyone's satisfaction. They are also easy-going and like quiet surroundings at home or work, but although they may appear vulnerable, they are in fact quite tough and ensure that they follow their own plans.

Libra is an airy sign, and is ruled by the beautiful planet Venus. Its symbol is the scales, typifying balance, justice and harmony, which form the keynote of those born under this sign. Such persons have a natural ability to weigh, compare and estimate facts, and to arrive at an unbiased decision, while it is a remarkable fact that they are able to judge the weight of material objects and can match shades of colour more accurately than people of any other type. Though full of sentiment, they seldom allow their own feelings to interfere with what they consider to be just; and they are broad-minded, tolerant and lenient to the faults of others, realizing that errors and failings are natural to the human race. But they detest injustice, cruelty and unfair treatment, and are always ready to take up arms on behalf of anybody who has been wronged.

In most of the activities of life they are inclined to take a middle course and to avoid extremes of any kind. Under the influence of Venus, the planet of concord and harmony, they constantly crave peace and happy surroundings, and their horror of all strife, worry and unpleasantness makes them invariably pliant, accommodating and complaisant; this trait may easily degenerate into a fault, and it would do the majority of Libra subjects no harm to cultivate some of the tougher moral fibre that distinguishes, for example, natives of Aries and Virgo.

Subjects of Libra are gentle, courteous and affectionate in their manner and speech, and are not easily roused to anger, except by the contemplation of injustice. They cannot maintain a quarrel for long, and seldom feel resentment afterwards. In religious matters they are very tolerant, setting the spirit and relative moral value of any doctrine far above the observance of rites and formulas. They dislike monotony and are fond of change, travelling and seeing interesting and beautiful sights, but if chained by circumstances to one place or occupation, their unfailing good humour enables them to make the best of the situation.

If you suggest to a Libran that it must be much better to live in a town than in the countryside, he or she will immediately start singing the praises of fresh air and healthy country life and how marvellous it is to live somewhere where everyone knows everyone else. And then they'll point out the endless problems of living in a big city with all that traffic, noise and pollution!

You might then propose that it would be wonderful to live in the country, and he or she will then give you a long lecture on how boring it is to live out in the country, where everyone gossips about each other. No, the big city is where the action is, with discos, cinemas and concerts: no time to be bored there!

It is one of the Libran's most typical traits that he or she will always see both sides of a case. This is what makes Librans such good mediators in any quarrel, for even though they love a good discussion they cannot bear disagreements.

Libra

Another Libran trait is the ability to go on talking incessantly, or until someone begs them to shut up. But to be fair, they are also good listeners.

Do you think that sounds pretty confusing? Well it is. Librans can be very confusing people. For they are always trying to balance things, to weight the scales evenly. So they can change from being sweet, charming and calm to restless, irritating and stubborn.

Librans often have a weight problem. They love sweet things and find it hard to resist temptation when there are chocolate, sweets or cakes around.

It can sometimes be difficult for people to work out how Librans really feel about things, which is not surprising when they often don't know themselves. Perhaps it's because they try so hard to please others, and are therefore willing to sacrifice their own needs and suppress their own feelings to make others happy

Libra subjects are natural homemakers, and can settle down anywhere, provided their surroundings are congenial; they then hasten to collect around them as many beautiful ornaments, furnishings and other pleasing things as lie within their means.

Intellectually, they are highly developed, and not infrequently of a scholarly turn of mind, with a decided love of the past, which their rich imagination endows with colour and life. However, their tendency to avoid unpleasantness of all kinds may impel them to seek the easiest road through life, with the result that they often turn out indolent and too easy-going, and so neglect and fail to make the best of their fine talents.

Librans are often accused of being lazy, but this is not really justified. If they are interested enough, they will happily work until late at night. But afterwards they sink into a kind of stupor, and wild horses won't get them moving again, especially not to help around the house. They will slouch in front of the TV, or perhaps read a magazine. But then all of a sudden they come to life again and become just as energetic as before.

The strong imagination of Libra folk makes them intuitive, inventive and ingenious, and when their well-balanced reasoning power is added a strong scientific or philosophic genius may be produced. Of this type were Michael Faraday and G. B. Beccaria, the pioneers of electricity; George Westinghouse and Robert Stephenson, the engineers; Noah

Webster, the lexicographer; Hugh Miller, the geologist, and Sir Christopher Wren, the famous architect.

Relationships and love

Libra subjects make loyal, cheerful and affectionate friends, who are always ready to put their own interests last. They are, as a rule, probably more happy and contented in marriage than any other type, for their deep fund of affection triumphs over difficulties and conflicts of temperament that would wreck the majority of marriages.

Good friends are often born under the same sign, or at any rate belong to the same element. Libra is an air sign, so this means that Librans get on well with the other air signs, Aquarius and Gemini.

Librans always want to do others a good turn, but they also care about other people's opinions of them. So they risk acquiring friends who really only want to exploit their kindness. Librans find it hard to distinguish between true and false friends, so they sometimes experience terrible disappointments in their relationships.

They tend to look for friends among the smartest and most popular people, because they are so unsure of their own feelings. These are usually only superficial friendships but if Librans manage to find true friends, they can be relied on to be faithful, considerate and keen to preserve their friendships.

In relationships with a partner, Librans can be complete romantics and regard this relationship as very important, so much so that even the Libran indecisiveness can be overcome for a time. They tend to fit well into the domestic scene, being quite capable of organizing the household with their usual equable approach to all things, including money.

If you are a girl who has fallen for a Libran, do not expect him to rush up and invite you to go to the cinema. No, you might as well jump in at the deep end and ask him out instead. And you need not fear that he'll feel that you have offended him by taking the initiative. On the contrary, he will just be grateful that he has been spared the job of making a decision.

Librans of both sexes are very romantic. And they set great store by everything being perfect. So the first time you invite your friend home to tea, do not offer him milk from a carton or bottle, but try to borrow a tea-set with a proper jug and sugar bowl.

Libra

Librans do not like being alone and love to have someone to look after and care for. But they often find it difficult to understand their own feelings and may therefore mistake friendship for love.

They are prone to jealousy and want you all to themselves. Watch out, otherwise you may lose all your other friends. It can be hard work having a Libran sweetheart, because they are so romantic and expect you to live up to their ideals.

When Librans fall in love seriously, they will do anything for their beloved. They make so many sacrifices that it can end up having a stifling effect on their partner. So it is important to stress that the Libran must learn to satisfy their own needs as well.

Librans make kind parents, although they must ensure that they are strong-willed and insist upon children doing as they are told. The Libran indecision might irritate some children, and every effort should be made to answer a child's queries.

The most congenial types to mate with Libra people are those born between January 21 and February 21 and between May 21 and June 21.

Good advice

As already mentioned, Librans are willing to suppress their own needs in order to satisfy those of other people. But sometimes it is all just too much for them and they become absolutely furious, perhaps with the wrong people. If you are a Libran, you should learn to say no when necessary. You will be a lot happier yourself, and in the long term you will get on better with others, because they will respect you more.

Air and earth compatibility

People born under an air sign or an earth sign often find it hard to get on. The first category dream up airy plans and ideas, and cannot understand why the more down-to-earth Virgos or Capricorns do not immediately fall for their crazy ideas.

They will, however, be able to cooperate on individual projects where, for example, the thoroughness and methodical nature of the Taurean will harmonise well with the imagination of the Libran. But as soon as one of them tries to take on the dominating role, they are asking for trouble and the friendship may collapse.

Of all the earth signs, Librans get on best with Taurus.

Air and fire compatibility

Air nourishes fire and fans its flames even higher. And the warmth of the fire makes the air rise.

So it would seem that these two signs are compatible and can offer mutual support. On the other hand these two signs often lose touch with reality when they discuss their ambitious plans.

Of the fire signs, Librans get on best with Leos and Sagittarians.

Air and water compatibility

You cannot breathe under water, so a water sign can have a suffocating effect on a Libran. On the other hand a Scorpion or a Cancerian may be able to teach the Libran to understand and handle his feelings better.

Of all the water signs, Librans get on best with Pisceans.

Occupations

As mentioned, the tact and evenhandedness of Librans make them ideal as diplomats, in public relations, or any profession requiring these qualities. Their appreciation of art and beauty lends itself to a career in the arts or literature, and fashion, beauty and related professions are all possibilities for them. Although they like to work with other people, especially those of a like mind, they are sufficiently ambitious to reach for the top, although any isolation that this might produce would be unwelcome.

Being apt at learning, adaptable, level-headed and capable of calm decision, Libra subjects can make a success of almost any career. Preferably, however, they should follow some line in which their strong artistic tastes and good sense of proportion have full scope. Thus they make excellent artists, musicians, writers, poets, sculptors, landscape gardeners, florists, and dress designers. Others will seek to develop the Libran interest in people and become health workers or psychologists. As a general rule, they work better when in employment or partnership than when alone. They often find a talent for the law, and their strong judicial powers may carry them to great heights The gift of cool and rapid decision imparted by Libra has also produced many great naval and military commanders, including Augustus Caesar, Pompey, Lord Clive, Lord Nelson, Lord Collingwood, Frederick III of Germany, Lord Roberts, and Marshal Foch.

Health

Libra rules the kidneys, lumbar regions and skin, and its subjects are liable to suffer from disorders affecting these parts, such Bright's disease, nephritis, diabetes, eczema and skin eruptions. Their nerves, also, are liable to be overstrained, and they should avoid worry and depression of spirits.

To attract good vibrations

Blue and violet are the colours that accord best with Libra, and they should be used freely in order to attract harmonious astral vibrations.

Scorpio

Dates

24 October to 22 November. The Sun enters Scorpio on or about October 24 each year, and leaves it approximately on November 22. Persons born between October 24 and 27 are, however, also ruled to some extent by the preceding sign, Libra, whose influence does not die away entirely until the latter date.

Origin and glyph

The origin of the scorpion is unknown, although it appears in numerous guises in ancient history. The glyph symbolizes a serpent's coil and is linked with the male genitalia.

Ruling planet and groupings

Pluto; feminine, fixed and water.

Typical traits

Scorpians can show rather a mix of behaviour and character, on the one hand being very determined and strong-willed, and on the other being obsessive, awkward and arrogant. Once committed to something, whether a person or an ideal, they will be very faithful, although they are susceptible to being melodramatic, and when emotions become involved logic suffers. They are usually energetic, wanting the most out of life, whether at work or play, and will not relinquish their goal easily. Although they are perfectly capable of sacrificing others, they do hold on to what is right and will exhibit a strong sense of fair play and reason.

Scorpio, whose symbol is the stinging scorpion, is a negative and watery sign, but is ruled by the fiery planet Mars. Its subjects are a mass of extremes and contradictions, and even at the best are always difficult to size up or classify. Powerfully magnetic, brimful of energy, intense in their emotions, and subtle and involved in their actions and manner of thought, they have perhaps the strongest personalities of all the zodiacal types. The willpower which their can exert over other people is enormous. Not only by their gift of rhetoric—in which they excel—but by means of something far deeper, some strange psychological power, they can mould and twist other people to their will, either individually or in the mass.

Most people do not like losing at games, but if you meet someone who considers any defeat to be a total catastrophe, that person will probably turn out to be a Scorpio. Scorpions hate to lose.

Scorpions also hate false modesty, so if you ask one whether they are good at something or other and they think they are, they will say so straight out. And if you want their opinion about your latest hairstyle or boyfriend, you will get an equally honest answer. Scorpions will not resort to flattery just to obtain something. That is beneath their dignity.

Some people are too embarrassed to admit that they are Scorpions, because the Scorpion is a creature who attacks his victim and kills it with the poison sitting in its tail. If it finds itself cornered it will even turn its poison onto itself.

But there really is no reason to be ashamed about being a Scorpion. A Scorpion who has had a loving home will develop into a friendly, caring person.

Scorpions are incredibly inquisitive. For instance they want to know what other people are thinking, and they will go on asking until they get an answer. And there is no point in trying to fool a Scorpion, because they will see through any deception straight away.

Scorpio people are nearly always inclined to be haughty, vain, and self-satisfied, and often nourish for their associates a contempt which they do not hesitate to display in harsh and biting words. They often seem to be possessed with a demon of perversity, and they love to impress and 'shock' people by some dramatic and unexpected action, usually of an unpleasant nature.

They have amazing powers of tenacity and resistance, and are seldom discouraged when their plans go awry and success seems far away. They will meet the most crushing blows without cringing or changing expression; in fact, they always know when and how to conceal their emotions, although there are few people who live on their emotions so much as those born under Scorpio.

Idealists and humanitarians at heart, the more developed types among these subjects are ever eager to defend and champion the weak and oppressed; but they often speak slightingly of those whom they uphold and protect, and affect a contempt of charity and kind actions! Naturally gifted with dramatic ability, many of them act throughout their daily life and, in a spirit of perversity, seem anxious to give the world an entirely wrong impression of their character and temperament. They have little use for convention, and often fly deliberately in the face of established custom and propriety, a course which seems to afford them keen pleasure.

Scorpions have good memories, and will remember your kindnesses as well as your cruelties. Your generosity will be richly rewarded, but you can expect dreadful revenge to be taken if you have been nasty. Just try to make fun of a Scorpion in public and you will find that you will receive a dose of your own medicine—with interest.

They are hard workers and never spare themselves, and if they are gifted with ambition—as is usually the case nothing can stand in the way of its realization. They lay their plans with calm deliberation, meet and overcome obstacles with the greatest coolness and ingenuity, and often look upon other people as pawns to be sacrificed to their own success.

Natives of Scorpio often have pronounced psychic gifts, and feel drawn towards a study of the occult. Many of them can sublimate their intense vital force into religion or mysticism, and this process produces personalities which are outstanding and unique. As examples we may cite Saint Augustine, William Cowper and Samuel Taylor Coleridge, the poets, and Alexander I, tsar of Russia, each of whom had a pronounced strain of mysticism in his or her nature.

A notable person born under Scorpio is usually remarkable in many other ways than that in which his or her particular talent or genius has distinguished him or her; he or she is the sort of man who is fated to make his or her mark in the world, no matter how he or she chooses to do so. This strength of character is observable in Theodore Roosevelt, Captain Cook, Danton, Gambetta, Franz Liszt, Benvenuto Cellini, Martin Luther, Edward VII and William Hogarth, all of whom were born under the rays of Scorpio.

Relationships and love

Those born under Scorpio have an intense love nature, which, if they value their happiness, they must not allow to get beyond control. They should guard against sudden and impulsive attachments that have no basis of real affection. Scorpio subjects are critical and not easy to please, and are liable to become violently jealous with little or no cause, but they may be successfully handled by a tactful partner who knows, and allows for, all the vagaries of their strong personality.

The Scorpian's desire to stay with a relationship holds good for partnerships, although their energy may need to be channelled if it is not to prove disruptive. They prefer people who are equally strong-willed but, despite outward appearances, may themselves be weaker than they look. They are certainly prone to depression, from which they find it hard to emerge, and this may contribute to the apparent extremes in marriage—some are very good, others less so.

If you are a man who has attracted a Scorpio woman, you must be someone really special. Because she will not settle for any old Tom, Dick or Harry. And if you break up, your next girlfriend will have quite a lot to live up to because Scorpions are never boring companions. They are very emotional and when they fall in love they do so with such ardour that it can quite take one's breath away.

But there is also a reverse side to their emotions. Scorpions get jealous very quickly, and their anger will erupt like a volcano if they have even the slightest suspicion that you have been flirting with somebody else. And even if you are quite innocent, the suspicion can be so powerful that it will break up your relationship.

Scorpions love to be in control of their lives. They want to run everything themselves, even their love lives. You must expect that your Scorpion sweetheart will want to satisfy his or her own needs first before considering yours. But once committed, he or she will be extra sweet and loving.

Good friends are often born under the same Sun sign, or at any rate belong to the same element. Scorpio is a water sign, so this means that Scorpions get on well with other water signs, Pisces and Cancer.

Scorpions often do not have a lot of friends, because they are very fussy and can easily see through people. On the other hand, once you have been accepted by a Scorpion, he or she will become a very faithful friend.

If you are friends with a Scorpion, do not expect to keep many secrets. For instance, if you have fallen for the new person in your class, it will not be long before your Scorpio friend has sussed it out. He or she is not only good at guessing other people's feelings, but is also extremely inquisitive.

But do not try to stick your nose too deeply into the Scorpion's private life. Scorpions do not like that at all. For as much as they like to guess your secrets, they want to guard their own.

As parents they will do their utmost for their offspring, but they can push a little too much and should consciously develop a balanced approach to parenthood, allowing their children some freedom.

Their closest affinities are formed with people born between February 21 and March 21 and between June 21 and July 21.

Good advice

Scorpio people would do both themselves and others a favour if they learned to control their tempers. That goes for when they are playing games and think they are about to lose, as well as when they think they have been unfairly treated by others.

Water and air compatibility

The air signs, Gemini, Libra and Aquarius, can learn a lot from the water signs, and vice versa. For example, Scorpions find it hard to grasp that other people are different to them and don't think the way they do. Air sign people are much more understanding. But water sign people can teach air sign people to recognise their own emotions.

Water and air get on well with each other, but just as water can have a suffocating effect on air, for you cannot breathe under water, a Scorpion can be so dominating that an air sign person feels stifled.

On the other hand, the air can whip up great storms and high seas. And this can happen if an Aquarian or a Libran is not sufficiently aware of Scorpion sensitivity, which may provoke a Scorpion tempest.

Of all the air signs, Scorpions get on best with Geminis.

Water and earth compatibility

Water is necessary for all growth on earth.

This means that people born under an earth sign usually get on well with Scorpions. Earth sign people are down-to-earth and sensible, and Scorpions are more emotional. So if they do not pressurise each other too much but respect each other's idosyncrasies, they can derive much pleasure from each other.

But just as a plant will wilt and die if it is not watered, a friendship will also flounder if the Scorpion gives free rein to his emotions without showing consideration for his more down-to-earth Taurean friends.

Of all the earth signs, Scorpions usually get on best with Capricorns or Virgos.

Water and fire compatibility

These two signs are not normally well suited. Water puts out fire. Scorpions just cannot cope with an Arian or a Leo who comes charging in with some half-baked project to be carried out right away.

In return, fire sign people are irritated by the thoroughness and systematic nature of the Scorpions.

Occupations

Both Scorpio and its ruler, Mars, favour success in the army and navy. Other congenial careers include those of government official, overseer, magistrate, butcher, iron-founder, brazier, brewer, chemist, photographer, and dentist, while the most skilful of surgeons are produced by this sign. A love of secrecy and intrigue is inherent in the Scorpio nature, and this may produce excellent detectives, spies and secret service agents, as well as prominent Freemasons and members of secret societies.

They do not always aspire to the top jobs at work. But they do like to be in control and so they prefer to pull the strings and direct things the way they want.

Scorpions are also attracted by danger in their choice of jobs. Many of them attempt to realise their childhood dreams and end up as soldiers, policemen or firemen.

But their great interest in other people's emotional lives also leads them to jobs as psychologists, lawyers or social workers.

When running a business, a Scorpian will work to his or her very limit to help ensure success and, to a certain extent, they welcome challenges and problems. They can employ charm when necessary but can also be hard and demanding at times. They also like financial security and are willing to work for it. Scorpians are well suited to being in the medical profession or in a profession where analysis and research are required.

To attract good vibrations

The deeper shades of red harmonize best with Scorpio, and russet-brown is also beneficial. These colours should be incorporated in the clothes of Scorpio subjects, and in their household decorations, in order to attract the maximum of good fortune.

Wider aspects:

The character of a Scorpian is built up of a fine balance of attributes, which, in a positive sense, can yield a tremendous achiever but conversely may produce someone riven with jealousy.

Sagittarius

Dates
23 November to 21 December. The Sun enters the zodiacal sign Sagittarius about November 23, to leave it a month later, about December 21. However, the full power of Sagittarius does not begin to take effect until about November 27, for until that date the influence of Scorpio is also active, though declining. Hence, persons born between November 23 and 27 are partly ruled by Scorpio, and should consult the properties of that sign as well as those of Sagittarius.

Origin and glyph
The origin is unknown, but the glyph, represents the arrow of the Centaur.

Ruling planet and groupings
Jupiter, masculine, mutable and fire.

Typical traits
Sagittarians are essentially gregarious, friendly and enthusiastic, with a desire to achieve all goals that are set. They are rarely beset by depression, but their inborn enthusiasm can sometimes take them too far, and they may take risks. Although they are versatile and intelligent, their desire to jump from the task in hand to the next may result in some tasks being unfinished. In excess, their good qualities can become a nuisance, leading to tactless, hurtful comments (without the intent to hurt) and jokes that go too far.

Sagittarius is the third of the fiery signs, and is symbolized by an archer, or a centaur, drawing his or her bow. In magnetism it is positive, and it is under the rule of the benign and expansive planet Jupiter. Natives of this sign are distinguished by frankness, sincerity and optimism; they have a strongly developed sense of justice, and are tolerant, philanthropic and humane. They display great sympathy with human nature, and are generous and charitable to a degree. They like being made a repository of other people's troubles, and are very fond of giving advice, but are apt to become sententious and patronizing, which often lessens the appreciation of their kindness. They are intensely hard workers, though in the pursuit of their aims they are apt to run along a somewhat narrow track, so that much escapes their notice that might be helpful to them.

They are very sociable, and are popular in friendly and convivial gatherings, though they are apt to affront their individual friends by their extreme outspokenness. They are essentially honest and hate deception and trickery in any form, and usually they lead very respectable lives and bow unfailingly to convention. Always ready, and even anxious, to shoulder responsibilities, they are solicitous in their regard for the welfare of those under their tutelage or in their employ.

Being gifted with considerable strength of will, they show great independence and insist on conducting their affairs and living their lives in their own way. They are both versatile and impulsive, and therefore frequently make sudden decisions or change their occupations or interests in a totally unexpected way.

Many people born under Sagittarius are deeply religious, and their faith in moral and spiritual matters seldom falters. Others are fond of philosophizing, and in this direction often display great depth of thought. Examples of the highest type of keen and philosophic intellect given by Sagittarius can be seen in John Milton, Thomas Carlyle, Jonathan Swift and Heinrich Heine.

Sagittarians are strangely prone to theorize and make shrewd guesses as to the outcome of events. Indeed, their intuition and foresight are often considerable, and reliance upon them is amply justified by the success achieved by the higher types of Sagittarians when guided by their own impulses. Many Sagittarius folk display the curious characteristic of completely altering their occupation or habits of life, quite irrespective of advancing age, change of abode and other circumstances, and often without any obvious motive at all; and they are quite as sincere and successful in this new existence as they were in the former. A few notable Sagittarians in whom this peculiarity may be observed are General Monk, who achieved fame first as an able general and then crowned it by restoring the supremacy of England on the sea; Prince Rupert, the dashing cavalry commander, who later became an admiral and eventually retired to the seclusion of the chemical laboratory; and Thomas Becket and Lope de Vega, the Spanish dramatist, both men of pleasure who became rigid ascetics.

Sagittarians are very often of athletic build, with long and well-developed legs, and they are extremely fond of sport; they are at their happiest in the open air and in the company of dogs and horses.

Sagittarians are restless. They hate sitting or standing still. They love fast cars, dangerous jobs and violent sports.

There is an old saying that truth comes from the mouths of babes. It also could be said about Sagittarians. Not because they want to be outspoken, but rather because they are slightly naive and just cannot imagine that others could be offended or hurt by their remarks. They are often rather tactless but in fact think themselves to be very diplomatic.

Sagittarians are prone to very erratic moods. One moment they are floating on cloud nine and feel they are totally in control. And then, if they are given a lot of boring tasks to do, they will suddenly become fed up. If they are able to pass their work on to others, they will do so quite readily.

Sagittarians often have money problems. They behave as though money grows on trees, and they get very annoyed when they discover that it doesn't.

The undeveloped types of Sagittarians are inclined to be pretentious, vain and patronizing. They love to make a parade of any generous actions which they may be called upon to perform, and are full of religious cant and smug self-satisfaction. They do not hesitate to commit the meanest of actions, and are quite unscrupulous in the pursuit of their ambitions; but they endeavour to conceal the unpleasant side of their nature with a cloak of hypocrisy and bluff, for the good opinion of the world is very precious to them.

Relationships and love

Sagittarians have a great capacity for friendship, and are popular among their associates, but they are apt to lose friends through want of tact. They make good husbands, wives and parents, who never shirk the responsibilities of family life, but they often marry unhappily, probably being carried away by a passing impulse. However, their proud and independent spirit can be depended upon to hide their unhappiness from the eyes of the world, and they will endeavour to make the best of things in order to preserve appearances. They are fond of home life, and take a great pride in the comfort and adornment of their home.

Freedom is important to Sagittarians, so much so that it may inhibit long-term relationships. After settling down, however, they are good in the family context, and their enthusiasm can help lift boredom or depression. Sagittarians will enjoy a friendship or partnership more if they are given a loose rein to enable them to do what they want. Often their ultimate goal is not materialistic but more spiritual.

Sagittarians have a strong sense of independence, so it is not easy to trap one. This is not because the male Sagittarian does not like women, on the contrary, but that doesn't mean having to be tied hand and foot to one.

If you are a woman who has fallen for a Sagittarian, and he suggests you go on a camping tour together, don't for one minute believe that he is a boy scout. He may have very different plans in mind, so you had better 'be prepared'!

Sagittarians find it hard to talk about or to display their feelings, so if you fall in love with one, do not expect to spend your evenings together holding hands and discussing your beautiful future. But you definitely will not be bored.

Good friends are often born under the same Sun sign, or at any rate belong to the same element. Sagittarius is a fire sign, so this means that Sagittarians get on well with the other fire signs, Aries and Leo.

Sagittarians usually have lots of friends, because they are so honest about their feelings and opinions. And even though some people may be taken aback by the Sagittarian's outspoken remarks, they soon realise that these are never ill-meant.

Sagittarians are not easily offended, perhaps because they are both optimistic and somewhat naive. If friends try to play a trick on a Sagittarian, say by sending a box full of polystyrene chips, the Sagittarian will not be upset, but simply believe that they forgot to include the present.

Sagittarians make exciting friends, because there is usually something happening when they are around. They are always hatching some plot, and even though this may seem quite daft, Lady Luck seems to be on their side, and they succeed where others would fail. This could be because they have total faith in their own ideas.

Sagittarians love to talk and discuss things with their friends, but if the conversation gets too close to the subject of emotions, especially their own, they immediately try to change the subject.

As parents, their approach to life means that they encourage their children to be outgoing, and this is fine providing a child is not nervous or shy.

Sagittarius folk mate most harmoniously with those born between March 21 and April 21, and between July 21 and August 21.

Good advice

Because of their tendency to leave the more boring, everyday tasks to others, Sagittarians are often accused of being lazy and self-centred. So they would be well advised to realise that you have to learn to take the rough with the smooth.

With their lack of economic sense, adult Sagittarians would do well either to leave money matters to their partners or to make a conscious effort to change their attitude.

Fire and earth compatibility

There is nothing as annoying as someone saying "Stop making such a fuss", when you have pulled out all the stops to convince them of your brilliant idea. Or who just reacts to your grand plans with some derisive remark.

People born under a fire sign often lack respect and understanding for the world in which they find themselves. "It'll work out" they say, and run the sort of risks that a Virgo or a Capricorn wouldn't dream of. But these two signs can learn a lot from each other. The Sagittarian could do with a bit of common sense and thoroughness, whilst people born under an earth sign could benefit from following their hearts sometimes, not just their minds.

Of all the earth signs, Sagittarians get on best with Taurus.

Fire and air compatibility

While an earth sign can have a suffocating effect on a fire sign like Sagittarius, the air signs fan their flames so they burn even brighter. And the strong sense of independence which they share creates a mutual attraction, though usually more as friends than as partners.

However, they may lose touch with reality, and the grand plans which a Sagittarian and Aquarian cook up together could end up as nothing more than hot air.

Of the air signs, Sagittarians get on best with Aquarians and Librans.

Fire and water compatibility

People born under these two signs find it hard to understand each other, and thus a Sagittarian will rarely count a Scorpio or a Piscean amongst his or her best friends.

Sagittarians are in too much of a hurry to make allowances for the water sign people, whom they consider to be too 'wet', and too timid to take a risk now and again. On the other hand the water sign people think that the Sagittarian's plans are too risky for their taste.

Of all the water signs, Sagittarians get on best with Cancerians.

Occupations

Sagittarians are naturally fitted for positions of authority in which their advice, aid and judgment can be sought by others. Thus they excel in medicine, the law and the Church, and as employers of labour, naval and military officers, technical experts of all kinds, politicians, missionaries, relieving officers, inspectors, nurses, matrons, modistes and officials of charitable organizations. Many veterinary surgeons and dealers in dogs and horses are found under this sign.

They often have a deep love of music and make excellent musicians. In this connection it is interesting to note that the great Beethoven was born under Sagittarius, as also were Weber, Rubinstein, Edward McDowell and Sir Hamilton Harty.

Sagittarians usually have lots of interests, but they are all designed to satisfy their drive for excitement and exploration. Adventures such as mountain-climbing or parachuting are ways of testing their own limits.

Sagittarians may look for a career to satisfy their insatiable curiosity. But as they are also individualistic, they prefer to work on their own. Law and education are areas which many Sagittarians like. But deep down they may dream of becoming astronauts.

Sagittarians are not interested primarily in material gain and because they are particularly interested in education and travel, that is where money may be spent. Work of a varied nature is preferred, but care should be taken to make sure details are not omitted in the race to move on to something new. There is a natural desire to help others, which may manifest itself in a career in teaching, counselling, lecturing, the Church, law, and publishing.

Health

The hips, thighs, nerves and arteries are under the rule of Sagittarius, and its subjects may suffer from rheumatism in the lower limbs, as well as from sciatica, gout and nervous disorders. The lungs and throat may be delicate, and the native may be prone to bronchitis and lung troubles. The commonest accidents suffered by Sagittarians are those affecting the lower limbs, such as sprains, dislocation of the hip and fracture of the thigh.

To attract good vibrations

Orange is the colour most in tune with the vibrations of Sagittarius, while mauve and purple harmonize best with Jupiter, its ruler. Good fortune should ensue if these colours are freely used.

Wider aspects

When both mind and body have a certain degree of freedom, Sagittarians are at their best and will then employ their versatility and intellectual strengths to the full.

Capricorn

Dates

22 December to 20 January. The Sun passes into Capricorn on approximately December 22 and leaves it about January 20. People born on the cusp of the sign—between December 22 and 27—are, however, also influenced to some extent by the gradually declining power of the preceding sign, Sagittarius, and they should consult the qualities given by this sign as well as those with which Capricorn endows them.

Origin and glyph

It may have originated with a mythical sea-goat from ancient Babylon. The glyph, is said to represent a goat's head and a fish's tail.

Ruling planet and groupings

Saturn, feminine, cardinal and earth.

Typical traits

It is said that there are two types of Capricornian, one of which has greater and higher hopes of life. In general, they are patient, practical and can be very shy, preferring to stay in the background—but, they are strong-willed and can stand up for themselves. Capricornians have a reputation for being mean, ambitious and rather hard people. A mean streak may often be directed at the self, and ambition, if tempered with realism and humour, can be positive. Usually the character is enhanced by other elements of the chart to produce a warmer personality.

Capricorn is an earthy sign, and is ruled by the secretive and restraining planet Saturn. The symbol of Capricorn is the goat, an animal which delights in climbing the highest mountains and the most precipitous rocks. Even so do the patient, persistent and dogged subjects of Capricorn seek the steepest and most arduous paths through life to reach the summit of their worldly ambition or spiritual salvation. Hard work, fatigue, and self-denial are counted as nothing, and all their energies are bent towards one object. Practical, shrewd, and calculating, and of a grave, self-contained disposition, they scorn all forms of extravagance and display and all unnecessary expenditure of energy. They are reserved, secretive and taciturn, and very averse to taking anybody into their confidence or imparting their thoughts and opinions to those around them.

Capricornians scorn effusiveness and are unmoved by flattery, and they seldom express wonderment or surprise; but they are amid of knowledge in all its branches, are keenly interested in science and philosophy, and are impelled towards the study of all that is ancient, such as archaeology, history and folklore. They are painstaking and methodical in all they do, and although their researches may be animated by enthusiasm, this is of a quiet and prosaic order and is seldom revealed. Johann Kepler and Sir Isaac Newton, both subjects of Capricorn, are excellent examples of this patient, undemonstrative, but indefatigable spirit of inquiry.

Natives of Capricorn are quick to take the lead in their particular sphere of activity, and their right to do so is usually accepted without question, for their implicit faith in their own powers is rapidly communicated to those about them. If baulked of a position of authority and obliged to work under the domination of others, they become gloomy, morose and mordantly critical.

Though most of them are strongly material, many Capricornians are also idealists at heart, and their love of moral and intellectual freedom often impels them to back up an apparently worthy but hopeless or unpopular cause, even though it is plain that their own interests may suffer thereby. This type of idealism, in a greater or less degree, may be observed in Joan of Arc, Edmund Burke, Alexander Hamilton, Marshal Ney, W. E. Gladstone, President Woodrow Wilson and David Lloyd George, all of whom, at some period of their life fought for their convictions in a difficult or apparently losing battle.

The image of the mountain goat or Capricorn climbing up to the highest peaks also fits the human Capricorn, who sets his or her sights high and is prepared to undertake the long climb upwards to reach his or her goal.

In other words, Capricorns are the ambitious types. They are persevering and patient, and don't mind waiting to fulfil their goal.

Capricorns admire competent and successful people. So they are sometimes regarded as snobs. In turn they often feel that other people are slightly superficial and stupid, but they will not express this opinion in public. There is no point in creating enemies!

Capricorns tend to be pessimists and never embark on any risky or dangerous venture, believing it is bound to fail. They frown on those who take risks and who refuse to plan their lives down to the last detail. But they also tend to become envious when they see how lucky other people can be.

Natives of Capricorn are not easily roused to anger, but, on the other hand, they are very slow to forgive, often nourishing their wrongs in secret for years until the time is ripe for the revenge which they never hesitate to reap in full measure, since they are vindictive beyond the ordinary. They are also inclined to be jealous, suspicious and morose. Extreme melancholy and depression of spirits are perhaps the worst enemies of the Capricorn type, and may colour all their thoughts and actions. Edgar Allan Poe is a striking example of this type, as is also, though in a lesser degree, Thomas Gray, author of the *Elegy Written in a Country Churchyard*.

When badly developed, they may become the most hateful of mankind—timid, callous, tyrannical, intensely selfish, miserly, morbid, lustful, and full of low cunning and duplicity. The superior types are, however, among the noblest members of the human race.

Relationships and love

Subjects of Capricorn make good and true friends, though they are bitter and implacable enemies. In love and marriage, they are capable of deep and passionate affection, though no type is more undemonstrative. They are advised not to marry young, such marriages often proving unfortunate. Much domestic friction can be avoided if they will contrive to overcome their selfishness and cultivate good humour and cheerfulness.

Capricornians make good partners, although they may come late to marriage to ensure a career has been established and that the correct choice is being made. Once set up, they are likely to be happy and to provide well, if economically, for the family. This aspect of caring can extend well outside the immediate family, and although there may be a lack of confidence, a Capricorn subject will not allow him or herself to be pushed around.

Love

A Capricorn always thinks everything over carefully before taking action, and that goes for love affairs too. Like everything else, love is a serious matter, not to be trifled with by simply giving way to one's feelings!

If you fall in love with a Capricorn do not expect him or her to be romantic. You will not be invited for an expensive meal or be showered with red roses for no particular reason.

If you take the initiative and invite a Capricorn home for a romantic dinner by candlelight, do not be surprised if he or she turns all the lights on before sitting down to eat. After all, you need to see what you are eating, don't you?

On the other hand, once a Capricorn has found his or her true love, he or she will be very faithful.

If you have a Capricorn boyfriend, do not attempt to show up on the beach topless. He hates causing a stir.

If you have a Capricorn girlfriend, you will do your cause no good if you start making fun of her. She will probably not appreciate the joke, and will definitely not be amused. Nor does she like the type who pretends to be a regular Don Juan and charm the pants off all the girls. She generally prefers the more stable type who keeps a check on both his finances and his love life.

Good friends are often born under the same sign, or at any rate belong to the same element. And as Capricorn is an earth sign, this means that Capricorns get on well with the other earth signs, Virgo and Taurus.

Capricorns are often loners. When they are young they tend to be very serious and think that their peers are either too childish or too irresponsible. They feel that others should concern themselves with the future instead of larking around. And they cannot stand their wild ideas and plans.

Capricorns become more relaxed as they grow older, so by the time they are old, they tend to think their peers are too old for them! And, contrary to most other people, they do not make friends at work, but rather stick to their own or their spouse's families.

Never be disparaging about a Capricorn's family. That makes a Capricorn really mad, and he or she will take immediate offence.

But if you should manage to make friends with a Capricorn, he or she will be a very loyal and faithful friend, who will be prepared to help you when you are in need.

As parents, they can be too strict. However, they encourage their children and will make sacrifices to assist their child's progress.

Those most in harmony with the Capricorn type, both in friendship and marriage, are born between April 21 and May 21 and between August 21 and September 21.

Good advice

Capricorns always want to plan everything down to the minutest detail. And whilst planning is a good thing, it is also wise to follow one's heart instead of one's mind now and again. Otherwise one can easily miss out on all the exciting things in life.

Earth and water compatibility

Water is necessary for all growth on earth, so people born under an earth sign usually get on well with those born under a water sign. One lot is down-to-earth and sensible, the other is more emotionally sensitive. And if they can avoid putting too much pressure on one another, then any cooperation will usually lead to a positive outcome.

But just as a plant can wither from overwatering, a relationship will founder if the Capricorn starts to feel that his or her Cancer or Virgo friend is being carried away by their emotions without due regard for the more down-to-earth Capricorn.

Capricorns get on better with Pisceans and Scorpions than with Cancerians.

Earth and air compatibility

These two signs are not very compatible. The practical, cautious and down-to-earth Capricorn finds it hard to stomach the airy ideas which Geminis and Librans come up with. These will soon be dismissed by the Capricorn's common sense and eye for detail.

For their part, air sign people find Capricorns incredibly boring. And far too serious and never willing to have any fun.

They may be able to cooperate on the occasional project, where the Capricorn common sense can combine with the lively imagination of air sign people to good effect. But they do not make good partners in love. Of all the air signs, Capricorns get on best with Aquarians.

Earth and fire compatibility

Fire sign people tend to bubble with life and the desire to do lots of exciting things. Capricorns never do anything unpremeditated or unplanned. So these two signs will often find it hard to get on. The Capricorns cannot understand how others can love new and exciting projects, especially when decisions have to be made quickly. They prefer things as they are, or at any rate to consider everything very carefully before making any changes.

Occupations

Subjects of Capricorn are fitted by their prudence, tact and extreme caution to be diplomats and negotiators of delicate business of all descriptions (Disraeli, Benjamin Franklin and Lord Curzon were all born under this sign). As officials, especially in the government, they are industrious and methodical, and usually rise to a position of authority. Other professions and trades which they may follow with profit are those of editor, actor, detective, architect, farmer, farrier, miner or mining official, metallurgist, dealer in lead or wool, and plumber.

Capricorns put a lot of effort into their work. They are not born leaders, but thanks to their hard work and single-mindedness, they often make it to the top anyway.

But they will not gain success at the expense of others. Capricorns will not push others aside in order to be first at the goal post. They prefer to make themselves indispensable.

Many Capricorns seek work in the educational field or in business. But there are also quite a few Capricorns in the art world.

Capricorns put so much into their work that they do not have much energy left for leisure activities. However, many of them enjoy music, either as performers or listeners.

Although they make very good back-room people, Capricornians can make good leaders and do well in their own businesses. Many have an affinity for scientific work and pay attention to detail. They work well with people, although they tend to have an isolationist attitude, taking advice only grudgingly. One might well find them in local government, finance, publishing, building or politics.

Health

Capricorn folk tend to be weak and ailing in childhood, though when they reach adult life they usually enjoy good health. The commonest ills of this type are injuries and diseases affecting the knees (which are ruled by Capricorn), as well as skin disorders, chills, rheumatism, constipation, toothache and earache. They should guard against anxiety and depression, for their complaints are often induced or aggravated by worry and introspection.

To attract good vibrations

The colours that will bring the most harmonious vibrations to Capricorn folk are black, grey and violet; all shades of the last two colours may be used.

Wider aspects

Those with Capricorn as their Sun sign are generally happy alone in leisure pursuits and therefore enjoy music, reading, etc.

Aquarius

Dates

21 January to 18 February. The Sun enters the zodiacal sign Aquarius about January 21 and passes out of it on approximately February 18 each year, but since or about a week after its entry the influence of the previous sign, Capricorn, still remains in force, those born on the cusp—between January 21 and 27—are also ruled by Capricorn, and should consult the pages devoted to that sign as well.

Origin and glyph

There are several links with the water carrier, and the glyph clearly resembles water waves, although the similarity to serpents has also been noticed.

Ruling planet and groupings

Uranus; masculine, fixed and air.

Typical traits

Aquarians are renowned for their independence and the fact that they like to operate according to their own rules. This can lead to them becoming very stubborn, but they can be inspiring because they do not easily lose hope. Aquarians are friendly, although they may not be totally reliable when circumstances become difficult, and highly creative in terms of ideas. However, they are not necessarily sufficiently practical to see through the ideas. Overall, they may be a little perverse or paradoxical, but beneath it all is a gregariousness and a real wish to help.

Aquarius is the last of the airy signs. It is positive in magnetism, and is ruled by the mighty planets Saturn and Uranus; it is symbolized by a man holding a pitcher of water, which he or she pours upon the ground.

Persons born under Aquarius are generally idealistic, generous and humane, and are quick to relieve the distress or wants of others. They are very shrewd judges of human nature, and are acutely sensitive to outside impressions, with a natural gift for immediately sensing the magnetic auras of any persons or places with which they come into contact.

Seeking eternally after truth and beauty, they are strong champions of progress in every direction, longing to sweep away all that is corrupt and burdensome, even though it may have become sanctified by age and long custom, and to replace it with something more serviceable to the needs and welfare of humanity. Three leading examples of this type are Abraham Lincoln, Charles Dickens, and Philip Melancthon, the reformer.

Though gifted with great insight and intuition, their reasoning powers are also active, and they do not depend upon feeling alone for their impressions or opinions, but must debate everything in their own mind in a logical fashion. When once they have formed their conclusions, however, their opinions are unalterable.

Aquarians are cheerful and reliable friends and are usually very popular, since they have social gifts of a high order. They deeply appreciate the affection of others, and respond eagerly to the least show of friendship; but at the same time, their feelings are easily affronted, and slights and injuries which would leave many people unaffected are nursed and brooded over for a long time.

Aquarians are usually strong intellectually, and though they are eager to welcome fresh and novel ideas, they refuse to take anything on trust, but insist on its being demonstrated fully and satisfactorily before they will accept it. They are keenly attracted by science especially by electricity and magnetism—and by any invention or new line of thought that promises to increase the happiness of humanity. Among leading scientists, thinkers, and others who have helped the human race, Francis Bacon, Swedenborg, Copernicus, Charles Darwin, Ernst Haeckel, Sir Hiram Maxim and Thomas Alva Edison were all born under the sign of Aquarius.

The dual rulership of this sign—by both Saturn and Uranus makes its natives contradictory in many ways. Under the influence of Saturn, they may be cautious, indolent, restrained in their passions, and rather slow-going and dull. But at other times, under the sway of Uranus, the same people may surprise their friends by an entire alteration of character for a time, when they defy convention, break old ties and habits, and probably display eccentricity or strange flashes of genius.

Aquarians often have fine talents or incipient genius lying latent and undeveloped in their subconsciousness, and unfortunately it may be on rare occasions only that these are ever called to the surface—usually in emergencies and at the urge of necessity. Many such people, apparently quite ordinary and undistinguished, might rise to a high place in the world if they would but apply themselves to developing these hidden powers.

Not surprisingly, Aquarians like the freedom to do whatever they want, and they tend not to heed anyone who tries to boss them around. They are highly inventive and are generally good with any subject of a technical nature. They are also highly competent at practicalities. This makes for a considerable range of occupations, and Aquarians often turn their hand to science, communications, teaching, social work and general administration.

Have you ever come across a girl who turns up at parties in her grandmother's old dresses? Or a boy who likes to flaunt new and quite outrageous hairstyles? If you have, then they are bound to be Aquarians.

But you should also realise that that crazy hairstyle or that weird notion of wearing granny's old clothes may become the fashion in a couple of years. For Aquarians have a knack of being ahead of their time. One could even say that they live in the future.

Aquarians hate anything ordinary and detest doing the same as everyone else. They love to shock people and to create scandals.

Aquarians are unpredictable. You can never be certain of how an Aquarian is going to react. If an Aquarian girl decides to knit a sweater, she won't bother to use a pattern. And even if she does, she is bound to try to 'improve' on the original idea. Nor will she have much use for a cookery book, preferring to create a new dish by trying various combinations of her own creation.

Aquarians are sometimes regarded as slightly eccentric by other people. But it is a fact that more geniuses have been born under the sign of Aquarius than under any of the other signs.

Inferior or undeveloped subjects of Aquarius may be indolent, timid, neurotic, revengeful, dishonest, unscrupulous and false to their word. In financial matters Aquarians are usually fortunate, but, whether they be rich or poor, money is often a worry or a source of misfortune to them.

Aquarians are happy and successful in any kind of scientific research, but especially in connection with electricity. This sign also produces talented musicians, actors, and poets, such as Mozart, Schubert, Mendelssohn, David Garrick, Sir Henry Irving, Joseph Jefferson, Lord Byron and Robert Burns were also born under Aquarius.

This sign particularly favours the callings of psychologist, company promoter, aviator, electrician, ship's carpenter and nurse or keeper of the insane.

Relationships and love

Aquarius folk are romantic and idealistic, and are apt to set the object of their affections upon a pedestal, so that they are bitterly disappointed and grieved when their beloved's human frailties become apparent. The consequent disillusionment gives rise to much unhappiness, until the partners become adjusted to one another by the process of time. Usually Aquarians are faithful and loyal in matrimony, but they may be quite the opposite. At the best of times their sudden moods and caprices are liable to cause perplexity and pain to friends and marriage partner alike.

Good friends are often born under the same sign or at any rate belong to the same element. Aquarius is an air sign which means that Aquarians get on well with the other air signs, Libra and Gemini.

Aquarians need a lot of security, which they try to reinforce by surrounding themselves with other people. A true Aquarian will often have a lot of friends, but will not necessarily form emotional attachments to many of them.

If you ask an Aquarian friend for a word of advice or his opinion, you will get a straightforward, honest answer. But if this upsets you he or she will not shed a tear with you in sympathy. Nor will he or she try to change you. An Aquarian thinks that that is your problem and your responsibility, and would not want anyone to try to run his life for him.

If you make friends with an Aquarian, you will find him a very loyal person. He will not be moved by gossip. He might listen to your enemies having a bitch about you out of sheer curiosity. But you can safely assume that he will rely on his own judgement rather than others.

Because of their independence, Aquarians may find it difficult to establish an emotional tie. However, providing they find the right type, who is not weak but capable and sensible, personal relationships can be very successful. They are usually totally faithful.

Aquarius

Aquarians are not great romantics, who dream of the great love of their life. If you fall for an Aquarian, your chances will be greater if you are also best friends. And should you by any chance be planning on spending the rest of your life on a desert island together with the Aquarian of your dreams, you will probably find yourself rowing out there on your own.

Aquarians cherish their independence, so there is no point in fooling yourself that you can have one all to yourself. On the other hand, Aquarians are happy to let you have your own friends and interests without interfering. They are not at all inclined to jealousy .

Aquarians find it quite hard to express their emotions. For instance, if you haven't seen your partner for a long time and are expecting a great love scene when you are reunited again, then you will certainly be disappointed. The old cliché 'out of sight, out of mind' fits the Aquarian like a glove. Your partner may well seem quite cold, even though he or she really does like you.

If you want to hold on to your Aquarian then you mustn't be jealous or possessive. Never say: 'You can't do that—what would other people think?', if you do, you can start looking for someone else straight away.

With children, they are supportive but may find it difficult to cope with emotional problems.

They should mate, if possible, with those born between May 21 and June 21 and between September 21 and October 21.

Good advice

Aquarians like working with other people, but still think they should be the boss. It wouldn't be a bad idea for Aquarians to try listening to what others have to say instead of thinking that they are the only ones who are right. Nor is it always such a bright idea to go for every new thing that turns up, believing that everything new is automatically good and everything old useless.

Occupations

Aquarians are often frustrated when trying to reconcile their childhood dreams of performing great deeds or their ambitions of achieving great fame with the real world. The boys dream of becoming deep sea divers and astronauts, and the girls long to become great politicians or the

Prima Ballerina. This does not make it easy to settle for a job as a clerk or till lady.

The Aquarian has lots of different interests, but tires of them very easily. He or she is always interested in the latest ideas and fads, and loves science fiction books and movies.

Ideal jobs for Aquarians are those which deal with people like teaching. But they prefer unusual careers such as inventor, research worker or writer.

Not surprisingly, Aquarians like the freedom to do whatever they want, and tend not to heed anyone who tries to boss them around. They are highly inventive and are generally good with any subject of a technical nature. They are also highly competent at practicalities. This makes for a considerable range of occupations, and Aquarians of ten turn their hand to science, communications teaching, social work and general administration.

Air and earth compatibility

Those born under an air sign or an earth sign often find it difficult to understand each other. The first group have all sorts of pie-in-the-sky plans and ideas, and can't comprehend why the more down-to-earth Taureans or Capricorns don't fall for these ideas straight away, but tend to be regular wet blankets.

But just as the plants and animals of the earth benefit from the oxygen in the air, air and earth sign people can profit from one another. But they are heading for trouble as soon as one tries to dominate the other.

Of all the earth signs, Aquarians get on best with Virgos.

Air and fire compatibility

Air signs are often somewhat frivolous, and fire signs barge ahead, not always allowing for thought before action. These two signs get on well with one another, because an Aquarius person would never dream of stopping an Aries or a Sagittarius person in mid flight. On the contrary, they are more likely to encourage any project or even join in, regardless of how daring it may be.

People born under these two signs do not seem to be bothered by the fact that they are somewhat detached from reality. But it does look as though they are destined to be best friends rather than partners.

Aquarians get on better with Arians and Sagittarians than with Leos.

Air and water compatibility

Air and water signs can learn a lot from each other. Whereas Aquarians are usually very self-confident, a water sign such as a Pisces person may often doubt his own worth. On the other hand the Aquarian person has trouble expressing his emotions, and can receive a lot of help in this respect from the more sensitive water signs.

It is a well-known fact that you cannot breathe under water, and this image is transferable to the water and air signs. They can have a suffocating effect on each other, if one of them tries to dominate.

Of all the water signs, Aquarians get on best with Cancerians.

Health

Aquarius rules the legs and ankles, and these members are more prone to injury—by sprains, fractures and the like—than any other part of the body. The circulation of the blood also comes under this sign, and may be liable to disorder. Uranus gives a tendency to electric shocks and danger from lightning. Aquarians are often keenly interested in hygiene, food reform, dietetics and similar subjects, and by practising these things are often able to keep themselves in splendid health.

To attract good vibrations

Electric blue and electric green are the most harmonious colours for Aquarius, and if worn on the person and freely used in other ways they will be found to act as receivers of beneficial astral vibrations.

Wider aspects

Aquarians are by their very nature a little out on a limb and unconventional, but their very positive qualities make this an interesting Sun sign.

Pisces

Dates
19 February to 20 March. The Sun enters Pisces about February 19 and leaves this sign about March 20. Persons born between February 19 and 27 are also partly ruled by the preceding sign, Aquarius, and they should, therefore, study the characteristics given by this sign as well.

Origin and glyph
There are numerous links between the two fishes and various deities from history, including Jesus Christ. The glyph represents two fish, linked, but also refers to the physical and spiritual side of the person.

Ruling planet and groupings
Neptune; feminine, mutable and water.

Typical traits
It is not easy to recognise somebody born under the sign of Pisces, for all the other eleven signs are combined in this one. In other words, sometimes a Piscean will behave like a Leo, and at other times like an Aries or a Gemini.

But traits which are common to most Pisceans are sensitivity and a caring nature. Pisceans are impressionable people and they are quick to express sympathy for others.

In March the weather can shift dramatically from warm and sunny to snow, frost, rain or fog. The Piscean's moods vary in the same way. Pisceans will shed floods of tears when they feel hurt, and can sink into such a mire of self-pity, that they are a pain to be with. But fortunately, just as the sun soon breaks through again, so too the Piscean's mood will brighten up.

Pisces people need lots of praise if they are to make a success of things. But where a Leo or an Aries will swallow it lock, stock and barrel, a Piscean will know whether your praise is sincere and deserved.

The Piscean person is really quite sensitive but above all is a highly sympathetic and caring person who invariably puts other people first, especially the family. They have great intuition and are good at understanding the needs of other people and make very good, kind friends. Sometimes they can take their idealistic and self-effacing stance too far, resulting in an unwillingness to face decisions, and sometimes they will rely on other, stronger, characters to lead for them. They are usually always tactful but should beware that helping others and becoming involved emotionally is not always a good thing.

Pisces is a watery and negative sign, and is ruled by the two planets Jupiter and Neptune. Its symbol is two fishes, attached yet turning in opposite directions, which typify the dual nature of those born under this sign, who often intend one thing and do another. Gifted with wide vision and a rich imagination, they are capable of conceiving lofty and grandiose schemes; but when they are called on to put them into action, grow timid and lose confidence.

Natives of Pisces are exceedingly romantic, kind-hearted and emotional, but are so lacking in stability and willpower, and are so sensitive to rebuffs and discouragement, that the amount of good which they achieve falls far short of their intentions. They are retiring, vacillating and sadly lacking in ambition, and yet, if constantly urged forward with encouragement and sympathy, they may easily climb the heights of fame and success, for they are often talented, are very apt at learning and accumulating knowledge, and possess a quiet sort of persistence which is peculiar to them.

Pisces subjects readily absorb impressions and take on the psychic auras of people with whom they are brought into contact, and thus their judgment is often clouded and their opinions are unreliable. For this reason, when they are obliged to make an important decision, they should ponder the matter carefully when alone and act resolutely upon their own intuition, without allowing it to be vitiated by the influence of others.

Pisces subjects are fond of comfort and a quiet life, and they will invariably take the easiest path that offers itself. But the superior Pisces folk—and even many of the weaker types—are capable of making the most signal sacrifices when necessity demands, and will then endure an extraordinary amount of suffering and privation without complaint.

A love of order and social convention characterizes those born under this sign, yet they are always ready to find an excuse for the transgressions of others; for, not having much real vice themselves, they simply cannot recognize it in the people around them.

Natives of Pisces are usually fond of animals and children and may have considerable influence over them, ruling them by kindness rather than severity. They may become powerfully attracted towards the study of the occult, and, if very weak, may be completely ruled by superstition. Their telepathic and intuitive powers are often highly developed, and they make good mediums, thought-readers and psychic investigators.

Many of the finest and most enlightened types of mankind are born under Pisces, and many of its natives achieve renown, high rank, honours and riches. But the great majority of those born under this sign are burdened with such a heavy inferiority complex that they stand constantly in need of a stimulus to bring them up to the mark.

Relationships and love
They like to be petted and fussed over, and are often very attractive to the opposite sex. But their vows, promises and affectionate ways are not to be relied on, and a measure of firmness on the part of their partner in marriage is usually desirable.

Good friends are often born under the same sign or at any rate belong to the same element. Pisces is a water sign, so this means that Pisceans get on well with the other water signs, Scorpio and Cancer.

If you need a shoulder to cry on, then it is handy to have a Pisces person as a friend. But you may find that the Piscean gets so caught up in your problems that he or she ends up crying twice as much as you. On the other hand you won't be criticised for whatever you have done. The Pisces person is very understanding and will not be shocked nor disappointed in you.

Pisceans often stand up for the weakest group, which also means that they are sometimes exploited because they find it hard to say no to others.

Pisceans cannot cope with disappointments, which anyhow they find difficult to avoid as they are so concerned with the welfare of others. Many Pisceans tend to console themselves with food. This is a vicious circle: they feel sorry for themselves because they are too fat, and so they need consolation, and eat even more.

In partnerships, Pisceans can be a little difficult to cope with, but with the right partner they will build a welcoming home. They like visitors and to visit others and their self-sacrificing attitude means that they will usually go a little further to make people happy, or an occasion just right. It is important that their lack of strong will is not exploited by a stronger character.

Pisces people are highly emotional and when a Piscean really takes a fancy to someone he or she will fall head over heels in love. But here too they find it hard to distinguish between fantasy and reality, and a Pisces girl will thus experience terrible disappointment when her knight on a white charger turns out to be just an ordinary guy on a rusty old bike. Pisces people want to believe in the best in others so much that they fit the old adage 'love is blind' better than anyone else.

If a Pisces' sweetheart does not live up to expectations, then the Piscean can always withdraw into a world of daydreams, just as he or she did as a child with no friends.

If you are going out with a Piscean then you cannot afford to have a jealous nature, because the Piscean tendency to listen and be sympathetic to others draws people to him or her. But do not let this confuse you, for Pisces people are faithful by nature. In return, you are expected to be just as loyal and reliable. Once you have understood this, you will find there is no more loving a sweetheart than a Pisces.

If you have a Pisces girlfriend you will find that she does not try to dominate or to change you. She will accept you as you are.

Pisceans love children and make very good parents providing they are not too soft. They do have an inner strength, and can be very tough and resourceful if the occasion demands it and when they rise to the challenge. Children often take second place to others and may need some help with their self-confidence. However, they can be very good in science and with parental encouragement can be good achievers.

Subjects of Pisces are most deeply in harmony with people born between June 21 and July 21 and between October 21 and November 21. They are full of sentiment, and their sympathy is easily excited.

Good advice

Pisceans are easily influenced, because they are so uncertain of themselves. The best advice one can give a Piscean is to stick by his or her own feelings and opinions.

Water and air compatibility

Air signs like Libra and Aquarius can learn a lot from the water signs, and vice versa. Pisces people for instance, find it hard to understand that other people are different to themselves and think in different ways. The air signs are much better at this. On the other hand the water signs can teach the air signs to understand their own emotions.

Water and the air signs can get on well with each other, although some air sign people find it hard to take the highly strung and emotionally unstable Pisceans.

Air can create high seas and wild storms. Similar things happen when an Aquarian or a Gemini shows too little consideration for the oversensitive Piscean. Then the Piscean atmospheric barometer plunges below zero!

Pisceans seem to get on best with Librans.

Water and earth compatibility

Water is essential for all growth on the earth. So people born under an earth sign usually get on well with Pisceans. One is down-to-earth, the other more emotional. So if they do not try to dominate each other but respect each other's idiosyncrasies, they can derive a lot of pleasure from each other's company.

But just as a plant will die from overwatering, a friendship can be destroyed if the Piscean gets wrapped up in his own emotions to the exclusion of the more materialistic concerns of Taurus, Virgo or Capricorn people.

Of all the earth signs, Pisces people get on best with Capricornians and Taureans.

Water and fire compatibility

These two elements are normally not very compatible. As we know, water extinguishes fire. A Pisces person simply cannot understand an Arian or a Leo who comes dashing in with some half-baked project to be carried out right away.

On the other hand, people born under a fire sign get very frustrated by Pisceans who always seem so passive and have to take so many things into consideration before making any decision.

Occupations

Travel, especially on the water, seems to exert a great fascination for Pisces folk, and this, coupled with their characteristic love of delving into the mysterious and unknown, may produce a genius for exploration; notable examples are David Livingstone and Arminius Vambéry. Pisces subjects may also have a strong gift for music, literature and philosophy, occupations in which their intense imagination can have full play, and this sign has produced such great artists and thinkers as Chopin, Handel, Rossini, Michelangelo, Ibsen, Victor Hugo, Longfellow, Montaigne, Cardinal Newman, Ernest Renan, Schopenhauer and Ellen Terry.

It is not surprising, with their caring instincts, that Pisceans make good teachers and members of the health and related professions. They tend not to be particularly ambitious but can have extremely good business minds. Success is usually more likely if they have a supportive business partner. Other professions that often attract Pisceans include acting, the ministry, and anything linked with the sea.

A Pisces person usually chooses a career which involves working with people, like a nurse or a doctor. Zone therapy and healing are also obvious choices, as the Piscean is strongly attracted by mysticism. Many Pisceans develop their creative talents and become artists, actors or musicians.

Pisceans also spend their leisure time on creative activities. They enjoy listening to music, or going to the theatre. And they like water, both for drinking, or swimming.

Among the more prosaic occupations favoured by this sign are those of commercial traveller, sailor, brewer, fishmonger, teacher, nurse, leather-worker and dealer in boots and shoes; also any occupation connected with children and animals.

Health

Pisces rules the feet and toes, and these parts are particularly liable to disease and injury. Among the most common ailments affecting subjects of Pisces are chills, gout, dropsy, sluggishness of the liver and infectious diseases. They should guard also against disorders arising from the pleasures of the table, of which they are usually very fond.

To attract good vibrations

The most magnetic colours for Pisces folk are purple, mauve, and sea-green; these should be freely used in clothing and in household decorations.

Wider aspects

Pisceans have to be careful that in helping and caring for others they tend to ignore their own pursuits or problems.

Your Birth Chart

Constructing a Chart

All the foregoing is background information that helps in the interpretation of a birth chart or horoscope. A typical blank chart is shown on page 509. The solid central line represents the horizon and the numbered segments are the houses, as described previously. On this chart are plotted the positions of the Sun, Moon and planets.

To begin with, the following information about the subject is required:
—the date of birth,
—the time of birth and whether it was British Summer Time or not, and
—the place of birth and the appropriate latitude and longitude.

From the information, the position of the ascendant and midheaven can be plotted, followed by the planets' positions. As each planet is placed on the chart there will be certain angular positions developed between them, and when these form specific angles they are called *aspects*. These aspects have considerable influence on the chart and therefore on its subject.

In addition to these factors, there are further interpretive factors depending on the placing of the planets in the various signs and the positions of that same planet in one of the twelve houses.

All these different parts of astrology are considered in further detail next.

Astrological aspects

The word 'aspects' has a particularly significant meaning in astrology. These are the angular relationships that planets make with each other and also with the ascendant, midheaven, descendant and nadir. On a birth chart the aspects appear as lines joining the planets to each other, and often these are also displayed in a grid, using another set of glyphs in a kind of shorthand notation.

Aspects form a qualifying statement about the planets and, depending on their effect, can be called easy or difficult, or, alternatively, the degree of their effect may be classed as positive, negative or weak. Hence, some aspects will make life easier for the subjects while others will introduce difficulties. Other factors should also be taken into account,

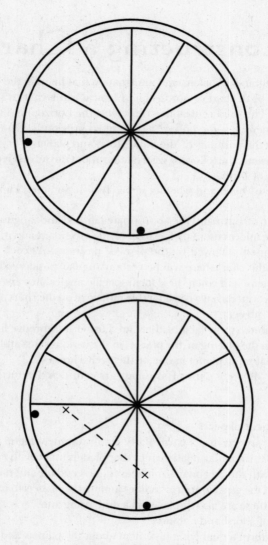

Constructing aspects

namely the nature of the planets concerned and the houses and signs in which they occur.

An aspect is considered valid only if the respective planets are within a certain number of degrees of each other. The width or range allowed is called the *orb*, and, not surprisingly, an exact aspect is much stronger than a wide one. There is some difference in the size of the orbs used by different astrologers, but major aspects commonly have an orb of 8 degrees while others are 4 degrees, and for those aspects with only a minor influence, the orb may be 2 degrees.

The different aspects with appropriate glyphs are listed below, starting with the *major aspects*:

Major aspects

Conjunction
Conjunction ☌ can be positive or negative. A conjunction is when two planets or a planet and the ascendant are located close to each other (within the 8 degrees orb). If the planets fall in the same sign then the aspect is strengthened. Conversely, it is weakened if one falls into an adjacent sign, although it does depend upon the planet. The conjunction is the most powerful of all aspects and confers a strong personality.

Oppostion
Opposition ☍ is negative. Opposition is when two planets are opposite each other, within the orb of 8 degrees. This is also a powerful aspect and can indicate problems in dealing with people or handling different facets of the personality.

Trine
Trine is positi ve. A trine is formed when two planets are 120 degrees apart and in general indicates that the planets work well together.

Square
Square ☐ is negative. When two planets are 90 degrees apart, a square is formed. This is quite a powerful aspect but may represent tension, disruption or difficulties, although it can equally be put to positive ends.

Sextile
Sextile ⚹ is positive. The sextile marks two planets or features that are 60 degrees apart. Like the trine, the sextile indicates a helpful, easing influence, although it is not as strong as the trine.

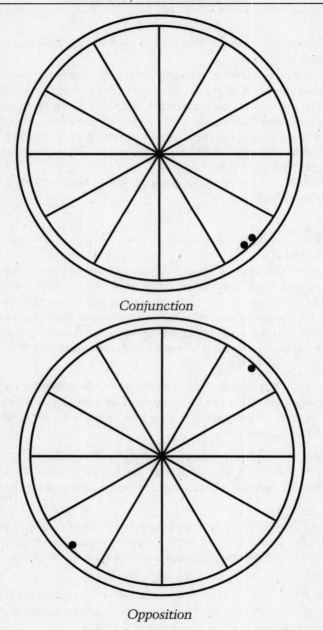

Conjunction

Opposition

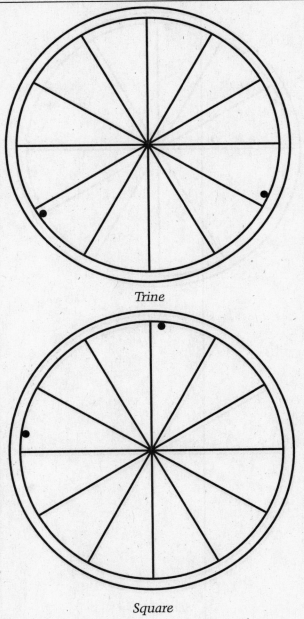

Trine

Square

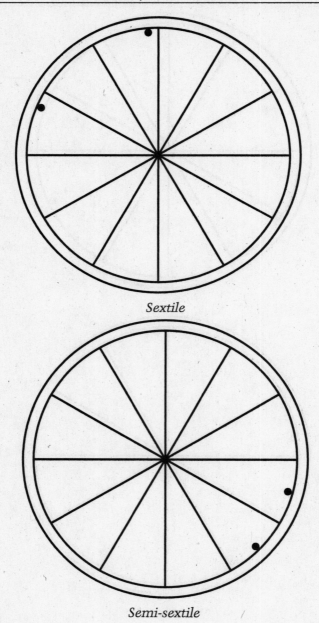

Sextile

Semi-sextile

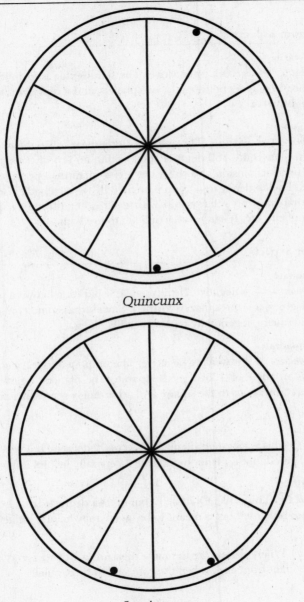

Quincunx

Semi-square

Medium aspects

Semi=sextile

Semi-sextile ✕ is weak to negative. The semi-sextile is formed when there are 30 degrees between the two planets, and it represents tension and slight stress.

Quincunx

Quincunx ✕ is negative. The quincunx (otherwise called the *inconjunct*) is when planets are 150 degrees apart within an orb of 2 degrees. It also represents tension and stress but less so than the opposition and square. The tendency to tension is created by the two bodies being in signs that have no relationship with each other through triplicity, quadruplicity, etc. It can be very difficult to live with.

Minor aspects

Semi=square

Semi-square ◁ is negative. If the angular separation between planets is 45 degrees, a semi-square is formed. Since it has some connection with the square, it generally represents difficulties.

Sesquiquadrate

Sesquiquadrate ⊔ is weak to negative. The sesquiquadrate, or *sesquare*, is when an angle of 135 degrees separates the planets. Again it has obvious connections to the square and accordingly represents difficulties.

Quintile

Quintile Q This is a strange angular aspect of 72 degrees. It is very weak and little used, but is meant to indicate a generally helpful influence.

Biquintile

Biquintile BC This is like Quintile Q but of 144 degrees. It is also very weak and little used but is meant to be a generally helpful influence.

Parallel

Parallel | | When planets are the same measurement above and below the ascendant from each other, they are said to be parallel.

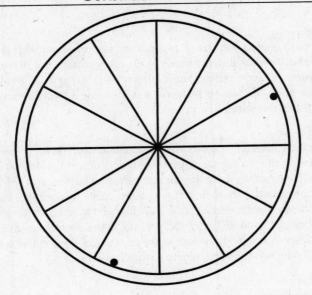

Sesquiquadrate

Aspect patterns

When a chart has been plotted with all the information, certain aspects will become apparent. By joining up the information in a particular construction, certain patterns are formed that have influence upon the subject's personality, and they can work to his or her benefit or detriment.

Upon establishing a particular aspect, a point is made midway between the centre of the chart and the planet on the periphery. Lines then join these points for each aspect, creating a chart with several geometric shapes that are discussed below. It is often the case that different aspects are drawn with different lines (solid, dotted, dashed, etc) or several colours are used to help differentiate between oppositions, trines, sextiles, and so on.

There are a number of *aspect patterns*, which may involve three or four planets. It is generally the case that all the planets form aspects. If, however, there is an unaspected planet it will be a very powerful feature but may represent personality problems. The main aspect patterns are:

Tee=square

This configuration consists of two planets in opposition with a third that makes a square aspect to both of the other planets. All the aspects so constructed are negative, but it often confers strength. A great deal depends upon the planets involved, but it can be a forceful, dynamic subject with this pattern.

Grand trine

The grand trine is a triangular aspect formation with three trine aspects. At first sight this is a positive aspect, but it does depend greatly on other factors. For example, there may be a tendency to laziness and weakness of character, and if more than three planets make up the trine, there is the tendency for the element that is highlighted to become too strong. Charts should be studied carefully, however, as there are often other patterns that compensate. For example, the presence of a tee-square pattern will add some solidity and strength to the character.

Grand cross

The grand cross is not a common feature, but when it does occur it forms a very strong influence. It is made up of four planets in a four-cornered square such that there are two oppositions comprising planets at opposite corners. In addition, the four planets make square aspects with their adjacent planet. The result is that it is a very powerful feature and can be disruptive, although its effect may be lessened by other aspect patterns.

Because of the separation of the four planets, each will fall in the same quadruplicity or quality, i.e. fixed, mutable or cardinal. This confers a slightly different perspective on the interpretation.

Fixed grand cross

The *fixed grand cross* suggests an individual who may be stubborn or at least someone who tolerates the *status quo*. It may be that he or she has been put upon and criticized so much that he or she has given up.

Mutable grand cross

The *mutable grand cross* implies adaptability and potentially an ability to overcome obstacles and work around problems. There may still be nervous stress because although the subject will opt for an easy solution and a straightforward life, other factors may prohibit this, such as a feeling of duty.

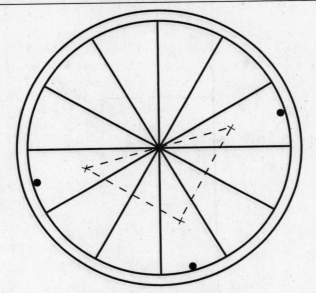

Tee-square aspect pattern

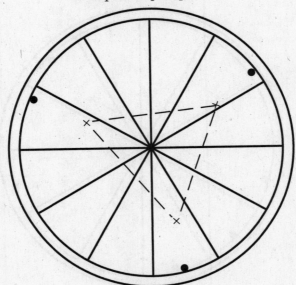

Grand trine aspect pattern

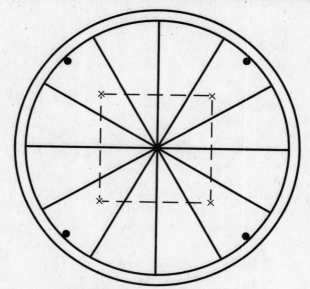

Grand cross aspect pattern

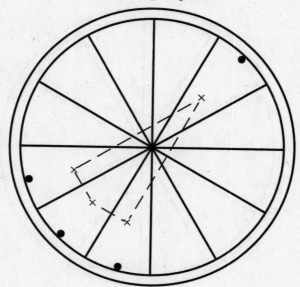

The pointer aspect pattern

Cardinal grand cross

The *cardinal grand cross* essentially implies a desire and a will to overcome difficulties. A lack of self-confidence may prove a barrier, but, with sufficient determination, this can be overcome and result in considerable achievement.

Pointer

A pointer aspect pattern is made up of two planets in opposition and one of these two then forms quincunx aspects with two further planets, producing a pattern shaped like an arrowhead.

The quincunx and opposition are both indicative of tension and stress, and this is compounded by two semi-sextile patterns at the other end of the pointer. Overall, then, this is a stressful pattern, and in many cases it focuses, at its point, on the house of importance.

Stellium

A final pattern that may occur is when three or more planets occur in one house or sign, and this implies a reinforcing of the concerns of the house or the characteristics of the sign. This arrangement is called a *stellium*, and can cause a certain imbalance in a subject's chart because of the emphasis it applies. The extreme qualities of the sign involved may be accentuated, and it helps to look to other planets to counterbalance this effect.

Aspects of the Planets

In this section each planet is considered in relation to the others by way of the aspects formed. In each case the conjunction and then positive and negative aspects are described with regard to how they affect the overall picture. Reference can be made to the preceding list of aspects and whether they are positive or negative.

The Sun

Aspects made by the Sun to other planets are very important in interpreting charts, and planets aspected to the Sun will be strengthened. The effect of the planet or planets on the Sun shows how its own influence will be manifested. If the Sun aspects with the ruling planet of the chart then it is very important.

Sun/Moon aspects

In conjunction these planets generally confer harmony, and there is an emphasis on characteristics associated with the sign. The conjunction may not always be in the same sign or house. If this happens, it may reflect an inner conflict normally associated with negative aspects. Positive aspects between the Sun and Moon represent a coherence and oneness of the personality, while negative aspects mirror the likelihood of unsatisfied restlessness. Minor aspects will have little influence and will have a subsidiary role in the presence of other features.

Sun/Mercury aspects

Because the Sun and Mercury are never more than 28 degrees apart, the only aspects that can occur are a conjunction or semi-sextile. If the conjunction is close, less than 5 degrees, it is customarily taken that the subject will be a slow developer, although experience does not necessarily confirm this. In general these aspects confer an energetic and positive outlook. If the planets are in the same sign, the subject will think and express himself or herself in the nature of that sign.

Sun/Venus aspects

The Sun and Venus are never more than 48 degrees apart, so the only aspects possible are a conjunction, semi-sextile and semi-square. A conjunction represents affection, and the individual will probably enjoy the pleasurable aspects of life, often to excess. Other characteristics that may be strengthened or emerge are kindness and gentility, but, to excess, the overall result can be laziness and a certain irresponsibility. The semi-sextile will never be a strong feature, but it does indicate creativity and an appreciation of finer things, for example, art or music. If the semi-square occurs, it can indicate a rift in personal relationships.

Sun/Mars aspects

If the Sun and Mars occur in conjunction, there is a very strong positive, and cumulative, effect. Because of the individual effects of these planets, Mars for physical energy and the Sun for vitality, this conjunction is particularly forceful. This may also apply to the emotional picture of the individual. The bold, brave traits may be taken to the point of heroism but may equally result in overwork. Positive aspects have much the same effect but with a beneficial outcome and without treading on anyone's toes. Negative aspects include angry outbursts but more commonly the bad effects of overwork.

Sun/Jupiter aspects

In many ways a conjunction of the Sun with Jupiter can be regarded as highly fortuitous. It represents a general contentment, but more, people with this conjunction are held to be very 'lucky' as they will probably have considerable good fortune and opportunities in life. There tends to be a feeling that good luck can be expected. The outward-looking and expansive nature associated with Jupiter can result in an ambitious, intelligent and humorous individual. Positive aspects will have much the same result, and although the individual may not be particularly competitive strength may be seen in certain sports.

Negative aspects may include conceit, impudence and extravagance and a tendency to exaggerate, although these may be lessened to some extent if there are other, steadying influences in the chart.

Sun/Saturn aspects

It has been understood for some time that Saturn has a dampening effect on the Sun, cancelling out to some extent its vitality. Thus, in conjunction, Saturn will cause the Sun's effect to be limited and the cumulative result will depend very much on other planetary aspects. If other aspects are mainly positive then the effect of Saturn will be limited. Positive aspects introduce patience and a practical outlook on life, and although there may be shyness, it can be overcome.

The negative aspects are often manifested in a lack of self-confidence, and this may result, with other factors, in a tendency to ill health.

Sun/Uranus aspects

The Sun in conjunction with Uranus can be extremely strong and result in someone who is rebellious or rather eccentric. It may, however, also confer originality and independence, and there is often a scientific ability. Positive aspects can have similar effects, with a leaning to leadership, flashes of inventive thought and even genius. There is a greater emotional and nervous energy, which can sometimes be seen in a somewhat erratic enthusiasm.

Negative aspects are manifested as awkwardness and stubbornness, and the subject can be difficult, although this may be lessened by other factors.

Sun/Neptune aspects

In conjunction this aspect shows sensitivity and an intuitive nature. If there are no negative aspects influencing the chart, there may well be a creative flair. There can, however, often be a tendency towards the impractical, and the individual may be thought of as having his or her head in the clouds. Positive aspects create a vivid imagination that can be used to good effect, but it may also verge into daydreaming and thus become less productive than it might be.

Negative aspects may produce vagueness and muddled thinking and quite often there is a deceitful aspect to the nature, whether it applies to the self or others. The daydreaming feature of such individuals may become a definite drawback in that issues and reality are avoided.

Sun/Pluto aspects

A conjunction between the Sun and Pluto can tend to produce obsessive behaviour and considerable self-analysis. Depending on where the conjunction falls, however, it can enhance an intuitive individual. Positive aspects reinforce the theme of self-analysis, and this may be extended into an ability to undertake research.

Negative aspects, on the other hand, may prove very frustrating, with a likelihood of the individual being very reticent to talk through problems and situations, even with family members and close friends. Obsession is never far away but can be countered by other influences, particularly involving Venus and the Moon.

The Moon

Planets aspecting the Moon are subtly altered, and any matters ruled by that planet will probably undergo changes and modest alterations, heightening or lessening a particular characteristic.

Moon/Sun aspects—see section on The Sun.

Moon/Mercury aspects

A conjunction between the Moon and Mercury has a marked, positive mental effect, resulting in good instinctive behaviour that can extend into an active mind producing a facility for writing or something similar. Positive aspects produce common sense and the ability to work out a problem or situation and choose a logical solution.

Negative aspects can lead to a restless mind and an acrimonious nature, and although intellectual powers are heightened they may be used negatively, for example, in more gossip and criticism.

Moon/Venus aspects

The Moon in conjunction with Venus is a particularly good aspect, resulting in a balanced person who is calm, friendly and popular. It also has a positive effect on partnerships, making the individual very aware of his or her partner's needs. Positive aspects will show the same characteristics exhibited by a conjunction, with the additional benefits of intuition and charm.

Negative aspects may cause some difficulty in the outward expression of affections, and this can result in troubled relationships.

Moon/Mars aspects

The conjunction with Mars produces a strong influence and results in a tendency to be direct and energetic. However, it can also render someone too quick, and liable to jump first and check the ground afterwards. Positive aspects result in good physical and emotional strength, which means that the individual can make progress, whether in work or life generally.

Negative aspects lead to moodiness and a tendency to quarrel and also an impulsive nature that may lead to the necessary rescue of hastily made decisions.

Moon/Jupiter aspects

In conjunction these planets confer a helpful, kind nature to the individual, who is generally optimistic about events and often has a relatively trouble-free journey through life. Positive aspects have the same effect, particularly the trine, and the mental faculties are enhanced.

Negative aspects create a slightly destructive slant to these qualities so that the nature may be essentially the same, but judgement is affected and gains may be squandered.

Moon/Saturn aspects

A rather serious, cautious and even pessimistic outlook can be engendered by a conjunction between these planets. There is a desire for order and for things to be correct, so much so that the individual may be tagged a perfectionist. There may also be a timidness to the character and an underlying feeling of inadequacy, but loyalty can be relied upon.

Positive aspects include a commitment to duty willingly given and an ability to work reliably, thereby gaining a good reputation that is usually rewarded with progress. A lack of self-confidence, shyness and difficult relationships with the opposite sex all reflect negative aspects. If the individual is not careful it is quite easy for depression to take over, and other aspects of the chart should be studied to find more positive, constructive influences.

Moon/Uranus aspects

If the Moon and Uranus are in conjunction, there will be tension and emotions may be strained. Alongside the quite scintillating effects that may occur, there is a perversity and desire for the unusual, and often an independence in behaviour. Positive aspects result in a strong intuition and a need to achieve, which can be channelled constructively in almost any direction. Mood changes are common but are usually for the better.

Tension, an overpowering will, frequent (if only temporary) disagreements with friends all reflect the negative aspects. Flair and creativity may be present, but they need to be handled in the correct way.

Moon/Neptune aspects

Idealism, sensitivity and kindness all reflect a conjunction between the

Moon and Neptune. These can be so dominant in the make-up that it can work to the subject's detriment should others take advantage of him or her. It is important to avoid deceptions that may be perpetrated in order that others are not hurt.

Positive aspects frequently add imagination to the character, but this must be controlled to avoid a muddled approach. A seriously muddled mind is typical of a negative aspect, as is the non-fulfilment of positive traits.

Moon/Pluto aspects

A conjunction between the Moon and Pluto commonly produces someone who is changeable and prone to highly emotional outbursts. Even so, this may act to his or her benefit in that a fresh start can be made uncluttered by bubbling discontent. It may, however, prove no easy task for the individual to express his or her true feelings if other planets restrict the conjunction.

Positive aspects create a similar tendency; outbursts may occur but can ultimately prove beneficial while the need to 'clear the decks' every so often will enable something or someone to be exorcised from the person. Negative aspects result in an inability to express oneself and open up emotionally, which can be frustrating and ultimately destructive unless countered elsewhere in the chart.

Mercury

Since Mercury is the planet of the mind, communication and general mental capacity, it is often feasible to find a positive outlet in this area.

Mercury/Sun aspects—see section on The Sun.

Mercury/Moon aspects—see section on The Moon.

Mercury/Venus aspects

In conjunction there will be an ease of mind rather than worry and a harmony and understanding of other people. A pleasant manner and charming speech result in good abilities to communicate. These planets are never separated by more than 76 degrees so the positive aspect that may be found is the sextile. This results in a friendly and affectionate nature and often an appreciation of, and ability in, craft pursuits.

The negative aspects may be the semi-sextile, which is very weak (and thus of little consequence), or the semi-square. The latter similarly has little adverse effect, save perhaps a critical manner, but depending on the configuration it may actually produce a greater balance of emotions in the character.

Mercury/Mars aspect

In conjunction with Mars, Mercury takes on the forceful, energetic nature of this planet. This produces someone who is mentally sharp, decisive and agile and able to take decisions quickly. Such individuals will probably prove effective in discussion or debate, which may serve them well in business. Aggressiveness may appear but will usually be manifested in strong opinions that the individual is quite happy to voice. Positive aspects produce much the same results with a lively mind but in addition an ability to handle stressful situations.

Negative aspects may result in moving too quickly, resulting in premature action, and incisiveness can become a more destructive carping. The mental faculties can be overloaded, resulting in tension and even a breakdown.

Mercury/Jupiter aspects

This conjunction confers very good mental creativity and potential, which may reflect a writer or any sort of literary occupation. There tends to be an appreciation of broader concepts rather than fine detail, although this will depend to a certain extent upon the remainder of the chart. A cheerful optimistic individual with a sense of humour reflects positive aspects, and in such cases challenges are necessary to stimulate the mind and obtain the best. Otherwise there may be a tendency to laziness.

In general, the negative aspects are not particularly problematical, but there can be carelessness if the mind is overloaded, or a tendency towards absent-mindedness.

Mercury/Saturn aspects

The conjunction of these two planets has a contradictory effect in that there is a mix of communication and limitation. It creates someone with a serious and thoughtful perspective on life, but he or she can become pessimistic. If combined with a good chart, there will be common sense and an attention to detail; conversely, a bad combination can result in mental slowness. Saturn will also inhibit and limit positive aspects, but there is often an enthusiastic nature combined with a useful reliability.

Negative aspects may force these characteristics to excess, causing obsessive behaviour in many ways, such as orderliness, self-discipline and depression.

Mercury/Uranus aspects

This conjunction is a particularly dynamic one and leads to a very quick mind, rich in inventive and innovative thought. It may also impart independence and a little stubbornness, and can produce an unconventional character who prefers the unusual and unorthodox. This is also seen with positive aspects, leading to originality and inventiveness, especially in a scientific context. Such individuals are self-assured and may be good with their hands.

The ability to communicate may become too sharp and almost isolated under the influence of negative aspects, and reaction to delays or difficult situations may be quite out of proportion to the problem faced. The preponderance of following the unusual can seem to others to be eccentric, which in itself becomes counterproductive.

Mercury/Neptune aspects

Mercury and Neptune in conjunction produce a fascinating result. The sensitivity and inspiration of Neptune confer on the individual a highly flexible mental attitude, resulting in creativity, intuition and a fertile imagination. There will not, however, necessarily be the rationalizing effect of common sense, and this may result in daydreaming. Positive aspects have a similar effect—sensitivity, kindness and an intuitive feel for people's aspirations and even thoughts.

Negative aspects lead to gullibility and unwillingness to face reality, and the thinking may operate in a scheming, deceptive way.

Mercury/Pluto aspects

The conjunction of Mercury with Pluto produces an individual capable of dispensing with worries easily and someone who enjoys the mental challenge of solving a mystery. A similar vein is seen with positive aspects, and there is a fascination and thoroughness when dealing with a topic that has once caught the individual's interest.

Negative aspects tend to be manifested as a secretive nature, perhaps with obsessive or stubborn sides to the character.

Venus

In general any planet aspected by Venus will be softened, resulting in an enhancement of certain characteristics, such as the expression of love and dealing with possessions.

Venus/Sun aspects—see section on The Sun.

Venus/Moon aspects—see section on The Moon.

Venus/Mercury aspects—see section on Mercury.

Venus/Mars aspects

These two planets have a limiting effect on each other when in conjunction so that Mars limits the delicate beauty of Venus, and Venus limits the robust, coarse nature of Mars. As a result, the individual is enthusiastic, while sensitive to a partner's needs and also able to enjoy sexual relationships and all things of beauty. Positive aspects work in much the same way, with the further introduction of warmth into relationships.

Negative aspects may increase tension in relationships, often resulting in hurt and quarrels. If Venus is the stronger planet then the subject may be oversensitive to the comments of others.

Venus/Jupiter aspects

A conjunction between Venus and Jupiter is a very beneficial aspect and confers popularity, an artistic inclination and an affectionate nature. Such individuals work better in partnerships rather than alone and may lead a busy love life. Positive aspects produce similar results, and the individual will be popular, charming and happy.

Negative aspects tend not to be too detrimental because of the beneficial nature of both Venus and Jupiter. In most cases it will be an excess of a particular characteristic, thus the charm will be overplayed or an excessive number of love affairs will cause problems or there may be a discontent with being alone.

Venus/Saturn aspects

When Venus is in conjunction to Saturn there is often some factor that inhibits the complete and open expression of affection or love, and this may produce disappointment in such affairs. There may also be a strong sense of duty, which, although it may bring its own rewards, can be traced back to strong inhibitions. Positive aspects tend to be less restrictive than the conjunction, and while there is a serious side to relationships, a particular partnership can benefit from faithfulness.

Negative aspects are also restrictive, to the point where it is difficult to express affection, although more positive characteristics elsewhere in the chart may help overcome this barrier.

Venus/Uranus aspects

In conjunction, these planets confer an element of inconsistency and an inability to focus the attention. In addition, emotions and tension may run high, and this really needs to be channelled and controlled. Although considerable personal appeal is possible, commitment may be lacking. Positive aspects lead to a less compulsive and magnetic personality and a tendency towards creativity and often considerable achievements.

The personality may retain its magnetism and dynamism, but under the influence of negative aspects there may also be a dramatic temper and impatience, which can cause nervous tension and strain.

Venus/Neptune aspects

There is a sensitivity and idealism when Venus is in conjunction with Neptune and an inclination towards pleasant or amiable behaviour. If the subject lives too much in the clouds, however, there will be self-delusion and a likelihood that partnerships and associations are not as solid and secure as perceived. When positive aspects are found, these will increase the chance of success, particularly in artistic pursuits such as music. Ideas and hunches may occur during periods of apparent daydreaming, but in many cases these can prove more realistic than at first believed.

Negative aspects can produce problems, in that restlessness can turn to discontent if other areas of the chart reinforce this trait. There is a possibility of self-delusion unless common sense appears elsewhere, and confusion can occur in personal relationships.

Venus/Pluto aspects

The conjunction of Venus with Pluto is often a powerful one when it comes to emotions. It is quite likely that love will be felt deeply and passionately, but unless it is reciprocated there may be upheavals. Both planets influence money affairs, so this area may form a theme for a career. Positive aspects produce a very similar effect on personal relationships, especially those of the heart, while negative aspects tend to block these factors. The emotions may well be present, but there is an inability to talk above them and this can lead to frustration.

Mars

Mars will strongly affect any planet it contacts and will tend to create extremes in its positive and negative aspects.

Mars/Sun aspects——see section on The Sun.

Mars/Moon aspects——see section on The Moon.

Mars/Mercury aspects——see section on Mercury.

Mars/Venus aspects——see section on Venus.

Mars/Jupiter aspects

A conjunction between these two planets has very strong effects, resulting in energetic, decisive, enterprising individuals who tend not to miss opportunities. In addition, they will probably be willing to take on challenges that others would not even consider. There is a tendency for individuals to be almost daring, although they may be more argumentative. The influence of positive aspects is very good, leading to good humour, enthusiasm and the constructive taking of opportunities, whether physical, material or intellectual. Unless it is countered by controls shown elsewhere in the chart, the negative aspects can be quite destructive, with excesses in action and thought.

Mars/Saturn aspects

There tends to be something of a conflict when these planets are in conjunction, with Saturn limiting and Mars enlivening. As a result there may be mood swings from determination to frustration, from gloom to optimism. There may also be obstinacy. Positive aspects create a slightly more harmonious character such that the individual will be very determined. If put to good use this can lead to achievement in certain fields.

Negative aspects tend to result in a stern attitude, but this also means that hardships are endured. Selfishness is another trait that may be seen.

Mars/Uranus aspects

The combination of Mars and Uranus in conjunction produces very strong attributes, with determination, often obstinacy and frankness. Although this may not make the most pleasant of individuals, there will be a desire and ability to reach goals, but there may also be undue haste, which can result in accidents. Positive aspects confer independence and a magnetic character, but this may be a disadvantage unless used well. Flair and creativity can be manifested in engineering or science.

Tension and nervous strain result from negative aspects, and an argumentative nature is very likely. Personal relationships may be strained because of tactlessness, and an awareness of other people's feelings has to be engendered.

Mars/Neptune aspects

The conjunction of Mars with Neptune stimulates the imagination and strengthens the emotions. It can also make the individual somewhat lazy. In general there tends to be an interest in the arts, dancing and similar pursuits. Positive aspects lead to a creativity and original thinking that would be well employed in design. The emotional side of the individual is also enhanced.

Negative aspects can all too often result in escapist ways that can lead to problems. There may also be moodiness, and hard work undertaken possibly for perfectly altruistic motives may come to nought, perhaps because the idea had little substance at the outset.

Mars/Pluto aspects

An almost explosive nature can result when Mars is in conjunction to Pluto. Certainly there will be a determined, stubborn outlook, and it may be necessary to find a controlled outlet for the excessive energy. The temper is likely to be fierce, and obsessions are always possible. The character may even be flawed by a cruel streak. Hard work and ambition characterize the positive aspects, even to the point of the subject becoming a 'workaholic'.

Because both energy and emotions are increased by negative aspects, the subject may become someone who works almost obsessively to achieve a goal.

Jupiter

Jupiter's influence tends to be one of expansion and the provision of greater scope, and is often associated with understanding and knowledge.

Jupiter/Sun aspects—*see section on* The Sun.

Jupiter/Moon aspects—*see section on* The Moon.

Jupiter/Mercury aspects—*see section on* Mercury.

Jupiter/Venus aspects—*see section on* Venus.

Jupiter/Mars aspects—*see section on* Mars.

Jupiter/Saturn aspects

The conjunction of Jupiter with Saturn brings together seemingly opposing principles of limitation and expansion. If the influence of each is balanced, then common sense, a balanced approach to life and positive thinking will result. If the influences are not balanced there can be swings between optimism and pessimism, but in any event there is usually application to the task in hand and the ability to stay to the end. Positive aspects emphasize the constructive combination of common sense with optimism, producing a rounded character for whom little cannot be achieved. The intuition is good, as is their ability to plan and bring ideas to fruition.

Negative aspects introduce dissatisfaction and restlessness allied with a lack of self-confidence. There is also a tendency to press on regardless, even when caution is called for.

Jupiter/Uranus aspects

This conjunction produces an individual who is positive in his or her thinking, independent, and with a considerate approach to others. There may also be a good sense of humour, and such people are unlikely to be lost in the crowd. Many of these features are also produced by positive aspects, but in addition there is determination, self-belief and possibly an eccentricity bordering on genius.

Eccentricity can work to the individual's detriment under negative aspects, with an associated streak of pomposity. Such an individual may consider that everyone is wrong except he or she.

Jupiter/Neptune aspect

In conjunction these planets convey a kindness and desire to help others combined with idealism, although the effect of the latter trait will be shaped by the rest of the chart. In general there is optimism, and while there is a tendency to dream, a practical side should be sought.

The positive aspects tend to be quite similar in effect, with an added altruism in their efforts.

The negative aspects often result in the beneficial qualities of kindness and sensitivity being overridden by lack of attention. In the extreme there may be escapism, foolishness or deception.

Jupiter/Pluto aspects

Jupiter in conjunction with Pluto produces a desire for power, material gain and an obsession in attaining goals. If it goes too far, it may verge on the fanatic, but if controlled these traits can prove very beneficial. The individual may well show leadership potential, and there may well be prominence in life at some time. Positive aspects provide similarly useful features, such as determination, the ability to lead and organize, and great strength of character.

The fanatical side of a character can develop under negative aspects, and if this is combined with an ability to lead and draw people, problems may arise. There may be a compulsion to gain what is wanted by violent means and to break away from existing constraints. Such tendencies must be tempered.

Saturn

A key feature of Saturn is its limiting effect, and this possibly relates to its being at the edge of the universe until late into the eighteenth century when the 'modern' planets were discovered.

Saturn/Sun aspects—see section on The Sun.

Saturn/Moon aspects—see section on The Moon.

Saturn/Mercury aspects—see section on Mercury.

Saturn/Venus aspects—see section on Venus.

Saturn/Mars aspects—see section on Mars.

Saturn/Jupiter aspects—see section on Jupiter.

Saturn/Uranus aspects

This conjunction has very great potential and, depending on the position of the conjunction, can result in great achievers. A practical outlook combined with persistence and other beneficial aspects can create brilliance. In certain circumstances the aspects can combine to produce someone with true leadership qualities, possibly a leader of their generation. There could always be nervous tension because of the conflict between limitation and freedom, which has to be countered. A balanced, perhaps more integrated, whole is generated by positive aspects, with persistence, patience and yet originality.

With negative aspects there may be a conflict, producing a stubborn nature and someone who is awkward and has a tendency to suffer from nervous tension.

Saturn/Neptune aspects

The conjunction of these two planets is interesting in that Uranus lies between the two for this period of the last generation, and this has a considerable effect. The overall result is an individual with a strong character who has ideas and imagination but controls them to the greatest benefit for all. There is a similar result with positive aspects, and there is a kind and caring nature. An aptitude for science is common.

Negative aspects render these traits weaker, leading to confusion and a lack of application. There may be self-deprecation and shyness.

Saturn/Pluto aspects

Aspects involving these two planets occur rarely and last a long time when they do happen. The conjunction occurred last early in the 1980s when both planets were in Libra. This results in a determination allied with a pushing drive. Positive aspects confer a more determined outlook and also stubbornness.

Obsessional behaviour is typical of any negative aspects, and there is a tendency to avoid facing problems through misplaced fear, which makes the individual appear to waste time.

Uranus

Aspects between Uranus and the remaining planets Neptune and Pluto stay within orb for a long time (for example, from 1989 to 1998) because of the immense distances and separations involved and also the slow movement of Uranus. This means that such aspects will apply to the charts of people born within a long period.

Uranus/Sun aspects—see section on The Sun.

Uranus/Moon aspects—see section on The Moon.

Uranus/Mercury aspects—*see section on* Mercury.

Uranus/Venus aspects—*see section on* Venus.

Uranus/Mars aspects—*see section on* Mars.

Uranus/Jupiter aspects—*see section on* Jupiter.

Uranus/Saturn aspects—*see section on* Saturn.

Uranus/Neptune aspects

In conjunction there is the combination of independence, imagination and intuition with sensitivity, which produces an individual with inspirational qualities. Positive aspects often result in creatively or scientifically gifted people because logic, flair and similar attributes are strengthened.

Negative aspects may result in nervous tension, and the individual may be rather absent-minded. In such cases it is good practice to seek compensatory traits and activities elsewhere in the chart.

Uranus/Pluto aspects

This conjunction occurs very infrequently, roughly once every 115 years, and because of the slow relative movement of the planets the effects are relevant for a generation. In many charts it will therefore not be a particularly strong feature. However, it may result in general frustration within the house in which the conjunction falls. Positive aspects may result in a likelihood to seek change while negative aspects can result in this trait being overdone and leading to disruptive behaviour.

Neptune

The majority of cases in which Neptune aspects with other planets have been covered in the preceding pages under the other planets. Just one planetary aspect remains.

Neptune/Pluto aspects

Because of the relationship between these two planets, conjunctions were formed many years ago but now Neptune is ahead of Pluto in their respective orbits around the Sun. As such a conjunction will not occur for some considerable time.

The only aspect that Neptune makes with Pluto is the sextile, and this occurs quite a lot in charts. Depending on the general construction of the chart, this may have little effect or it may strengthen intuition. However, the sextile is a weak aspect as other factors will tend to override it.

Aspects to the Ascendant and Midheaven

Other aspects that are important in interpreting charts are those between the planets and the ascendant and midheaven. In general, those to the ascendant have a personal implication while to the midheaven the implication applies to self-expression. It is essential that an accurate time of birth is known to allow a full interpretation. If this is not known, aspect to the ascendant and midheaven are better not included. The primary features and possibilities of these aspects are summarized below.

Sun/Ascendant aspects

Conjunction	rounded character, amiable; could be domineering, reticent.
Positive	depends on house position, but usually a strengthening effect.
Negative	depends on house but can be ambitious. Love of home but can be problematic.

Moon/Ascendant aspects

Conjunction	moody and often easily influenced. Secretive but intuitive.
Positive	good intuition, common sense with an adaptable character.
Negative	impatient and often discontented.

Mercury/Ascendant aspects

Conjunction	mentally sharp, versatile, communicative and imaginative.
Positive	similar to the conjunction.
Negative	tense and prone to worry and be over-talkative.

Venus/Ascendant aspects

Conjunction	affectionate and loving with an appreciation of things artistic. Care necessary not to overdo food or drink.
Positive	similar to the conjunction, with an understanding nature.
Negative	this may cause excesses in behaviour and personal relationships.

Mars/Ascendant aspects

Conjunction	a strengthening of physical or emotional energy. May be selfish but can be altruistic.
Positive	physically active, independent.
Negative	prone to quarrelling. May overdo things, for example, in work.

Jupiter/Ascendant aspects

Conjunction	depending upon the house, can be optimistic and lively but also fair-minded. May be a risk-taker.
Positive	effects similar to the conjunction.
Negative	may be prone to showing off to the detriment of relationships.

Saturn/Ascendant aspects

Conjunction	self-consciousness; practical with common sense neverthe-less. Can be moody but also content, particularly in the home surroundings.
Positive	common sense and practical nature; also cautious.
Negative	may be pessimistic with a tendency to complain.

Uranus/Ascendant aspects

Conjunction	original and independent but can be prone to being irrational and nervous.
Positive	lively and creative usually with a strong need for independence.
Negative	unpredictable and possibly melodramatic.

Neptune/Ascendant aspects

Conjunction	variable effects but may include creativity, ill-discipline, or irrational behaviour.
Positive	quite inspired but may be tempered by forgetfulness.
Negative	possibly self-deceptive, and blinkered in situations where logic and analysis might be more appropriate.

Pluto/Ascendant aspects

Conjunction	strong emotions. May be secretive and prefer being alone.
Positive	can be precipitate in actions; caution is required.
Negative	desire for change may become strong.

Sun/Midheaven aspects

Conjunction ambitious and hopeful and usually self-confident. Can also be 'too big for their boots'.

Positive ambitious but in a constructive way.

Negative difficulty in achieving, great effort required.

Moon/Midheaven aspects

Conjunction a strong character with possibility of leadership qualities.

Positive a strengthening of traits associated with the sign containing the midheaven.

Negative dissatisfaction; should be overcome with encouragement.

Mercury/Midheaven aspects

Conjunction highly communicative, this talent can be applied to a career.

Positive similar to the conjunction, also a balanced view of objectives.

Negative may be prone to tension and worry.

Venus/Midheaven aspects

Conjunction works well with people; considerate; may not have full powers of concentration and organization.

Positive similar to the conjunction; more constructive effect than the conjunction for self-employed.

Negative can be arrogant; prone to overreacting.

Mars/Midheaven aspects

Conjunction thirst for success; energetically pursues the career.

Positive enthusiastic, particularly in work.

Negative hard-working but may be argumentative.

Jupiter/Midheaven aspects

Conjunction content and optimistic; usually popular and fair. Successful, usually enthusiastic in whatever venture is in hand.

Positive good at meeting challenges, which enhances self-esteem. Optimistic and enthusiastic.

Negative may exaggerate, thereby losing standing with people around.

Saturn/Midheaven aspects

Conjunction ambitious and can be high achievers; can handle responsibility but may let other aspects of life pass them by.

Positive common sense and practicality; a good worker, who looks for promotion but reckless.

Negative may experience frustration in reaching for goals; can be self-conscious and too cautious.

Uranus/Midheaven aspects

Conjunction independent, perhaps with an inclination to rebellion, but may be creative and clever. Changes of direction possible, as is a liking for control.

Positive similar to the conjunction, but with an innovative quality. The urge to change should be tempered, as it may become detrimental.

Negative tension and a resultant over-caution may impede progress.

Neptune/Midheaven aspects

Conjunction changes in direction may become frequent although this will not necessarily restrict progress.

Positive imagination and flair will help appropriate careers.

Negative liable to deceive, the subject may use dubious methods to achieve his or her aims.

Pluto/Midheaven aspects

Conjunction a desire for influence may predominate. Careers may be marked by sudden, quite remarkable, changes of direction.

Positive an ability to handle unexpected change.

Negative life may throw up challenging situations with which some will cope and others not. It will all depend upon the remainder of the chart.

Constructing
the Birth Chart

The construction of a birth chart is essentially a fairly elementary mathematical exercise. There are computer programs that enable it to be done simply, but in undertaking the task manually there is greater understanding and achievement.

Before beginning, a number of items are required:

- a blank chart; the one shown (*see* page 189) is of the equal house system. It can be drawn up quite easily using a pair of compasses.
- pen, pencil and ruler (and to begin with, probably an eraser).
- an atlas for determination of longitude and latitude.
- access to Raphael's ephemeris, which provides data on the position of the planet by month and year. Also known as the ephemerides, they are contained in some astrological books or you may have to consult a library. They are also available on computer.
- detailed instructions to follow or a computer program to use.

The following stages provide an overview of the process involved without complicated guidelines. It shows essentially how the data is derived but allows us to concentrate on the interpretive aspects of the subject.

Stage 1
The central horizontal line marks the horizon, and starting in the house below this line, the houses can be numbered 1 to 12, moving in an anticlockwise direction.

Stage 2
The position of the ascendant is now calculated. There are a number of calculations to be made, but the first task is to determine the longitude and latitude of the place of birth. The time of birth is also vital

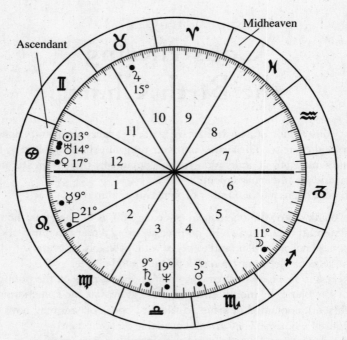

*The birth chart with initial placings of the ascendant,
midheaven and planets*

and should initially be stated as the birth time in Greenwich Mean
Time. To find the ascendant and mid-heaven, the birth time is con-
verted to sidereal time (that is, in relation to the stars) with minor ad-
justments for the year. Because the sidereal time from the tables relates
to midnight it must be changed to the sidereal time at the time of birth
by adding the sidereal time to the time of birth. Again, minor amend-
ments have to be made at this point, both for minor changes in sidereal
time and the precise geographical location of the place of birth. Again,
tables are used for this latter correction. This calculation produces a
true sidereal time of birth, and by referring to a *table of houses*, degree
values can be found for the ascendant and midheaven.

In this example the ascendant is 22 degrees Cancer and the midheaven is 20 degrees Pisces. Referring back to the chart, the 22 degrees are counted clockwise around the chart from the horizon line and the ascendant is marked. This is the cusp (that is, junction) of the first sign, and the remaining sign divisions can be drawn in from here, every 30 degrees around the chart. The glyphs of the sign are then added and the midheaven is also positioned.

Stage 3
The next stage is to determine the positions of the Sun, Moon and other planets. By reference to the ephemerides, the positions can be found, and these are given as a number of degrees in a particular sign. The example here results in the following, rounded to the nearest degree for simplicity:

Sun	13 degrees	Cancer
Moon	11 degrees	Sagittarius
Mercury	9 degrees	Leo
Venus	17 degrees	Cancer
Mars	5 degrees	Scorpio
Jupiter	15 degrees	Taurus
Saturn	9 degrees	Libra
Uranus	14 degrees	Cancer
Neptune	19 degrees	Libra
Pluto	21 degrees	Leo

Each planet is now marked on the chart in the relevant sign, counting anticlockwise from the sign division. Each plot should be marked and the appropriate planetary glyph inserted. The chart, completed to this point, is shown opposite with all information calculated to date.

Stage 4
When the planetary positions have been established, the aspects can be determined. As described earlier, there are various aspects that may be apparent, and when constructed as described their significance can be determined from the other sections of the book. On the sample chart there can be seen conjunctions (the Sun with Venus and Uranus), sextiles (the Sun, Uranus and Venus, all with Jupiter; Pluto with Neptune),

squares (Neptune with Venus and the Moon with Saturn), and so on.

The complete picture of a chart, and the personality, is built up from information such as this but also the details gleaned from the position of the planets with respect to the signs and houses. The Sun's sign influence has already been covered in reasonable detail, and below the remaining planets are dealt with. It is possible to give only the briefest indication of influences here, but more comprehensive details will be found in other publications. The next section therefore deals with the planets through the signs and houses, beginning with the Sun through the houses.

The Planets Through the Houses

The Sun

The energy of the Sun is very important, and it shows by its house position in which facet of life the energy will be focused.

The Sun in the . . .

. . . First house

Indicates the strong, self-centred type who is good at giving orders—and may therefore be successful in business—but not so good at taking them.

. . . Second house

Very acquisitive, both in terms of money and other possessions and with a desire to flaunt it a little. This may also apply to a partner, that is, the partner is also regarded as a possession. The motivation may be a wish to be wealthy or a fear of being poor.

. . . Third house

At whatever level, the mind will be active and the person will be a communicator.

. . . Fourth house

Seeks the security of a good home and happy family life, and may also work from home.

. . . Fifth house

Creativity needs to be expressed and enjoyment will be gained from that. Spontaneous and proud but generous and may be upset easily. There is a desire to feel important and wanted.

. . . Sixth house

Such people are hard workers and often commit themselves to the local community, or their employer and, of course, their family. Personal health is a feature of this house, whether for good or bad, but it may also show as employment or voluntary work in the health sector.

. . . Seventh house

Relationships with others become very important whether it is on a personal level or concerned with work. Emotional dependence may actually become a problem.

. . . Eighth house

An interest in self-development, which may relate to money or the personality. Strong emotional tendencies with a perceptive mind.

. . . Ninth house

Education and travel are both associated with this house and both help to broaden the mind. There is a strong desire to learn and possibly to teach.

. . . Tenth house

A strong commitment to ambition, work (may actually overdo work) and possessions, with a desire for progress in a career. Secure family life is also important.

. . . Eleventh house

Is drawn to cooperative ventures, working with other people and is often a good communicator. Very close relationships are however often avoided.

. . . Twelfth house

Tends to like quiet and seclusion but can be creative. The most withdrawn of all the houses. Usually wants to improve life for others even though the subject may have no great ambition for himself or herself.

The Moon in the . . .

. . . First house

A natural instinct to care for others but not to the detriment of self-interest. Likes travelling. Is susceptible to mood changes.

... Second house

There is a need for security through money and possessions and often a desire to collect the latter. Emotions will affect judgement on money.

... Third house

Usually a good communicator and often turns to teaching. Shrewd but could be a deceiver. Intelligent and humorous but commonly restless and always on the move.

... Fourth house

A strong feeling exists for the home and family and a safe, solid base is essential. Caring and protective in nature, but may become obsessive and retiring.

... Fifth house

An outlet for creativity is vital, which may manifest itself in parenthood. Socially active and may be something of an extrovert but with quick reversals of mood.

... Sixth house

Good workers who often opt for charity work or the health field. Emotions frequently affect health and work.

... Seventh house

Usually look for close emotional ties, although in so doing their individuality may be lost. Subject to mood swings. Job variety and interest is sought.

... Eighth house

Emotional and intuitive, often to the point where they have a 'sixth sense'. Usually a good business sense. Strong sexual needs.

... Ninth house

An interest in things foreign, be it travel, language or culture. Also a tendency for higher education and for religion.

... Tenth house

An ability to lead and a desire for status and power. An understanding of those being led, which can lead to being highly esteemed.

... Eleventh house

Tends to get involved in activities involving groups, which they themselves may lead. Politics commonly appeals.

. . . Twelfth house

Time alone is always valued. In working for others it is usually 'behind the scenes'.

Mercury in the . . .

. . . First house

Talkative and quick-witted though with some nervousness. Versatile and keen to learn and to present own ideas. May be prone to excessive worry.

. . . Second house

Financially astute with an aptitude for financial dealings and the creation of wealth.

. . . Third house

Usually communicative and often employed in a profession where such skills can be used. Mentally agile with an interest in education.

. . . Fourth house

The home is particularly important and may base work there. Interest in the family and its past and history generally. Can be restless.

. . . Fifth house

Highly creative in a literary or craft pursuit although may be lacking in attention to detail. Generally at ease with children, something that is usually reciprocated.

. . . Sixth house

Excellent at communication and in analysing situations and problems. Makes a good employee, working carefully, and also a good employer who maintains an interest in employees, their health, etc.

. . . Seventh house

Seeks a sharing, caring relationship whether in marriage or pastimes. Can be a good business person with an ability to act as intermediary. Often interested in other's problems but not necessarily out of totally altruistic motives.

. . . Eighth house

May have an interest in mysterious things, for example, psychic phenomena, mystical teachings or divination, but can also prove to have a good business sense. An enquiring mind with good powers of concentration.

. . . Ninth house

A thirst for knowledge and understanding is very strong and may lead to a career in research with considerable academic achievements. Also may have an aptitude for languages.

. . . Tenth house

Variety is necessary, particularly in the career, and there may be changes in career direction. Generally a good approach to business, although financial reward is not necessarily the primary motivation.

. . . Eleventh house

A very friendly type who enjoys social contact and the opportunity to discuss ideas. This may lead to involvement in local groups, organizations or politics.

. . . Twelfth house

Tends to be emotional and shy, almost secretive and lacking a little in self-confidence.

Venus in the . . .

. . . First house

An attractive and charming character, which in part is a means to securing friendship. Kind and sympathetic, often interested in the outward appearance, that is, fashion and beauty.

. . . Second house

Likes to collect possessions, especially things of value and beauty. A competent approach to business in the main, but this is often used to impress.

. . . Third house

Very friendly and sociable with an ability to communicate effectively. Welcomes a mental challenge.

. . . Fourth house

The home is central and is a focus of pride. Every attempt is made to make it nice and secure and comfortable. Dislikes arguments and can be quite effective at defusing situations likely otherwise to end in quarrels.

. . . Fifth house

Likes luxury and glamour and participating in social events. Gets on well with children. Creative with an affinity for the arts.

. . . Sixth house

The working environment must be pleasing and conducive to work. A steady pace in all things is ideal. Socially correct and critical of those who are not.

. . . Seventh house

An interesting combination of shrewdness and affection. Often popular with their peers, they can sometimes rely too much on a partner and make unreasonable requests.

. . . Eighth house

An increase in emotions and sexual matters can be uplifting or totally problematic. Generally sympathetic but can become jealous and secretive.

. . . Ninth house

A strong interest in other cultures with a desire for foreign travel, which may lead to residence or even marriage abroad. Varied contacts in social circles with a relaxed attitude in general.

. . . Tenth house

Socially adept with positive spin-off in the career, forming good relationships with work colleagues.

. . . Eleventh house

Large number of social contacts and an enjoyment of communal ventures, fund-raising, etc. Good organizer of events.

. . . Twelfth house

Shy and incommunicative with secretive emotional feelings.

Mars in the . . .

. . . First house

Very energetic and positive although sometimes impulsive and even hot-headed. They usually put themselves first although can be very helpful to others.

. . . Second house

A desire to build up possessions and wealth but often an extravagant spender. Very competitive in business and may be likely to take risks.

. . . Third house

Competitive and often argumentative. Also inquisitive and may have a temper. In being argumentative, they may also lack tact.

. . . Fourth house

Much effort is spent on the home in decoration and improvements. On occasion restlessness may precipitate moving home.

. . . Fifth house

Energetic in all aspects of life whether social, creative or romantic. A keen sportsperson who enjoys leisure time. Tends to be good with children but often pressurizes his or her own children to succeed.

. . . Sixth house

A hard worker who gets on with the task in hand. Quite ambitious and competitive but can be rather impatient when faced with delays. They will also be difficult when disagreeing with colleagues.

. . . Seventh house

Forceful in partnerships and can prove argumentative. Can be popular through their energetic participation but they can offend or upset people through their outspoken nature.

. . . Eighth house

Interest in investigative work or financial occupations. Highly intuitive. Strong sex drive.

. . . Ninth house

Adventurous and interested in travel. Also intellectually very capable and may find education rewarding. Usually have strongly held views and beliefs.

... Tenth house

A very strong character and a hard worker, which in regard to the career means ambition, success and an achiever. Although they make good employers, they can on occasion be a little too ruthless.

... Eleventh house

Likely to get involved in various groups and organizations where they will probably become leaders. Friends are important but their basically argumentative nature may cause temporary rifts.

... Twelfth house

A desire to help others, perhaps in the caring professions but often working behind the scenes. Can become secretive, too much so, which leads to problems not being discussed and solved.

Jupiter in the ...

... First house

Honest, optimistic and generally outgoing with a tendency to offer encouragement to others. A possible weakness may be overconfidence.

... Second house

Money is a central theme although the emphasis may vary. In some, money is made effortlessly while in others it is of secondary importance. Generous in partnerships and with a desire for comfort in the home.

... Third house

Welcomes mental challenges, shares ideas and opinions but may force them on others. Can be restless but there is often a desire to continue in education, possibly through self-teaching.

... Fourth house

Strong ties with the family and home life and may have ambition for a large house.

. . . Fifth house

Enthusiastic and optimistic, and may also be creative. Generally self-confident but in excess this can lead to risk-taking and someone who shows off.

. . . Sixth house

Helpful and generous and particularly so in work when a good rewarding job will take precedence over the financial return.

. . . Seventh house

Friendly and quick to form new contacts, although sometimes with an ulterior motive. Good in business and assertive, with plenty of ideas for development.

. . . Eighth house

Often a good business person who invests wisely. Can be over-demanding where a partner is concerned and may also like freedom to the detriment of a relationship.

. . . Ninth house

May have an interest in travel and foreign cultures. There is also a continuing desire to find out, acquire knowledge or study. Can become self-opinionated.

. . . Tenth house

An ability to grasp the significance of situations and take a long-term view. Tend to work towards their goals, becoming wiser en route. Can be rather melodramatic with a tendency to show off.

. . . Eleventh house

Very sociable with many superficial friends and acquaintances, and just a few real friends. Quick to offer encouragement and provide ideas.

. . . Twelfth house

Can be rather idealistic, finding the material world unsatisfactory. Prefer in many cases to work alone although they will have an excellent mind.

Saturn in the . . .

. . . First house

Shy and lacking self-confidence although with common sense and responsibility. Can often meet with repeated setbacks but through dogged perseverance can succeed.

. . . Second house

Works hard to make the money that is gained but little comes easily in this respect. There may be a tendency to possessiveness, and over-caution can lead to lost opportunities.

. . . Third house

Success usually comes later in life through sheer hard work as a lack of confidence is overcome. Usually practical-minded and sensible with a caring attitude to brothers and sisters.

. . . Fourth house

A potentially unhappy early life may link at a later stage with the need for domestic security. Intuitive, although the individual may have to learn to accept intuitive judgements.

. . . Fifth house

A latent creativity may need to be encouraged. May find dealing with children difficult, possibly because of their own childhoods.

. . . Sixth house

Usually committed to hard work, although possibly in a complaining way, but goals are commonly met. Avoidance of change. May be excessively concerned about their health.

. . . Seventh house

Regards partnerships very seriously and may choose an older partner, but tends to be very faithful. Occasionally there will be problems in relationships.

. . . Eighth house

A generally serious perspective on life, with the potential for depression. Very good at financial pursuits, particularly in their responsible attitude to the money of other people, thus suited to banking or insurance.

. . . Ninth house
Thinks seriously and sensibly about important matters, but with a conventional, traditional approach to most matters. There is a tendency to travel, although in some this raises problems and even phobias.

. . . Tenth house
Ambitious, with high hopes and an ability to take responsibility. These people make good, dependable workers who can progress through hard work, overcoming difficulties on the way.

. . . Eleventh house
Hard-working and often a little shy. However, a definite effort may be made to be more sociable, which frequently results in membership of numerous committees. A concern for all good causes is evident.

. . . Twelfth house
Can withdraw into his or her own world but in any event will welcome the security of home. Good, supportive workers in whatever they do.

Uranus in the . . .

. . . First house
Intelligent, freedom-loving and individualistic, so much so that they may prefer competition to cooperation. Quite unpredictable, but original and often brilliant.

. . . Second house
This has financial implications and may result in the unexpected gain or loss of money. Can be emotionally cool with a possessive streak.

. . . Third house
Original and mentally alert and likely to respond negatively to the orthodox system of education. Seeks logical answers to problems, can be inventive. A stubborn, awkward streak may also be apparent.

. . . Fourth house
A rather perverse, mixed-up influence with the subject wanting a stable secure home life but also considerable freedom. They may be brilliant but moody. However, it is best to encourage and develop the intuitive ideas of such a person.

... Fifth house

A creative individual with flair and originality. Their children tend to be clever but may be demanding. Emotionally rather fearless, these people will often take risks.

... Sixth house

May experience health problems, perhaps associated with tension. There is an affinity for work that is slightly out of the ordinary and that requires invention, flair or idealism.

... Seventh house

Relationships are affected greatly. Often the individual will not want to be tied down and partners need to be very understanding. There may be mixed emotions about such ties that can lead to mistakes, although there can be a generally romantic outlook.

... Eighth house

Commonly a relaxed attitude to money, which may result in unpredictable actions that subsequently cause friction. Fickle sexually and possibly obsessive in analysing problems.

... Ninth house

Often clever with a flair for science or the arts and an appetite for challenges. Travel is sought with possible attraction for a foreign culture resulting.

... Tenth house

Career direction may change abruptly, particularly if there is not the scope for their talents. Not averse to holding positions of power, leadership is handled well.

... Eleventh house

Superficially friendly with a varied social life and often a hard-working commitment to a cause or organization. Dislikes inaction and lethargy in others.

... Twelfth house

Highly imaginative, often in a strange way with an interest in the unusual or mysterious. Often takes to a humanitarian cause to the detriment of a personal relationship.

Neptune in the . . .

. . . First house
Imaginative and sensitive with a tendency to daydream. In general such people are kind and unselfish, but may be rather gullible.

. . . Second house
A potentially varied and unpredictable attitude to money including a susceptibility to be misled. May be sentimental and loving.

. . . Third house
Imaginative and communicative, particularly with respect to artistic careers or pastimes. May achieve later rather than sooner through lack of application in the early years of education.

. . . Fourth house
Chaos may reign at home in both organization and general provision of domestic routine but also in giving guidance to children. Usually imaginative and a lover of animals.

. . . Fifth house
Creative, with imagination. Romantic associations can be a little too consuming and would benefit from a wise head.

. . . Sixth house
Can be attracted to work in the caring professions but may not be very good at meeting deadlines. Tend to be self-sacrificing and often work hard for little recompense but can be impractical at times. Health may be a problem, particularly with allergies.

. . . Seventh house
Too much may be expected romantically, and disappointment may result, or there may be a tendency to rush in without considering the implications.

. . . Eighth house
Romantic/sexual activities can be quite dominant. In money matters there will be generosity, but the individual may prove easily led, perhaps by a business partner.

. . . Ninth house
Inspired and imaginative with a fascination for other cultures and mysticism. May find a career in religion. Travel often features strongly.

. . . Tenth house

An idealist and romantic, which in a career can lead to unrealistic hopes or success if the idealism can be used to good effect. There are likely to be many changes of emphasis and direction in life.

. . . Eleventh house

Sociable but not very perceptive in such circumstances. There may be some shyness and an aversion to taking on responsibility as this can result in stress.

. . . Twelfth house

Kind and caring, which may be reflected in the choice of career where they can readily understand the problems of other people. Often creative with an affinity for the arts.

Pluto in the . . .

. . . First house

Strong and dynamic with a determination to work hard and achieve targets. Can also be moody and obsessive with an emotional intensity. Strongly developed motivation with an excellent ability to bounce back after setbacks.

. . . Second house

There is usually a good aptitude for business and money matters, which when allied with a determination to succeed can lead the individual to considerable success. An intense emotional life, although may be manipulative.

. . . Third house

Can be very good at communicating although often the urge to be quiet and contemplative masks this. Perceptive and curious, which may lead to a career in research.

. . . Fourth house

Strong feelings about the home although there may be concealed frustration from his or her early life. Intuitive, and this will help deal with any emotional or family problems.

. . . Fifth house
Usually creative and with a determination to use their potential to the full. Too much may be expected of romantic/emotional associations.

. . . Sixth house
A disciplined individual who works hard and to a routine if applicable and may be rather hard on himself or herself. May experience health problems.

. . . Seventh house
An aptitude for the financial aspects of a business. Can appreciate others, with understanding and sympathy, but must be careful not to dominate a partner.

. . . Eighth house
A good business sense. Intuitive and logical but may experience sexual problems.

. . . Ninth house
Frequently shows connection with or interest in foreign countries and different faiths. Seeks mental challenge. Quite a strong personality.

. . . Tenth house
A strong desire to succeed, which may be shown in the career, where personal power will be sought. An interest also in money and politics. May be ruthless.

. . . Eleventh house
A tendency to become involved in groups or societies, and possibly in politics. There may, however, be a predominance of these interests over domestic concerns, to the detriment of the latter.

. . . Twelfth house
A likelihood that the individual will be secretive, whether in financial or romantic matters. Habitually searching and analysing, which may be directed on themselves.

The Planets Through the Signs

The positions of the planets with respect to the Zodiac signs are unique for each chart. Each planet has twelve expressions through the signs, which follow a basic pattern, so in Aries, planets act assertively and powerfully.

The planets in Aries

Moon
Quick in reaction, thought and temper and rather impulsive. Can be good partners but may also be selfish.

Mercury
Quick-thinking and strong-willed with an enjoyment of debate. Decisive and to the point.

Venus
Affectionate, even passionate, with a generous nature. Lively socially and generally popular.

Mars
Energetic, even aggressive, and usually leading the way. They can be impulsive and obstinate although friendly, and they may create problems through carelessness.

Jupiter
Optimistic and enthusiastic with a love of freedom. Can be generous, but these traits to excess can lead to recklessness and extravagance.

Saturn
Assertive and strong, and very determined, thus more than able to cope when circumstances become difficult.

Uranus
Originality with self-confidence, although there may be impatience and a tendency to behave foolishly.

Neptune

This is an impossible placing because of the slow motion of Neptune.

Pluto

The same applies as for Neptune.

The planets in Taurus

Moon

A solid base is required to counter any emotional ups and downs, but otherwise very practical with lots of common sense.

Mercury

Stubborn but with an ability to consider problems of a practical nature and work steadily. Generally cheerful.

Uranus

Warm and affectionate and generally faithful. Likes craft and the arts, including music. Aims for financial security, through hard work if necessary.

Mars

Quick-tempered and passionate. Such individuals work very hard and can be very determined, almost stubborn. Works at making money.

Jupiter

Appreciates good living and usually has the flair and good judgement to use and invest money well. Generous but can be possessive.

Saturn

Very patient, with caution and discipline, but can become too stubborn. Ambitious and materialistic.

Uranus

Stubborn yet sound and with some flair. May be erratic with money, splashing out and then saving every penny.

Neptune

This placing cannot occur for living subjects because of the slow orbit of Neptune.

Pluto

The same applies as for Neptune.

The planets in Gemini

Moon
Quick to respond and versatile. There is a reluctance to get too involved emotionally. Can be impatient and restless.

Mercury
A desire to communicate and exchange ideas. A quick thinker, decision maker and quite inventive. Can be impatient with slower people but adaptable.

Venus
A good communicator and a lively personality. Can be flirtatious but often avoids emotional ties through constant analysis and thus does not face the real issues. May be restless.

Mars
A good mind but has a tendency to take on too much, thereby reducing effectiveness. Usually versatile and capable but can be nervous and impatient.

Jupiter
Inventive and clever but can skip from one area to another and grasp only superficial knowledge Often takes to teaching as communication is good.

Saturn
Good mind with a logical approach to problems. May be a late developer and generally good at the physical sciences computing, mathematics, etc.

Uranus
A quick thinker who has original and often brilliant ideas. However, he or she may be nervous and tense.

Neptune
Very few people will have Neptune in Gemini, unless very old.

Pluto
Applies only to the elderly (born before 1912).

The planets in Cancer

Moon

Highly instinctive, emotional and affectionate. A secure, stable home life is very important, and these individuals are adept at homemaking. Can be moody and a little possessive.

Mercury

Kind and thoughtful with a good imagination. Intuition and opinions are strong, as is the dislike of change. A good memory is not unusual.

Venus

Sympathetic and affectionate, but if overdone can be possessive and clinging. They love the home and make it as comfortable as possible and are likely to make sensible investments.

Mars

Great commitment, physical and emotional, to see things through. Although they need security and a strong family life, they are ambitious. Occasionally very short-tempered.

Jupiter

Kind and sympathetic, and also dutiful. Quite good at business and generally ambitious on behalf of and for the family.

Saturn

Can be self-pitying and suspicious, and there is a need for emotional stability. May be a worrier, but there is also a financial aptitude and general shrewdness. Hard-working and ambitious.

Uranus

Imaginative and original though logical. Can be moody and unpredictable and difficult to work with.

Neptune

This placing occurred in the early years of the twentieth century. It confers intuition and sensitivity although the individual may be too imaginative and prone to worry.

Pluto

Generally emotionally strong and intuitive. Can be a good business person with staying power, although some may fall prey to excessive worry.

The planets in Leo

Moon
Confident and with a desire to impress, but can be self-centred. Enthusiastic and lively but may, in their ambition, start taking over. Can be stubborn and difficult.

Mercury
Creative and well organized in a practical sense. A good communicator but can be arrogant and patronizing. Generally happy and with a positive outlook.

Venus
Lively, generous and faithful, this person will adore his or her partner and will love children and material things. May be a tendency to show off and be extravagant.

Mars
Looks for leadership because of organizational ability and enthusiasm. Socially active with a touch of drama that can be overdone. May be too pushy and overbearing.

Jupiter
Usually generous and enthusiastic with a positive outlook on life. Can also be ambitious but melodramatic and overpowering.

Saturn
Determined, well-organized and faithful apply here. Can often be bossy and arrogant, especially if they are pursuing a long-held goal.

Uranus
Quite dynamic, which can result in good leadership qualities. However, there will almost certainly be stubbornness. Often creative but with mixed personal outlook on relationships.

Neptune
Enthusiastic and creative with a good imagination. Commonly an interest in the visual arts, such as photography or film.

Pluto
May succeed in business through flair rather than calculation. Interested in technology. Commonly shows leadership qualities although occasionally these may degenerate into empire-building tendencies.

The planets in Virgo

Moon
A strong tendency to be well-ordered, neat and with a dislike of bad behaviour. Can be lacking in self-confidence and a worrier but with a practical streak.

Mercury
An analytical mind and practical, which makes these people good at solving problems. May become bogged down in detail when wanting to be precise but generally able to cope with demanding tasks.

Venus
Often shy and with few close friends, perhaps because they tend to be critical of other people, often due to their own lack of self-confidence. Good at business and communicating.

Mars
A hard worker who pays attention to detail but lacks imagination. The emotions and personal relationships may not run too smoothly.

Jupiter
Patient but can be overconcerned with detail, critical but kind. There may be worry and mental conflict when facing a problem because of lack of self-confidence. Tends to be kind and matter-of-fact.

Saturn
Patient, modest, with attention to detail and duty. Hard work is not avoided and personal standards are kept high. Can be too hard on others, for example, employees, and may be a little detached from others.

Uranus
Can lead to originality but the familiar is not rejected. Depending upon other placings, the individual can be dynamic and somewhat restless.

Neptune
Imaginative and expressive, but there may be a lack of self-confidence and an associated dissatisfaction.

Pluto
An ability to see, grasp and solve problems, although some individuals may find difficulty in talking about their own worries. Can be very critical of others.

The planets in Libra

Moon
Sympathetic and understanding, to the point where they will help to sort out problems for other people. Clear thinkers, very charming but can be moody.

Mercury
Peace-loving, sympathetic, can see many possibilities, but this can leave them indecisive. Gentle and affectionate. Often good at business but will need application and discipline.

Venus
Kind and understanding, and tactful in helping others with a dislike of argument. Quite generous with money but fond of luxuries. May be lazy and indecisive.

Mars
Affectionate, keen to promote and maintain unity, but can themselves be argumentative. Perceptive and friendly.

Jupiter
Sympathetic, kind and generous; a naturally warm person. Has a relaxed attitude to life with a love of luxuries that can lead to self-indulgence.

Saturn
Understanding with a feeling for what is right and wrong, kind and fair. May be some intolerance and difficulty with relationships.

Uranus
Friendly and caring, and unselfish when someone is in need. May be independent and unsure of being committed to a partnership.

Neptune
Sympathetic, peace-loving and kind. May be lacking in self-confidence and self-deceiving.

Pluto
A tendency to start arguments, particularly with a partner to prove a point. Can be jealous.

The planets in Scorpio

Moon

Very emotional and may be jealous. Determined with a strong ambitious urge. Tend to be a little retiring socially but in personal relationships can be very committed.

Mercury

Intuitive with a logical mind although can be obsessional and possessive. Usually loyal in relationships.

Venus

Passionate, possessive with occasional jealousy. Often a flair for business, investment and money, but obstinacy could interfere.

Mars

Full of potential with a strong character. Hard-working with ambitions but self-discipline may be lacking. Perceptive with, occasionally, a critical nature. Can be secretive but with strong motivation and commitment.

Jupiter

Determined, with a will to succeed, especially in the career. Lives a full life but in many cases may need to ease off a little.

Saturn

Committed to goals, determined and with a very good ability in business. Can be ruthless, stubborn and obstinate, and consideration should be encouraged if they are to succeed.

Uranus

Emotional but afraid to show it, courageous and may take risks. May be a liking for power but potential must be developed in the correct direction.

Neptune

Emotional, but can be ambitious and even inspiring if this is also shown elsewhere in the chart. May be fortuitous with money.

Pluto

A desire to make money and achieve a powerful position in some way. Usually strong emotions and quite intuitive.

The planets in Sagittarius

Moon
A liking for freedom and also travel, which may result in living abroad. A challenge is always enjoyed, and the individual is enthusiastic and positive with a desire to maintain progress. May be restless and a little offhand.

Mercury
Can be unrealistic and superficial but, on the positive side, will always be learning, and is broad-minded. Grasps situations quickly, versatile.

Venus
Emotional freedom is required, and may not like to be tied. Idealistic and imaginative but may be thoughtless.

Mars
Very ambitious, often on a grand scale. Very energetic and independent but with a non-traditional approach. Can be argumentative and heavy-handed.

Jupiter
Enthusiastic and positive with a tendency to look for intellectual development. Often intuitive and with a good sense of judgement.

Saturn
Study is a primary aim, assisted by a capacity for concentration. Honest and forthright, these people will not be afraid to challenge the thinking of the majority.

Uranus
Original in thought and welcomes a challenge, caring in an altruistic sense and with this is a good sense of humour.

Neptune
Generally understanding and caring with an idealistic streak. Also enthusiastic and positive-thinking.

Pluto
This occurs only from 1995 until well beyond the millennium. Likely to be independent and generally sensible, possibly wise.

The planets in Capricorn

Moon
Unable to show feelings easily and may find partnerships difficult although good at homemaking. Ambitious to some extent but with a tendency towards arrogance, but with a good sense of humour.

Mercury
Down to earth, practical and to the point. Determined and careful, but can be restless. Often a tendency to scientific pursuits.

Venus
Tends to stick with tradition and conventional relationships. Good in business with a careful approach, although occasionally showing off.

Mars
Very ambitious, seeking targets, and with a liking for power. Generally practical-minded but can be stubborn and cold.

Jupiter
A good worker who sees the job through. Very sensible and responsible, with ambition and reliability. Can be stubborn.

Saturn
Ambitious, practical, hard-working and well-organized. May like power. Can be pessimistic and likely to complain, but has a good sense of humour.

Uranus
A careful thinker but with occasional lapses. There may be a hard side to the character, which could be tempered by a concern for good causes.

Neptune
Possibly creative. Determined and positive with a cautious streak but may be subject to self-deception.

Pluto
It is unlikely that this placing will be found.

The planets in Aquarius

Moon
Independent, dislike of being tied down emotionally and may reject